Ulster Football &

THE PATH OF CHAMPIONS

HENRY DOWNEY, Derry captain 1993

Jerome Quinn has gone to great lengths to ensure that Ulster has a book that details, reports and commemorates the history of Ulster's football and hurling achievements.

There has been a longing for this book for some time and it could not have arrived at a more appropriate moment when Ulster football and hurling is at an all-time high.

I hope Ulster will have more history makers in the not too distant future and I wish Jerome every success with his book.

Henry Downey

ANTHONY MOLLOY, Donegal captain 1992

This book is most welcome and overdue. It is fitting that such a committed GAA supporter from the great county of O'Neill should take on this huge task and deliver it with such distinction. An excellently produced book that explores, commemorates and celebrates the special significance of Ulster football.

Ulster Football and Hurling is a must for the library of all GAA fans and an excellent read.

Well done, Jerome.

Anthony Molloy

PADDY O'ROURKE, Down captain 1991

This is a most enjoyable book. The photographs are excellent — the statistics incredible.

The book has to be a 'must' for all supporters of Gaelic games, especially all Ulstermen. It gives great reference and discussion value to all sports fans.

Paddy O'Rourke

Ulster Football & Hurling
THE PATH OF CHAMPIONS

Jerome Quinn

WOLFHOUND PRESS

First published 1993 by
WOLFHOUND PRESS Ltd
68 Mountjoy Square
Dublin 1
Reprinted 1993

British Library Cataloguing in Publication Data

Quinn, Jerome
    Celebrating Ulster Football: Path of the Champions
    I. Title
    796.33409416

    ISBN 0-86327-395-5

The publishers gratefully acknowledge support from Guinness Northern Ireland Ltd towards the publication of this book.

PHOTOGRAPH CREDITS
The author and publishers acknowledge with thanks the assistance received from the following both in research and in supplying photographs for this book. The pictures reproduced are sourced and identified as follows:
Oliver Mc Veigh, Frontline Photo Agency, Donaghmore, Co Tyrone [0868 - 767612] for photos on pages: 10, 14, 17, 22, 23, 24 bottom, 26, 29, 30, 31, 38, 40, 41, 67, 68, 69, 74, 95, 98, 109, 112, 116, 123, 128, 139, 143, 144 bottom, 147, 156, 157, 163, 164, 166, 171, 176 top, 183, 197, 211 top, 213; and colour sections photos on pages: i top & bottom, ii top, iii, iv top, vi bottom right, x top.
The Irish News, Belfast: 54, 58, 73, 77, 80, 90, 93, 102, 125, 126, 134, 135, 136, 137, 138, 144 top, 151, 152, 196, 199, 201, 203, 210, 211 bottom, 212, 218.
Sunday Life, Belfast: colour section photos on pages: iv bottom and v.
The Donegal Democrat, Donegal, and photographer **Michael O'Donnell**: photos on pages: 19, 23, 105, 158, 162, 169, 172, 176 bottom, 179, 180; and colour section pages x bottom, xi top, xii bottom right.
Inpho, Dublin: for colour section pages ii bottom, vi top, xiv top, xii top and bottom left, xiii top, xv top left, bottom; and for the cover photographs.
The Derry Journal and **Tom Heaney**: page 24 top.
The Daily Star: for colour section pages xiv centre, xv top right,
BBC Northern Ireland, Belfast: for colour section pages vii bottom, xi bottom left and right, xiii bottom, xvi top; and page 84.
Louis McNally, Rostrevor, for colour section page vi bottom left; and pages 127 left.
Jim Connolly, Dublin: pages 43, 44, 49, 60, 130, 165, xvi bottom.
We are grateful to various people for supplying pictures including Art McCrory [colour section page viii] and Pat Nugent [pages 56 and 63] Every effort has been made to identify and contact the copyright holders and where we have been unable to do so, we request that they would contact the publisher.

Cover photographs: Inpho
Cover design: Jan de Fouw
Typesetting: Wolfhound Press
Colour separations: Pentacolour
Printed in the Republic of Ireland by Colour Books, Dublin
Bound by Betaprint International Ltd

Contents

Contd.

HURLING

STATISTICS for ULSTER Football and Hurling

Acknowledgements

'Apologies' might be a better title here than 'Acknowledgements' as the first thing I must do is say 'Sorry' to my wife Justine, and children Matthew and Kathryn, for abandoning them for the past eight months or so. Writing a book is not only time-consuming but it also dominates your mind; you are effectively on another planet!

I could not have had a better 'mentor' and friend than Paddy O'Hara. We travelled all over Ulster to football and hurling evenings with top players and personalities, from Newry to Killybegs and from Ballybay to Garvagh. Paddy's knowledge of the games and his wise counselling will be obvious on reading the book, especially to those who know him.

There are many interviewees to thank: suffice to say that as I said on leaving Ross Carr in Newry after the first 'football evening' at the beginning of March, I hope I have done you all justice.

One of the difficulties in writing about different counties was balancing and authenticating opinions and information. I have been fortunate to have been able to call on invaluable and dedicated GAA people in each county. I must list some of them:

In Derry, Bernie and Seamus Mullan; in Donegal, Peter Campbell, Father Seán Ó Gallochóir, Ken Dooley and Michael Daly; in Down, Michael Keenan, Sheila McAnulty, Ray Morgan and Seán Óg McAteer; in Tyrone, Frank Rodgers; in Armagh, Pat Nugent; in Fermanagh, Peter Watson; in Monaghan, John Graham; in Antrim, Gerry McClory; in Cavan, Owen McConnon, Father Dan Gallogly and Barney Cully.

Without the above persons, the statistics section would have been impossible to compile. Most counties have records of their own games but I have attempted here to unite the information, for example, with all Ulster Senior Football Championship Results on file and teams in Ulster finals, including players' Christian names. Where there has been a conflict or absence of information, I can only ask for your tolerance. An amusing instance of how much effort is required to track down the smallest detail, is the search for the captain of the Down Senior team in the 1964 Ulster final. Nobody seemed to know — not even the manager or half of the team! I am told that it even became a topic of conversation among the 1968 Down team as they were being introduced to the crowd on All-Ireland final day last month at Croke Park. Eventually Fintan Mussen, the former Down PRO, uncovered a photograph taken on the day, with George Lavery sitting in the middle of the front row with the ball.

Many long days were spent in the Central Library, Belfast, and the *Irish News* where Kathleen Bell was ever helpful. Further details were gleaned from Mick Dunne, Owen McCann, the *Down Recorder*, Ulster Council Secretary Michael Feeney and from other books. To name a few, Raymond Smith's *Sunday Independent Complete Handbook of Gaelic Games* and Con Short's *Ulster GAA Story*, as well as County histories in Down, Derry and Tyrone. Mick Dunne and Owen McCann (UUJ), Ray Morgan (Newry), Vincent Lee (Monaghan) and Adrian McGuckin (Maghera), assisted with the collection of colleges results and teams.

My employers, the BBC, were most kind in granting permission to use stills from 'The Championship', while the *Donegal Democrat, Daily Star, Sunday Life, Derry Journal* and *Irish News* have, I feel, added considerably to the book with some of their outstanding photographs. Louis McNally from Rostrevor also contributed. The majority has come from Oliver McVeigh from Donaghmore. His alert camera work often tells the story in a way words never could.

The quality of the overall production was aided by support from Guinness Northern Ireland, while Seamus Cashman, Sean Rafferty and Josephine O'Donovan at Wolfhound Press deserve credit for their professionalism and co-operation.

Preface

'The great appear greater to us,
because we are on our knees. Let us rise.'

This inscription, under the statue of James Larkin on O'Connell Street, caught my eye on a visit to Dublin earlier this summer. It seemed to say in just fifteen words what I had been trying to say in as many chapters about Ulster football and hurling.

Throughout the seventies and eighties, Northern football teams were indeed on their knees, easily dismissed by the great Dublin and Kerry sides who must have appeared greater with every continuing year of their astonishing reigns. So too Northern hurling with Antrim's return to the All-Ireland scene in the early eighties greeted with numbing defeats and Down trapped in the lower divisions of the National League.

I grew up with this background, never really believing it was possible for an Ulster football team to win the Sam Maguire or that an Ulster hurling team could reach an All-Ireland final. In 1977, I saw Armagh's fairytale dreams crushed by Dublin; in 1984 and '86 Tyrone promised but failed to deliver. What opportunity missed! The light at the end of the tunnel seemed to fade further into the distance as three Ulster champions lost heavily in Croke Park.

This is why Down's success in 1991 appeared so incredible. To see an Ulster team perform with such style and steel to beat Meath, the team they said couldn't be beaten, restored faith and inspired a generation.

Almost overnight, other Ulster teams rose from their knees to contest the next five national finals, winning four of them. Donegal's first ever All-Ireland success was also unexpected but when Henry Downey became the first Derryman to lift the Sam Maguire, it was almost a case of 'we knew we would'. Derry have now won five games in succession in Croke Park — as many as they had won in the previous thirty-two years.

Ulster's resurgence is a truly remarkable story — one which inspired me to write this book. I felt the Down, Donegal and Derry successes deserved to be fully recounted in detail, while in hurling, the dramatic emergence of Antrim and Down has run almost parallel to the football success. Antrim bridged a gap of 46 years to reach the 1989 All-Ireland final while both they and Down are currently riding high in Division One of the National League. It is a success that continues

— even as I write this preface, Ulster defeats Munster in hurling's Railway Cup for the first time ever — the first victory in twenty meetings since 1942!

The first chapter records the latest adventures, the 1993 All-Ireland Football Championship, before the roots of the modern revolution in football in this province are traced back to the forties and fifties.

My elders tell me that the excitement of Down's first All-Ireland triumph in 1960 — the first by an Ulster team outside of Cavan — was even greater than the same county's victory in 1991. The Mourne men's contribution is followed by 'The Barren Years' from 1968-91 with detailed looks at three counties through the eyes of leading personalities — Jimmy Smyth, Armagh captain in 1977, Art McCrory, manager of Tyrone in 1986, and Sean McCague, the man who brought Monaghan out of the wilderness and to the verge of an All-Ireland final.

There are many reasons why Ulster came good and one of them is explored in a look behind the scenes of 'The Championship', the BBC television programme which gave Ulster football a new platform in the nineties. However, television pictures do not tell the full story: the thoughts and experiences and humour of the players and personalities behind the scenes, their lows and highs. I have tried to record this side of things in Chapters 9-20 which chronicle Down and Donegal's All-Ireland wins and Derry's National League triumph in 1992.

A reborn Ulster Championship has been the platform for these successes and hopefully the thrills, spills and sheer drama of the competition will become clear. Increasing crowds, television coverage and the continued presence of the Sam Maguire have made Ulster the envy of the rest of Ireland. The province has been tremendously proud to host the famous trophy this past few years, with the scenes greeting its arrival on each occasion testament to its importance and significance, especially to people within Northern Ireland. Small populations, as in Derry, have been rewarded for years of dedication and commitment. Facilities in that county were among the best in Ireland before their team became the best.

Success in modern Gaelic games means money, and Chapter 10, 'The Boots Story' tackles the treatment of players and creeping professionalism in the GAA.

Chapter 21 lists nine All-Time Ulster football teams, as selected by a chosen player/manager from each county. From the aggregate number of votes for each player, I have compiled *the* All-Time Ulster football team.

In hurling, there have been two main characters involved in the resurgence of Antrim and Down in the last ten years — Sean McGuinness and Jim Nelson. Chapters 22-24 are essentially told through their eyes, while Chapter 25 records their Ulster selections.

A Statistics Section began as a passing idea but mushroomed into a major part of the book. I have gone into considerable detail on Ulster results, teams, All-Ireland winners, All Stars, etc. My intention is to provide a wide-ranging Ulster-only reference point, not in an insular way but in a celebratory way.

It has been a pleasure to compile and write this book: I sincerely hope you enjoy the read.

Jerome Quinn

As a long-standing fan of sports of all kinds, I am delighted both on my own behalf and on behalf of Guinness Northern Ireland that our company's first ever sponsorship involvement with a book should be with Jerome Quinn's excellent work, *Ulster Football & Hurling.*

Jerome has subtitled his story *The Path of Champions* and indeed the book itself champions the players and the games down the decades covered by that pathway. It is evident from the outset that his knowledge of the Gaelic sports scene in Ulster is accompanied by a genuine respect for the games and a commitment to understanding their development. He clearly brings to his subject a lively and independent expertise as sports analyst, as well as a simply amazing capacity for research, information and statistics. And he writes well too!

The result for the reader is an entertaining, informative, and often exciting story which does credit to great teams and to their training, management and support. Beginning with the Derry triumph of this year, Jerome's story goes back to the early sixties and all the ups and downs of in between, from county to county across Ulster, returning again to the 1990s to relive the great excitement of 'the break through' with Down's and Donegal's capture of the Sam Maguire Cup.

Guinness connections with sport are well known not just here in Northern Ireland but throughout the world, and it is with great pleasure that we continue our strong commitment to the games of football and hurling in Northern Ireland through supporting the publication of this book by Wolfhound Press, a publishing house well known in this field for its classic hurling title, *Giants of the Ash.* Jerome Quinn's *Ulster Football & Hurling* is, I suggest, a book for every Ulster shelf.

You will enjoy reading and talking about it!

John Lavery

Above: 'Do youse boys know anything about football!' Derry manager Eamonn Coleman lectures Dublin pressmen at Newry.

Below: The banner says it all.

1

1993: Ulster wins again!

Down 0-9 Derry 3-11, 30 May, Newry. Derry manager Eamonn Coleman emerged from the winner's dressing-room to talk to a group of newspaper men from South of the border. They wanted to know how he had motivated his team to such an impressive victory. 'I didn't,' declared Coleman, 'Youse did. Youse all tipped Down!'

Over the following months the Dublin-based media came to enjoy the Ballymaguigan bricklayer's acerbic one-liners. They quoted his strong country accent verbatim, so that 'media' became 'meejah' and 'man' became 'maawn'. A wealthy hotelier he is not, nor an articulate teacher, but with a basic and boyish charm, Eamonn Coleman became the outstanding character in the 1993 Championship race.

'They're wary of me, ye know,' he told me in July, puzzled by the reputation he had won for himself among the Dublin scribes. But, by the time Derry had defeated Dublin in their semi-final, Vincent Hogan of the *Irish Independent* admitted a 'strange fondness' for the entertaining Coleman, despite his latest attack on media judgement: 'I don't know why I'm even talking to you boys. I told youse, I told youse we were as good a team as any in the country, but youse wouldn't listen.'

Coleman enjoys putting the media in their place. There's a glint in his eye as he scolds, as there was when he welcomed another newspaper group to Dessie Ryan's pub in Ballyronan. 'Don't tell them anything,' the Derryman warned the barman, 'these boys are from Dublin!' Another victim of Coleman's sense of fun and playfulness was a Clones official who stopped him outside the Derry dressing-rooms. 'Are you the Derry manager?' he asked. 'No,' answered Eamonn with a straight face, 'he's in there.'

The Derry players would be lost without Eamonn Coleman. He's not just a manager, he's their friend and inspiration. 'I'm happier playing cards at the back of the bus than sitting at the front with the County Board men.' He was the players' choice as leader, the man they wanted to give them direction and purpose. Therefore, Coleman's pledge at their first meeting in February 1991 to win both the National League and the All-Ireland was music to their ears. The story goes that he points to a pillar in the middle of the dressing-room and says to his players, 'I don't want you going round that. I want you to go through it!' There are no back doors, no messing with Coleman; the players appreciate his competitiveness and discipline.

Coleman has twice been banned from the GAA for twelve months. In 1985, the defeated Derry Under-21 manager was judged to have moved forcibly towards the referee when one of his own players intercepted him at the end of their All-Ireland final with Cork. Coleman insists that the referee, Carthage Buckley, was a friend, and that he only wanted to question a particular decision. In the late seventies Coleman was found to have played for three clubs in one year. His weakness is a dislike of red tape; he has little time for the establishment.

Coleman's record is impressive. In thirty-three League and Championship games up to September this year, twenty-seven have been won, four lost (Down, Galway and Donegal twice) and two drawn. Yet, Derry were ten to one outsiders to win the Ulster title and slight underdogs in Newry to a Down team that had lost to Clare and Kerry in the League. Perhaps the bookmakers were judging Derry by their collapse to Donegal in their League quarter-final at Breffni Park when they scored only once in the second half to go down by 0-10 to 2-3. Question marks hung over Derry's composure, belief and ability to go the distance.

'It's up to you now,' the manager told his team before the Championship. 'I have given everything I can and have nothing more to give.' Derry handed Down their heaviest Ulster Championship defeat since 1952.

Coleman's Record

1991

National Football League
Derry 2-4	Leitrim 0-7
Derry 1-7	Tyrone 1-6
Derry 2-16	Longford 1-11

Senior Football Championship
Derry 1-9	Tyrone 1-8
Derry 0-13	Monaghan 0-8
Derry 1-10	Down 0-13
Derry 0-9	Down 0-14

National Football League
Derry 1-9	Meath 1-7
Derry 3-6	Kildare 0-7
Derry 1-8	Kerry 0-8

1992

Derry 2-13	Offaly 1-7
Derry 1-11	Down 0-7
Derry 1-11	Cavan 0-7
Derry 0-12	Meath 1-8
Derry 1-10	Tyrone 1-8

Senior Football Championship
Derry 1-10	Tyrone 1-7
Derry 1-14	Monaghan 3-8
Derry 2-9	Monaghan 0-7
Derry 0-15	Down 0-12
Derry 1-9	Donegal 0-14

National Football League
Derry 0-11	Dublin 0-9
Derry 2-8	Wexford 1-8
Derry 1-14	Limerick 1-8
Derry 0-9	Galway 1-8

1993

Derry 2-12	Sligo 2-8
Derry 2-9	Antrim 0-7
Derry 2-9	Louth 0-10
Derry 2-3	Donegal 0-10

Senior Football Championship
Derry 3-11	Down 0-9
Derry 0-19	Monaghan 0-11
Derry 0-8	Donegal 0-6
Derry 0-15	Dublin 0-14
Derry 1-14	Cork 2-7

Anthony Tohill epitomised the new spirit and maturity of the Derry squad. Four years after winning an All-Ireland Minor medal, the twenty-one-year-old was ready to deliver on the Senior stage. Helped by a spell in Australian Rules football, the 6'4" midfielder from Swatragh had developed into a finely-tuned athlete. In the spring Tohill was timed at 64 seconds for 400 metres on grass.

In Newry, he leapt highest to field the very first ball at the start of the game, as he did at the start of the second half. Such was his control in the middle that the pressure exerted on a susceptible Down defence began to tell early on. After twelve minutes, Damien Barton took advantage of a slip by full-back Conor Deegan and transferred quickly to the unattended Dermot Heaney for the first goal. Had Deegan read a preview of the game that morning by Liam Hayes in the *Sunday Press*? 'Conor Deegan is not quite the insurmountable figure he has been painted by full-forwards and newspaper men alike ... Some day soon he will pay a heavy price for his unbounded playfulness in front of his own goal'. Hayes' article was headlined 'Derry have a point to prove' and not for the first time in the Championship, his assessment of the Northern scene, and of Derry in particular, made the former Meath captain stand out among the media experts.

Ross Carr converted just enough free-kicks to keep Down in touch but their only real source of joy was Mickey Linden whose pace was too much for Tony Scullion, just back from injury. He was replaced after twenty-five minutes and Gary Coleman snuffed out the danger. Derry's other regular corner-back, Kieran McKeever, was missing through suspension but John McGurk stuck close to James McCartan. The fact that Derry could manage without two of their vital links emphasised the strength of their squad.

Minutes before the break, Carr had a goal chance blocked by Derry goalkeeper Damien McCusker, who showed the benefits of coaching from former county keeper John Somers. 'Stand up until the last minute,' was the advice he put into practice on this occasion and again in the Ulster final when John Duffy burst through on a one-on-one. McCusker kept four clean sheets up to the All-Ireland final.

In the second half at Newry, Richard Ferris and Eamonn Burns turned the screw with two more goals. Down's John Kelly vented his frustration when surrounded by Derrymen and was sent off.

Disgruntled Down supporters left the ground early, angry at the margin and manner of the defeat. Their team had failed to match Derry's attitude and were beaten in every department. Just twenty months after winning the All-Ireland title, Down had slid all the way back down the ladder.

McGRATH'S WRATH

'Our performance was a complete shambles,' Pete McGrath admitted. 'I think Down fans are owed an apology by everyone connected with the team. The players worked hard for this game and I felt the frame of mind was good but they lacked hunger out there. It's a bit of a mystery but I feel the players will have to come to terms with it and try to sort out in their own minds exactly where we went wrong.'

Several theories cropped up in the following months. One was that Down had gone into the game with too many unfit players who had carried niggling injuries during the build-up. Barry Breen injured a hamstring in a challenge the previous Sunday; DJ Kane had ankle ligament damage from another challenge a week before that, and John Kelly was not quite back to match fitness after a shoulder injury he received against Kerry in the quarter-final of the National League. Eamonn Burns had a cast removed from his wrist (broken bones) on the Friday before the game and Gary Mason had hamstring trouble.

Above left: Mark Gallagher gets to the ball first, Fermanagh v Armagh. *Top right:* Jim McCorry, Armagh's manager. *Bottom right:* Peter Canavan and Adrian Cush of Tyrone sit out the Championship.

Eamonn Coleman was of the opinion that Donegal in 1992 were a much better team than Down in 1991, and although I would not for a minute undervalue their magnificent achievement in winning the All-Ireland, the same players have failed to produce the goods since. Thirteen of the team that beat Meath played in Newry, but as John Kelly confesses, 'it's just that little bit harder after you've been to the pinnacle.'

Some felt Pete McGrath had been too loyal to his '91 team. Brendan Mason was used in the League but with ten minutes to go in Newry, he upped and left the Down dug-out. Peter Withnall was retained, even though his refusal to 'knuckle down' had caused friction in the camp. Later, in August, Withnall was dropped from the Down panel for the 1993/94 National League.

After Newry, some Down players remained unhappy at McGrath's comments on television. They felt the blame had been left squarely with them, and in August there was talk of players meeting just before the manager was reappointed. Paddy O'Rourke departed the management team and County Chairman Danny Murphy joined it. A new panel was drawn up, with many new faces brought in by McGrath who vowed to lift Down from their low point back to the top, as he had done before.

Elsewhere, the most dramatic game of the Championship was the replay between Armagh and Fermanagh at the Athletic Grounds on 23 May. With eight minutes to go, Fermanagh were 1-15 to 1-7 ahead and coasting. Mark Gallagher, Collie Curran and Brian Carty were running the show with a fluent, confident short-passing game, while young Raymond Gallagher scored a goal on his debut and had another effort stopped on the goal-line. Armagh had been a man short since the opening minutes when Dominic Clarke was sent off. Midfielder Jarlath Burns was stretchered off at the start of the second-half, and Neil Smyth had a penalty blocked by Cormac McAdam. The contest was as good as over, so what harm could a fresh pair of legs do on either side?

Armagh sent on Denis Holywood for his Championship debut and the Fermanagh manager Hugh McCabe replaced Raymond Curran with Michael McCaffrey in the thirty-first minute of the half. Suddenly, the Fermanagh defence fell apart at the seams and Armagh found acres of room in front of goal. The first chance fell to Ger Houlihan but he blazed the ball wide. Moments later, Holywood shot unchallenged to the net when put through by Houlihan. The sequence of events from that moment went like this:

32:50 Holywood goal for Armagh	2-7 to 1-15
35.02 Gallagher point for Fermanagh	2-7 to 1-16
35.32 Holywood point for Armagh	2-8 to 1-16
36:04 Holywood goal for Armagh	3-8 to 1-16
37:00 McAdam blocks goal effort from Barry O'Hagan	
37:28 Grimley goal for Armagh	4-8 to 1-16
40:27 Full-time.	

Houlihan was also the provider for Holywood's second goal, taking possession after John Grimley had charged down a casual clearance by McCaffrey. The winning goal came when Ciaran McGurk launched a high ball into the Fermanagh goal area. Houlihan palmed the ball into the path of John Grimley and the big man picked his spot in the corner of the net. As Grimley and Houlihan embraced, the crowd looked on in disbelief. Many had left the game early, only to hear the astonishing news on their car radios.

'I'm absolutely devastated,' Fermanagh manager Hugh McCabe told Owen McConnon on BBC television (see colour photo section). 'I changed the team when I brought on a sub: it didn't work and could have been responsible for losing the game. I have taken a lot of plaudits for this team but today was my fault.' Shocked viewers watched as the visibly distressed McCabe choked on his words. 'I would take the criticism for that defeat and will have to consider my position.'

Messages of support were sent and phoned to the McCabe home in the days that followed, Brian McEniff for one urging his neighbour not to resign. Fermanagh's County Executive called a meeting to 'make sure we learn from our mistakes and to let the players and management know that the board is fully behind them'. Players insisted that in no way were they blaming McCabe for the defeat, and that they were the ones who lost the game on the pitch. McCabe agreed to stay.

'THE DREAM TEAM'

Tyrone were next up for Armagh. National League finalists in 1992, All-Ireland Under-21 winners in 1991 and '92, and guided by the 'dream team' of Art McCrory and Eugene McKenna with Dessie Ryan, Tyrone were widely tipped as the team of the future. However, the team emerged from an arduous winter almost unrecognisable as the one John Donnelly had built to almost win the League in '92. Some supporters argued that the new managers had 'destroyed a good team,' but others were prepared to be patient. The new managers had assessed more than forty players over the winter, with Art McCrory testing their durability and commitment. His eyes were firmly on the Championship, though the short-term results were not encouraging. Defeat in Laois meant a drop to Division Three, while Derry were twelve-point winners in the McKenna Cup.

Morale was low and the panel reduced itself to less than thirty, with former regulars such as Enda Kilpatrick and Kevin McCabe quietly departing the scene. Management accepted blame for the Laois game, they had worked the players too hard. Worse was to follow. Star forward Peter Canavan cracked a bone in his ankle just weeks before the Armagh game and so joined Adrian Cush on the sideline. Cush had a disc removed in a back operation and was ruled out for a year. Defenders Paul O'Neill and John Lynch were also injured.

Tyrone gave seven debuts against Armagh, including two in the central defensive positions and the entire half-forward line.

Eugene McKenna admitted there were 'a lot of questions I really won't know the answers to until the game starts.' With five minutes to go to half-time, the new boys had Armagh on the ropes, leading by 1-7 to 0-4. Tyrone also had reason to complain when Mattie McGleenan's second 'goal' was ruled out by referee Tommy McDermott for square ball in the twenty-seventh minute.

The game swung in the closing minutes of the half, as Armagh reduced the deficit to four points before the interval. For the second half the home captain John Rafferty moved to midfield to counter Tyrone's dominance in that area and, slowly but surely, Armagh whittled down Tyrone's lead. Tyrone's Championship looked over when Finbarr McConnell dropped a ball under a challenge outside his area, but the referee again ruled out the score. In another exciting climax, John Toner kicked the equaliser from a 45 in the last minute.

Armagh manager Jim McCorry made a bold move for the replay in Omagh, awarding debuts to All-Ireland Minor stars from 1992, Diarmuid Marsden and Des Mackin. Most of his injured parties had recovered but McCorry gave youth its chance. At half-time, Armagh led by 1-5 to 0-6 but Tyrone hit a purple patch in the second period with six points in a row.

Faced with yet another crisis, the 'Player of the Championship' Ger Houlihan struck the kind of goal Armagh knew he was capable of scoring. Taking possession twenty yards from goal, seven minutes from time, he ambled forward with only a goal on his mind. Houlihan sidestepped a defender and thumped the ball past McConnell and into the roof of the Tyrone net. The goalscorer gave the goalkeeper a playful nudge on the way past, 'because moments earlier big

Tyrone captain, Plunkett Donaghy, leads from the front watched by team-mates Barry McGinn and Sean Teague with Armagh's Des Mackin in pursuit.

Finbarr had booted his spare ball over the stand to waste time.' It was fast turning into Houlihan's Championship, a fact acknowledged by supporters from his home club, Pearse Óg, who carried a large banner reading 'Telegraph it Houly!' The explanation for the cryptic message is that Houlihan's girlfriend is the daughter of John Campbell, sports journalist with the *Belfast Telegraph*.

Ironically, the losers took credit from their Championship display against Armagh. Tyrone are still without a Championship win in the 1990s — perhaps they have suffered from too much team-building — but the 'new' young charges gave a strong enough hint of hope for the future. Inexperience and missed chances (eight bad wides in the second half of the replay) had been their downfall while Art McCrory lamented the harsh sending-off of 'our steadying man' Colm Donaghy in the first match and the loss of Canavan and Cush. 'If we'd had those two in Armagh we would have won the game.'

'GET IN THERE AND DO THE DAMAGE'

Resident television expert Liam Austin caused a stir by tipping Armagh to dethrone All-Ireland champions Donegal in the semi-finals of the Ulster Championship. The former Down midfielder reasoned that Armagh were the team on a roll, with a confident panel and a proven matchwinner. Donegal had only three points to spare in beating a lively Antrim side, and they had a long list of injuries.

Brian McEniff's team were showing all the signs of wear and tear from a demanding All-Ireland and League campaign. Donegal would have been content to bow out of the League at the quarter-final stage to almost anyone else but Derry: then Clare gave Donegal an easy passage into a final which dragged a tired team through two games. Club demands on players exacerbated the situation with Martin McHugh claiming that players were 'too tired to train'. Others picked up injuries. Anthony Molloy needed a fourth operation on his troublesome knee while Martin Gavigan, Tony Boyle, Barry Cunningham and James McHugh had various problems.

After the Antrim game, McEniff expressed his dissatisfaction with the club situation to the County Board and they agreed to abandon relegation in the Donegal leagues for the year.

The champions were not in the clear. Just before the semi-final John Cunningham cried off with injury and eighteen minutes into the game, Barry McGowan pulled up with a hamstring injury. Donal Reid took a hefty challenge from John Grimley which would keep the All Star out of the remainder of the Championship, and Noel Hegarty was sent off for a late and high tackle on Jarlath Burns.

Donegal also contrived to shoot eleven wides in the first half, yet still lead by 0-8 to 1-3. In the second-half, Armagh produced their best football of the championship. Houlihan tapped over a lovely score off the outside of his left boot, Martin McQuillan pointed from distance and Des Mackin put Armagh in front on forty-eight minutes, 1-7 to 0-9. The sight of Armagh's large and colourful support behind the goals rising to mark each score left Brian McEniff looking worried. Manus Boyle inexplicably failed to raise a fourteen-yard free above the crossbar while John Toner's accuracy from greater distances had Armagh in front by 1-12 to 0-11.

Entering the closing stages, Armagh led by two points. The Donegal manager turned to his bench and gambled. 'Get in there and do the damage,' he said to John Duffy. McEniff remembered Duffy scoring three goals against Bundoran as a fourteen-year-old in 1985, and he won a London Championship for Tír Chonaill Gaels almost single-handedly in 1992, but was not 'overly-committed'. With his first touch, Duffy slipped the ball to Martin McHugh to score.

With time fast running out, referee Michael Cranny awarded a free to Donegal. Michael Gallagher delivered the ball into the hands of John Duffy who swivelled and split the posts, almost in one movement. The champions were alive. 'You never realise how much you want something until you see it draining

Martin Gavigan in 'The Cage' bandaged from ankle to thigh.

away,' observed panellist Sylvester Maguire.

Brian McEniff promised himself coming away from Newry that he would not play unfit players. He stuck to his word for the replay, preferring to blood new players such as Declan Boyle who had not even togged out in Breffni. Boyle holidayed in Greece only three weeks earlier, before receiving a note: 'Drop round to training. We want to see you.'

Boyle proved a capable replacement for Donal Reid while Duffy and Mark Crossan (debuted in drawn game) all started. And, with several of the more established players returning to form the second day, Donegal destroyed Armagh. Matt Gallagher, Brian Murray and Martin McHugh redeemed themselves, with McHugh featuring in a match-winning tactical move. Released from the hurly-burly of the central area to full-forward, the 'wee man' pointed after twenty seconds. The rest of the team was instructed to 'hit Martin with the early ball' and by the thirteenth minute, Donegal led by 2-5 to 0-0. John Duffy and Mark McShane (another new name) grabbed the goals.

Houlihan replied with his fourth goal of the Championship in the second half *(See colour photo section)* but Armagh's spectacular contribution to the Ulster Championship, over six games, petered out. Donegal were in the Ulster final.

'WE'RE ON A MISSION'

With all the fuss and drama diverted by the Armagh side of the draw, Derry moved quietly into the Clones final, in contrast to their over-worked summer of 1992. They eventually shook off a determined challenge from Monaghan when Joe Brolly's point within seconds of his introduction nine minutes into the second half put Derry 0-10 to 0-9 in front. From there, Derry romped home by 19 points to 11.

Painful memories remained vivid in Derry minds of the 1992 Ulster final, when they failed to meet the promise and expectation among their support. Sitting in the traffic in Clones, Henry Downey and his team had seen 'pain on people's faces and tears in the eyes of the young.' After the 1992 League win and the toppling of All-Ireland champions Down in the Ulster semi-finals, Derry had been defeated by Donegal in 1992. They had lost to Down in 1991. 'We've just got to do it this time,' declared Eamonn Coleman. 'We've got to go all the way. We're on a mission!'

On the Monday night before the Ulster final, Danny Quinn was taken to one side and told that he would not be playing. Donegal's nippy forwards had given him a torrid time in '92 and the big full-back had been substituted in the semi-final with Monaghan. Strangely, Quinn was still named in the team given to the press and it was only when the players lined out at Clones that it became clear he was not on the team. Quinn would be recalled for the All-Ireland semi-final with Dublin only to be withdrawn after nineteen minutes.

SUMMER IN CLONES

Derry put in a spirited display to win the Ulster final but the occasion is best remembered for the awful conditions in which it was played. Twelve hours of rain, including a torrential downpour at lunchtime, left pools of water on the surface. Spectators wondered whether the games could be played. Word circulated that the referee of the Minor match did not want to go ahead. Unfortunately, such fears were realised when Derry Minor Cathal Scullion sustained a broken shin-bone. With no first aid readily available, apart from that from the Derry camp, the player was carried off the pitch by his team-mates and the Derry chairman.

After the lowest-scoring final in forty years, Eamonn Coleman and his players were united in their condemnation of the pitch. 'I think it was ridiculous to bring this Ulster final here today,' said the manager, 'to ask men who have trained since February to play in conditions like that.' Henry Downey said they had been accustomed to playing on rock-hard pitches all summer while Enda Gormley suggested that the Ulster Council should review its policy.

The issue was not just the weather on the day of the game, but the fact that this was the first game played on a new pitch. After the 1992 final, St Tiernach's Park had undergone phase one of a major facelift which included the digging up of the playing surface and its replacement with a new sod. Its maturity was not aided by a poor summer.

GAA President Peter Quinn admitted that there was 'always a fear that if it rained we might have a problem.' The gamble on the weather did not pay off. Rainwater was unable to seep through the undersoil of the fresh sod and consequently it sat on the surface *(See colour photo)*. However, Quinn defended the decision to play the game on the new pitch. 'I was here yesterday and found the pitch in marvellous condition. You could have played billiards on it. No pitch anywhere in Ireland could have taken the rainfall of the last twelve hours, roads in some areas were even flooded.'

Off-the-pitch organisation was makeshift, to say the least. New dug-outs were in place but were not covered. Nobody in the 27,500 crowd was protected from the elements apart from the media, some of whom were housed on the back of lorries. A tannoy announcement urged people on the Hill to be careful on their way to the portable toilets. Phase two of the Clones development will rectify this situation but in 1993 there is little doubt that the venue was not ready for such an occasion. Had the weather been kind, the problem might not have arisen.

Most observers wanted to know why the Ulster Council had not 'played safe' and taken the game out of Clones for one year. Martin McHugh had suggested Croke Park as a venue (before the Leinster Hurling final was drawn) while Casement Park was put forward by most parties as the 'logical choice'. Jack Boothman, President-Elect of the GAA, lauded the Belfast setting after the Down-Derry semi-final in 1992 when the attendance was estimated by seasoned supporters at 30-35,000. Many players and fans favour this venue, for its playing surface and easy access. Before the decision was made to develop Clones as the premier ground in Ulster, a poll in the *Irish News* drew 3,000 replies with 92% in favour of Casement Park, Belfast.

The Ulster Council insist the Casement capacity is only 22-23,000 and that some of the counties with the biggest 'potential' support (Monaghan, Cavan, Donegal) prefer Clones. Brian McLernon, President of the Ulster Council, revealed that some council members had suggested moving the 1993 Ulster final venue some weeks beforehand, but the majority voted to stand by their aim to play the game in Clones.

You had to feel sorry for Donegal, losing their All-Ireland crown in these circumstances. Ironically, a request by Brian McEniff to postpone the Ulster final for one week had been turned down flat. Donegal might not have won seven days later (even with Tony Boyle, Noel Hegarty and the rest) but the furore over the venue might have been avoided.

Anthony Tohill was again Derry's match-winner in a burst of brilliance directly after half-time. During the interval, manager Eamonn Coleman had reminded Tohill of the previous Ulster final when he had been unfit to come out for the second half. Within ten seconds of the restart, the midfielder won a free which he then converted from fifty-five yards to make it 0-5 each. In the next six minutes, he carried the game to Donegal, winning ball and laying it off for Cassidy, Barton and Gormley to score. Derry did not score again but Donegal only managed one point in the entire half, a tribute to the Derry defence. Tony Scullion dived full length to block a late goal effort by Manus Boyle. Their half-backs played a vital role in carrying the ball forward, beating Donegal at their own short game: 'we practised that since last year and anyway, there was no point in trying to kick-pass the ball because it wouldn't bounce,' said Eamonn Coleman.

'CROKE PARK'S MY STAGE!'

Joe Brolly was dropped from the Derry panel at the start of the Ulster Championship. 'Get your act together,' was the message to the Dungiven man who was just another face in the crowd at Newry on May 30. Recalled soon after, Brolly made his mark in the last 26 minutes against Monaghan, he came on for the last sixteen minutes against Donegal in Clones and then played the entire match against Dublin. 'You've gotta play me, Croke Park's my stage!' he

Derry trainer Mickey Moran rushes to the changing rooms at half time in the semi-final to give a very strong team talk.

repeated to Eamonn Coleman in the weeks before the All-Ireland semi-final. Just like Manus Boyle the year before, Brolly's nerve and confidence is best suited to the big occasion.

The media adore him. Holding court in the middle of the Derry dressing-room after the Dublin semi-final, Brolly gave the pressmen an abundance of great quotes. 'We were swanning around like superstars in the first half,' said Joe. 'It's a cauldron out there, you don't hear anything. We were like headless chickens.' He stopped. 'Does anybody else want to get a word in?' 'No, no, no, keep going, Joe!'

The Dungiven man likes to joke around. Beating Dublin was 'a great laugh, great crack. Sure it doesn't happen often!' He also likes to perform. After scoring goals he used to run back with a beaming smile and arms flagging up and down, airplane-like. A Down player remarked that 'one of these days he's going to get thumped.'

His team-mates don't really listen. 'There goes Joe again!'; but they also knew that without Brolly they might not be in the All-Ireland final. Almost every ball went into the right corner of the Derry attack in the second half and Brolly won almost every one of them. Sometimes he started five yards behind his man, sometimes in front and sometimes alongside. It didn't matter, Brolly's speed and timing had different markers at a loss.

He scored just one point, but the possession he won and distributed between the 21- and 50-yard lines was the vital cog that turned the Derry machine into action on its magnificent comeback.

THE MOMENT OF TRUTH

Five points behind Dublin at half-time, Derry supporters feared the worst. Gormley's early free-kicks and Anthony Tohill's gem of a point (rifled over from under Hill 16) were forgotten as Dublin led 0-9 to 0-4. The Leinster champions won the last twenty-five minutes of the half by nine points to one, hence Brolly's 'swanning around like superstars' assessment. 'We believed we were there and forgot that we have to work hard. We play good football but we cannot deceive ourselves that we are a brilliant team. We must sweat blood and tears.'

ALL-IRELAND SEMI-FINAL 1993		
SECOND-HALF	Derry	Dublin
37 mins - Tohill (F)	0-5	0-9
38 mins - H.Downey	0-6	0-9
39 mins - Heery	0-6	0-10
40 mins - Coleman	0-7	0-10
42 mins - Redmond	0-7	0-11
47 mins - McGilligan	0-8	0-11
48 mins - Clarke	0-8	0-12
49 mins - Gormley	0-9	0-12
52 mins - Gormley	0-10	0-12
56 mins - Redmond	0-10	0-13
58 mins - Gormley (F)	0-11	0-13
60 mins - Brolly	0-12	0-13
63 mins - Gormley (F)	0-13	0-13
64 mins - H.Downey	0-14	0-13
65 mins - Redmond (F)	0-14	0-14
68 mins - McGurk	0-15	0-14
FULL-TIME		

'Where will I kick this one?' Derry's Brian McGilligan and Manager, Eamonn Coleman in Croke Park, 1993.

At half-time, Derry listened. 'You either run away from the game or start to play football,' challenged Eamonn Coleman. Team trainer Mickey Moran, normally a reserved background figure, angrily stepped forward to take the floor from the manager. 'Are you going to throw away all the work we've done? Are you going to die on the big day like other Derry teams of the past?'

Moran had played on the Derry sides of the mid-seventies, which many felt had the talent to win an All-Ireland. This young team also had talent, and had won a National League, but playing against the Dubs in Croke Park in front of more than 60,000 was something else again. 'The welcome we got when we came out at the start should stay with us for the rest of our lives,' said Damien Cassidy. 'I would say it was unparalleled in the history of Derry football. Apart from the Hill, it was as if we had the whole ground.' Could Derry rise to the occasion?

Derry needed leadership and a touch of good fortune. The latter came from referee Tommy Sugrue in the shape of a fortunate free in front of the Dublin goal just after the restart: the former came from centre-half-back and captain, Henry Downey.

In front of him, McGilligan had faded after a super start; Tohill looked as if he was wary of the ankle problem he picked up in training; Barton and Cassidy were easily contained on the half-forward line; Heaney had not settled in his new position of right-half-forward and some observers would have switched him with Seamus Downey, the surprise selection at full-forward who had not played in the Championship for more than a year. None of the forwards had managed a single score from play. Henry stormed through the ineptitude, accepted a pass and coolly lobbed the ball over the bar. Easy! He did it again in the closing stages

Above: The winning point. Anthony Tohill (8) celebrates before McGurk's kick sails over the Dublin crossbar. *Below:* The break-through! At the final whistle the Derry bench delight in their victory over Dublin in the semi-final.

to put Derry ahead, his first points of the Championship. Joe Brolly joked that he had been giving him lessons. 'It beats me how someone like Henry could send a pinpoint pass from forty yards but not take scores.' Henry formed a match-winning half-back-line which did the job the half-forwards could not do, running at the Dublin defence to win frees and take scores, including a

memorable fisted point from Gary Coleman.

Still, Derry could not reduce the gap to two points until midway through the second half when they took a firm grip of the contest. Charlie Redmond ended up fighting a lone battle as Heaney dropped back to form a three-man block across the middle of the park which no Dubliner was to pass. Sheedy faded after feeling the full force of a Brian McGilligan shoulder charge and Tohill caught a few important balls. Substitute Dermot McNicholl picked up the pieces and ran aggressively at an unsettled Dublin defence.

Eamonn Coleman called the right shots on the touchline. As well as McNicholl for Cassidy, Damien Barton was removed directly after having an effort blocked down in front of goal. He also resisted the temptation to switch Seamus Downey, and earlier moved the ever-reliant Tony Scullion onto Vinny Murphy. It was a confident manager that watched the last quarter unfold, 'When we came within two points, I felt we were going to win. The work done on the fields of Ballymaguigan and Maghera in February worked for us.' (Derry, in fact, had fifty-eight training sessions up to the end of June.)

THE McGURKS FROM LAVEY

With seven minutes to go, Seamus Downey was fouled and Enda Gormley brought the sides level. Henry Downey and Redmond then exchanged points as a thrilling second-half kept the crowd on their toes right into the last ninety seconds. Joe Brolly roamed inside and the ball was worked out to McNicholl on the right. His pass to the overlapping John McGurk (now right-half-forward) was overhit but the Lavey man was allowed to collect and work off his left foot. A Derry supporter seated in a line behind McGurk had a perfect view, 'you wouldn't believe how much the ball curled when McGurk hit it. It started towards the far post and came in to drop over the bar, crossing the black spot.' Put simply, it was the mother of all winning points in an All-Ireland semi-final.

'The McGurks are a special breed of family,' said Eamonn Coleman of John and his six brothers. Collie is in the 1993 squad, Hugh Martin captained Derry in the eighties and Anthony won two All Stars in the seventies. 'Every one of them gives his life for Derry and Lavey.'

Joe Brolly shed a tear as the Derry fans celebrated. 'Imagine the excitement of a small county like ours on the brink of something really big. It was sheer pandemonium, an amazing atmosphere and very emotional. It was too much really.'

Derry's victory carried with it two important side-effects. First, it maintained the balance of power within Ulster (Dublin had threatened this state of affairs by beating Donegal in the National League final), and second, it finally put Derry on the All-Ireland map. Earlier defeats of Down and Donegal had put the record straight in Ulster, but coming from five points behind to beat Dublin in Croke Park, proved what Eamonn Coleman had been saying all along. They *were* as good as any county in Ireland.

Derry covered every possible angle in 1993. Team doctor Ben Glancy deleted chips from the food menu because of the fat content, the players imposed a drink

Backroom support: Dr Ben Glancey, team doctor; Harry Gribben, assistant; Craig Mahoney, team psychologist; and John Somers, goalkeeping coach.

ban on themselves (most stuck to it religiously, others had a few after games), and a Sports Science Lecturer was enrolled from Queen's University.

Craig Mahoney, an Australian with associations in Rules football, joined the team. Derry had a reputation for choking when under pressure, yet in four of their five championship games this year they showed remarkable composure and mental toughness to come through vital, testing periods. Mahoney pinpoints a squad meeting on the evening after the National League quarter-final defeat by Donegal in April as a turning point. 'Our problem was one of communication between players and management, but after the first two hours we had some real honesty and some players even became verbally abusive, which was exactly what I wanted. At the end of the night we had communication.'

Eamonn Coleman attributes Derry's composed look to their short game, which had become second nature to them. He also recognises the *overriding* importance of his back-up team, from Mickey Moran, 'the best trainer in Ireland', to Eugene Young and goalkeeping coach John Somers, and to Harry Gribben and Dinny McKeever, his trusty mentors. Together they made up a formidable team on the sideline, most especially during Championship matches when they made crucial and correct moves.

THE FINAL STEP

The Derry manager was a happier man in the months of August and September, mainly because the ghosts of '92 had been buried. Derry had finally come out of Ulster and beaten Donegal, 'the best team in Ireland apart from ourselves. That win gave me most pleasure this year, it made people sit up and take us seriously'. Derry carried with them the confidence and organisation necessary to go all the way, the manager was left to pick his team for the last step to Sam.

Criticism of his forwards was flatly rejected, even though twelve different men had been used in four games. Cassidy and Barton had both been replaced in the semi-final and none of the forwards managed to score from play for two-thirds of the contest. 'The important thing is that we got the scores and won the game.' Coleman named the same six forwards for the final, resisting the temptation to start Dermot McNicholl.

He studied videos of Cork games and exchanged notes with Brian McEniff, as he had done for the Dublin game. The Derry manager saw possibilities for his forwards against the Cork defence; full-back Mark O'Connor was really a wing-back, Cahalane had 'lost a bit of pace' and Stephen O'Brien 'might suit Damien Barton'. At midfield, Coleman was confident of Derry's superiority while he reckoned his revered defence would be capable of shackling Cork's attack which had looked impressive in totalling 5-15 in their semi-final with Mayo.

At the Derry press night in Glenullin, Coleman's main problem was in keeping Joe Brolly away from the spotlight. The fluent, frank assessments of the barrister from Dungiven were not considered to be helpful in the run-up to the game. The manager kept a sceptical eye on all the media people, even spotting the lone Corkman, Michael Ellard from the *Cork Examiner*. Coleman bent an ear to a television interview with Ellard but walked away scornfully when the opinion was offered that Cork's experience gained in previous All-Ireland finals would carry them through. Elsewhere, Seamus Downey revealed that his mother does not go to watch her sons play. 'She goes to pray in the chapel but on the day of the semi-final she left too early and heard from a radio in a shop that Dublin were leading with seven minutes to go. She headed back to the chapel!'

Johnny McGurk tried to repeat his left-footed point during training but, much to the amusement of his colleagues, he was unable to do so. More seriously, at the very end of the press evening, the half-back pulled a hamstring. Intensive treatment over the next week averted the scare. There were no more worries until a few days before the final when Enda Gormley was laid low by a virus. If the game had been on the Saturday, Gormley may not have played, and on the Sunday morning he had to drink a green 'cocktail' of vitamins.

The players were very aware of the groundswell of support within and without of their own county. Huge crowds sent them on their way from Dungiven, Maghera and Moneymore while Malachy McAfee, a former Derry player now exiled in Sydney, Australia, arrived home for the game. Some of the team watched Phil Stuart, a midfielder on the only previous Derry team to play in an All-Ireland final, explain on a BBC television preview programme that it would mean more to him now to see Derry take the Sam Maguire than when he was a 21-year-old in 1958. Stuart's emotion was evident as he said that 'it would make me very proud'. Damien Barton remarked to his team-mates, 'If that's what it means to Phil Stuart, what does it mean to us?'

On Sunday afternoon, Derry's team bus took just seven minutes to get from the International Airport Hotel to Croke Park, thanks to a Garda escort. When Henry Downey bounded out from the tunnel onto the pitch and towards Hill 16 it became clear which of the red and white flags were from Derry and which were from Cork.

In the pre-match parade, Derry's number 15 gave rise to concern as he appeared to haul his right leg at the back of the queue. However, a Derryman assured me that 'Gormley's always like that'. Later, the forward revealed that he needs another operation on his right knee and that he had 'hardly used the right leg all year'.

Henry Downey was at his third All-Ireland final, the last viewed from near the front of the Nally Stand in 1991. This time, the Derry captain won the toss and played into the same end of the ground, with the advantage of the swirling wind. Before the start, Gary Coleman switched onto the Cork dangerman, Colin Corkery, but neither the wind nor the switch seemed to matter as Cork raced into a five-point lead. 'They were better than I thought,' admitted Eamonn Coleman after the game. John O'Driscoll and Corkery won the first few high

ALL-IRELAND FINAL 1993		
FIRST HALF	Derry	Cork
1 min - T.Davis	0-0	0-1
5 mins - Kavanagh	0-0	1-1
6 mins - Corkery (F)	0-0	1-2
7 mins - McGurk	0-1	1-2
11 mins - McGilligan	0-2	1-2
13 mins - Gormley (F)	0-3	1-2
14 mins - Tohill (45)	0-4	1-2
15 mins - S.Downey	1-4	1-2
18 mins - Tohill	1-5	1-2
19 mins - Fahy	1-5	1-3
21 mins - Corkery (F)	1-5	1-4
23 mins - Gormley (F)	1-6	1-4
24 mins - Brolly	1-7	1-4
27 mins - Kavanagh (F)	1-7	1-5
28 mins - Corkery	1-7	1-6
34 mins - Gormley	1-8	1-6
37 mins - Gormley	1-9	1-6
HALF TIME		

balls in the full-forward line while Joe Kavanagh burst clear of Henry Downey for a stunning goal. 'My legs felt like lead,' revealed the Derry captain who had been suffering from a bout of flu for the previous three days.

Johnny McGurk calmed Derry hearts with their opening score on seven minutes. Brian McGilligan tapped over another after a slip by Teddy McCarthy and Derry were in business. In the eleven minutes from McGurk's point to the eighteenth minute, they scored 1-5, all from play and without reply. The sequence included an opportunist goal from Seamus Downey when he capitalised on confusion in the Cork goal area. John Kerins and Mark O'Connor both stopped and watched as Downey's fist met Damien Cassidy's goalward lob. A minute earlier, Damien Cassidy had another goal chance blocked by Kerins after a superb set-up by Dermot Heaney. Tohill pointed from the resultant 45.

Derry goalkeeper Damien McCusker shouted to his defenders to concentrate on the game as spectators spilled onto the side of the pitch from one corner of the Canal End. Tony Scullion and Henry Downey barely noticed as they broke Cork hearts with vital interceptions, stalking the man with the ball before prising it from his grasp, perfect examples of how to tackle in Gaelic football.

Still, the game could have turned again critically towards the Leesiders but for a point-blank save by Damien McCusker from Michael McCarthy in the twentieth minute. A goal would have put Cork in front and jolted Derry's confidence once again, but as it was, Derry maintained their slight advantage with scores by Enda Gormley and Joe Brolly.

What followed is not in the textbook. Four minutes from half time, Enda Gormley crashed to the floor after a left hook from Niall Cahalane. Referee Tommy Howard consulted his umpires and booked the Corkman, much to the derision of the Derry support and television viewers who saw the incident clearly on replay. Leaving the pitch at half time, Eamonn Coleman was adamant. 'Cahalane shoulda gone. If you strike a man in this game, you have to go.'

The minutes leading up to the half-time whistle were the most telling of the entire final. Within a minute of his booking, Cahalane was dispossessed coming

All-Ireland Final winners 1993 -- the Derry team. *Back, left to right:* Joe Brolly, Dermot Heaney, Anthony Tohill, Damien McCusker, Seamus Downey, Tony Scullion, Damien Barton, Brian McGilligan. *Front, left to right:* Enda Gormley, Johnny McGurk, Henry Downey (captain), Kieran McKeever, Gary Coleman, Fergal McCusker, Damien Cassidy.

out with the ball. Gormley ran free near the left touchline, took a pass and coolly lobbed over a marvellous point, wagging his finger at Cahalane on his way back outfield. Gormley was alert again moments later when Gary Coleman's kick rebounded off a post, the Maghera man rising bravely to punch the ball over the bar. Derry stretched their lead to three but more importantly, they had kept their discipline (they had just one booking in the entire Championship) and answered Cork in the best way possible.

Cork were also reduced to fourteen men in this brief flurry of activity, Anthony Davis being sent off after crashing into Dermot Heaney. Most people viewed that Davis had suffered for Cahalane's sins, that the referee had put pressure on himself by only booking Cahalane for the earlier incident. The Games Administration Committee appeared to agree, as they later 'exonerated' Davis by giving him the minimum two-week suspension, and Cahalane two months.

In the Derry dressing-room Eamonn Coleman asked Dermot McNicholl whether he was ready to come on. 'Bloody right' replied the former All Star. 'I've been ready for weeks.' 'You couldn't score furniture,' cracked Adrian Logan (Ulster Television) after the game, yet McNicholl was the only Derryman to hit the target for twenty-five minutes of the second half, and a magnificent effort it was too. A neat interchange with Henry Downey was followed by a driven point from out on the right side.

Cork's half-time substitution was also successful. Danny Culloty showed why many observers felt he should have been on from the start, instead of the ineffective Teddy McCarthy. Ten minutes into the half Don Davis split the Derry defence with a crossfield pass. John O'Driscoll, running forward from his new

Enda Gormley scores a point from a free in the final

midfield position, took the ball in his stride and rifled an unstoppable shot into Damien McCusker's net to put Cork ahead. For the second time in the game, Derry were asked how much they really wanted and believed they could win the All-Ireland.

38 mins - Corkery (F)	1-9	1-7
42 mins - McNicholl	1-10	1-7
44 mins - Corkery (F)	1-10	1-8
45 mins - O'Driscoll	1-10	2-8
55 mins - Gormley	1-11	2-8
57 mins - Tohill (F)	1-12	2-8 **
62 mins - McGurk	1-13	2-8
65 mins - Gormley (F)	1-14	2-8 **

Eamonn Coleman beckoned Johnny McGurk and instructed Derry's extra man to stop 'getting in the way of the forwards'. Instead, McGurk was told to make himself available every time his fellow defenders came out with the ball. Derry's approach appeared over-elaborate with as many as eight short passes required on one occasion to find a man in a clear shooting position. Yet, this was a Derry team in control of the situation. In 1992 they learned that the direct route has an element of risk, especially against clever opponents. Now they were prepared to work hard and play the percentage game.

Scullion and McKeever swept up at the back, 'we just know where each other is all the time', while a fully revived and inspirational Henry Downey repeatedly set up and later joined Derry attacks. Still, for ten a half long minutes after O'Driscoll's goal, Derry failed to score. The forceful Dermot Heaney took one of Downey's clever lay-offs but John Kerins saved bravely in the Cork goal. Brolly fisted against the upright and from the rebound Seamus Downey pawed the ball wide.

Then, the pressure told. Gormley found his range in the swirling wind to level the scores, Anthony Tohill pointed a simple free after Barton was grounded and Johnny McGurk struck another left-foot special. With five minutes to go, Gormley curled a wonderful free-kick over the bar, Derry 1-14, Cork 2-8. Cork needed a goal but 'it seemed like there were twenty-five Derrymen in their goalmouth,' commented John O'Driscoll afterwards.

Grown men burst into tears within seconds of the final whistle. They never thought they would see the day a Derryman would lift the Sam Maguire. 'At last,

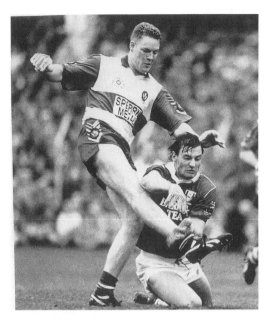

DERRY 1993			
Player	Matches	Minutes	Score
Gary Coleman	5	350	0-1
Henry Downey	5	350	0-2
Enda Gormley	5	350	0-25
Damien McCusker	5	350	-
Brian McGilligan	5	350	0-3
Anthony Tohill	5	350	0-15
Damien Barton	5	342	0-2
Dermot Heaney	5	311	1-1
Tony Scullion	5	305	-
Damien Cassidy	5	291	0-6
Fergal McCusker	5	207	-
John McGurk	4	280	0-3
Kieran McKeever	4	280	-
Joe Brolly	4	181	0-5
Dermot McNicholl	4	137	0-2
Karl Diamond	3	191	0-1
Danny Quinn	3	145	-
Eamonn Burns	3	81	1-1
Seamus Downey	2	128	1-0
Richard Ferris	2	105	1-0
Brian McCormack	2	105	-
Stephen Mulvenna	1	55	-

Dermot Heaney's goal bid blocked.

at last,' yelled Henry Downey as he looked at the cup above his head. In his acceptance speech, the captain declared that 'Derry needed this All-Ireland a lot more than Cork did.' Derry folk knew what he meant, years of toil finally seemed worthwhile; their craving to be recognised with the ultimate reward was the single greatest reason why Derry became champions. In the words of former World Champion boxer Dave McAuley, 'I'm not hungry to win, I'm starving!'

Restrained joy was the order of the day in the winners' dressing-rooms. There was even a touch of anti-climax 'because the semi-final was like a final and we really expected to win today,' explained Joe Brolly. As the media honed in on Eamonn Coleman, his players chanted 'I told youse boys, I told youse,' while Damien Barton revealed that a rendition of the 'Derry Air' the previous evening at the team hotel 'would have taken a tear from a stone', so deep was their pride and love for their county. Joe Brolly looked forward to taking the cup to the Bar Library in Belfast and showing it to the Lord Chief Justice (he received a round of applause when he returned to work at the Library after the semi-final). In a quiet corner, Man of the Match Johnny McGurk reflected on his good fortune to be the first of seven brothers to win an All-Ireland senior medal, 'This is for my mother who lost our father last year. I'm sure he's looking down on us today, so this one's for him as well.'

The party moved on to the post-match banquet at the Shelbourne Hotel where a comical-looking Eamonn Coleman was stopped on the way in by the doormen. 'No more allowed in for a minute,' they shouted to the crowd, not recognising the All-Ireland winning manager at the very front of the queue! Once inside, Coleman listened as his players took plaudits from RTE's 'Sunday Game' and Dermot McNicholl paid particular tribute to 'two men who deserve this day more than any others, Brian McGilligan and Tony Scullion'.

Scullion indeed was the happiest man in Dublin that night, beaming from ear to ear and willing to talk all night. He was annoyed about O'Driscoll's goal, 'I so nearly got to it', and regretted that 'poor Kieran (McKeever) wouldn't get an All Star because he had been sent off in the League,' but he hoped Derry would get at least as many as Donegal in 1992 (seven). Apart from himself, the certainties would appear to be McGurk, Henry Downey, Tohill (if his suspension case is appealed successfully) and Gormley, while Damien McCusker, Coleman, McGilligan, Barton, Heaney and Brolly fall into the list of 'possibles'. Midfield will be interesting: only once before have the selectors given both positions to one county (Kerry in 1981), yet Anthony Tohill is rated 'the best player in Ireland' and many support Eamonn Coleman's theory that the one man Derry would not have won an All-Ireland without, is Brian McGilligan.

In the longer-term, Coleman took pleasure from reading John O'Keeffe's assessment of his team in the *Irish Times* on Monday morning: 'The best Ulster team I have seen in all my time watching football ... Derry have the capacity to be a powerful force for years to come'. Finally, Derry were beginning to get the credit their manager always said they deserved. 'Youse boys' were starting to believe him.

On the drive North that afternoon Eamonn Coleman did not sit 'playing cards with the boys at the back of the bus'. He was perched proudly at the front, beside the Sam Maguire, waving at the thousands of smiling faces along the route.

On the steps of Drogheda cathedral, they made their first stop. After a presentation and a brief rendition of 'Back Home in Derry' from Joe Brolly, the bus rolled towards Dundalk for a similar stop. This time, the crowd covered the main square, and again Mr Brolly took to the microphone.

Arriving at the Carrickdale Hotel near the border at Newry, the players had difficulty in getting through the gathered masses from the bus to the function room. 'It's just unbelievable,' muttered Brian McGilligan, taken aback by the welcome and enthusiasm on the journey from Dublin. Anthony Tohill tried to imagine what the scenes were going to be like in their own county.

Back in Maghera, the town had been closed off from mid-afternoon as a massive crowd assembled for the champions. The schools had a day off, the pubs ran dry despite ordering three times their normal stock of beer, people danced and drank in the street. Publicans gave away drink at 1958 prices, 10p a pint!

The Sam Maguire had not strictly been beyond Newry and County Down until now, and on the streets in Armagh city, the Moy, Dungannon and Cookstown was evidence of the delight of the rest of Ulster at Derry's victory.

After Moneymore and Magherafelt, the All-Ireland champions edged into Maghera just after 3am. Upwards of twenty thousand people crammed into the town which was bedecked in red and white. Every vantage point was taken as the cup was held aloft on top of an open-decked double-decker bus for the greatest reception of the entire journey.

That week, the rest of the county celebrated in turn. Joe Brolly spoke for twenty minutes in his home town of Dungiven and was joined by his team-mates for a rousing chorus of 'The town I loved so well' and 'The Gem of the Roe', a song written by Brolly's proud parents.

However, parties like this one always have a touch of madness and irregularity about them and the said entertainer was again responsible. As the day broke early next morning, somebody pointed out that Joe had disappeared. Hours later, Brolly phoned from Belfast, explaining that he had hitched a lift with some workmen travelling from Dungiven to the city, and that they were having a great time on a building site!

Fourteen of the players brought the Sam Maguire back to their old school and team coach, Adrian McGuckin at St Pat's Maghera. Twelve thousand people watched the GOAL match at Bellaghy. Later Ballymaguigan welcomed the team and manager, and on the Friday evening, a civic reception at the Guild Hall in Derry city was preceded by what Henry Downey described as 'fantastic support from the people of the city'.

It was a week to be remembered by the whole county, a week that will be relived for many years to come. Derry may win another All-Ireland but this was the first. The players' names are engraved into Derry football history.

ULSTER CHAMPIONSHIP 1993

DOWN 0-9 DERRY 3-11 May 31st First Round, Newry: DERRY: D. McCusker, McGurk, Quinn, Scullion, Diamond, H. Downey, Coleman, Tohill, McGilligan, Ferris, Barton, Cassidy, McNicholl, Heaney, Gormley. *Subs:* F. McCusker for Scullion, Burns for McNicholl. DOWN: Collins, Magill, C. Deegan, Higgins, Kelly, B. Burns, D.J. Kane, Breen, E. Burns, Carr, Blaney, Mason, Linden, Withnall, McCartan. *Subs:* G. Colgan for B. Burns, G. Deegan for E. Burns. SCORERS: *Derry:* Tohill 0-4, E. Burns, 1-1, Ferris, Heaney 1-0, Cassidy 0-3, Gormley 0-2, Barton 0-1. *Down:* Carr 0-5, Mason 0-2, Linden, Withnall 0-1.

ULSTER CHAMPIONSHIP 1993, SEMI-FINAL

DERRY 0-19 MONAGHAN 0-11 June 20th. Casement Park: DERRY: D. McCusker, McKeever, Quinn, Scullion, Diamond, H. Downey, Coleman, Tohill, McGilligan, Ferris, Barton, Cassidy, Burns, Heaney, Gormley. *Subs:* McCormack for Ferris, Brolly for Burns, F. McCusker for Quinn. MONAGHAN: Thompson, Bernie Murray, McGuirk, Sherry, Hoey, Loughman, King, F. McEneaney, Byrne, Edwin Murphy, McCarron, Slowey, McGinnity, Mone, G. Flanagan. *Subs:* D. Flanagan for King, McShane for Slowey, Brendan Murray for Hoey. SCORERS: *Derry:* Gormley 0-7, Tohill 0-5, Brolly 0-3, Cassidy, Diamond, Heaney, McGilligan 0-1. *Monaghan:* McCarron 0-3, Mone, Murphy 0-2, G. Flanagan, Hoey, McGinnity, Slowey 0-1.

ULSTER CHAMPIONSHIP 1993, FINAL

DERRY 0-8 DONEGAL 0-6 July 18th Clones: DERRY: D. McCusker, McKeever, Scullion, Coleman, F. McCusker, H. Downey, McGurk, Tohill, McGilligan, McCormack, Barton, Cassidy, Mulvenna, Heaney, Gormley. Subs: McNicholl for Heaney, Brolly for Mulvenna, Diamond for McNicholl. DONEGAL: Walsh, J.J. Doherty, Matt Gallagher, McGowan, Crossan, Carr, Shovlin, Murray, Michael Gallagher, J. McHugh, M. McHugh, McMullan, Bonnar, M. Boyle, Duffy. *Subs:* McShane for Bonnar, Gavigan for Michael Gallagher, Molloy for McHugh. SCORERS: *Derry:* Gormley 0-3, Cassidy 0-2, Barton, McNicholl, Tohill 0-1. *Donegal:* M. Boyle 0-2, Bonnar, Duffy, M.McHugh, McMullan 0-1.

ALL-IRELAND SEMI-FINAL 1993

DERRY 0-15 DUBLIN 0-14 August 22nd Croke Park: DERRY: D. McCusker, McKeever, Quinn, Scullion, McGurk, H. Downey, Coleman, Tohill, McGilligan, Heaney, Barton, Cassidy, Brolly. S. Downey, Gormley. Subs: Diamond for Quinn, McNicholl for Cassidy, F. McCusker for Barton. Dublin: O'Leary, Walsh, Deasy, Moran, Curran, K. Barr, O'Neill, Sheedy, Bealin, Heery, Gilroy, Clarke, Farrell, Murphy, Redmond. Subs: Deegan for Deasy, Galvin for O'Neill, J. Barr for Clarke. Scorers: Derry: Gormley 0-7, H. Downey, Tohill 0-2, Brolly, Coleman, McGilligan, McGurk 0-1. Dublin: Redmond 0-8, Gilroy 0-2, Curran, Bealin, Heery, Clarke 0-1

ALL-IRELAND FINAL 1993

DERRY 1-14 CORK 2-8 September 19th Croke Park: DERRY: D. McCusker, McKeever, Scullion, F. McCusker, McGurk, H. Downey, Coleman, McGilligan, Tohill, Heaney, Barton, Cassidy, Brolly, S. Downey, Gormley. Subs: McNicholl for Cassidy, Burns for S. Downey. CORK: Kerins, Cahalane, O'Connor, Corcoran, O'Sullivan, O'Brien, T. Davis, Fahy, T. McCarthy, D. Davis, Kavanagh, Coffey, Corkery, O'Driscoll, M. McCarthy. Subs: Culloty for T. McCarthy, Cleary for M. McCarthy, Counihan for Corkery. SCORERS: Derry: Gormley 0-6, Tohill 0-3, S. Downey 1-0, McGurk 0-2, Brolly, McGilligan, McNicholl 0-1. Cork: Corkery 0-5, Kavanagh 1-1, O'Driscoll 1-0, T. Davis, Fahy 0-1.

2

Where it all began

'I firmly believe Ulster can go on to dominate the All-Ireland Championship over the next ten years. Tyrone have a crop of brilliant Under-21s coming through, Derry and Down are still quite young and Donegal have a great depth of talent within their county.' This was Down captain Paddy O'Rourke speaking after Down's All-Ireland triumph in September 1991.

Ulster football has indeed never looked so well as it does today.

Led out of the ashes by Down, it is loving every minute of its new status as the leading province in Ireland. Derry and Donegal backed up O'Rourke's prediction by showing that more than one Northern county is capable of winning national titles, and in 1992 Ulster almost made a clean sweep of all the major football trophies. It is remarkable to think that in the twenty-three seasons from 1968 to '91, the province won no senior All-Irelands and just two National Leagues.

In those barren years, the province maintained a vitality and a desire which, along with a flow of talent, just had to come good again. To fully understand the re-emergence it is necessary to go back to the start of the 'new wave' of Ulster football, to a revolution in the middle of the century.

Before 1956 only four counties had lifted the provincial crown: Antrim, Armagh, Cavan and Monaghan; from 1956-59, Tyrone, Derry and Down all won their first title. The former giants were pushed aside, and with Donegal emerging

ULSTER TITLE BREAKDOWN								
	1920s	1930s	1940s	1950s	1960s	1970s	1980s	1990s
Cavan	7	8	9	3	4	-	-	-
Monaghan	3	3	-	2	-	1	2	-
Antrim	-	-	1	2	-	-	-	-
Armagh	-	-	-	2	-	1	2	-
Down	-	-	-	1	6	2	1	1
Derry	-	-	-	1	-	3	1	1
Tyrone	-	-	-	2	-	1	3	-
Donegal	-	-	-	-	-	2	1	2
Fermanagh	-	-	-	-	-	-	-	-

in the seventies, the 'new boys' have taken twenty-eight of the last thirty-eight Ulster Championships.

The reasons for the resurgence are many, from the influence of the Catholic Church in schools to better organisation within counties, the opening up of the education system, Queen's University, and individuals such as Maurice Hayes and Jim McKeever.

Christian Brothers and priests kept Gaelic games alive in Northern schools from the 1920s. For example, Brother Rice first entered Abbey CBS, Newry, for the MacRory Cup in 1926. His encouragement and the work of his predecessors reaped success for the school in the Rannafast Cup in 1938 and MacRory triumphs in 1954 and 1959, years when Down football was gathering momentum. Ex-pupils include Barney Carr, Down manager for their 1960 and '61 All-Irelands, Gerry Brown, manager in 1968, and Sean O'Neill.

Father John Treanor is another prime example. He joined the staff at St Colman's, Newry in 1942 and in the following twenty-eight years he helped make the college into the force they are today. A first MacRory Cup arrived in 1949 and a first Hogan Cup in 1967. Father Treanor's workload included the running of Cór na nÓg and Rannafast teams, though he had an assistant in Gerry O'Neill for the latter-day success.

The very first Hogan Cup was won in 1946 by St Pat's, Armagh, who had Father Rouahan in charge of a talented group of boarders. Iggy Jones and Eddie Devlin came from Tyrone, Tommy Gribben and Larry Higgins from Derry, Pat O'Neill from Armagh. In time, these young men returned to their clubs and county teams with knowledge and discipline in great store.

Elsewhere, the organisational skills of Maurice Hayes were first becoming evident in County Down. This is the man credited with the foresight and dynamism that lifted the Mourne men from obscurity to a unique place in the history of the GAA. Back in 1946, he joined the staff of St Pat's (De La Salle), Downpatrick, where he helped to establish hurling in what had been a 'rugby school' until the war. In 1949 Hayes became Assistant Secretary of Down and soon after he set up an All-County Football League, the first of many initiatives which culminated in All-Ireland glory.

Other counties were also paying more attention to organising their games. Tyrone, for example, established a foothold right across their county in the thirties. Seven clubs became twenty-eight, debts were paid off and foundations laid for the future. Kerry visited the county in 1932 for an exhibition and a first Ulster final was reached in 1933. Cardinal MacRory is credited with driving the reorganisation from Ulster Council level, helped by dedicated officials on the home front. In 1942, Tyrone won their first major trophy, the Lagan Cup, and after winning the Minor All-Irelands of 1947 and '48, they formed a new Juvenile Board in the fifties and new club competitions. County grounds opened at Dungannon, Pomeroy and Coalisland.

Tyrone were still being hammered by Cavan (8-7 to 0-3 in 1950) but with Paul Russell from Kerry introducing the concept of collective training and with outstanding talents like Iggy Jones and Jody O'Neill coming through, the good days were just around the corner. O'Neill was only nineteen when he captained the 1956 'breakthrough' team. In the final, he passed to Donal Donnelly and on to Jackie Taggart for the first goal after two minutes against Cavan. After the 3-5 to 0-4 demolition of the kings of Ulster, huge bonfires raged in Coalisland, home town of Jody O'Neill and Eddie and Jim Devlin.

Many of that Tyrone team were nearing the end of their careers and so the success lasted only a few years, but they had inspired a generation. Derry has a similar story, winning the Lagan Cup in 1944, the National League in 1947, and maintaining the momentum to their first senior provincial title in 1958. Neighbours were inspired by one another's success, higher goals were set and reached. Antrim showed what could be done when they beat Cavan in the Ulster Championship final of 1946, the first time in thirty-three years that the title went outside Monaghan or Cavan.

The 1947 Education Act is one of the more unlikely origins of the emergence of counties within Northern Ireland. It made education free to everyone and raised the school-leaving age from fourteen to sixteen years. Before this, most Catholics left school early to earn their keep in the home, only the rich few being fortunate enough to be sent to boarding schools in Newry, Armagh, Derry or Belfast. Now, new secondary schools sprouted up across the six counties with sport, for the first time, on the curriculum.

Into the fifties, a supply line was established into third level education with the increased number of Catholic boys progressing through the system. Queen's University became the destination for the likes of Donal Donnelly from Tyrone, Mick Brewster from Fermanagh, Tom Scullion, Phil Stuart and Gerry O'Neill from Derry and Sean O'Neill from Down. The first four went on to manage their counties, Gerry O'Neill took Armagh to the 1977 All-Ireland final and Sean O'Neill's contribution to Northern football is second to none.

QUB Sigerson Cup Winners, 1959. Seán A. O'Kane, Peter Quill, Christy Mallon, Phil Stuart, Seán O'Neill, Patsy McDonald, Shay McMahon, Henry McCorry, John O'Neill, Tom Scullion, Barney McNally, Paddy McGuckian, Mick Brewster, Frank Higgins, Gerry O'Neill, Charlie Murphy, Leo O'Neill, Eamonn Flannagan, Jessie O'Rourke, (Hon Sec), Kevin Halfpenny, Paddy O'Hara (trainer), Hugh O'Kane (captain), Dr John A. MacAuley (President), Seamus Mallon (Vice captain), Brendan Donaghy (Hon Treasurer).

Jim McKeever coming onto Croke Park, All-Ireland semi-final day, 1987.

Queen's Gaelic Football Club had battled to stay above water in the thirties and forties. Without a grant and having to call on guest players like Kevin Armstrong to make up the numbers, they won nothing but kept the game alive until the fifties' influx. Even then, the club had only one pitch, in such a poor state that they had to rely on the kindness of the rugby club to let them play on one of their pitches. Winning the Sigerson Cup in 1959 was therefore a considerable achievement, and a milestone for Ulster football.

Brewster, Scullion, Phil Stuart and Sean O'Neill all played on the team that beat UCD in the final. So did John O'Neill, who would win an All-Ireland Junior medal with Fermanagh the same year, and Frank Higgins who played on Tyrone's 1956 and '57 Ulster winning teams. Other team members were Peter Smith who played with Scullion and Stuart for Derry in the All-Ireland Senior final of 1958, and Brendan Donaghy and Kevin Halfpenny who played in the 1961 Ulster final for Armagh. The defeat of a southern team (UCD) containing well-known county names fuelled the realisation in Ulster that success could be found outside the province.

Most teams in this generation were organised by a group of officials or selectors. Queen's had a relatively new concept — a coach. He was Paddy O'Hara, who had won an Ulster medal with Antrim in 1951 and was alert to modern coaching methods. Dr Eamonn O'Sullivan of Kerry was a pioneer in the coaching field, and O'Hara remembers his practice of bringing the county team together a full two weeks before a game. Maurice Hayes also took note and in 1958 he sent each member of the Down team a copy of O'Sullivan's book, *Coaching Gaelic Football.*

Another extremely influential character was 'Gentleman Jim' McKeever. Captain of the Derry team that lost to Dublin in the 1958 All-Ireland final and

Hogan Cup winners, 1993: St Colman's College, Newry.

one of the greatest fielders ever seen, his effect on modern-day Ulster football is incalculable. Coaching became his profession at St Joseph's Teacher Training College in Belfast (now St Mary's), where he arrived at just the right time, 1957. Physical Education teachers were in demand for new schools setting up throughout the North, and an increasing number of students were ready to learn. The problem was that there was no training centre for them. Jim McKeever had to go to Loughborough College to learn his trade, but then the authorities realised it would be more economical to set up a centre closer to home. McKeever was the obvious man for the job.

Some still opted to travel for their education (Gerry Brown and Derry's Adrian McGuckin qualified in Manchester) but the majority of Physical Education teachers qualified at St Joe's. In McKeever's thirty-five-year stay (1957-1992), hundreds of young men returned from the college to benefit their schools, clubs and counties, and by the early seventies the successful Derry county team had no fewer than a dozen graduates from the college, Peter Stevenson, Tom Quinn, Eugene Laverty and Hugh Niblock among them. The accusation was actually levelled that there were 'too many teachers' on the team, that they could have done with more men from a working-class background.

Among the first batches to come out of St Joe's in the early sixties were Leo Murphy and Fintan Mussen from Down, and Frank Rodgers and Arthur McCrory from Tyrone. Murphy went on to win All-Ireland Senior medals; Mussen's brother Kevin was Down captain in 1960; Rodgers is Games Administration Secretary in Tyrone and McCrory led his county into the 1986 All-Ireland final. Back in 1957-58, they were young men in a hurry.

'I was very interested in this new coaching idea and all of us at the college were anxious to get on the move with it,' recalls McCrory. 'We were shown a new type of football, no longer was it a simple game where you caught the ball and kicked it up the field. Now there was this new thing called tactics. As well as being a strong man's game, it became a thinking man's game.'

McCrory also took instruction outside the college, with courses organised by Jim McKeever and Maurice Hayes, 'the ideas man'. In 1964, he received a National Coaching Certificate under Down All-Ireland winner Joe Lennon at

Top: Adrian McGuckin, St Pat's Maghera coach [centre] visited by fourteen of his former PE pupils, now All-Ireland winners with their trophy. *Left:* Ray Morgan, St Colman's Newry coach.

Gormanston. Within his own county McCrory was one of an enthusiastic band of teachers who promoted Gaelic games in schools throughout the decade. Results were dramatic, with an All-Ireland vocational schools title and an Ulster Minor Championship won in 1967. The following year, St John's, Dromore, won the Ulster secondary schools senior Championship. Help came from various sources, such as an active Minor Board and individuals, such as John McCusker at the Dromore school, and even Fermanagh man Mick Brewster who taught at Omagh Technical College. Tyrone went on to dominate the seventies at youth level, winning six Ulster Minor titles and reaching six Ulster Under-21 and three All-Ireland Vocational finals. Omagh CBS also won the MacRory Cup.

Many others took the same route as McCrory, from the McKeever 'academy' back to their roots — Liam Austin, Colm McAlarney, Ray Morgan, Jimmy Smyth and Peter McGinnity in the sixties and seventies, and more recently Damien Barton, John Reihill, John Rafferty and Benny Tierney. All of these ex-students are spread across the province: Austin in Warrenpoint, Smyth in Lurgan,

Eddie McDevitt *(centre)* and *(from left)* Martin Gavigan, Sylvester Maguire, P.J. McGowan and Anthony Molloy.

McGinnity in Enniskillen, Barton in Dungannon and Rafferty in Belfast, though none have had the success of Ray Morgan in Newry. Just as Father Treanor departed St Colman's in 1970, Ray Morgan came in to uphold the tradition. Assisted by Pete McGrath from 1978, the school has added another seven MacRory Cups and four Hogans to its trophy cabinet.

Morgan's main adversary on the Ulster scene is Adrian McGuckin at St Pat's, Maghera. The former Derry player has been in charge for all of his school's eight MacRory Cups and two Hogans since 1977, a remarkable record for a school founded only in the late sixties so that pupils from South Derry did not have to travel to the city for their education. McGuckin and Maghera's contribution to football in the county is clearly marked by the fact that eighteen of the Derry Senior panel in the 1993 Championship are ex-pupils.

In recent years, the supremacy of Newry and Maghera has been tested, with schools in Belfast, Enniskillen and Dungannon re-emerging. In fact, the MacRory Cup has visited five of the six Northern Ireland counties since 1986, Armagh being the exception, though they had a team in the 1985 final. This healthy competition mirrors the Senior inter-county scene.

What is most noticeable is the absence of a Cavan or Monaghan school in a MacRory decider since 1975. St Pat's, Cavan and St Macartan's, Monaghan were frequent winners of the competition up to 1956, with eight and seven wins respectively. Since then, the Cavan college has won just three, the last in 1972, and the Monaghan college none. These statistics take us full circle, back to the revolution in Ulster football. Just as Cavan and Monaghan's stranglehold on the Ulster Senior Championship began to weaken from the mid-fifties, so too did their schools as Northern neighbours stepped out in front with modern coaching techniques and qualified PE teachers. Emigration was another major problem for these counties from the mid-forties; their population seriously declined and rural clubs that had been their backbone were eroded.

Boarding schools like St Pat's and Macartan's also came in for competition from new vocational schools in the fifties. In what was equivalent to the emergence of secondary schools in the North, the southern establishments provided a cheaper alternative to a wider section of the community. In the early seventies, free education was introduced and vocational schools prospered further.

Donegal football has benefited more from this system than Monaghan or Cavan, partly because Donegal has more schools and pupils, and partly because they developed firm ties with the County Board from the early days. Eddie McDevitt was primarily responsible for this marriage in Donegal when he liaised between the county's newly-formed Minor Board (late sixties) and the vocational schools. McDevitt looked after the county Minors, helped by Brian McEniff, and also the Vocationals from 1964 until 1979. P.J. McGowan and Michael Lafferty then arrived on the scene and the eighties brought unprecedented success.

Lafferty was a mentor to the 1982 All-Ireland winning Donegal team. McGowan managed teams who reached the finals in 1984 and '85 and the next All-Ireland success in 1987. 'We became better organised with people in different schools putting their shoulder behind the wheel,' explains McGowan, chairman of the Donegal Vocational Board. 'Manus Brennan, Packie McGinley, Barry Campbell in Carraig and Colm O'Donnell in the Rosses all worked with young fellas like James and Martin McHugh, Anthony Molloy, Declan Bonnar and the Boyles, Manus and Tony.'

Twelve of the Donegal team that started the 1992 All-Ireland final passed through this system, which involves more than twenty schools.

What becomes abundantly clear is that no matter which education system you are under, success can be achieved, but there must be co-ordination, enthusiasm and numbers. Down had the talent in the fifties, so too did Donegal in the sixties when they reached their first Ulster Senior final, and Derry and Tyrone. However, meaningful long-term benefits did not accrue until an effective infrastructure was established.

3

Down's Glorious Sixties

James McCartan passed the ball to Sean O'Neill in the right corner of the Down attack. O'Neill picked out Paddy Doherty in space, but entering the square he was pulled down by Kerry defender Tim 'Tiger' Lyons. 'Penalty,' ordered referee John Dowling.

Down was leading Kerry by three points in the second half of the 1960 All-Ireland final, and another three points would clinch a famous victory. Doherty possessed one of the sweetest left pegs ever seen in Gaelic football and his shot travelled low and true to the Kerry net.

Sean O'Neill of Down in action, second from the left.

James McCartan, snr, Down.

'I'll never forget that penalty kick,' reflects Down defender Kevin O'Neill. 'Supporters were seated behind the goal in the Nally Stand but when the ball went in they all jumped up and threw their hats and coats into the air. It was a marvellous sight and gave us a great lift.'

Mick O'Dwyer scored a point for Kerry but Doherty hit back with three more for a final score of 2-10 to 0-8, Kerry's heaviest defeat in an All-Ireland final this century. Thousands of Down fans spilled onto the Croke Park field to see Kevin Mussen become the first man from the six counties to lift the Sam Maguire. Two daring young Down fans scaled an upright at the Railway End to secure a red and black flag to the top, others danced and cheered long after the presentation. O'Connell Street was taken over that night and the following afternoon as the journey home began with a long cavalcade through the capital's main street. At the Customs Post, there were fears that the Cup might not be allowed across the border, but the 50,000 crowd in Newry was not disappointed.

The crossing of the border by Sam Maguire was a landmark in GAA history. Down had only become Ulster champions for the first time in 1959, yet now they had turned the world of Gaelic football on its head. They played a new short-passing game, breaking the ball instead of catching it in the middle of the field and man-marking in defence. 'Soccer dressed up as Gaelic football,' scorned the traditionalists, but the fact was that Kerry's catch-and-kick game could not compete.

Down had six marvellous forwards. Sean O'Neill, 'King James' McCartan and Paddy Doherty made up one of the greatest half-forward lines ever seen, while Tony Hadden, Patsy O'Hagan and Brian Morgan completed the attack. Evidence of their long-lasting impact on young spectators such as Brian McEniff, Sean McCague and Art McCrory is found in their All-Time Ulster Selections in Chapter 21.

In 1961, Down beat Kerry again, this time by six points, in an All-Ireland semi-final. In so doing, they proved that Kerry's injury problems before the 1960 final had little to do with the eventual outcome. In the '61 final, Offaly were handed a two-goal start but goals from McCartan, O'Neill and Morgan gave Down a half-time lead of 3-3 to 2-3. They became double All-Ireland champions.

Further glories came their way in the sixties, starting with the National League in 1960, to be repeated in 1962 and '63, as well as the All-Ireland Championship in '68. The Ulster final was an annual occurrence as Down played in every decider from 1958 to '69 inclusive, an incredible run considering their only previous appearances had been in the early forties.

Down's Ulster Final Run 1958-69		
1958	Derry 1-11	Down 2-4
1959	Down 2-16	Cavan 0-7
1960	Down 3-7	Cavan 1-8
1961	Down 2-10	Armagh 1-10
1962	Cavan 3-6	Down 0-5
1963	Down 2-11	Donegal 1-4
1964	Cavan 2-10	Down 1-10
1965	Down 3-5	Cavan 1-8
1966	Down 1-7	Donegal 0-8
1967	Cavan 2-12	Down 0-8
1968	Down 0-16	Cavan 1-8
1969	Cavan 2-13	Down 2-6

Maurice Hayes is the first name to whom Down people give credit. He was not team manager — that was Barney Carr — but the county secretary's influence in those days was much greater than it is today. Organisation was the key requirement for the post. Hayes demonstrated his powers in this area when he was assistant secretary in the early fifties. He effectively pulled the county together, forming a new All-County League in 1950 and later calling a halt to the practice of 'holding players' off the Senior team so that they could play in the Junior Championship. Coming into the full position in 1956, the secretary turned his ideas to the development of the county team. They were ideas ahead of their time.

'Maurice Hayes was the first man I heard saying we would win an All-Ireland, and that was after we had lost heavily to Donegal in the first round in Ulster in '57,' recalls Kevin O'Neill. 'I thought he was mad but that autumn he came round the houses of a lot of young fellas and told us about a plan he had, and said we were going to start this thing called "collective training". We wondered if it wasn't illegal!'

Despite the 3-2 to 0-3 defeat by Donegal, Hayes and Barney Carr had devised a five-year plan to bring the Sam Maguire to the Mourne county. They were given the green light at the 1958 Down convention, as part of a three-man selection committee with Brian Denvir. A year later, Carr was appointed manager with the other two as selectors, Danny Flynn as trainer and Dr Martin Walsh as medical adviser.

The management team insisted upon the relatively new concept of collective training. Training indoors was another novel idea, in halls or schools in Dundrum and Castlewellan. Players were asked to train twice a week, and in return, they were well looked after. 'You stick by us and we'll stick by you. If you're hurt we'll get you to hospital, if you have trouble getting off work we'll see about it,' said Hayes. Players were made to feel important, even in small matters such as being provided with tea and sandwiches after training and matches, a luxury in those days. A solidarity developed from the fact that they were doing things nobody else was, they were a step ahead of the rest.

In 1956, Down had hinted at their potential in a defeat of Carlow in a challenge game. Nine of the 1960 team played that day and this nucleus remained until the performance was repeated in a meeting of the same counties in 1958. Kevin Mussen, Jarlath Carey and Paddy Doherty were some of the reasons behind the growing opinion that this team was bound for greatness. In the '58 Championship, Down avenged themselves on Donegal with a 3-11 to 3-5 victory, their first in the Ulster Championship since 1950. In the semi-finals, they put a lid on Tyrone's glories but lost to Derry at Clones by four points.

On 10 May 1959, Down gave the first real sign of what was to come when they sparkled in front of a 32,000 crowd at Wembley Stadium. In the final of the Whitsun Wembley Tournament,* Patsy O'Hagan scored two spectacular goals and Sean O'Neill another as they beat the 1956 All-Ireland champions Galway by 3-9 to 4-4. 'Rarely has a crowd given out its affection so warmly as it did to "wee" Down. These men of Ulster fought like terriers against mighty and campaign-hardened opponents', said the *Sunday Press*.

Down had a positive, exciting game-plan which they carried over to the Ulster final to overwhelm Cavan by 2-16 to 0-7. Their forwards mesmerised the Cavan backs by constantly changing the direction of their attack. In the All-Ireland semi-final, Galway were better prepared for the upstarts and won by 1-11 to 1-4, but Hayes was not concerned. His five-year plan allowed for such an experience, just as losing in the Ulster final the previous year was part of the natural progression. Logically, Down would next reach an All-Ireland final.

1960 was to be Down's year, starting with their first National League triumph. They beat Cavan in the final after a superb semi-final against Kerry, when a teenage Sean O'Neill showed signs of greatness.

As chance would have it, Down travelled to Kerry two weeks after the League final for the opening of the ground at Listowel. A large crowd turned up to have a closer look at the Northerners, some intrigued and others sceptical. They were none the wiser after the hour. Kevin O'Neill takes up the story:

'We had taken the match before winning the League but saw no point in engaging Kerry in a furious battle; we thought of meeting them later in the year. Our strategy was not to try too hard. Kerry scored freely and at half-time they actually asked us what was wrong! We were laughing but they were fooled into believing that this was the real Down. Sure enough, later that summer we met Kerry and running out of the tunnel we shouted to one another "Remember Listowel!".' Kerry won the Listowel challenge by 6-6 to 0-9, but Down won the re-match.

The very fact that Down had the wherewithal and self-belief to turn the situation to their advantage indicates a characteristic which Down teams still possess. The sixties team developed it from winning and from the positive thinking of Maurice Hayes: losing was never considered and the big names never feared. Croke Park was to be looked forward to, a place to perform.

Down also enjoyed breaking the mould, from revolutionary tactics to a new colour of shorts. They caused a bit of a stir when they appeared in black shorts, as all teams had worn white shorts up to then. One theory was that black togs helped Down players to recognise their team-mates whenever the ball was in a ruck of players. In 1968, the trend-setters first used black numbers on their

*The Whitsun Wembley Tournament was played from 1958-76, peaking in 1963 when 42,500 watched the final. The GAA hired the stadium and qualifying games were played in Ireland for the London decider.

jerseys and in the seventies they were among the first to wear short-sleeved shirts.

The net effect is that Down people always feel they can win, that they are as good as anybody else, and the further they go in a competition the more confident they become. Outsiders accuse them of being 'arrogant' but Pete McGrath has another theory. 'It is not arrogance. It is confidence in one's own ability and one's team's ability to play well and to win.'

Ross Carr describes the extra dimension as a 'sixth sense', a belief born out of the Down tradition. 'Without being big-headed, I know the Down jersey can play anywhere. In 1991 going into the All-Ireland I could relate to and identify with Patsy O'Hagan who lived next door and my former headmaster Kevin Mussen. They had both conquered Ireland before me. Martin O'Connell had two All-Irelands and is a fantastic footballer but he didn't have what I have. He had five senses with two All-Irelands, I had a sixth sense without having played there before. I suppose it was cockiness but it was also the belief that when you go down to Dublin you own it. I knew in my heart that Down were going to win.'

Self-belief did not however mean self-reliance in 1960. After surviving against Offaly in the All-Ireland semi-final with a controversial penalty, Down saw the need to bring in an outsider. Peter McDermott of Meath had trained the 1946 All-Ireland Junior champions from Down and was a friend of Barney Carr. He had captained his own county to the 1954 Senior All-Ireland. 'Peter was introduced to us in a classroom in Castlewellan', remembers full-back Leo Murphy. 'Here was a man who had been through All-Ireland semi-finals and finals (four) and after he spoke to us the team no longer felt they were on a journey into the unknown.'

Kevin O'Neill learned two things in particular from the Meathman. 'He had a great bearing on our style of play and he made us more streetwise. He reckoned that our short game was too complicated, that we were nearly as bad as the Antrim team in the forties who he said wanted to go all the way through and set the ball down behind the line. Peter told us to shoot from further out and channel the ball early down the lines.

'Defensively, we got blown for fouls any time we touched a forward, while if we got a ball and looked up the field Paddy Doherty or one of the others would already be on the ground or being held. The philosophy here was to foul early, not when the ball is falling on you and the referee is watching. Also, when the ball came down the left, we had to hold our men on the right side of us and not let them past. You watched the referee and dropped your hands when he looked round.'

McDermott's message was not in the handbook but he was merely passing on the 'cuteness' that other counties had. He told them that they must be prepared to do what he said if they wanted to win. Kevin O'Neill went home and wrote down everything McDermott had said. Down football changed that night and they beat Offaly by two points in the replay.

The 1960 final was a special occasion, Down in their first ever All-Ireland final against the nineteen-times champions and reigning title holders, Kerry. The red and black mixed dramatically with green and gold, adding to a highly-charged atmosphere among the near 88,000 crowd. Down scored in the second minute, George Lavery setting up Tony Hadden for a long-range point. A scoring spree of five points in five minutes gave Down an edge they held to half-time, 0-9 to 0-5. Turning round with a wind advantage, Kerry levelled early on and forced three fifties. Kevin Mussen relieved the pressure by sending a sideline ball to James McCartan under the Hill, forty yards from goal. Kerry goalkeeper Johnny Culloty reached for the high ball coming into his goalmouth but let it slip through his hands into the net, a fortunate but vital goal for Down. Minutes later came Paddy Doherty's penalty kick.

Excuses were offered on behalf of the losers but all queries about their authenticity were cast aside in the very first minute of Down's 1961 semi-final with the same Kerry team. Sean O'Neill slammed the ball to the Kerry net and Down gave their finest performance to date. Over most of the decade, Down sustained their new-found lofty status, winning five more Ulsters, two more National Leagues and another All-Ireland.

In 1962, they thrilled thousands of Down exiles on a four-week coast-to-coast tour of America, winning five games. A fortnight after returning, they were sixteen points better than Fermanagh in Irvinestown. Tyrone were next but a surprise awaited Down in the final, when they were thumped by ten points by Cavan, 3-6 to 0-5. Early goals by Mick Brady and Jim Stafford came either side of an injury to Down goalkeeper Eamon McKay while substitutes Kevin O'Neill and Kevin Mussen were badly hampered by injuries. It was an undignified close to the greatest chapter in Down football.

The 'breakthrough' team stayed together but found national honours elusive in the next few years, losing two league finals in 1963 and '64 and three All-Ireland semi-finals in 1963, '65 and '66. Gradually, a transitional period saw the likes of Maurice Hayes and James McCartan leaving the scene, so that by 1968, only four players from the winning Double team remained. Fortunately, another breed of talented young players matured quickly, thanks in no small measure to the excellent schools set-up in the county. Nurseries at St Colman's and the Abbey in Newry supplied players such as Peter Rooney and John Purdy, who were on the first Hogan winning team from Colman's in 1967. Colm McAlarney, Ray McConville, Danny Kelly and Jim Milligan prospered under the leadership of Brother Justin at St Pat's (De La Salle), Downpatrick, reaching the 1966 MacRory Cup final. This foursome played in the 1968 All-Ireland final for Down, just as in 1991 four more ex-Downpatrick pupils represented their county.

McAlarney was the jewel in the crown, one of the first of the mobile midfielders, pacing up and down the field with unbounded athleticism. He excelled on the first county Minor team to reach an All-Ireland final, in 1966. On Ulster final day he won a Minor medal and came on as a substitute for the Seniors, and a week later he played in an Ulster Under-21 final.

Rising young stars such as McAlarney lacked experience, but they did benefit from the knowledge within the county of how to prepare for an All-Ireland final and the self-belief instilled by the 1960-61 team. 'The 1968 team were at an advantage, they had the tradition of winning in Croke Park. It's like beating the four-minute mile, it becomes easier the next time,' reasoned Maurice Hayes. In

The All-Ireland Winners, 1968: Down, captained by Joe Lennon. *Back, left to right:* Tom O'Hare, John Murphy, Ray McConville, Willie Doyle, Danny Kelly, Seán O'Neill, Jim Milligan, Dan McCartan. *Front, left to right:* Brendan Sloan, Peter Rooney, Mickey Cole, Joe Lennon (captain), Paddy Doherty, Colm McAlarney, John Purdy.

charge this time were George Lavery from the Double team, T.P. Murphy who had worked for two years with Maurice Hayes as Joint Secretary, and others like Dan Rooney, Gerry Brown (Manager), Des Farrelly (Trainer) and Paddy O'Donoghue (Chairman).

Sean O'Neill now operated at full-forward for Down and his intelligent play blended effectively with the young stars around him. In the 1968 semi-final with Galway it was O'Neill who made room for Peter Rooney as he carried the ball towards goal late in the game. The eighteen-year-old flicked the ball to his colleague and the resultant Down goal put them a point ahead. They won by two points. Of the other survivors from the early sixties, Paddy Doherty was still his reliable free-scoring self at thirty-three years of age, Dan McCartan as immovable as ever at full-back and captain Joe Lennon still inspirational at left-half-back. At corner-back, Tom O'Hare had been a regular since 1964 and won the Telefís Éireann 'Player of the Week' award for his performance against Galway.

The Kingdom were once again waiting in the final and, like Down, they had older players such as Mick O'Dwyer and Mick O'Connell surrounded by a new generation of promising young men who would win the next two All-Irelands, in 1969 and 1970. Perhaps the '68 final came too early for Kerry because Down led by eight points after just eight minutes. Jim Milligan fielded from the throw-in and passed to O'Neill for the first point; minutes later the same scorer stunned Kerry with a much-talked-about goal. Observers said O'Neill was 'lucky' when a rebound from Peter Rooney's shot struck the post five feet above the crossbar and appeared to bounce off O'Neill into the net. The full-forward insists that he followed the ball 'just in case' it stayed alive and that his reflex action to deflect the dropping ball was deliberate. Kerry were still reeling when John Murphy struck another goal soon after. Down captain Joe Lennon retired at half-time and Kerry came to within four points in the second half, but a last-gasp goal gave the misleading appearance of a close contest, 2-12 to 1-13.

Down had again rocked the whole country by toppling the favourites with a new team. They seemed bound to stay at the top of the tree for years to come, but county secretary T.P. Murphy anticipated problems. In his report to County Convention the following January, he pointed to the large number of younger players on the team gaining All-Ireland Senior honours early in their careers. 'Therein lies the danger, this might result in a sense of anti-climax, and cause a lessening of effort in 1969. Such an attitude would be disastrous to the team's prospects in the coming year.'

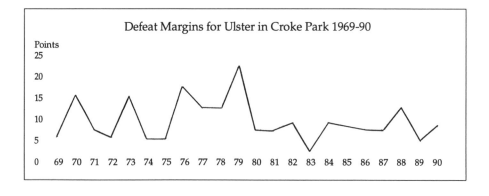

Defeat Margins for Ulster in Croke Park 1969-90

4

The Barren Years

3 October 1968. The victorious Down All-Ireland squad was being afforded an official civic welcome by Alderman William Geddes, Lord Mayor of Belfast. Eileen Paisley, wife of Ian, led a picket outside in protest at what was seen as an action of betrayal by the Mayor.

5 October 1968. The front page headline of the *Irish News* read, 'Civil Rights March to go ahead'. The Troubles were starting, in the midst of a glory time for Ulster football.

Derry were the All-Ireland Under-21 champions, Ulster held the Railway Cup and Down were holders of both national Senior football titles. The Dublin press predicted an extended period of dominance by Ulster, such was the youth of the Down team and the development of facilities in the North.

Unfortunately, the Northern press was more prophetic than its Southern counterpart. Tension and fear gripped Northern Ireland as the troubles began, society became increasingly polarised and the image of the GAA suffered. 'We were very definitely seen as being on one side of a divided community,' contends GAA President Peter Quinn. 'That is still the reality of the situation and it is because of this that our clubs continue to be attacked.'

One line of thought is that 'the Troubles' caused an intensification of commitment within GAA membership in the six counties, that it became more vibrant in order to preserve its cultural identity. Peter Quinn disagrees, 'I have no doubt that the Troubles have had a negative rather than positive effect on the Association. Players have been harassed on their way to training and clubs have been burnt down. The GAA in Belfast has suffered most of all.'

Clubs like St Paul's, Sarsfields, Rossa, St John's and St Gall's have seen the worst of the Troubles in the west of the city, and Antrim's county ground, Casement Park, was taken over by the British Army for an entire year in 1972. The venue has not been used for an Ulster Senior final since 1971. Antrim's last major football Championship success was at All-Ireland Under-21 level in 1969. A year later, their Seniors played in the Ulster final but have not been back since.

St Malachy's, Belfast and St Mary's CBS competed in successive Hogan Cup finals in 1969 and 1970, but not since.

Elsewhere, St Oliver Plunkett Park, Crossmaglen, has been part-occupied by the British Army since 1971. Lying adjacent to the GAA grounds, the Army base took over an area for use as a helicopter pad and to extend the base. Helicopters landed on the pitch, sometimes during games. A gate was opened onto club property and tension ran high within the local community. The Carryduff club on the outskirts of Belfast is still searching for a home, more than ten years after turning up at their first grounds to discover glass embedded in the pitch and goalposts bent over. St Peter's, Lurgan, had a seven-year battle throughout the eighties with Craigavon Borough Council to get permission for a new pitch. At one stage, the council set conditions that no game would be played at the pitch on Sundays and that an eighteen-foot wall would be built around it. Eventually, the issue went to court and St Peter's were awarded more than £100,000 in compensation. In Derry two clubs were burnt to the ground in 1988: Dermot McNicholl's Glenullin and Anthony Tohill's Swatragh.

Ciaran Barr left such problems behind when he moved to Dublin four years ago. Antrim's first hurling All Star swopped the O'Donovan Rossa club on the Falls Road in Belfast for St Vincent's of Dublin. 'I go to matches where policemen turn up in their uniform and strip off to play. Everyone plays or has played Gaelic games in the South, it is the number one sport, an accepted phenomenon.

'The difference is that hurling in the North is on the fringe of society: in the South it is woven into the fabric of society, especially in the country. Yet, the people down here imagine it's the same in the North as it is in the South: they don't realise how hard it is to get success.'

Ulster football during the Troubles has experienced mixed fortunes. The absence of Sam Maguire for so long caused frustration and sorrow, but the seventies also brought hope and joy to counties which reemerged on the home front. Derry, Tyrone and Armagh all regained the Ulster Championship they had last won in the fifties, Monaghan bridged a gap of more than half a century and Donegal were first-time winners. In all, there were six different champions in this decade.

Cavan and Down were well and truly upstaged after their domination of the sixties, with Cavan's demise the more dramatic. Down managed to maintain some momentum in reaching five finals and winning two in the seventies, but Cavan's name vanished from the honours list. They had always been at the top of the tree along with either Monaghan, Antrim or Down, but now the Breffni blues were left standing. Some say it was Cavan's own fault, that they refused to move with the times. The popular jest is that 'Cavan are still playing away in the Polo Grounds', implying that the county dwelt for too long on the celebrated defeat of Kerry in the 1947 All-Ireland final in New York.

Cavan traditionally had strong, physical players who were well-suited to their catch and kick game. However, the type of men who made Cavan famous slowly disappeared due to emigration from rural communities. Still, they persisted with their familiar gameplan rather than adapt to the modern running game. Additional theories exist, such as the feeling of despair in Cavan after they fell at the line in the All-Ireland semi-finals in 1967 and '69; Cork beat them by a point in the former, Offaly won after a replay in '69. The standard in club football also declined because of the unhealthy domination from the mid-sixties of one club, Crosserlough. The net result was that through the new two decades, Cavan lost the art of recognising what it takes to win, looking instead for instant results.

In direct contrast to Cavan's fading fortunes in the seventies, the rest of Ulster enjoyed a new lease of life in a revolution which had its roots in the sixties. Most counties took a leaf out of Down's book and organised themselves better, with under-age boards and competitions set in motion. Combined with the continuing benefits of an improved education system, this meant that more and more well-coached young players became available to county Senior teams.

Derry, for example, drew seven players from the St Columb's side that won the Hogan Cup in 1965. The seven contributed largely to the Derry revival, from the winning of All-Ireland Minor titles in 1965 and '68 to the recapturing of the Anglo-Celt in 1970. Similarly, Tyrone's positive planning paid off in 1973 when their name was on every inter-county football trophy in Ulster. Eugene McKenna and Patsy Kerlin won All-Ireland Minor medals. Fermanagh also had success at youth level with St Michael's, Enniskillen reaching five MacRory Cup finals from 1968 to '74 and the county's Under-21s playing in successive All-Ireland deciders in 1969-70. The Seniors went on to win the 1977 McKenna Cup, their first since 1934. Donegal's breakthrough in 1972 owed much to progress on the field in the sixties and to Brian McEniff who took on the job of player-manager when 'nobody else wanted it'. More soccer-minded Donegal folk will point to the lifting of the 'Ban' in 1971 as helping the cause of Gaelic football.

The Ulster Senior Football Championship became the most competitive provincial competition in the country. Most of the nine counties started on the line together with the knowledge that each of them was capable of landing the title. Every single county made the final between 1970 and 1982. Contests were close and defeats were regularly avenged the following year. For example, Tyrone reconquered Donegal in 1973, only for the tables to be turned twelve months later. Local rivalries intensified, with Derry/Tyrone and Down/Armagh battling for supremacy and pride.

There were two casualties of the new era. First, the quality of play gradually suffered as the importance of winning grew. Fast, open games became the exception, with neighbours afraid to lose to one another. With the talent so evenly spread, coaches discovered that they could negate the opposition by taking care of their 'quality' men. Secondly, success in Croke Park eluded Ulster. Its representatives often resembled a spent force, their energy expended in scaling the peak within Ulster, though their misery was shared by most of the country as Dublin and Kerry proved untouchable.

'The difficulty for Ulster's representatives was that they could not develop a winning habit,' explains Jim McKeever who took Derry teams to All-Ireland semi-finals in 1970 and 1987. 'They were denied the opportunity of turning their first-time experience of Croke Park to good use.'

Retention of the Ulster title proved near impossible, with only Derry managing the feat from the mid-sixties. They were arguably the best-equipped in

Left: Armagh's Colm McKinstry with the Anglo-Celt in 1982. *Right:* Tyrone's captain, Eugene McKenna with the Anglo-Celt in 1984.

Ulster in the seventies, coming out of the province three times. In 1970, they matched Kerry into the second half of the All-Ireland semi-final but were overrun after Seamus Lagan shot wide from a penalty. Sean O'Connell's penalty had earlier been saved. League semi-finals were reached in 1971 and '72, and three successive McKenna Cups were won from 1969-71, but the crime was that this classy team could not get out of Ulster again. 'Maybe we were a couple of players short of All-Ireland quality,' reflects McKeever. 'That was nearly always the case with Ulster teams and certainly with Derry from 1958 through to 1987.'

An even better Derry team emerged in 1975 and '76 to win successive Ulster Championships. Backboned by half of the 1970 side, including Anthony McGurk, Gerry O'Loughlin and Peter Stevenson as captain, they had additional young talent in Gerry McElhinney, Mickey Moran and John Somers. They looked capable of winning a national title but were unlucky to run up against two rising forces, Dublin and Kerry. 'Heffo's Army' were too strong in the 1975 All-Ireland semi-finals and the following year the Dubs squeezed home in a classic National League final. Derry led 9-3 at half-time but lost by 2-10 to 0-15. In the 1976 Championship, the Northerners headed Kerry going into the second-half, but crumbled after a Mike Sheehy goal.

Derry's near-misses should be judged alongside other attempts to break down the big two. Armagh, Down and Monaghan were well-beaten in the three years after 1976 as Dublin and Kerry took over the scene, winning every All-Ireland bar one from 1974 to 1986. 'We may as well pack up and go home and forget about it for the next ten years,' said Art McCrory after watching Dublin destroy Down in 1978.

The picture changed little in the early eighties, on and off the field. Political tragedies and tension continued to affect most counties. The H-block protest spread across the province and a huge 'H' was cut on the Clones pitch just before the 1980 Ulster final. The Anglo-Celt floated merrily from county to county as before, and Croke Park remained a graveyard for Ulster champions.

Armagh should have done better against Roscommon in 1980; Down totalled a mere six points against Offaly in '81 and the Dublin-Kerry barrier blocked Armagh in '82 and Tyrone in '84. Only a promising Donegal team, with Martin McHugh and Anthony Molloy on board, came within a point of Galway in 1983.

Ulster still maintained its enthusiasm and hope in these lean times, its ideals reinforced by success in the Railway Cup and the National League. Eight counties were represented on the Ulster team in 1980 and the top players revelled in their ability to pull together as a unit and defeat the other provinces. Between 1979 and '84, the Railway Cup came North four times.

The National League came North in 1983 and '85 with Down and Monaghan the successful counties. Armagh contested and lost both finals while Derry and Tyrone played regularly in Division One. Winter victories over the big names from the South were common enough, as they were in the Centenary Cup in 1984. Derry beat Cork and Kerry (away) en route to the semi-finals where they were joined by Cavan and Monaghan.

However, League was different from Championship. Ross Carr of Down recalls a day when Kerry took a sixteen-point hammering in Newcastle. 'On the way off the pitch our supporters gave Mick O'Dwyer some awful stick. They asked what he thought of Down now, he answered that they were a "good league team".' The Kerry manager knew that his team could find another gear come the better weather, but then again, they were working from a different timetable. Whereas the Ulster Championship began in mid-May with a preliminary round, Kerry and Cork were so far ahead of the rest in Munster that they could afford to gear themselves towards the provincial final. Kerry and Cork contested every Munster final between 1969 and 1991, while in stark contrast, seventeen Ulster champions lost their crown in the same period without even making the final. Those who did manage to survive the minefield were found to lack the mental sharpness of their southern counterparts in late summer.

Significantly, the picture changed dramatically when the open draw system was introduced in both Munster and Leinster in the nineties. Clare broke the Kerry-Cork monopoly in Munster

Armagh (in foreground) and Fermanagh parade at Clones, 1982, before the Ulster final with Peter McGinnity half hidden and Paddy Moriarty the third Armagh man.

while Dublin and Meath met for the first of their four first-round epics in 1991 on 2 June, a week earlier than Down's first game in Ulster. The 'shorter summer' advantage was gone.

Championships in Leinster and Connacht were more akin to Munster than Ulster in the twenty-three years since, with their titles shared between just three and four counties respectively. At one stage, Ulster was considered the only remaining 'true championship'. Even the Cinderella county of Fermanagh came within a whisker of taking their first title in 1982. Peter McGinnity's goal midway through the second half levelled scores with Armagh and a point put them in front. But Fermanagh's lack of tradition and belief failed them at the vital moment. 'Opportunities like that only come in cycles for our county,' reflects McGinnity. 'We have only eight Division One clubs and eighteen in all. Therefore, we do not have the same turnover as others.'

Nevertheless, Fermanagh embodied the open nature of the Ulster Championship, as proven again a year later when they toppled National League champions Down in the first round. Down's lesson was a familiar one as League success became a sure sign of a fall in the Championship. There simply was not sufficient time to catch breath between the closing stages of the League and the start of the Ulster Championship in mid-May.

Ulster counties tended to speed their own downfall because of counter-productive preparation work. Down, for example, over-exerted themselves in training on the Thursday night before the 1983 loss to Fermanagh. 'Going out onto the pitch I remarked to Greg Blaney that my legs were dead,' recalls Liam Austin. 'He replied that his were the same.' The word came North that Kerry and Dublin were doing four nights a week, but they were not running all the time, they were playing with the ball. 'Ulster teams were not as thorough as the southern ones, not as professional in their approach,' declares Art McCrory.

Down were one of the major failures of the decade. Much was expected of them in the eighties — probably too much — with Greg Blaney, Liam Austin and Paddy O'Rourke coming through from their All-Ireland winning Minor and Under-21 teams in the late seventies. They won Ulster in 1978 and '81 and the League in 1983, but then had eight barren years to 1991. 'We got into a rut where we forgot how to win,' says Paddy O'Rourke. 'In 1977 with the Minors, I had no doubt we would win in Croke Park, a self-belief carried over from the sixties, but then it evaporated in the eighties. Luck went against us too, as in the 1986 final when Tyrone beat us with a dubious goal.' Tyrone held the upper hand over Down throughout the decade, their battle-hardened defenders able to contain a forward line in which the critics suggested that 'too many did not fancy the physical battle'. A further theory was that Down club football was 'cleaner' than that in Tyrone because of different refereeing standards.

National success arrived in the Mourne county in the form of O'Rourke's Burren club. All-Ireland Champions in 1986 and '88 and Ulster Champions five times from 1983-88, the contrast between club and county could not have been greater. Some argue that the connection is not mere coincidence. Consider that Down's two Ulster Championships (1978 and '81) slotted in between periods of domination on the home front by Bryansford and Burren, and that the county only re-emerged when Burren faded. Certainly, it is unusual for club and county to challenge for national honours at the same time.

Outside Down, there were signs that the gap was closing between North and South. Success at Croke Park was still limited to the League and to Tyrone's defeat of Galway in the 1986 All-Ireland semi-finals, but the slayings had stopped. Monaghan and Tyrone managed to build on previous visits to centre stage and had realistic chances of winning. They discovered that Dublin and Kerry were no longer indestructible, yet Ulster teams lacked the necessary conviction to finish the job. Their failures represented a time of missed opportunity and sentenced the province to further depression. The next three Ulster Champions (1987-89) fell some way short in their visits to Croke Park.

It is difficult to imagine what path Ulster football would have taken if either Monaghan or Tyrone had made a breakthrough. The overall standard had dropped, as Mick O'Dwyer admitted after the '86 final, but it was Cork and Meath who stepped forward to take the next four All-Irelands. Ulster remained its own worst enemy with Monaghan and Tyrone unable to return to the All-Ireland stage until they were near their sell-by date. New talent was coming through, in Derry for example, but they still had to endure the painful initiation process in 1987 of losing in Croke Park. The Oak Leaf county had won All-Irelands from the turn of the decade at Vocational and Minor levels but on reaching their first Senior semi-final in eleven years, they had the misfortune to run up against Meath at their peak. Derry's best chance disappeared when Dermot McNicholl aggravated a hamstring injury in the warm-up.

In 1988, Tyrone might have fared better than Monaghan if they had come out of Ulster, but when the opportunity did come a year later, Donal Donnelly's team collapsed inexplicably against Mayo. Most of the '86 names had carried Tyrone to memorable victories in Ulster over Armagh, Down and Donegal, but there was nothing left for Mayo.

Outside the Senior Championship, Ulster excelled. Down won another All-Ireland Minor title. The Sigerson, Hogan and Railway Cups took up residence in Ulster, and in the 1988-89 National League, five out of the eight Division One teams were from the Northern province. Even former greats Antrim and Cavan stirred from their slumber to appear at Croke Park. Antrim won Division Three and played well against Kerry in the 1989 quarter-finals, yet manager Eamonn Grieve's patient team-building counted for little as his team continually flopped in the Championship. Also in 1989, Cavan gave Dublin a run for their money in a League semi-final but Donegal quickly arrested their progress with an eight-point victory in Breffni in the Ulster Championship.

Donegal were a re-emerging force. Brian McEniff succeeded Tom Conaghan as manager later in 1989 and the next summer Donegal salvaged some of Ulster's lost pride in the All-Ireland semi-finals. Level pegging with Meath entering the last quarter, McEniff's hungry team showed that the breakthrough was possible once more. Meath were no longer invincible and Cork looked like two All-Irelands might just do them. After twenty-three years, Ulster was poised to return from the wilderness.

One of Tyrone's eighties' stars, Kevin McCabe evading Down's Barry Breen in the 1989 Ulster Championship.

5

The Boys from County Armagh

Thump, thump, thump, came the rap on the door of the Armagh dressing-room, just after 3 o'clock on All-Ireland Final day, 25 September, 1977. 'Time to go out on the field,' was the coldly delivered message in a Dublin accent. The northerners stayed where they were.

Two minutes later. Thump, thump, thump, 'Time to get out on the field lads,' in a raised voice. This time the wide-eyed Armagh men heeded the call and duly raced out onto the pitch, into the heated cauldron that was Croke Park. 'The noise was like an explosion,' recalls team captain Jimmy Smyth.

'The crowd had been waiting for us for hours, singing right through the Minor game and they just went daft when we finally came out. You just felt this "thing" hitting you and you became completely disorientated. I did one thing I had never done before or have done since. I booted a ball straight up into the air as I ran out.'

Smyth's team was carried along on the wave of emotion coming down from the stands and the Canal End. Nobody seemed to notice the rain lashing down, neither the supporters nor the players who ran free around Croke Park. But where were Dublin? The champions had stayed in the cover of their dressing-room. Eventually the rain stopped, the sun came out and so did the Dubs.

'If you look at the photograph of myself with the referee Johnny Maloney and the Dublin captain Tony Hanahoe before the match you'll notice our differing appearances,' explains Smyth. 'Maloney and I have one thing in common, we're soaked to the skin! The rest of the Armagh players were the same, our gloves and fashionable long hair were wet, but if you look at Hanahoe he is standing there like a model, dry, fresh and gleaming in the sun.

'The rain factor may seem like a small thing but on reflection it was a big thing. It told me more afterwards about the preparation for an All-Ireland than anything. We went out when we were told to, Dublin went out when *they* wanted to. They were drawing up the guidelines before the ball was thrown in.'

The handshake, 1977. All-Ireland final captains Jimmy Smyth and Tony Hanahoe with referee, Johnny Maloney.

Let the hicks from the sticks run about out there.'

Not many years later the authorities would lay down a stricter schedule for pre-match formalities, so ensuring only three minutes between the teams appearing on the pitch. But in 1977, Dublin were on top of the situation, very much at home in their fourth final in a run of six. Armagh were there for the first time since 1953 and simply did not have the same know-how.

'Even when the captains were called together by the referee, Hanahoe tried to use his experience to unsettle me,' says Smyth. 'He stared at me but said nothing, the old boxer's psychology. That's why I'm looking at the camera and he isn't!'

Dublin won the toss and played with the slight breeze and strong sun on their backs. After just 90 seconds they succeeded in stamping their authority on both the occasion and the game, Jimmy Keaveney's goal reinforcing the idea of the champions being in charge. This was the Dubs.

'Some things are frozen in your memory and Keaveney's goal is one of them. I can still see and feel it, as I watched from down the field, Tom McCreesh our full-back slipping on the greasy surface and Keaveney flashing the ball from near the touchline across the face of Brian McAlinden, whose vision was impaired by the sun, and into the far top corner of the net.

'The Hill went whoosh behind the goal with an explosion of blue. You just felt a real downer and our aspirations had gone after just a minute and a half.'

Armagh did come back, Paddy Moriarty blasting a penalty past Paddy Cullen after five minutes. This lifted the underdogs but not up to where they had been at the start. The Dubs were always in control. If Armagh scored, Dublin scored, and by half-time further goals from Bobby Doyle (14 minutes) and John McCarthy (33 minutes) gave them a lead of 3-6 to 1-2. Game over.

Armagh's fairytale year had come to an abrupt end within just 35 minutes. Disbelieving eyes stared down from the crowd, cheated of the vision they had so effortlessly embraced that summer, of Armagh lifting the Sam Maguire.

Logic did not enter the equation, even the fact that Armagh had come out of Ulster for only the second time in sixteen years while Dublin were All-Ireland champions in 1974 and 1976.

It had only been five years since Armagh had been rated 31st in Ireland by a Dublin newspaper, a laughing stock within their own county. 'How did the circus do today?' was the common inquiry on a Sunday evening. A newspaper report in 1971 had described their defeated team as 'donkeys' and although a revival was sparked in 1974, Armagh were still a Division Three team in 1976.

But what did these facts matter when the gods are on your side? Tomás Ó Fiach was a devoted Armagh Gael, seldom missing a game until the semi-final replay with Roscommon, when he was summoned to Rome and appointed Archbishop of Armagh. The story went round that only when an Armagh man was on the 'see' (the chair of St Patrick) would the county win the All-Ireland.

There had also been an unreal expectation that Roscommon would not be a problem, purely because Armagh had beaten the men from the west in the 1953 All-Ireland semi-final! 'We're as good as in the final' was the attitude.

Armagh lost the '53 final to Kerry and since then, their neighbours from Down had won the Sam Maguire three times, so providing plenty of ammunition for rival supporters to poke fun in Armagh's direction. Now they had an opportunity to put an end to this inferiority, another reason why it was to be Armagh's year.

Supporters felt they had a team good enough to beat the Dubs. Hadn't they annihilated the Ulster champions from Derry in the Ulster final *and* given the Dubs the runaround in a challenge game earlier in the summer? Never mind the fact that Armagh had caught Dublin just after a bruising challenge with Wexford.

All-Ireland euphoria swept through Armagh. Everybody wanted a ticket for the game; one man stood outside Jimmy Smyth's front door for an hour and a half in the hope of receiving a ticket. Nine years later Smyth would write to the Tyrone manager, Art McCrory, advising him to do himself and his players a favour by informing the press that they had no spare tickets.

Media interest was as novel as it was intense. Phones never stopped ringing. Sports companies tried to get in on the act and Armagh training sessions had to be moved from the college fields to the Athletic Grounds, because of the crowds coming to watch. Signing autographs was a new thing and flags, jerseys and footballs were passed into the Armagh dressing-room to be signed.

When All-Ireland day arrived, it seemed as if every one of those supporters had succeeded in securing a ticket, such was the colour and excitement in Croke Park. It's a cliché to say it but the Canal End was 'a sea of orange and white'. I was there as a 13-year-old, almost smothered by the thousands of Armagh fans, most memorably when Paddy Moriarty's first penalty struck the top of the Dublin net.

Most of the Armagh support had been in the ground for hours and all were in position by half-time in the minor game when all the emotion welled up from the terraces and burst into song.

'There's one fair county in Ireland,
with memories so glorious and so grand,
where nature has lavished its bounty
in the orchards of Erin's green land ...
but where are the boys that can court them
like the Boys from the County Armagh'

'When the Armagh supporters saw us, they went completely berserk,' recalls Smyth who emerged from under the Hogan Stand with his team. They had to make their way around the pitch to the dressing-rooms under the Cusack Stand. 'I'll never forget the flags and colour. Anything that was orange was there. Only Clare's appearance in the '92 semi-final rivalled that scene for excitement, emotion and novelty value. We simply had to be affected by it.'

Well before this point Armagh had fallen all too comfortably into the role of innocents abroad. 'Myself and Denis Stevenson were brought down to Ulster Television in Belfast and asked how we were going to play against the Dubs,' recalls the captain. 'I said that their full-backs might be vulnerable, that we could do this and that in other areas. What an idiot!

'Gay O'Driscoll, the Dublin corner-back was sitting at home watching and listening to these comments about himself and Robbie Kelleher and Sean Doherty. Gay said to himself "Will they now?"'

Small things attached to All-Ireland final preparations took up vital time and energy. Being measured up for new blazers was uncharted territory. 'We were sidetracked. Training continued but the whole thing overwhelmed us.'

Armagh were amateurs in the true sense of the word. While others were realising the benefits of proper training and diet, they plodded along, unconcerned. Jimmy Smyth stood at his cooker frying sausages when Bob McEvoy came to visit. Bob had been with Offaly in 1971. 'On the night after the final Bob told me that he became worried when he saw me that day in the kitchen. He said in '71 the Offaly players ate nothing but steaks in the run-up to their final.'

On the night before the final Armagh travelled down to Dublin and accepted an invitation to appear on the RTE television show, 'Trom agus Éadrom', with Liam Ó Murchú. It was the done thing, or so Armagh thought, for while they baked under the intense heat of the studio lights the Dublin players were far away from the cameras. The next morning the observation was made to Jimmy Smyth that the camera had caught him yawning towards the end of the programme. Armagh's base at Trinity Hall had also been found by their supporters. More distractions.

Still, Armagh would hardly have won even if they had been more streetwise. They did have some very good players and others who would improve but on that day their few weak links were ruthlessly exposed by the best team in the land. The speed of Bobby Doyle and the poise and experience of Jimmy

Keaveney tormented the Armagh defence with the constant pressure coming from further up the field. Smyth just about held his own against Kevin Moran but on the wings Tommy Drumm and Pat O'Neill were able to drive forward at will.

Armagh's plan had been to run at the Dublin defence while Paddy Moriarty would stop Tony Hanahoe, the brains of the Dublin attack. In the second half Armagh showed great fight. Sean Devlin drop-kicked the ball against a post, Joe Kernan scored two goals in a row to bring Armagh within eight points, and Paddy Cullen saved a penalty from Moriarty two minutes from time.

Maybe Dublin sat back on their big lead but no team likes to concede as much as three goals and six points in an All-Ireland final. Armagh argue that they exposed a few cracks in the Dublin team that day (it was their last All-Ireland win for six years) and that they kept Dublin on their toes right to the end. Anton O'Toole and Keaveney responded with goals, the Belfast-born full-forward setting a new personal scoring record for an All-Ireland final of 2-6.

Most of the Armagh squad stuck around to win another couple of Ulster titles in 1980 and 1982, unlucky not to scale the heights again as on the first occasion. The county played in five Ulster finals in the eighties, making considerable progress from the bad old days.

The resurgence in Armagh's fortunes dates back to 1974, when former county chairman Tom Lynch invited Father Peter Makem to take over the county team in 1974.

Makem knocked on players' doors to tell Brian McAlinden, Noel Marley and his new captain Jimmy Smyth about his exciting new plans. Father Sean Hegarty, the minor star of the fifties from Blackwatertown, took over training and Kilrea-born Gerry O'Neill, who had left the scene, was coaxed back.

Smyth had learnt the basic principle that success came from training, from his time in St Colman's in Newry, at St Joe's in Belfast and with his club Clann na Gael in Lurgan who won Ulster titles in '72, '73 and '74.

'I remember coming down to Lurgan on the train from Belfast for county training but very few others were turning up. Armagh's reluctance to train changed with the new organisation.' The success of the Clanns at Ulster level also began to rub off on other clubs who adopted the 'train to play' policy.

Father Makem stayed only eight months but left an indelible impression on the county set-up. Up to then players from the north of the county, nearest to Antrim, played a running, short-passing game while in the south the traditional catch and kick game prospered, most notably at Crossmaglen. The result was that when they joined forces on the county team you had a fast runner calling for a short ball while the man in possession launched it fifty yards up the field. Makem's new-look Armagh team was coached to play the running game.

Morale improved among the new young panel and Father Makem encouraged wives, girlfriends and families to become involved. Match days were looked forward to, the camaraderie was healthy and a bond was formed. Results followed in Division Three, with the most important victory over the twice-Ulster Champions Donegal. Taking a 'big name' scalp helped to fuel the revival. March 1976 was another marker. Not only did Armagh win the Division

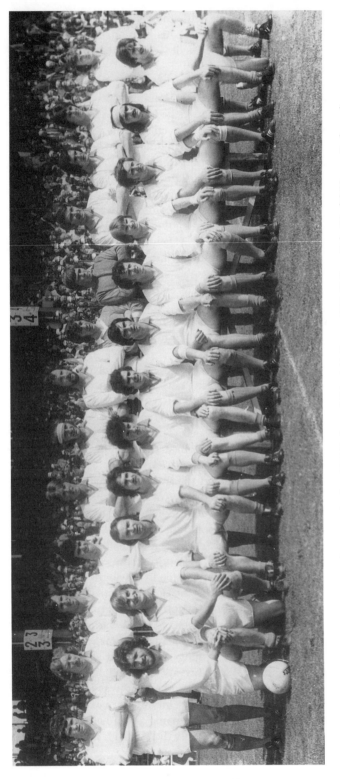

The Armagh squad before the semi-final in 1977. *Back row, left to right:* Eamon O'Neill, Sean Daly, Noel O'Hagan, Redmond Scullion, Fran McMahon, Larry Kearns, Colm McKinstry, Malachy Heaney, Brian McAlinden, Tom McCreesh, Noel Marley, Thomas Cassidy, Kevin Rafferty. *Front row, left to right:* Sean Devlin, Peter Trainor, Peter Loughran, Frank Toman, Joey Donnelly, Denis Stevenson, Joe Kernan, Jimmy Smyth (captain) Paddy Moriarty, Jim Finnegan, Jim McKerr, Jim Loughran.

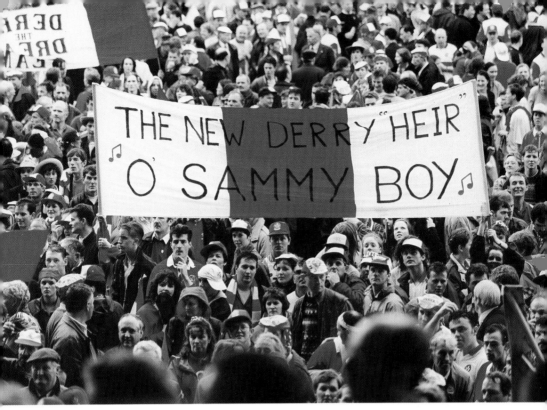

ULSTER AGAIN! DERRY 1993

Above: Derry's 1993 triumph. *Below:* Derry captain Henry Downey sights the prize.

Above: Red *v* red — Cork players break away from the Hill, home to the Derry fans.

Below: Derry's Captain Fantastic, Henry Downey, All-Ireland final 1993.

Facing page: Rain did not stop play. Surface water sprays around Derry's Damien Cassidy as Donegal's John Joe Doherty slides along the Clones pitch, Ulster final 1993.

Above: The Sam Maguire Cup.

Below: Goal maker and goal scorer; Mickey Linden and Barry Breen (8) celebrate Down's goal and Peter Withnall looks on, 1991 All-Ireland Final.

Facing page: Down players parade under Hill 16 — 'I felt like God. We had to deliver because they had put their trust in us.' Ross Carr (10)

Top: Greg Blaney celebrates Down's semi-final victory over Kerry.

Above: Liam Austin wearing Down's new gear: see 'The Boots Story', chapter 10

Left: Down captain Paddy O'Rourke limbers up before the 1991 All-Ireland final.

Top: Sam's new home: Paddy O'Rourke and friend Noel Murdock return with the cup. Job done!
Bottom: Which way to go? Armagh goalkeeper Benny Tierney poised for Mickey Linden's penalty for Down, Ulster Championship 1991, captured by the BBC's in goal camera.

A goal — almost! A penalty — almost! During the first half of the Dublin v Tyrone All-Ireland semi-final 1984. Patsy Kerlin, on the ground in front of Mick Holden and John O'Leary, punches the ball towards the Dublin goal. Damien O'Hagan (11) and Patsy O'Neill (15) follow up but the ball rebounds off the post, out to Gerry Hargan (3). Frank McGuigan appeals to the ref for a penalty.

Three title but they also played in Croke Park three weeks on the trot, drawing with and then beating Clare and losing to Cork.

Championship progress was not so straightforward, and they were beaten by 11 and 15 points by Derry in 1975 and '76. Management changed direction; The League had been useful as the platform for their resurgence but now it was time to target the Championship. Instead of training through the winter Armagh would begin after Christmas.

A Colm McKinstry goal tied up a first round win over Cavan in 1977 and set up a semi-final with neighbours Monaghan. A new confidence filled the camp, partly because an Ulster final was not an unreasonable possibility and because Armagh were avoiding Down and Derry. They had beaten Monaghan often in the leagues and not even a young Nudie Hughes on his debut, marking Jimmy Smyth, could stop them.

Armagh prepared well for the Ulster final and convinced themselves that previous defeats by Derry had not been as bad as they looked. Jimmy Smyth enjoyed being an underdog. 'I remember a radio interview with myself and Anthony McGurk of Derry where I said all the usual nice things about this great Derry team, but afterwards when Anthony left I whispered to the reporter that we would stuff them! We just knew we would win.'

Jimmy's confidence and coolness betrayed him for one amusing moment at the start of the game on 24 July. Returning to his team-mates after taking the toss the captain was asked by his goalkeeper what way Armagh was playing. 'I don't know whether it was the occasion of my first final or what but I had managed to walk up to the middle of the park and all the way back without having a clue who won the toss! I told Brian (McAlinden) to watch whatever goal the Derry keeper John Somers went into!'

Derry were without the injured Mickey Moran and Brendan Kelly and, when Gerry McElhinney missed an early chance, Armagh sensed it would be their day. Playing a free, running game, Armagh took control and grabbed two goals within as many minutes when Paddy Moriarty and the lightning-quick Noel Marley latched onto half chances. With 33-year-old Man of the Match Tom McCreesh watertight in defence, Armagh finished the job when Smyth used the famous hill on the Clones pitch to full advantage.

'If you hit the ball onto the rise it would not run away from the incoming forward so I sent the ball through and up it sat for Larry Kearns to score.

'The Armagh fans went crackers at the end of the game. Con Short handed me the cup and it disappeared, the lid going one way and the cup the other, both eventually rescued and re-united half an hour later by a photographer who maintained that it would be a good idea to formalise the photo of the captain with the cup.'

Armagh's first title in 24 years awakened a dormant interest in the county, a point not lost on Smyth: 'When we won the National League trophy in '76 I took the cup along to an old man from Lurgan called Sam Coleman. The tears ran down his face when he looked at it. It brought another world flooding back for him. Unfortunately he died in February of '77 and was one of the first people I thought of in Clones.'

In their All-Ireland semi-final Armagh started badly against Roscommon, six points down after twenty minutes. Peter Rafferty was hauled down in the square for a penalty. Paddy Moriarty came up from centre-half-back to take the kick and no sooner had 'Mo' struck the ball to the net than he was sprinting back down the pitch, hair blowing in the wind and Michael O'Hehir telling viewers that 'that's the reason he's an All Star'. Three glorious points from Smyth in the dying minutes rescued Armagh from impending defeat, the score 3-9 to Armagh and 2-12 to Roscommon.

Yet there was time for one further dramatic twist: a brilliant block by Moriarty, denying a certain point for Tony McManus, presented Dermot Earley with a fifty. As the Roscommon player set the ball for the important kick Gerry O'Neill, the Armagh manager who had been on the pitch to treat a player, appeared from nowhere to run across the kicker and mouth something towards Earley. To his credit Earley insists O'Neill did not affect his subsequent miss though the Armagh man was severely ticked off by the authorities and the *Evening Press* ran a competition on 'what O'Neill said to Earley'. Surprisingly the Armagh players were not aware of the incident until they saw it on video the following Tuesday night.

Armagh drew confidence from the knowledge that they could come from behind and win, which they did in the replay by 15 points to 14. The tailbacks on the way home at Drogheda were three abreast but the Orchard County fans didn't give a hoot. Armagh were back in the All-Ireland final.

ALL-IRELAND FINAL 1977

ARMAGH 3-6 DUBLIN 5-12. 25 September: ARMAGH: McAlinden, Stevenson, McCreesh, McKerr, Rafferty, Moriarty, Donnelly, Kernan, McKinstry, Kearns, Smyth, Marley, Devlin, Trainor, P. Loughran. *Subs:* J. Loughran for Donnelly, F. Toman for McKerr and S. Daly for Marley. DUBLIN: Cullen, O'Driscoll, Doherty, Kelleher, Drumm, Moran, O'Neill, Mullins, Brogan, O'Toole, Hanahoe, Hickey, Doyle, Keaveney, McCarthy. *Sub:* Paddy Reilly for O'Neill. SCORERS: *Armagh:* Kernan 2-1, Moriarty 1-0, P. Loughran 0-2, Devlin, Smyth, Trainor 0-1. *Dublin:* Keaveney 2-6, Doyle 2-2, McCarthy 1-2, O'Toole, Hickey 0-1.

6

How Great Thou Art

There's a bookmaker in Dungannon who takes out his video of the 1986 All-Ireland final every once in a while. He enjoys the first half and the first minute or so of the second half, up to when Paudge Quinn scores the goal that put Tyrone six points ahead of Kerry. Then he switches off the tape, happy that his county looked certainties to lift the Sam Maguire. No need to watch the rest.

The late Pat Shields from Coalisland, who was a valued friend and helper to the Senior set-up, would not settle for leaving the game at that point. He couldn't accept the dramatic turnaround in events, 'How did Tyrone throw it away?' He told Art McCrory that one night when he couldn't sleep he actually got up before breakfast to watch the video again but Tyrone were still beaten!

It's not that unusual for teams to come back from a six-point deficit, but this was more than an ordinary game. After the Quinn goal Tyrone had a penalty to go *nine* points clear and at that moment the shock of the century looked likely.

Art McCrory, Tyrone manager, under the spotlight as he emerges for the second half of the All-Ireland final, 1986.

Tyrone's Collapse All-Ireland '86 SECOND HALF:		Tyrone	Kerry
45 seconds	Quinn Goal	1-7	0-4
3 mins	McCabe (Pen)	1-8	0-4
4 mins	Spillane	1-8	0-5
7 mins	Spillane Goal	1-8	1-5
8 mins	M. McClure	1-9	1-5
10 mins	Sheehy (F)	1-9	1-6
13 mins	Sheehy Goal	1-9	2-6
16 mins	Spillane	1-9	2-7
			(Kerry ahead)
18 mins	Sheehy (F)	1-9	2-8
19 mins	Sheehy	1-9	2-9
21 mins	Power	1-9	2-10
23 mins	Moran	1-9	2-11
24 mins	O'Dowd	1-9	2-12
26 mins	Rice	1-10	2-12
27 mins	O'Dowd	1-10	2-13
28 mins	Liston	1-10	2-14
34 mins	Moran	1-10	2-15
FULL-TIME			

'Kerry were definitely on the rack,' recalls Eugene McKenna, 'experienced defenders were running over to Mick O'Dwyer looking for advice.'

The supermen from Kerry, five of them going for their eighth winners' medals, were tottering on the brink of defeat. The Kingdom had won 28 of their 44 previous finals, six of them since 1978. Tyrone were in their first final and had come from nowhere, overcoming the loss of their greatest talent Frank McGuigan in a car accident in 1985 to come within sight of an All-Ireland Championship.

It was too good to be true. Kevin McCabe's penalty kick flew over the bar, a point for Tyrone, but Kevin may as well have tapped the ball to Charlie Nelligan and told him to play on while Tyrone left the pitch for the next thirty minutes. The score was 1-8 to four points. *Four points!* That's all the most revered attack in the country had managed in the first forty minutes.

The rest, as they say, is history. The records show that Kerry added 2-11 from then to the final whistle with Tyrone scrambling a pitiful two points in reply. Kerry wiped out the nine-point advantage within nine minutes and streaked

The vital moment — Kevin McCabe's penalty rises over the Kerry crossbar, 1986 All-Ireland final.

Watching the agony unfold — Tyrone's injured men, John Lynch *(sitting)* and *far right* Eugene McKenna, 1986 final.

home to win by eight points, a 17-point turnaround. Tyrone scored only one point in the last 27 minutes of the game. Remarkable statistics.

Explanations for the 'great collapse' are many, from injuries to key players at crucial stages, to lack of self-belief, to inexperience, though the McCabe penalty was a watershed if ever there was one.

The cocky Clonoe man had converted a memorable late penalty in the semi-final to see off Galway and was an automatic choice to take the kick in the final. However I can reveal that McCabe carried a stomach injury into the final, which had prevented him from practising penalties for a few weeks beforehand. The ligament damage was deep-seated and ironically came from practising penalties, the pain affecting the kicking leg. Medical experts were unable to freeze the problem area.

McCabe does not use the injury as an excuse and maintains that he felt all right to take the kick. He stands by the explanation he gave to me directly after the game, that he 'did not opt for a point. The ball just flew up from my boot like a balloon and sailed high over the bar.'

Charlie Redmond can sympathise with McCabe, having blazed a penalty high and wide in the '92 All-Ireland final at the same Canal End, the bogey end for penalty-takers. Redmond also missed from there in a Leinster final, Eugene McKenna missed one in '84 and in the same '86 final Jack O'Shea cracked a second-minute spot-kick onto the Tyrone crossbar. Redmond's miss in 1992 came much earlier in the proceedings than McCabe's but was as much an inspiration to the losing team as the Tyrone man's kick in 1986.

The Kerry magic instantly returned, Pat Spillane firing over an immediate point and adding a goal three minutes later. A second goal came from Sheehy six minutes later and Tyrone's lead had vanished.

'We just needed to hold them for five or ten minutes,' laments Eugene McKenna who was brought out to midfield to steady the rocking Tyrone ship when the gap closed to three points. McKenna caught one ball but then looked towards the sideline with arms outstretched as if to say 'I'm gone'. He was in trouble by the time Kerry went ahead and left the field 21 minutes in, with the lead moved on to four points.

Like McCabe, McKenna carried a well-concealed injury into the game, hidden from his team-mates; he did a lot of work separately from the others. The injury came from an Ireland trial on 31 August in Croke Park for the Australian Rules series, after which he was told that the probability was that his achilles tendon would snap under pressure. The Augher man had waited a long time to play in an All-Ireland final and would take the risk.

Early in the game the tendon tore slightly, forcing the immobile McKenna to move into full-forward from centre-half in a swop with Damien O'Hagan. His courage won a second-half penalty: 'I had no feeling in the foot but played on. In an All-Ireland final you do these things,' but when the tendon ruptured completely his final was over. McKenna left Croke Park on crutches, had an operation on the Tuesday at St Vincent's Hospital in Dublin and did not play again for twelve months.

John Lynch left the action eight minutes before his captain, injured in a challenge on Eoin Liston just before Kerry's first goal. The corner-back was unable to cover the danger area exploited by Pat Spillane and was powerless when his man, Mikey Sheehy, turned in space before picking his spot for the second goal. Lynch went off before the ball was kicked, out though a broken bone in the back of his leg was not diagnosed until two weeks later. His retirement meant that Sean McNally had to retreat from his half-forward position, taking power from the attack.

'We lost it because of the injuries, particularly that to McKenna,' reasons Art McCrory in hindsight. 'Eugene was our father figure and when he went off, the team lost its way. There are no reserves for people like McKenna and Lynch. Early on Eugene and Damien had done well, getting in behind the defence, but against the strong breeze we could not find the full-forward and so he became isolated.

'The penalty miss was crucial too but maybe we went too far ahead too early in the second half. We were programmed for everything except going seven points ahead and obviously had no experience of the situation. Kerry had vast experience and that's what pulled them through.'

Five years later McCrory was asked for his opinion midway through the second half of the 1991 All-Ireland final when another Ulster team, Down, were in a similar position to that of Tyrone in '86, well ahead and with most of the half to play. He said, 'We were seven points ahead yet lost because we lacked confidence in our own ability. Down don't lack that.' Down had the advantage of tradition within their county while Tyrone had no-one to compare notes with. They simply did not believe that they could win.

Joe Martin had unwittingly written the Tyrone '86 epitaph two years earlier when he finished his book '*The GAA in Tyrone 1884-1984*' with these words:

'Tyrone will achieve a measure of success, will reach a plateau and will then stop short at that level of attainment. What seems to be required is an attitude of mind, an atmosphere such as that which enabled Kerry over the years to produce one great team after another ... or which enabled Down and Offaly to make the breakthrough to glory in the 1960s.

'It is a vision which motivates and sustains, which is inspired, at least in part, by the memory of past achievements, and which catches glimpses, even in its hour of defeat, of its own potential for greatness ... With awareness of its present potential and a total belief in itself Tyrone can attain the ultimate success — the winning of the Sam Maguire Cup.'

Tyrone had done everything right in preparation for the game, confident and clever enough to lull Kerry into a false sense of security. At every media opportunity Art McCrory and his team voiced the opinion that Kerry were the finest bunch of players they had ever seen: 'We set out to give the deliberate impression that we were just down for the day, to make up the numbers. I knew Kerry studied us and all they would see was that we absolutely adored and admired them. I have no doubt that this worked to an extent in that Kerry were complacent going into the game.'

Mick O'Dwyer tried to snap his players out of their relaxed approach before the game by pinning eight copies of a newspaper sports page onto their dressing-room walls. It read, 'Kerry — Over the Hill'.

O'Dwyer was in his tenth final as a manager, McCrory in his first. The Dungannon man admits his energies were used up in dealing with peripheral issues in the build-up, such was his determination to do most of the work off the field himself 'to make sure things were done right'. When he returned to the management set-up in 1992 McCrory insisted on being part of a triumvirate to share responsibilities.

Thirty thousand Tyrone fans went south for the '86 final, most of them taking over Hill 16. They behaved impeccably, notably for Mikey Sheehy's free-kicks, and inspired a letter from Superintendent Garda Mick Francis who was in charge that day: 'I must tell you that your Tyrone supporters were the best behaved people that I have ever worked amongst'. One abiding memory was when the team came onto the field: thousands of red and white flags were held aloft on the Hill, effectively forming one huge flag with faces hidden underneath.

McCrory, the physical education teacher, had his team in excellent shape for the final. Eugene McKenna described it as 'a fitness level reached over a number of years' while Brian McGilligan and Dermot McNicholl, who joined the Tyrone training to prepare for the Australian Rules series, remarked on the toughness of the training routine. Most of the Tyrone team were in their prime: McCabe was 28, O'Hagan 26, Donaghy and McGinn 24 and Harry McClure 23.

Tyrone decided well in advance to play positively, attacking Kerry in every part of the field. Direct, fast and simple football led to Quinn's goal, Harry McClure and McNally had their best games in Tyrone shirts and Ciaran McGarvey was unlucky not to get an All Star. However there was one tactical decision that still invites question, 'Why did Tyrone put Kevin McCabe on Pat Spillane?'

Spillane rated his performance as his best in ten finals. He scored 1-4 from left-half-forward on the attack-minded Tyrone right-half-back. McCabe, a former All Star in the position, was as good an exponent of the attacking wing-half-back as you could find but was not born to man-mark.

Meath manager Sean Boylan warned that McCabe would have to play Spillane at his own game: 'They are both fit and skilful, and both like to roam. The head-to-head could have a major bearing on the game'. Others close to the Tyrone manager tried to persuade him to move McCabe off Spillane. Sean McCague of Monaghan had this advice when Art McCrory came to visit, but McCrory pointed to *his* player's strengths. He hoped that their similar styles might cancel one another out and anyway McCabe was the kind of player who would have had absolutely no qualms about taking on Spillane.

To his credit the Tyrone manager did not blame the referee after the game though he does maintain that the Corkman Jim Dennihan made a vital error in not penalising a 'blatant foul on Plunkett Donaghy by Ger Power from which Kerry immediately scored their first goal'.

So many talking points yet the result, as on the video, remains the same. Tyrone failed to bring Sam 'among the bushes' of County Tyrone. Eugene McKenna refuses to dwell on regrets from '86 though he does offer the opinion that 1985 should have been Tyrone's year. 'We learnt a lot from the semi-final defeat in 1984 and were ready to do something but went out in the first round in controversial circumstances to Derry. In '86 we still had the same team but it was coming towards the end of that team.'

Art McCrory had built the team; in fact he had led the renaissance of Tyrone football throughout the eighties. Hence the famous banner of the '86 final, 'How great thou Art.' On coming into the post of manager in late 1979, he had instant knowledge of the successful Minors coming through; after all he co-managed Tyrone to six Ulsters and one All-Ireland in the seventies. One of his young charges, Aidan Skelton, was now Drumquin's top scorer but would return to his position as goalkeeper in the county team. The manager scoured the county from top to bottom, finding John Lynch and Sean McNally at the bottom of Division Three, and he gave a chance to the likes of Plunkett Donaghy and Harry McClure who had not played Minor football. Donaghy made his championship debut as a 21-year-old corner-forward in 1983.

'As long as you have the right attitude and a combination of football and athletic ability it doesn't matter where you come from. You must also be prepared to live football,' was the philosophy of the manager building his team.

'After those basics you need an engine in any team. It's alright having lovely players but you must have internal motivation and you must be prepared to work. Work-rate is the hallmark of any team in the modern game, the fella without the ball is vital, either in tackling back or getting into a position to receive a pass.'

Frank McGuigan returned from the States in the early eighties. Before emigrating the immensely talented 18-year-old had made history by captaining his county to the 1973 Ulster Senior Championship. Now he would be the outstanding figure when Tyrone won their next Ulster title, in 1984. Eleven

The master, Frank McGuigan, Tyrone v Armagh, Ulster Final, 1984.

wonderful points he scored, all from play, two off the right boot, eight off the left and one fisted. Frank McGuigan was in a class of his own. Two different markers were tried on him, Thomas Cassidy and Kieran McNally, but they either bounced off the powerful upper body of McGuigan or were fooled by his dummy-solos on either foot.

McGuigan was a marked man for the All-Ireland semi-final with Dublin and failed to make a match-winning impression. His manager was unhappy with the lack of protection from the officials. 'The Dublin full-back was all over Frank. Before half-time I went round to the umpires to tell them to point it out to the referee. They must have told him at half-time because at the start of the second half we got a free and the full-back was booked when Frank was fouled from the first ball to come in. But by then most of the damage had been done.'

Tyrone had failed to score in the first 26 minutes of the game despite being warned against repeating the mistake of the 1973 team which took 32 minutes to score. P.J. McGrath, the referee, denied Tyrone a penalty when Patsy Kerlin was hauled down by Mick Holden as he bore down on the Dublin goal. Kerlin punched the ball against the post as he fell, the rebound falling kindly to Gerry Hargan. *(See colour section)*

The *Irish News* reported that 'for most of the match the referee was never in a position to take correct decisions as he was so far removed from the play'. Twelve minutes from time Plunkett Donaghy was dispossessed by Brian Mullins for Joe McNally to score Dublin's second goal. Donaghy was taken to hospital suffering from concussion. Tyrone may not have beaten the All-Ireland champions even if a free-kick had been given and with a first-half goal, the end margin being nine points, but they felt sore that any chance they had had on their first opportunity in eleven years to reach the final was denied by refereeing errors. There was one talking point before the game when

Art McCrory on the sideline during the 1986 All-Ireland final — 'the man who invented dug-outs should be left in them'.

Tyrone went straight to the Hill end for their warm-up. Word was passed to Kevin Heffernan in the Dublin dressing-room and he sent his team down after Tyrone with the result that about forty players were kicking-in together, a potentially dangerous situation.

Tyrone admit to plotting the move to show they were not no-hopers from the North. Possibly they were barking up the wrong tree as Dublin were the masters of the psychological battle but the incident did raise an interesting point. Should Dublin automatically have the right to kick into the Hill goals just because they play their home games there? The Dublin media condemned the Northerners for their cheek, though a few months later Art McCrory perplexed a correspondent at a league match in Newcastle by asking which goals he thought Tyrone should shoot into, so as not to offend the locals!

McCrory's wont was to challenge officialdom at Croke Park, in contrast to Armagh's naivety in 1977 when they went along with the flow. The Tyrone man's attitude arose out of years of experience of going to headquarters with the Minors.

'Maybe we were a bit paranoid but we felt we had to beat everybody when we went to Croke Park. Every time there would be a new set of regulations, each more restrictive than the previous one. One year I had to get Audi Hamilton (one of the Tyrone substitutes) onto the bench with our County Treasurer's ticket, and the rest of the substitutes had to sit in the Cusack Stand.

'Southern teams always had more subs in the dug-outs and it was worse when you played Dublin as the officials or "wee green men" showed their power more. Heffernan was allowed to parade up and down the touchline yet I seemed to have a personal steward appointed to keep putting me back in the dug-out!' Art was not content to remain in the Croke Park dug-outs which are below ground level and make communication and vision very difficult. 'The man who invented dug-outs should be left in them!'

On another occasion Big Art came to the rescue of a couple of pressmen from his own county who were being denied access by a steward to a Minor match. After confronting the 'wee green man' McCrory announced, 'Come on boys, we'll all go home,' and putting his hand on the steward's arm he added 'You play the All-Ireland!' Permission was granted.

His experience of Hill 16 in 1984 was not pleasant. 'Some of the Dublin support was very nasty in those days as other counties also found. Whenever I had to walk under the Hill I was pelted with stones and anything they could find. At the end of the game some of them got onto the pitch and virtually intimidated our supporters in the Hogan Stand.'

In 1984 the Tyrone chairman spent 45 minutes arguing with an official before tickets were handed over for the team. In 1977 there was a serious altercation when a steward in the tunnel blamed a section of the Down Minors' support for throwing a bottle. Sean O'Neill, the Down manager, knew that the steward in question had not even seen the incident and confronted him. Fortunately such incidents are rare nowadays, though Donegal goalkeeper Gary Walsh was the target of a small section of fans from Hill 16 during the 1992 All-Ireland Final. Brian McEniff protested to officials as coins were thrown towards his player.

1986 ALL-IRELAND FINAL

KERRY 2-15 TYRONE 1-10. 21 September: TYRONE: Skelton, J. Mallon, McGarvey, Lynch, McCabe, McGinn, Ball, Donaghy, H. McClure, M. McClure, McKenna, McNally, Mickey Mallon, D. O'Hagan, Quinn. *Subs:* Rice for McKenna. Conway for Lynch, A. O'Hagan for M. Mallon. KERRY: Nelligan, P. O'Shea, Walsh, M. Spillane, Doyle, T. Spillane, Lynch, J. O'Shea, O'Donovan, Maher, Moran, P. Spillane, Sheehy, Liston, Power. *Sub:* O'Dowd for O'Donovan. SCORERS: *Tyrone:* M. Mallon 0-4, Quinn 1-0, McNally 0-2, McCabe, D. O'Hagan, M. McClure, Rice 0-1. *Kerry:* Sheehy, Pat Spillane 1-4, Moran, Liston, O'Dowd 0-2, Power 0-1.

7

Sean McCague

Sean McCague bought himself a new set of golf clubs in 1977 with the intention of spending more time on the fairways and greens of County Monaghan. Three Ulster Senior Football titles later, the clubs are still in the cupboard.

Golf never really had a chance with a man who has Monaghan football in his blood. Even now, in the lofty position of Chairman of the Games Administration Committee, McCague cannot beat the habit, becoming involved with the county management set-up earlier this year for the fourth time.

Even when he stands in the front room of his elevated Scotstown home, overlooking a panoramic countryside view, he cannot avoid noticing any activity directly below at the impressive Scotstown GAA pitch and premises. It was at this home club that McCague led the modern revolution which woke the sleeping giant that was Monaghan football.

The Farney county had been one of Ulster's big four in the first half of the century, regularly competing in finals and winning their fair share. But in the fifties the well dried up and Monaghan were overtaken by the chasing pack, not making a single final from 1953-78.

Other competitions tell the same story. The McKenna Cup was won eight times from 1927-52 but not again until 1976. Monaghan's last Ulster minor title came in 1945, St Macartan's won the last of their seven MacRory Cups in 1956 and the Ulster Under-21 Championship, which began in 1963, took eighteen years to come to the county.

The origin of Monaghan's earlier success was rooted in strong rural clubs. Like their neighbours in Cavan, healthy internal competition provided ready-made material for the county team. However, these small clubs were unable to remain potent forces over long periods and when they faded, so too did Monaghan. It was only when they began to amalgamate that the supply line was re-opened.

Scotstown is a prime example. The club was unknown before 1960 when a few junior clubs combined to become a new force in Monaghan football and later the

Sean McCague, Casement Park, 1989.

backbone of the county team that would bring back the Anglo-Celt in 1979.

Sean McCague was not an outstanding player, not even for his club, disposing of the myth that you must have experience of playing at the top level to manage there. 'You don't have to born in a field to be a farmer,' are his words. Any shortcomings on the playing side are made up for by a self-confessed 'total love and obsession with the game', and by an uncanny talent for reading a game.

This, combined with a schoolteacher's ability to organise, understand and get the best out of his charges, was a major factor in Scotstown's emergence and domination of Monaghan club football from 1974-84, a hat-trick of Ulster titles coming from 1978-80. Inevitably McCague's fresh approach was requested at county level, to see if he could work the same magic with a team rated in a national poll in 1978 at 26th out of 32.

McCague reasoned that Monaghan were not quite that bad, that Scotstown had shown the players to be there, and he set out to streamline the system. Before this the county team had been run by a five-man selection committee, now this was narrowed down to a team manager and a trainer. The new man began to relate to his players on a new level.

'I worked on a one-to-one basis with the players, encouraging them to think about what they were doing wrong on the field and how they could eliminate basic mistakes. Man management as opposed to team management,' he explains.

The Monaghan players responded well to his novel techniques, such as watching video tapes to analyse their play. They were keen to learn after years of endeavour without reward, the very reason some of them had lobbied McCague to take the job in the first place.

Other facets of the modern game required attention, such as fitness and the treatment of injuries. 'Because of having to train harder there was a greater physical awareness of the sporting body, where injuries came from and how to treat them. The talk was all about hamstrings and groins and how unhealthy it was to train after sitting behind a desk all day.'

Monaghan's style of play also moved with the times; they concentrated on the ball instead of the man.

Still, resources were limited with only 29 clubs to pick from and self-confidence was in equally short supply. What Monaghan needed was an injection of self-belief, someone with the presence of mind to fearlessly rub shoulders with the best. Enter Nudie Hughes.

'The first time I saw Nudie was in the county final of 1975 when you could not help but notice this 17-year-old corner-back standing thirty yards in front of his man,' recalls his greatest admirer. 'He was totally unorthodox, ignoring his man, yet the ball never got past him. He was like a magnet.'

Hughes was loud and super-confident on and off the pitch; Sean McCague had to have him in the Monaghan team, if only for the enjoyment he drew from watching his running commentaries at training matches.

'The ball comes in, Nudie has it, pretends to go left, he goes right, Nudie beats his man, goes past him and puts it through the keeper's legs!'

Outlandish antics such as these would normally draw anger from team-mates and opponents but they could only laugh at his comical nature. At another county final Nudie grew impatient of watching his defence being given the runaround: 'Get it up to me, I'll beat them on my own'. He did not intend to be disrespectful, he meant what he said and proved it.

One of Nudie's best tricks was reserved for the 1988 Ulster Championship first-round game with Cavan in Clones. By this stage he was a double All Star and a tall order for a fresh Cavan defender called Damien O'Reilly. As they stood side-by-side watching play at the other end of the pitch Nudie looked over at the famous hill and wondered out loud, 'Have you ever seen so many on that hill?' O'Reilly looked over to see for himself and suddenly Nudie was gone, the ball over the bar and the scorer teasing his embarrassed marker, 'Aren't you some eejit coming here to watch the crowd!'

In the early days results did not come immediately to McCague's Monaghan but in 1979 they beat the champions Down and neighbours Armagh to reach the Ulster final. The tough passage served them well in the final against a poor Donegal team but only after Monaghan had overcome the psychological barrier of not believing that they were as good as the Monaghan team of 1952. Up to this point their entire footballing lives had been burdened by tradition.

McCague and senior members of the team such as Paddy Kerr, who had played in third level education in Dublin, worked on convincing the players that they had the ability to win the Ulster title. Monaghan eventually shook off their anxiety to win easily, 1-15 to 0-11, with Kieran Finlay the scoring hero on a tally of 1-9.

Forty-one years of waiting showed on the faces of Monaghan players and supporters at the final whistle, relieved that the Anglo-Celt had finally been regained. Older players such as Paddy Kerr, Eamonn Tavey and Sean Hughes knew what it meant. The younger players were distracted by the euphoria of the celebrations, to the despair of a manager with an All-Ireland semi-final to prepare for.

Mind you, Kerry were not the best county to meet in your first All-Ireland semi-final in five decades, especially when they were in the middle of a four-in-a-row. Monaghan's ageing team was badly exposed by Kerry's speed, skill and experience, 5-14 to to 0-7.

'Our defence was totally overrun. Kerry came at us relentlessly in waves, laying the ball off and going for the return. We had seen nothing like it and could have done nothing to prepare for it.'

The 'Bomber' Liston got an early goal, Ger Power another and Mikey Sheehy helped himself to 3-6, but one of the Kerry forwards was kept quiet. John Egan was unfortunate enough to come up against the 21-year-old Monaghan corner-back Nudie Hughes. The Kerryman failed to score while Nudie, showing a total disregard for his esteemed company, set off up the field on the overlap and managed to score a point!

The semi-final defeat was not judged too harshly by the Monaghan support, grateful for the restoration of pride and position earlier that summer. The corner had been turned and they could look forward to more high points with Sean McCague at the helm. They were right but over the next fourteen years McCague would leave the post three times. His philosophy is that three years can be enough for any manager, then you start repeating yourself and the players fail to respond.

There were also personal reasons for McCague's first step-down, but he was never too far from the scene through his involvement with the County Board, which had begun in 1970 as Monaghan joint secretary. When his successor as manager, Tony Loughman, was suspended in 1982 during the League, McCague agreed to fill in 'for the rest of the League'.

The League ran into the Championship, then they won the McKenna Cup, reached the final of the Centenary Cup and before they knew it Monaghan and McCague were into 1985, which would yield the National League and another Ulster title. On paper it was McCague's best year with Monaghan though his one regret is losing after a replay to Kerry in their All-Ireland semi-final.

'The more I look back the more I realise that Kerry were there for the taking, as Tyrone showed the next year. We afforded them too much respect without realising we could reach the final. Once in a final Monaghan always seem to have the confidence to win, as in Ulster, but the trouble was getting there.'

McCague also admits he was short a couple of players to win an All-Ireland, in particular a corner-forward and a man on the '40.

His top forwards were Ray McCarron and Eamonn McEneaney, but they could be marked out of a game. This left Nudie Hughes, who didn't play well on the day. McEneaney's dramatic long-range kick forced a replay, but when Kerry scored two goals in the first eleven minutes the opportunity had gone. Eoin Liston was sent off in the twentieth minute but Kerry were already 2-3 to 0-0 in front and went on to win by five points.

Further regret followed in 1986 with defeat in the League final by just a point to Laois, 2-6 to 2-5. McCague departed again and Monaghan were beaten in the first round in Ulster twice in succession under Father McQuaid.

The talent was still there, Gerry McCarville, Nudie and Paddy Linden from '79 and most of the fresher '85 panel. There was another Ulster title in them and the players knew McCague was the man they needed to organise, discipline and inspire them.

In January and February of 1988 he set about licking his players into shape, training under floodlights in preparation for the Championship. Nudie had been a stone overweight but was soon back at his fighting weight as Monaghan sweated their way into the early summer, inspired by the thirst for revenge in the

first round of the Championship against Cavan who had beaten them 12 months previously. The combination of hard work and local rivalry saw Monaghan into a semi-final meeting with Down at Breffni.

The Mourne men were fancied to go further, having reached the League quarter-finals and relieved the champions Derry of their title in Ballinascreen under new manager Jackie McManus. McCague is nothing if not tactically aware and the danger men in the highly-rated Down

Left: Monaghan's Nudie Hughes rounds Tyrone goalkeeper Aidan Skelton to score the only goal of the 1988 Ulster final.
Below: Tyrone led by captain, Plunkett Donaghy, Clones 1988.

forward line were pinpointed. Nudie and McEneaney were on top of their game and Monaghan won by 1-11 to 0-9.

Tactics again played a major part in the final against a Tyrone team with ambitions of reaching another All-Ireland final. McCague admits they were a better footballing team but they were not allowed to function.

'Plunkett Donaghy was their link man, collecting the ball from defence, hitting it long and high without too much direction and by the time the forwards had brought the ball under control Plunkett was there again on the overlap. We brought P.J. Finlay into the team for the only time that year specifically to close Plunkett down, to prevent him from playing.

'After that there was Eugene McKenna but we were fortunate to have Ciaran Murray on him and he was very quick. We were lucky to have good players in their strong positions, Sherry on Patsy Kerlin who had been going well and Brendan Murray on Damien O'Hagan.'

McCague had done his homework and nullified Tyrone's engine room though Monaghan enjoyed the rub of the green at vital times. The otherwise faultless Aidan Skelton let a simple catch bounce out of his grasp and into the hands of Nudie Hughes for the only goal on 27 minutes, and late in the game Tyrone had strong claims for a penalty when Noel McGinn appeared to be impeded in a charge into the Monaghan goal area. Seconds later, the whistle blew for full-time, 1- 10 to 0-11 in Monaghan's favour.

The winning manager was not overly concerned with the television replays of the McGinn incident, as his mind was already tuned to an All-Ireland semi-final with Cork. His main concern was an injury to full-forward Eamonn Murphy who had missed the Ulster final and would not start against Cork. McCague knew he needed all the quality frontmen he could get, especially after failing to register a single score from a free-kick against Tyrone.

He was right to worry. Monaghan scored only six points in a game since labelled 'Gone with the Wind' in reference to the strong gale and the dramatic disappearance of Monaghan's chances in the second half. They had deliberately played against the wind in the first half and reached the interval within reasonable distance of Cork. The plan looked to be working early in the second period when Monaghan had their opponents on the rack. Substitute Eamonn Murphy hit the post but Cork looked ragged until the game turned on a refereeing error. Brendan Murray was intercepted coming out of defence with the ball. The challenge left the Monaghan defender nursing a broken jaw as Cork picked up the ball and fed it through for Dave Barry to score the game's only goal.

'I don't blame the referee, Seamus Prior. He made a mistake, probably should have given a free but referees are like players, they will make mistakes. It tore the heart out of us and lifted Cork who started playing the controlled game they should have been playing. That incident was not the only reason we lost, we may not have been good enough anyway, but it was certainly unlucky.'

McCague stayed for one more year but defeat by Down in the first round in 1989 brought the curtain down on term three for him and on the inter-county career of Nudie Hughes. For the next three championships McCague joined the

BBC television team as studio analyst on 'The Championship', before the urge took him yet again to get involved in 1993.

He wasn't named as manager this time but it became clear at training and in the first Championship game with Cavan that McCague was calling the shots; it was just too hard for the man with Monaghan football firmly embedded in his heart to stay away. Two other Ulster counties have asked him to manage them but he has refused.

'I would find it desperately difficult to prepare a team to meet Monaghan. If I have time at all it should be with Monaghan.'

8

'The Championship'

Billy Bingham stopped fellow guests Jimmy Smyth and Peter McGinnity as they left the set of the BBC's 'Sportscene' programme in Studio B, Belfast. The Northern Ireland soccer manager wanted to see the draw for the 1993 Ulster Championship which had just been made live on the show. After one glance Bingham's face took on a stunned look, 'Down v Derry ... Jesus Christ!'

That's what Gaelic football has become in the North of Ireland in the nineties, a high-profile sport accepted as one of 'the big three', along with rugby and soccer. A wider audience has become familiar with Ulster teams and players, mainly because of the popular BBC series, 'The Championship'.

A representative of the Down Supporters Club tells how he pushed his luck on a fund-raising tour in 1991 to raise money for track-suits. He approached a garage owner of the opposite religion who immediately stuffed £25 into his top pocket and said, 'You need to do something about that midfield.' He had never been to a GAA ground yet he knew every player on the Down team. There was also the Linfield Treasurer who complimented Ulster Council Secretary Michael Feeney on his games, though he could not understand them.

A new breed of Gaelic football personalities has emerged. Enda Gormley is recognised by his Protestant neighbours in Maghera as 'yer man on the Derry team'. Everyone refers to 'Ross Carr's pub' in Newry, though The Brass Monkey is part-owned, and Declan Bonnar is 'the red-haired fella who gets all the scores'. He also drives a large white car with his employer's name and logo all over it.

From 13 May, 1990, every move they made in the Ulster Championship was captured by BBC cameras for 'The Championship'. That was the day Monaghan played Antrim at Castleblaney in the preliminary round and at 10.30 that evening Mark Robson, parked on a Barry Norman-style chair, welcomed everyone to the first programme. Former All Stars Smyth and McGinnity commentated on 25 minutes of edited highlights. After-match interviews, analysis by Sean McCague, reaction from the defeated Antrim manager Eamonn Grieve live in the studio, highlights of the Minor game, an in-depth interview

Above: Jack Boothman, President-elect of the GAA visits the BBC Championship studio in June 1993 with Liam Austin and presenter Jackie Fullerton.
Left: Jim Neilly, BBC.

with President-elect of the GAA Peter Quinn, a quiz and a newsdesk filled the fifty minutes.

Four hundred postcard answers arrived in the BBC Sports Department that week, even though there was only one prize — an O'Neills football. Many entries included complimentary comments. The Bryansford club secretary was 'instructed by his committee to write to say it was the best GAA coverage ever'. Twelve clubs represented by the North Armagh Divisional Board sent their congratulations, as did county and club secretaries from across Ulster.

Jim Neilly was not surprised by the response. The BBC's former Head of Sport (appointed early 1989) had seen the potential for such a series and made it one of his primary objectives, presenting an attractive package to the Ulster Council. He came away with an exclusive contract to cover the entire Ulster Championship, even though Ulster Television had shown more interest in covering Gaelic games up to this point. Peter Quinn had stated in his outgoing speech as Ulster President in February 1989 that 'the BBC do not match their counterparts', and UTV were offered a formal deal before Neilly came along but they failed to tie it up.

Ulster Television offered more money but they had already surrendered the initiative. 'We were happy with UTV but the BBC offer was significantly better in every dimension other than finance,' recalls Peter Quinn. 'We could have had nearly fifty per cent more money but that was not our primary consideration. Myself, Father Dan Gallogly our President and Michael Feeney our secretary were swayed by two important factors — the facilities the BBC could provide and the time the programme would go out.'

In 1989, UTV's highlights of the Ulster final were broadcast at midnight. The BBC promised an attractive late evening slot.

The choice of programme presenter raised a few eyebrows. Mark Robson was regarded by GAA followers as a 'soccer-man'. He jokingly described himself as a 'North Down Protestant', but Jim Neilly persuaded the GAA that this could be used to their advantage, helping to attract a wider audience to their games.

Robson's enthusiasm and ultra-professionalism made him an instant hit. His quickfire 'two-way' chats with the knowledgeable Sean McCague became essential viewing. The former Monaghan manager's respected comments were lifted and printed in some provincial newspapers as part of their match reports. McCague was actually second choice after Kevin McCabe of Tyrone, who retired from inter-county football in 1989 and subsequently accepted an invitation to become the regular studio analyst for the new programme. However, when the former All Star reappeared for Tyrone in April 1990, he effectively ruled himself out of the television post.

Visual presentation of Gaelic football reached new heights with Alec Johnston, a former cameraman, directing the operation. Camerapersons were to be seen pacing up and down the sidelines and behind both goals. A dramatic fish-eye view was provided by a camera placed in the back of the net *(see colour section)*. New angles and techniques were copied from colleagues across the water as television coverage of sport began to get closer and closer to the action.

In only the second programme of the first series the cameras caught Anthony Molloy striking an opponent out of sight of the referee. He was subsequently banned for a month and for much of that season players appeared to be on their guard. The effect was short-lived, unlike the impact television made on ground presentation. Castleblaney were docked £1,000 of their share from the first televised game because of bald patches on the pitch and unpainted perimeter walls. Now most pitches are superbly turned out.

On the playing side Brian McEniff maintains that Ulster players go to Croke Park with increased confidence from seeing themselves and their teams put on a pedestal each week. Previously, they may have been unknowns, but now the top players are afforded star status. Jimmy Smyth noted that players in all Ulster counties were putting more effort into their championship preparation. They knew they would be seen on television and did not want to let themselves down.

Ryan Giggs has competition from Anthony Tohill, and schoolboys are seen wearing Down, Donegal or Derry jerseys instead of Liverpool's. This is one of the most satisfying benefits to the GAA. In their dealings with television they were keen to provide for the future, from the earlier broadcasting time to the showing of games from the Ulster Minor Championship and MacRory Cup finals. The latter is the schools showpiece of the year and under the BBC deal it is shown every St Patrick's Day on a highlights programme alongside its rugby counterpart, the Schools Cup final. Only four years ago Gaelic fans were outraged when one of the best MacRory finals ever was squeezed into a ten-minute slot after 11 o'clock that night on BBC1.

The programme continues to be popular with viewers. An independent telecommunications company reported more than two thousand phone calls lodged in one week for a quiz earlier this year. Live matches have attracted as much as half of the television audience yet this is an option which the GAA in Ulster remains unwilling to embrace.

Apart from 1992, the only live television broadcast from the Ulster Championship was the Down-Donegal final at Casement Park in June, 1966. The BBC had taken the 1961 All-Ireland final from RTE and were keen to make use of some new outside broadcast equipment. The match actually began at 3.45 pm, with Jim McKeever on commentary, though BBC1 viewers joined the game ten minutes in. Many Donegal supporters had stayed away from the game, unwilling to make the journey to Belfast. The venue had been set six months earlier but after the final the Ulster Council accepted a motion from Donegal to prevent television from dictating the venues of matches.

Television became less interested because of the GAA's indifference and with the advent of the Troubles, when occasional incidents at Gaelic grounds discouraged the broadcasters. By the time Michael Feeney began to make noises again, he found that he was back on square one. 'I remember one of the Belfast stations saying they would do the final in Clones but they wanted to know if I could guarantee two Ulster teams in the final! I said I was fairly sure that could be arranged. Then there was the television reporter who stood in amazement as the massive crowd filled up the ground and wanted to know where they had all come from.'

In October 1982 a media survey was carried out by Down's Communications Committee. They looked at sports coverage in the *Belfast Telegraph*, BBC and UTV over a period of one month, and found that Gaelic games averaged around 2 per cent of total sports coverage, compared with around 30 per cent for soccer, rugby and hockey. They also criticised the quality of Gaelic reporting and concluded that 'it would appear that there exists at editorial and director level a perception of Gaelic games as a very minor sporting interest in this community'.

Figures were produced from one weekend in April 1983 when Down and Armagh attracted 24,000 to Dublin for the National League final and Loughgiel drew 7,000 to Casement Park for the Club Hurling final. On the Saturday, rugby's Senior Cup final had a crowd of 2,000 and the All-Ireland hockey final 800. Government statistics were quoted comparing the province's 600 GAA clubs with 39 hockey clubs.

This was the first time researched figures had been presented and they caused quite a stir. Meetings were held with the media organisations surveyed and some coverage began to improve, albeit slowly.

'We were very frustrated that it took so long to get Ulster-based television coverage,' recalls Peter Quinn. 'RTE were only affording us token time on their

Jersey logos — Armagh's first sponsorship deal under the new 1991 rules. Included are the late Patsy Nugent, Ciaran McGurk, Manager Paddy Moriarty, Michael Mooney and Joe Canning.

highlights programmes, sometimes starting their series three weeks into the Ulster Championship, and feedback from the annual meetings with the BBC was not good. We felt that somebody was not favourable to us.' Those in position at the BBC at the time insist they were keen to cover Gaelic games but suggest that the GAA was asking too much money, an argument rejected by the sporting body. Whatever the case a stalemate persisted while around the corner Adrian Logan joined the staff of UTV.

From 1985, the Dungannon broadcaster began to report from Gaelic matches such as the National League final and early games in the Ulster Championship. He remembers being crammed into the back of the stands at Championship games with his cameraman, the only electronic media present. In 1986 a crew accompanied Tyrone to the All-Ireland final to record their historic journey, though the game with Kerry was not transmitted live within Northern Ireland. The BBC showed highlights of the game at 11.30 that evening.

Presentation of such programmes remained studio-based and basic. There was a frontman, Mark Robson, John Bennett or Jim Neilly, with Pat Blake, a reporter from Radio Ulster's 'Sunday Sportsound' programme. They linked into the game, chatted about it afterwards and said goodbye. It wasn't until the adventurous 1990 programmes that greater emphasis was placed on a large, colourful set taking up most of the studio, making full use of all available resources.

RTE revamped 'Sunday Sport' soon after, moved to an earlier starting time and in 1993 they extended their run to 21 successive weeks. The GAA also turned to a private company to market their games outside Ireland. Chrysalis, based in

London and Belfast and with Jim Neilly as presenter, broadcast a Saturday morning programme on Channel 4 from June 1993.

Radio leapt into the nineties arm-in-arm with big brother television with stations shooting up all over the Republic of Ireland. Along the border there is Highland Radio in Letterkenny, North West Radio in Sligo, Northern Sound in Monaghan and LMFM in Drogheda. All provide saturation coverage of Gaelic games, one even having commentary of the Tyrone county final in 1992. BBC Radio Ulster now carries commentary on all Ulster Championship games. Pete McGrath remarked that he 'never knew there was so many radio stations in Ireland', so frequent are demands for telephone interviews.

'Press nights' are common practice before big games, though Derry PRO Bernie Mullan sometimes wonders where they have all come from: 'Five years ago I called a press night but only one person turned up. Now everybody wants to come and they all want our team news and club results all year round.'

Along with the upsurge in media coverage has been the advent of sponsors' logos being carried on jerseys, first permitted in the spring of 1991 by Annual Congress. Money was paid up front and later the size of the logo increased but traditionalists despaired at the very thought of their wonderfully amateur game selling its soul to the greatest devil of them all, commercialism.

Down chairman Danny Murphy voted against the motion, 'one step away from professionalism'. Derry and Tyrone did not carry a sponsor's name for the first game of the Ulster Championship, but they soon realised that if money is available, and with the greater good of the Association in mind, it would be foolish to turn it away.

Murphy and his County Executive sought the best possible deal, first turning down an offer from O'Reilly Transport which was 'not quite what we were looking for', before teaming up with the Dutch shipping company Kersten Hunik for the semi-final with Derry. An option for the final was taken up, and qualification for the All-Ireland series gave Down the bargaining power to clinch a 'very substantial' long-term deal to cover the National League and hurling. The marriage ended in June 1992 but soon after Down were fortunate enough to find and clinch another top-class deal, with Ulster Bank. There are obvious difficulties for Ulster counties securing sponsorships in the North, especially in Belfast. When Antrim hurlers wore 'Mackies Foundry' on their shirts in 1993, Sammy Wilson of the DUP suggested that 'there must have been one hundred and one better ways for the company to spend their money than this'.

Outside top games, smaller sponsors can be found for under-age teams and club competitions; for example Armagh are backed internally by Guinness and the Carrickdale Hotel. However there is no doubt that at the top end of the scale 'big money' is available to successful county teams who are regularly found in newspapers and on 'The Championship'. The main deals are usually quoted as 'five-figure sums', which usually means £10,000, either as a set-figure for the 12 months (whether the championship lasts one game or ten) or graduated schemes. In one example, the county is offered £7,500 for reaching an Ulster final, £10,000 more for the All-Ireland semi-final and another £7,500 for the final. The county in question has not as yet reached any of the targets.

Ulster Senior County Football Team Sponsors 1990-93			
County	1991	1992	1993
ANTRIM	—	—	O'Neill Arms
ARMAGH	Mooney Windows	Carna Transport	Carna Transport
CAVAN	Holybrook Construction	Atlanta Conservatories	Cavan Mart
DERRY	Carhill Car Sales	Burns Clothing/ Sperrin Metals	Sperrin Metals
DONEGAL	Rocwell/Donegal Chips	Donegal Creameries/ Magee	Magee
DOWN	Kersten Hunik	Ulster Bank	Ulster Bank
FERMANAGH	Tracey Concrete	Tracey Concrete	Tracey Concrete
MONAGHAN	Poultry Products	Four ? Seasons	Westenra Hotel
TYRONE	——	Powerscreen	Powerscreen

Perimeter advertising has been another lucrative spin-off, with sponsors enticed by the presence of the cameras. An English company called Moreton Sports Media takes care of this side of things for the Council, though earlier this year there was an embarrassing scene when an advertising hoarding for *The Sun* newspaper, not the most diplomatic on Irish matters down the years, appeared for the Down v Derry game in Newry. It did not reappear.

Television, radio and sponsorship all contributed in some way to Ulster turning the corner into the nineties, while on the field there was another twist with the introduction of rule changes.

Perhaps Donegal prospered most, while some of Tyrone and Armagh's ageing campaigners found it a bit late to adapt to free-kicks and sideline balls taken from the hands.

Leaving all these factors aside, the most important reason of all for Ulster's awakening was the effort put in by players and teams. Donegal gave the best show by an Ulster team in Croke Park since Tyrone in 1986, when they matched Meath in their 1990 All-Ireland semi-final, standing toe-to-toe for nine rounds before being caught by two sucker punches. It was a physical game, and it put down a marker for Ulster football.

'Donegal hit us with everything,' said a drained and sore Liam Hayes after the battle. 'They badly want to do something at All-Ireland level and they damn nearly did it today. On that performance it won't be long before either they or another Ulster team makes the breakthrough at Croke Park.'

Ulster had suffered since 1968, but now the signs were good. Lavey, Queens University, St Pat's Maghera and Ulster were on top of their respective trees and Tyrone's Under-21s were on the way up. A Fermanagh man was about to become President of the GAA and he would appoint a Monaghan man to another lofty position. Ulster was about to take control!

BBC Players of the championship
1990 - Neil Smyth (Armagh)
1991 - Mickey Linden (Down)
1992 - Anthony Molloy (Donegal)
1993 - Ger Houlihan (Armagh)

BBC Score of the Championship
1990 - James McCartan for Down v Armagh (Goal)
1991 - Mark Gallagher for Fermanagh v Antrim (Goal)
1992 - Damien O'Reilly for Cavan v Donegal (Point)
1993 - Ray McCarron for Monaghan v Cavan (Goal)

It would be naive to say that 'The Championship' has healed all the wounds in Northern Ireland. Unfortunately there are barriers in our divided society which seem to be insurmountable, and which are certainly not going to be broken down by a television programme. On the contrary, the high profile and

success of Down in 1991 merely raised old problems in the North. On the Monday before the final a Unionist councillor complained to the press that there was 'too much Gaelic football being shown by the British Broadcasting Corporation'. Head of Sport Jim Neilly tried to explain that the large crowds merited coverage and that Gaelic sport provided the only major field games played in summer months.

Jealousy was mooted as a motive for the burning down of Greg Blaney's home clubrooms at Ballycran in the autumn of '91, while North Down Borough Council voted *not* to send a letter of congratulations to the Down team. 'The GAA as a body is associated with and supportive of the IRA', said a member of Belfast City Council, which refused a civic reception even though some of the Down players live and work in the city. Soccer players from Glentoran and Linfield were received in the City Hall without fuss.

The most sinister development was a threat issued by the UFF after the Ballycran incident, declaring that personnel within the GAA were 'legitimate targets'. After a howl of protest, this was withdrawn. Many Protestant neighbours joined in Down's success and were embarrassed by these events, though to many people in Northern Ireland the GAA remains a nationalist-dominated organisation (it excludes the British army and RUC from membership).

Lack of knowledge will always lead to wariness and suspicion and this is the case with Gaelic games. Protestants do not play Gaelic football at school, just as Catholics do not play cricket, hockey or rugby. The divisions continue after school level, each to his or her own club, with no need to know anything about the other.

'The Championship' has lifted the lid a little to show a broader audience that Gaelic football is an exciting, entertaining spectacle played by talented and articulate people who are dedicated to attaining the highest goals in their chosen sport, with politics a background irrelevance.

Facing page: In ruins again — a club member surveys the damage to Ballycran clubrooms in 1993.

9

Pete McGrath

Monday, 16 September, 1991, approaching midnight. Five thousand people pack Rostrevor town square to meet the Down victory bus. Their heroes have been delayed by an incredible reception in Newry, but the bus is now creeping along the three winding coastal miles from Warrenpoint towards the picturesque town.

A few hundred yards short of the town lies St Coleman's Gardens. Twenty-eight similar-looking houses, but tonight one of them stands out from the rest. Pete McGrath's house.

Red and black flags flutter against the backdrop of white house walls, lit up by lamps in the garden installed specially for the homecoming. The bus pauses to let the manager get off. Mrs McGrath embraces her son, proud for the joy he has brought to their people and proud that he has achieved a lifetime ambition.

In the 1974 Ulster final, Pete McGrath played alongside Sean O'Neill but a shot against the Donegal crossbar was the closest he came to glory. Discarded in 1977 for being 'too small', he began to explore the world of coaching. Early in 1978 he rejoined St Colman's College in Newry where he had captained a MacRory Cup team under Ray Morgan. In the next fifteen years they took the school to five MacRory and three Hogan Cups.

Down Under-16s provided McGrath's first solo managerial post in '78, and he was asked back twice after winning tournaments with a certain Greg Blaney on his team. Promotion to the Minors came, and after years of trying, the All-Ireland was captured in 1987. In 1993 in the space of five weeks he was with Down Under-21s in an Ulster final, St Colman's College in a Hogan Cup final and Down seniors in the Ulster Championship.

As the Down bus rolled into his hometown that night in 1991 the dedication seemed worthwhile. From then until Christmas, and beyond, he was showered with gifts. Crystal trophies and the like came from the County Board, Kersten Hunik, local schools, the Rostrevor club, the Ulster GAA Writers and Philips Electronics (Manager of the Year).

All of Ulster rejoiced in the Down success, not just because of the return of the

Sam Maguire after 23 years, but also because of the way Down had won with considerable style and on merit. Meath had been the strong favourites but Pete McGrath's team re-lived the halcyon days of Down football. In their first final in ten years they stood up to Meath, danced into an 11-point lead and refused to be broken by the famous Meath comeback. Down's eloquent and sincere manager won the praise and respect of a nation.

'There's one man who made this possible, one man who had the courage to take the Down job when many others turned it down, that man is Pete McGrath!' said Paddy O'Rourke on receiving the Anglo-Celt Cup in Clones earlier that summer.

The captain gave the manager credit for 'turning round Down football, from the soft touches in Ulster to All-Ireland winners'.

There were other reasons why Down came good. Many of the players had had enough of losing, and the likes of O'Rourke, Austin, Blaney made a pact to 'give it a real go' before it was too late. Luck was on Down's side at crucial times and with injuries. They played the entire Championship essentially with a stock of sixteen players, fifteen of whom played in all six games. Some of them emerged as outstanding performers, such as Peter Withnall in his first Championship and Paul Higgins who wasn't on the starting team for the first game with Armagh. Others became All Stars in new positions, such as Ross Carr in his first season as a forward, and Barry Breen who was an absolute revelation at midfield.

Many things fell into place but it was Pete McGrath who gave Withnall his chance and who went against the grain to move both Carr and Gary Mason into the half-forwards. He also had the courage to replace that most respected figure, the team captain, after only 35 minutes of the first game in Newry.

Paddy O'Rourke's dream of lifting the Sam Maguire seemed destined to remain a dream at that low point, though very few others could imagine what might happen four months later. For the first time in years, the tipsters and their own supporters had relieved Down of the favourites tag; too many promises had been unfulfilled. The mood of despair filtered into the squad and in May 1991, a month before the Championship, a mere seven players turned up for a training night at Kilbroney Park in Rostrevor. 'One of the lowest ebbs in Down football for many a year,' recalls Liam Austin. 'The League had gone badly and players were not in the right frame of mind to work. Certainly, they were not getting behind the manager at a crucial time.'

Some had university exams, some had problems getting off work and some were trying to shake off injuries. Plenty of excuses, all quite reasonable, but only seven? McGrath was as embarrassed as he was disappointed. He had not given up hope, he believed he had made progess in the League even if they only won one game in seven. The winter had been a time of restructuring, of preparing a squad for the Championship.

McGrath decided to take a more hard-line approach. After a McKenna Cup defeat by Donegal in Ballyshannon he presented a training schedule to the players, along with an ultimatum. 'They were told to make the most of it or forget it. The charade had to end.'

The next game was a challenge in Leixlip with Kildare, played in front of an enthusiastic home support just two weeks after the Lilywhites had been to Croke Park for the League final. Something clicked. Five of the Down forwards were in place, with only Gary Mason absent. Linden and McCartan looked lively, Withnall put himself about, Greg Blaney was back on song and Ross Carr fitted perfectly into the manager's idea of a strong, ball-winning half-forward. Blaney and Carr had both been enticed back into the panel after missing the League, Blaney having had a broken jaw.

McGrath's ultimatum had worked. All over the field his players fought with the kind of hunger and spirit needed for the Championship. A vital corner had been turned. It was a corner that had required turning for some time, in fact since the autumn of 1989 when Pete McGrath was appointed manager. A League final had been reached in his first season but Down were then relegated from Division One and had been beaten by Armagh in the 1990 Ulster Championship.

Pete McGrath did not come into the job in a blaze of glory. He was not one of the sixties heroes and had no managerial experience of senior teams, either at club or county level. His appointment ended a long search by the County Board who had been turned down at least six times before McGrath said yes.

Sean O'Neill was usually first choice. One of Down's favourite sons, he is arguably the greatest Ulster footballer of all time and had been a successful manager with Queen's University in 1982, Down Minors in 1977 and Ulster's Railway Cup team in 1979-80.

'"If only we could get O'Neill" was the attitude of the players,' explains Paddy O'Rourke. 'We felt that he was a great man, the man to do something with us. But in a way this had been a big problem for Down for years because every time he turned down the job there was a feeling of disappointment and whoever came in was always second choice.'

O'Neill again said no. So did Colm McAlarney, Tony Hadden, Peter Rooney and Ray Morgan. McGrath's name had been bandied around early on but, a month into the search, no approach had been made.

He recalls a chance meeting with a member of the sub-committee, but Barney Treanor did not bring up the subject. The only time he had been approached, even unofficially, had been in 1987 when he was in the middle of winning an All-Ireland with the Minors.

The start of something big. Down minor manager Peter McGrath with James McCartan in Croke Park in 1987.

Eventually, on the Saturday evening before the All-Ireland final between Cork and Mayo, Pete McGrath was sounded out. Would he be prepared to be part of a three or four-man team with assistance from County Secretary T.P. Murphy? After two days McGrath answered in the negative.

The next weekend he declined again when formally asked to be considered by a meeting of the sub-committee. Having weighed everything up, McGrath decided he was not ready; he was still playing for his club and had a busy workload. The fact that he was well down the list did not help.

However, McGrath continued to agonise over the decision and asked himself some searching questions. The answer he found deep down was yes. He rang Barney Treanor to say that he would take the job if he could pick his own backroom team. Treanor told him that the job had been offered to someone else and they were to have an answer by the following Saturday. The weekend was a long time coming but on Sunday morning, just two weeks before the first National League game, Pete McGrath was made Down manager.

Reaction from the players was not promising. Team captain Paddy O'Rourke did not believe McGrath was the man they needed. 'I was going to quit. It seemed a real no-hope situation, I felt I was wasting my time. I was thirty years old, had been in the panel for 12 long years and thought it might be better to let Pete work with the Minors he knew.'

To many, the appointment smacked of desperation. Some rated McGrath as a Minor manager but not a Senior, others said he had not been the 'right kind of Down player', the type who would have risked injury to win the ball.

O'Rourke was contacted by other players, asking his opinion. He told them to wait until an arranged meeting with the new management team and the players at Burren. 'I was intent on quitting and from the feedback I was getting I would say that at least half a dozen more would have gone with me. Only Greg Blaney was for him from the start.'

Pete McGrath came to the meeting prepared. He had heard rumours of discontent and half-anticipated their questions. 'The exchanges were very frank and sometimes brutal. The players wanted to know what made me think I could do the job and some indicated that they were not sure whether they wanted to be part of my squad.

'I said I would demand certain standards. I guaranteed that the squad would be managed and prepared in a certain way but if they were still not interested, then they should leave. I said it would take time but that I would do the job right, with them or with others outside the room.'

McGrath spoke for half an hour, Paddy O'Rourke listening attentively to the heated crossfire and the honesty of McGrath's message. 'I was impressed. He convinced me that he had a feeling for Down football and would do his damnedest for us. A lot of managers had come in before Pete because it was attractive to be in the position, but that was all. I said I was with him.'

McGrath's managerial career may not have been at Senior level but he had gained vast coaching experience over eleven years with successful under-age and school teams. Ray Morgan's role in the learning process cannot be overlooked though McGrath is very much his own man when it comes to running the Down team. 'We have shared experiences and have similar philosophies on football but don't discuss tactics or team selections.'

The St Colman's approach is uncomplicated, one of discipline and dedication. Work hard at the basics — tackle back, move the ball quickly, plenty of running off the ball, and get the best out of the limited number of players available to you. 'There's nothing better than seeing the basic skills performed well,' supports Ross Carr. 'Blocking, catching and kicking. The game in its purest form.'

Carr was impressed when McGrath applied the same approach to the Down team. 'One of the best people I played under was Sean Smith and one of the best trainers I played under was Jackie McManus, but the first to do effective ball training in practice was Pete McGrath. You got the ball and you shifted it in the general direction of your following number as fast as you could, moving the ball to the people who could do most damage.'

Ironically, Carr was one of the players dropped by McGrath for the 1990 Ulster Championship semi-final replay with Armagh at Casement Park. On the first day Down had been saved only by two magic moments from James McCartan late in the game, the second winning the BBC's Goal of the Championship. 'We were pathetic. We just lay down physically, the same old story with Down football. I knew changes were necessary.'

Carr, Shorty Treanor and Brendan Mason were the three to go, though Paddy O'Rourke pleaded with management not to make so many changes overnight. McGrath was determined to act. A few months earlier Down had outscored Meath in the final of the National League, 11 to nine (albeit 0-11 to 2-7), losing only because of inexperience. Now all the good work was going to be undone unless he addressed the problems.

'In the replay we were unlucky, losing by just a point, 2-7 to 1-12. I felt we were the better team but we had D.J. Kane sent off, conceded a dubious early penalty and don't forget we had already lost Greg and Paddy with injuries.'

Critics pointed to poor League results as proof that McGrath had been too hasty in the Championship. Two-thirds of those asked to join the panel for the winter refused, including Carr. He had night-classes but took a fair bit of coaxing back in the spring.

After a defeat in Roscommon in November, an irate Down supporter yelled in the manager's direction, 'Pack your bags and go, McGrath.' Within a year, Down were All-Ireland champions.

'That person did not realise that I was using the League to experiment. We were trying different moves, for example, playing to a stronger full-forward. Others, like Eamonn Burns, were left off the panel for their own good.' Down lost six games but still scored more than any other Ulster team in the League.

Peter Withnall was the 'stronger full-forward', not at all in the Down tradition of silky, stylish frontmen. He came from Division Three and was bullish and direct. 'A rough stone but when you knock off the edges you find a diamond,' observed Ross Carr.

He was just what the manager was looking for: 'I needed players who could compete and keep battling to win possession, the honest type of football Meath are very good at'. His new half-forward line also fitted the bill while James McCartan was never off the boot of the clearing defender. Down forwards were no longer 'classy but soft'.

Withnall played soccer with Reading reserves for three years until he broke a leg in an English FA Youth Cup tie. He drifted into Gaelic football at New Eltham and was a substitute for the London team beaten by Meath in the All-Ireland Junior Championship. A year later he came home and a phone call from a member of the Drumaness club persuaded Pete McGrath to have a look. He played centre-half-forward in a challenge against Meath before the 1990 All-Ireland final and scored a goal on his League debut in Cork a month later.

'Peter's newness and bubbliness lifted us,' reflects Carr. 'Alright, he may have been running round not knowing what he was doing, a bit like a headless chicken, but there was a whole lot of defenders running around marking him who didn't know what he was doing either! He could sprint ten yards and leave a man behind him, he mightn't get the ball but he immediately implanted a realisation in the defender's mind that he was up against an athlete. He didn't get many scores and was criticised for poor control, but lots of scores came off him. A great asset.'

'You always hope someone will come out of the blue and Peter was the one that year,' says McGrath. 'It happened in 1987 with Conor Deegan in the minors. Believe it or not Conor was a small fella and didn't play for his school in Downpatrick or for the Minors. He was more suited to golf, yet was spotted at Ballykinlar one day and the rest is history. Kevin Moran is another example, he was playing soccer when Dublin found him.'

McCartan and his hero Jack O'Shea swap jerseys after the 1991 All-Ireland semi-final.

Deegan came from the same All-Ireland winning Minor team as James McCartan, a likeable young man with his father's trademarks on the field and a maturity and confidence off it that belied his years. In 1990 he toured Australia with Ireland as a 19-year-old, a matter of months after making his debut against Cavan in the League and after putting two goals past both Roscommon in the semi-finals and Armagh in the Championship. McCartan's room-mate for the trip down under was Kerry great Jack O'Shea. When asked what it was like sharing a room 'with a legend', James cheekily advised the interviewer that he would be better asking Jacko. This was the same McCartan who shouted encouragement to the Down team as they ran out to play Tyrone at Castleblaney in the Championship in 1989. When Tom Hunt, a loyal Down supporter though from Roscommon, suggested that James should be playing, he slapped his chest and declared 'that's what is lacking in Down football'.

In 1991 the same perception was made by County Secretary Brian McEvoy. 'Too many players lack pride in wearing the red and black. Last year I was approached by a player within two hours of the defeat by Armagh, looking to get authorisation to go to America within days. That to me indicated a wrong frame of mind.'

Dublin came to Newcastle in February 1991 and conquered, 1-10 to 1-7 in the League. Cathal Murray and Paddy O'Rourke were sent off. In March defeat in Kerry by 2-10 to 1-10 technically relegated Down along with the All-Ireland champions, Cork.

The *Down Recorder* offered the opinion that 'Pete McGrath and his backroom team will have a massive job lifting the side and installing some sort of confidence. The Down forward line is still not correct, Jarlath Austin is not the answer and Shorty Treanor is to be recalled again. This current Down squad is not good enough to win titles.' Shorty Treanor was not a long-term recall, and he later went into Irish League soccer with Portadown.

Down played two challenge games in as many days near the end of May that year. On Saturday they lost in Derry, 1-10 to 0-9, with Breen and Eamonn Burns tried as an experimental midfield partnership. The next evening they lost to Cavan, 1-11 to 0-10. This time Conor Deegan was at midfield.

The weekend before playing Armagh in the first round of the Ulster Championship was spent at Gormanston in County Meath, organised by Joe Lennon. The group became a little closer and took in the first of the Meath-Dublin games at Croke Park. Little did they know.

Conditions were appalling at the Marshes, continuous rain making handling extremely difficult and tackles clumsy. The BBC showed only 15 minutes of highlights that evening, the shortest allocation in the series, so dour was the contest.

Mickey Linden's crisply-taken penalty after seven minutes gave Down a useful platform but they failed to capitalise, not registering another score for 28 minutes. Jim McConville rushed his shot in front of an open goal on 19 minutes and Armagh led by 0-6 to 1-1 at the break.

'I'm taking you out' are words Paddy O'Rourke will not easily forget. He knew the decision to replace him at half-time was the right one, as he had been too uptight, marking space instead of attacking the ball. Paul Higgins came into the left corner and Barry Breen moved to the pivotal defensive position.

Late points from Carr, Mason and Blaney hauled Down out of the Marshes, though television replay shows that the point which brought Down level was actually illegal. The referee gave a free for a foul on Carr who handed the ball to Blaney. He quickly kicked from his hands to Liam Austin who scored. Only the player fouled is permitted to take the free from the hands.

The important thing for Down was that they had survived, the motivation to avenge the previous year's defeat carrying them through. D.J. Kane was telling a television reporter that Down could win the All-Ireland. Not many believed him, but Pete McGrath was content that they had won their first game in the 1991 Championship.

ULSTER CHAMPIONSHIP FIRST ROUND 1993

DOWN 1-7 ARMAGH 0-8. 9 June at Newry: DOWN: Collins, McKernan, Deegan, Kelly, Kane, O'Rourke, Breen, Austin, Burns, Carr, Blaney, Mason, Linden, Withnall, McCartan. *Subs:* Higgins for O'Rourke, M. McCartan for Linden. ARMAGH: Tierney, Rafferty, G. O'Neill, Short, McQuillan, Smyth, O'Kane, M. Grimley, Burns, Toye, McGurk, Toner, Horisk, Houlihan, McConville. *Sub:* O'Rourke for Houlihan. SCORERS: *Down:* Linden 1-1, Mason, Carr 0-2, Austin, Kane 0-1. *Armagh:* Toner 0-5, Toye, Grimley, O'Kane 0-1.

10

The Boots Story

'I would not be in favour of Gaelic footballers being paid but if we want to get the best from our county players we must begin by treating them like professionals. Organisation must be as professional as possible and in return the players will adopt a more professional attitude to training and playing.'

These are the thoughts of Down captain Liam Austin in 1985, as written in a dossier requested by and presented to his manager Sean Smith. Austin continued: 'We must inject new and fresh ideas into our team, with a manager, selectors, medical adviser, two PRO's with responsibilities for organising sponsorship for the team, and twenty-five intelligent, mature young men who will eat, think and sleep football for the next year with their new family.

'Within this tight group we must develop comradeship and unity, on the training field and perhaps with ventures like social evenings with wives and girlfriends. The social aspect may be developed further with the planning of a holiday abroad which, on those cold winter nights, would give everyone something to look forward to, organised and financed by the players for the players.'

Two things are sure to raise the hackles of your average GAA traditionalist — the word 'professional' and the very thought of player power. He will insist that the Association is healthy and strong because it remains essentially amateur, a principle that no money can buy. He sees no need for the players to organise themselves, in fact it is simply not allowed, as the same Down footballer can recall from the early eighties when tentative moves were made by a handful of prominent players to form as a group.

In 1988, the Director-General of the GAA, Liam Mulvihill, again ruled out professional teams or players 'because it's not practical, either full-time or part-time', though he did accept that 'we are now in a new era when players deserve to be treated with dignity and respect. That means getting meals after training, receiving their full expenses and not having to wait months for them. A caring and sympathetic attitude is required'.

Liam Austin wanted this, and more, but very few of his suggestions were acted on. He envied the likes of Colm O'Rourke in Meath who was negotiating successfully on behalf of his team-mates. In 1991, the former All Star took the law into his own hands.

Together with Ross Carr and D.J. Kane, Austin gathered sponsorship money to buy boots for the Down squad. The benefactors said they wanted the money to be used on equipment for the team, arguing that previous donations had not always been used in this way. The boots arrived after the Armagh game. Soon after, the trio were beckoned over at the end of a training night at Rostrevor and asked to explain themselves to the county management and County Board. They were accused of collecting money 'on the side', of opening accounts, and asked to reveal their sponsors' identity.

'We were unhappy that the players circumvented the Board and we could not turn a blind eye. There are procedures for running county affairs, for which their kind of semi-professional organisation showed disrespect. It would only get out of hand,' explains county chairman Danny Murphy.

The players defended their initiative, pointing out that a third team soccer player at Newry Town could get boots and kit but that Down had consistently failed to provide for them. A furious Pete McGrath wondered whether he should turn up for the Derry game: 'I felt the players should have been concentrating on playing, and that the issue was disrupting our preparations close to the game.'

Would the Board suspend three senior members of the Down panel before an Ulster semi-final? Murphy contends that 'it was never a panic situation. We did not want to see the players hung out to dry,' though Austin, Carr and Kane felt very much under the axe. Stalemate ensued until John Murphy spoke up on the side of the players, followed by Pete McGrath. Despite his anger, he could see the positive side of receiving equipment, if money was available and within limits. The players were not suspended and the boots stayed, but in future the Board would deal with all such matters.

Liam Austin saw the outcome as a triumph, 'the first time in 17 years with the county that I got a pair of boots free'. Ross Carr said it was 'an important moral victory for the rest of the team who finally saw someone standing up for them'. After the All-Ireland, some players told the three that their putting themselves on the line was one of the things they would remember, bonding a squad whose commitment had been called into question only weeks earlier.

Other players took a dispassionate view, while the chairman maintains that nobody won, that it was not an issue of any great importance and that the Board saved the players from getting in deeper. Murphy accepts that the Board got involved in sponsorship of equipment from that point, supplying kit bags and boots, though he adds one salient point, 'to draw sponsors you need success, and around that time we became successful'. Down teamed up with Kersten Hunik for the Derry game.

Extra money came from the sale of headbands, Down jerseys and such paraphernalia, while a special account was opened for donations to a training fund. For the final, the entire panel of 42 people was kitted out in full with blazers and slacks, and another set of boots was acquired. Screw-in studs instead

Above: No expensive boots, no swapped jerseys from other counties, no matching tracksuits. Down and Liam Austin in the early eighties. Contrast Liam Austin in 1993 *(See colour photo.)*

of moulded were needed this time, and they got the best, ordered from Germany at £100-£200 a time.

Donegal and Derry have had experience of problems similar to those in Down. In 1990, Donegal players gathered money to buy boots and track-suits before their scheme was intercepted. In the twelve months surrounding their All-Ireland success, the squad received four pairs of boots from Puma, McElhinneys and Patrick, though they had to contribute to the first pair and a leading player negotiated for one of the later sets of boots.

Gardai were called to the scene of a row in the Derry camp at a challenge game in Meath before their All-Ireland semi-final in 1993. It's understood the subject of the disagreement, between a leading player and a county official, was the quality of track-suits purchased for the squad by members of the County board.

Football has become big business for those capable of progressing onto the All-Ireland stage. Donegal now have a major sponsorship deal with Magee Clothing; the partnership did not begin until the 1992 All Ireland semi-final. Interestingly, the eventual champions had no sponsor for their games up to the Ulster final.

Down in 1991 were without a jersey logo for their first Championship game against Armagh, while Derry did not sign up with Sperrin Metals until after winning the 1992 National League. The 'big three' now have three of the best sponsorship deals in the province.

Revenue has increased dramatically in Down, Donegal and Derry during their All-Ireland campaigns. For example, the Donegal County Board's 1992 income was a record £272,442, almost double the 1991 total of £140,153. In the same period, the Donegal Supporters Club more than quadrupled its income from £21,000 to £92,000, while sponsorship and fund-raising rose from £30,555 to £66,079. Expenditure on the senior team increased by £13,000 but the overall profit for the year was £155,845. Later, the successful 1992-93 campaign raked in £128,000.

However, the advent of sponsorship and everything that goes with it has brought particular problems for recent Ulster Champions. After 23 years of failure, three different counties have catapulted themselves into the limelight at a time when the game's face is changing. Down, Donegal and Derry have had to attempt to become streetwise in a very short space of time and inevitably, there have been some problems in adjusting. Players' expectations of what fringe benefits should come from increased revenue have clashed with the reluctance of some officials to shed their conservative attitudes. In another Ulster county, a treasurer stormed out of a meeting this year when ordered to sign a cheque for new boots.

Very few players want to be paid but many top inter-county representatives do want to 'see' some of the money. They wish to uphold the ethics of the Association, to remain amateurs, but when they look around packed stadiums and see money being generated by spin-offs, they want to know what's in it for them. They know that some coaches are receiving generous expenses and they hear stories from other counties where certain perks are enjoyed, so, 'If *they* get them, why can't we?'

The problem is that there is no equality in the area of perks. There are guidelines set down by the GAA but they are stretched and pulled in various directions. The stretching and pulling is usually done by players who resent their County Boards for not doing enough for them. They resent having to argue for some benefits. One leading footballer told me of his amazement at discovering that his counterparts in Waterford were receiving twenty-five pence per mile for travelling expenses while the rate in his own county was only fifteen pence per mile. Another player revealed that their post-training meals consist of a bottle of milk and a Mars bar while neighbours have first-class meals. Complimentary tickets are another bone of contention with Noel Hegarty complaining after this year's National League final that players had received only one free pass for the game. In August 1992, some Donegal players were unhappy when accommodation for their wives and girlfriends was not provided.

Having said that, Donegal players have been among the best-treated off the field in Ulster from long before their All-Ireland triumph. Full meals after training were insisted upon from the late eighties, while Brian McEniff's squad has a ritual of staying at one of his hotels on the Friday evening a week before a major game. They normally train in Ballyshannon and retire to Bundoran for a meal, a talk and to relax together on the golf course or leisure facilities. Before the

1992 All-Ireland final they were booked into a Dublin hotel frequented by the national rugby and soccer teams, while two weeks earlier the players benefited greatly from an overnight stop in Letterkenny.

Donegal's back-up team reaches double figures, from the manager to trainer Anthony Harkin, to selectors Noel McCole, Michael Lafferty and Seamus Bonnar, 'unofficial advisers' Pauric McShea and Sean Ferriter, physiotherapist Karen Crawford, team doctor Austin O'Kennedy, masseuse Angela McMenamin and assistant Maurice Hegarty. 'Professionalism' is a word that comes to mind and admittedly Donegal are fortunate to have a hotelier as manager but McEniff argues that players deserve proper care and rewards because of the demands of the modern game on their bodies and on their social lives. Furthermore, hotel get-togethers are good for team morale. Shades of Liam Austin, 1985.

Derry 'treated' their squad to weekends away before their All-Ireland semi-final and final this year. Throughout the rest of the year, the outlay on the Senior team is substantial but has to be viewed along with money spent on looking after Minors and Under-21s, as well as the hurlers. Derry have been a comparatively wealthy county down the years yet their willingness to re-invest and their excellent organisation at under-age level and in clubs has paid off at senior level. In 1993, Derry won the Ulster Under-21 championship in hurling and football while the Minor footballers reached the Minor final. The cost of running so many teams nowadays is considerable, especially when they are successful, but success also now pays for itself. Winning the '92 League brought not only financial gain to Derry but also a large sponsor.

Armagh and Tyrone also have long-term sponsorship deals which bring in five-figure sums annually and along with the three 'D's', they have dominated Ulster football at all levels in the nineties. Of the four remaining counties, only Monaghan have had a team in an Ulster final since 1989 (their Under-21s in 1992).

Monaghan have had financial backing, as have Cavan, Fermanagh and last to enlist, Antrim, though their agreements are on a different money scale from the Donegals and Derrys. 'Monaghan is not a rich county, there are many small companies but not multi-nationals. We have sponsorship deals but not worth anything like other counties', explains Sean McCague. A case of the rich getting richer and the poor getting poorer.

Two crucial questions. Are some players better treated than others? And, are successful players more deserving than those beaten in the first round of the Championship? The answer to the first is more obvious than the second.

The subject of team holidays is a revealing one. Antrim hurlers felt they deserved a continental trip as a reward for reaching the All-Ireland final in 1989, yet the very suggestion provoked uproar among some followers. 'They *only* reached the final', was the protest. However, it is not unusual to hear the cry in dressing-rooms that 'We must be owed a holiday now' after a team has been successful. Armagh's footballers in 1993 were an example of this, having come through six Championship games and helped to generate a couple of hundred thousand pounds at the turnstiles.

Armagh did not even reach the Ulster final but were they any more or less qualified to expect some reward for their efforts? In the two previous years, they had been beaten in the first round in Ulster and could not have expected quite the same treatment as other counties. Indeed, before the championship this year, the Armagh players were handed £25 vouchers towards new boots and taken to Bundoran. The weekend stay was increased from one night to two when the players contributed savings they had been given under a previous deal. Six games later, could they claim a new status? A manager from another Ulster county followed this logic when he said he would be going 'cap in hand' to his County Board after winning a Championship match. Certain perks had been refused before the game.

Traditionalists despair at this kind of talk. They argue that priorities are becoming confused and that some players down the line are expecting the same perks as those winning All-Irelands. Consequently pride in playing for the jersey is not as apparent as it used to be.

'My view is the original, basic one that you should not be in it for what you can get out of it, that playing is all about giving and ultimately you must want to give of yourself,' says Pete McGrath.

'Players have no right to a slice of the money coming in though they do have the right to better treatment because facilities are improving. By and large, players are well-treated,' says Peter Quinn.

Sean McCague has seen both sides of the coin as both a manager and a County Board officer in Monaghan. He's been able to keep a lid on murmurings of discontent in his own county but is saddened by problems elsewhere. 'My answer is that players must be well-treated but they in turn must realise when they are being well-treated. I draw the line at what is fair and reasonable. It is a situation

Donegal backroom support included (*top*) Seamus Bonner and Dr Austin O'Kennedy.

which must be carefully monitored as it could get to the stage where the money from sponsors and Supporters Clubs will go towards bigger and better perks for the players, and then we will have real problems.'

Many people within and without the GAA commonly ask the question, 'Where does the money go?' Senior players are often of the opinion that their Board is tight-fisted. The hurlers of Antrim and footballers of Armagh, to name but two, were warned not to swop jerseys at the end of Championship games this year because a new set costs £400. Surely this could have been paid for many times over by the estimated takings of £100,000 at Breffni Park for the first game between Armagh and Donegal? But this money does not go directly to the County Boards; they have to wait until much later when the Ulster Council shares out some of its income. For example, Donegal received £9,556 in 1991 and £12,780 in 1992. And the rest?

'It goes back into the Association,' explains Ulster Council Secretary, Michael Feeney, with one eye on modernisation work at Clones. It has to be said that grounds and facilities around the province are second to none, as a result of a re-investment policy over the decades.

'Our assets are our players,' counters Antrim hurling boss Jim Nelson. 'It's alright having great facilities and spending money on Croke Park and Clones but if only a fraction more of the money could be spent on coaching and equipment for schools and the like, what a lift it would give to our games.' Players I have spoken to insist that they would like to see more money spent on medical back-up at games, at county and club level.

The debate will continue beyond these pages. How best to spend the GAA's expanding coffers and how far can players go? What qualifies as fair and reasonable? And, how do you deal with grievances and prevent inequalities between the haves and have-nots?

In September 1993, the Derry manager, Eamonn Coleman, opened another can of worms when he made the front page lead story in the Sunday Press. 'Cash or I quit, says Coleman', screamed the headline, with the hero of just a week before reported to have threatened to leave for London unless 'I receive adequate compensation for the work and travelling I am putting in'. It's understood Coleman has been receiving a two-figure sum weekly from the Derry County Board, and has passed over work opportunities because of his commitment to Derry. The Ballymaguigan bricklayer feels he can earn 'good money' in the capital and that he may have to return there at some stage.

Brian McEniff backed up Coleman's argument by suggesting that ten thousand pounds a year would be a realistic figure to cover manager's expenses. The Donegal manager was not alone in sympathising with Coleman; many others pointed to the open secret that other high-profile managers were being handsomely rewarded.

Again more inequalities and more questions than answers. The noises may be coming from a relatively small number of players and managers at the moment but the stakes have become so high, that the GAA may find that the commercial door they ever so slightly opened themselves, cannot now be pulled shut.

11

Carr to the Rescue

'Ross Carr — bundles of talent, has been around the county set-up since the mid-eighties. When will he deliver?' This newspaper appraisal stuck in the mind of the Down number ten as he swaggered into the 1991 Ulster Championship. 'When will he deliver?'

If ever there was a time and opportunity for Carr to answer the question, it was the last kick of the Ulster semi-final with Derry on the 30 June, 1991 at the Athletic Grounds. Down were a point behind and on their way out of yet another Championship. 'The one moment in the entire year that I felt we were slipping away,' admitted Pete McGrath.

The side-lined Greg Blaney watched on anxiously. Conor Deegan lay in an ambulance with a suspected broken ankle, unable to see what was going on. Their summer depended on Ross Carr. He was 55 yards from goal, just to the right of the posts, kicking into the breeze and in injury time.

Carr didn't know it was to be the last kick of the game as he set the ball down. He paced five steps backwards, steadied his upright frame with feet together, took one look at the posts, breathed deeply in and out just once, bent both shoulders and launched himself at the ball with an almighty thump from his left boot.

Derry defenders and Down forwards crowded the goalmouth, half-expecting the kick to fall short or wide. They needn't have bothered. Carr's kick sailed straight as a die, beating Damien McCusker's crossbar with plenty to spare. Somebody shouted into the ambulance to Conor Deegan, Greg Blaney jumped in the air and the Down fans roared with a mixture of delight and relief. Ross Carr had delivered. *(see colour photo section)*

The family name is synonymous with Down football. His father, Aidan, was a substitute to the 1946 All-Ireland Junior winning Down side; Uncle Gerry was captain of the team; Uncle Hugh led the 1949 Junior team and was the Down Senior goalkeeper in the early fifties, while Uncle Barney captained the Seniors in 1951 and managed the county to their All-Ireland titles in 1960 and '61.

The home club, Clonduff, is also the home of Patsy O'Hagan, one of the stars of the sixties. Many times since, Ross has enjoyed hearing the story of how O'Hagan scored two goals for Down against Galway in the Wembley tournament, 'the only man from Clonduff to score at Wembley!' Ross Carr would follow in the same tradition though he only became aware of football in the seventies. 'At the age of five or six I remember entering a fancy dress competition as Sean O'Neill and being so delighted to wear his same number ten jersey. He appealed to me because he was the only player I knew who kicked with his left foot, though it turns out he was actually right-footed but learnt to play with his left.'

Twenty years later the number ten jersey was handed to Carr at the start of the Ulster Championship. Many were surprised that he had been selected in the forwards and that he was given the additional role of free-taker. Up to then his county career had been spent in defence and midfield.

Against Armagh, Carr scored just two points but no-one could be judged on the day that was in it and management stuck by him. They were rewarded with 16 points over two games with Derry, 12 of them from free-kicks. Carr did not look back, eventually winning an All Star in his new position and playing the best football of his career. He puts it down to hard work.

'For the first time in my days with the county we did circuit training in the winter. Star jumps, sit-ups, press-ups and a bit of weights. When it came to training in the summer I was able to sprint harder and run longer, I had power in my thighs and upper arms where I never had it before.

'One thing I could do as an under-age player was to catch a ball, now all of a sudden I was able to spring again. I firmly believe it was down to the foundation work we had done inside.'

The rest of the Down team evidently felt the benefits as well in the first Ulster semi-final game with Derry, 9 points to 4 ahead after what Pete McGrath described as 'probably one of the finest halves of football I had seen from any team'. Mickey Linden was at his lightning best, Greg Blaney won every breaking ball and D.J. Kane drilled a marvellous long-range effort between the Derry posts.

Ten minutes into the second half Down led 11 points to 4 when disaster struck. John McGurk of Derry took an innocuous ball from Brian McGilligan on a run out of defence but was crudely intercepted by a lunge from Blaney. Already booked, the Down man had to walk.

Down's world collapsed. Blaney had been their playmaker at centre-half-forward, spraying fast, intelligent passes to the rest of the attack. Carr and Gary Mason began to drift into the vacuum with the result that Down lost width and direction and Derry's half-backs found room to attack.

Liam Austin started to lose the midfield battle at the same time. He had been injured in only the second minute when he was pushed in the back going up for a ball: 'I felt an almighty rip in the bottom of my stomach.' He signalled to the bench but was told to battle on. 'Every movement was like a dagger going in, I really went through the pain barrier. I could catch balls but was not mobile and tried to hide the injury from Brian McGilligan.' (The groin injury became so discoloured after the game that Belfast physiotherapist John Martin wanted to take photographs of it for medical history. Austin would not play again until the second-half of the All-Ireland semi-final, despite travelling with his manager to the Omagh osteopath Jimmy Meyler every day for four weeks up to the Ulster final.)

Brian McGilligan sensed his chance and with substitutes Anthony Tohill and Joe Brolly they set about reducing Down's five-point lead. Tohill looked lean and fit from a winter in Australian Rules football. He reduced the lead with a point and played a part in Derry's goal. McGilligan won the ball from Austin in midfield, played a one-two with Tohill and fisted across the square for Eamonn Burns to volley into the net. Down 0-11, Derry 1-8, nine minutes left.

Brolly put Derry ahead with another quality score and then came another of those flashpoints that would be recalled when the Championship was all over.

Enda Gormley lobbed the ball towards the Down goal with just enough weight to carry it over the bar when goalkeeper Neil Collins stretched one-handed to scoop the ball away to safety.

'Usually you would not risk going for those kind of balls for fear of setting it up for the man coming in but we were already a point down with minutes left. It wasn't that difficult as the crossbars are a little bit lower at the Athletic Grounds.'

Three minutes on the clock. Peter Withnall and Cathal Murray found James McCartan. Shaking off Kieran McKeever, the Down man turned inside on his wrong foot and pointed. Level again. Then came one of the best scores seen in recent times in the Championship.

A long clearance out of the Derry defence broke to corner-forward Eamonn

Below: The pain barrier. Liam Austin in the Ulster Championship semi-final against Derry

Burns. With all the confidence of a 19-year-old he set off on a teasing run, leaving Down defenders falling over themselves in their anxiety to get to stop him. As the last Down man came within blocking distance Burns threw him with another outrageous toe-tap dummy, steadied himself and struck the ball over the bar with the outside of his right boot.

'Magnificent. You will never see a better score of skill, control and finish,' was Jimmy Smyth's commentary on the score he rated as the best in his four years in television. The following year the BBC changed their 'Goal of the Championship' competition to the 'Score of the Championship'.

Two minutes into injury-time Down were thrown a lifeline; Barry Breen was fortunate enough to get a free-kick. Ross Carr made it Down 0-13, Derry 1-10.

Down would live again and with Blaney and Deegan. The former received the minimum suspension, the latter made an amazing recovery from his ankle injury. Deegan found that running through water near his hometown of Downpatrick speeded up the process so that he could return to a full-back line that had struggled in the first game.

In the half-backs Paddy O'Rourke had done enough to justify his recall and keep his place for the replay, a personal victory for the man who lost his way against Armagh. Ever since then he had fought desperately to save his footballing life, training with the team four days a week and on his own the rest of the time.

'If you want to try to be the best you have to put in more time, for less results. You have to weigh up how much you really want it,' said John McEnroe, former Wimbledon tennis champion, on the difficulties of keeping a foothold at the top of his sport.

Pounding through Aughnamoira Wood in the heart of the beautiful Burren countryside, O'Rourke knew exactly what McEnroe meant. He had won every honour in the game bar one since captaining St Mark's of Warrenpoint to an Under-16 All-Ireland title in 1975, but was still prepared to push himself to the limits in his ultimate quest for the Sam Maguire.

At squad training Greg Blaney suffered when it came to backs and forwards, left black and blue after two weeks of close marking by O'Rourke. When the time came for the team to be named for the Derry game O'Rourke sat nervously and wondered for the first time in years if he was in. 'Number Six ... Paddy O'Rourke'. He did not hear the rest of the team and lay awake that night.

For the replay on 14 July, Derry named their usual team but shuffled the whole pack at the start of the game in a ploy which dramatically backfired. Tony Scullion moved onto Peter Withnall, Danny Quinn went out to centre-half-back, John McGurk to left-corner-back, Damien Barton to full-forward and Fergal McCusker from the forwards to right-half-back. Henry Downey was the only defender to line out as selected.

The intention was to man-mark the Down forwards but Derry looked uncomfortable and conceded seven straight points without reply. Down forgot they were missing Liam Austin because his replacement, Barry Breen, proved a revelation at midfield alongside Eamonn Burns. John Kelly found his niche at half-back, where he would stay for the rest of the championship, and Paul

Higgins held dangerman Eamonn Burns to one point from a free though the Derryman was injured from the first game and should not have played.

After 23 minutes Derry brought on Joe Brolly for Dermot Heaney and sent everyone back to their usual positions but the damage had already been done. Man of the Match Ross Carr popped over enough free-kicks to keep distance between the sides to the end.

Only when substitute Gary Coleman crashed a drive against the underside of the Down crossbar with four minutes remaining was there any reason for alarm.

Down responded immediately. John Kelly picked up the rebound and passed to Mark McCartan, James McCartan took up the running and slipped the ball to Greg Blaney at the other end. The Derry goalkeeper conceded a penalty which Mickey Linden joyously tapped over the bar to make sure of victory by 14 points to 9. Down were back in the Ulster final for the first time since 1986.

Greg Blaney could almost be forgiven for regretting his part in the triumph because the final clashed with another important date in his life. He was to be married on 25 July, just days before the decider with Donegal on 28 July — and to a Derry girl!

ULSTER CHAMPIONSHIP SEMI-FINAL 1991

DERRY 1-10 DOWN 0-13, 30 June, 1991, Armagh: DOWN: Collins, McKernan, Deegan, Kelly, Kane, O'Rourke, Breen, Austin, Burns, Carr, Blaney, Mason, Linden, Withnall, J.McCartan. *Subs:* Higgins for McKernan, Murray for Mason, Quinn for Deegan. DERRY: D. McCusker, McKeever, Quinn, O'Donnell, J. McGurk, Barton, H. Downey, Heaney, McGilligan, F. McCusker, McNicholl, Gormley, Burns, Cassidy, C. McGurk. *Subs:* Coleman for O'Donnell, Tohill for C. McGurk, Brolly for Cassidy. SCORERS: *Down:* Carr 0-7, Withnall 0-2, Blaney, Kane, Linden, McCartan 0-1. *Derry:* Burns 1-5, Barton, Brolly, McCusker, McNicholl, Tohill 0-1.

REPLAY - DERRY 0-9 DOWN 0-14, 14 July, Armagh. DOWN: Collins, McKernan, Deegan, Higgins, Kelly, O'Rourke, Kane, Breen, Burns, Carr, Blaney, Mason, Linden, Withnall, J. McCartan. *Subs:* M. McCartan for Withnall, P. McCartan for Mason. DERRY: D.McCusker, F. McCusker, Scullion, J. McGurk, K. McKeever, Quinn, Downey, Tohill, McGilligan, McNicholl, Heaney, Gormley, Burns, Barton, C. McGurk. *Subs:* Brolly for Heaney, Coleman for J. McGurk, S. Downey for Burns. SCORERS: *Down:* Carr 0-9, Linden 0-2, Blaney, Mason, P. McCartan 0-1. *Derry:* Gormley 0-3, Brolly 0-2, Burns, C. McGurk, McNicholl, Tohill 0-1.

12

Down on the March

Pete McGrath doesn't smile often, if at all, during football matches so when his guard slips you tend to remember the moment.

There were still a few minutes left to play in the 1991 Ulster final but the contest was over. Down were Champions and were turning on the style, picking off points at will, their supporters and manager thoroughly enjoying the show.

'That was the single most satisfying achievement for me in the entire Championship, including the All-Ireland final,' recalls McGrath. 'Our county had failed to win an Ulster title in ten long years. We were told we didn't have the bottle any more. It became an albatross around our necks but was removed that day in some style.'

Thumbs-up from Pete McGrath just before the final whistle of the Ulster final 1991.

Paddy O'Rourke played in the 1981 team, and in 1978, never thinking a decade would elapse before his third medal. 'This is the sweetest of them all. At times I thought I would never get another medal and some said I should have packed it in but I kept plugging away.' Just in case the Down captain might forget the man who showed faith in him only four weeks earlier, a large red and black banner in the crowd below read 'Ooh Ah Pete McGrath'!

In the Down dressing-room two of the backroom team, Martin Fitzsimmons and Gabriel Trueman, danced a jig of delight. Match programmes and hats were squeezed through the door to be signed by the champions. 'Bring in Mark Robson,' shouted the players, in reference to the BBC television presenter who was the only Northern pundit to back them to win the Ulster title. The irony was that Mark had been instructed to pick Down 'to balance things up' as the rest of the team on 'The Championship' had gone for Donegal or Tyrone!

When least expected Down had come good with flair, dash, skill and penetration. 'The best performance by any Down team in ten years,' said McGrath. 'Down could have won by twenty points, by far the most impressive team I've seen all year,' said the Kerry manager Mickey O'Sullivan. All the hallmarks of former Down greats had suddenly been rediscovered, appetite for the game, team-work, skilful interpassing and long-range scores.

Greg Blaney displayed all these qualities and more. In the tenth minute his early ball, launched at the heart of the Donegal defence, caused utter confusion. Sean Bonner and John Joe Doherty got in each other's way, Mickey Linden collected the loose ball, took three strides and shot left-footed under Gary Walsh.

Down were in business. A minute earlier D.J. Kane had drilled over the kind of score that lets your opponents know they're in a match. The goal made it 1-1 to 0-2 and within fifteen minutes Down led by 1-7 to 0-2. Carr pointed a free after a foul on Blaney and again after a brilliant field by Breen. Gary Mason sent over a radar-like kick after Eamonn Burns won a fifty-fifty ball. Withnall forced a 45 for Mason to convert and all the while Blaney was economy personified as he rounded off several Down moves. Corner-back Paul Higgins even managed to find himself in front of goal but he screwed his shot wide.

Seven points up at half-time, 1-9 to 0-5, Pete McGrath reminded his players that when he played in the 1974 Ulster final Down lost to Donegal after leading by nine points. The warning was not lost as his team continued to dominate, but they lost their way in front of goal, shooting eight wides in the first ten minutes of the half. Carr missed a couple of frees and Mason and McCartan fluffed while at the other end Manus Boyle and Declan Bonnar found their range. Suddenly there were only four points between the teams.

Next came sixty seconds of drama that would ultimately decide the outcome of the game. Donegal pressed forward and Barry McGowan found a yard of space in a crowded Down goalmouth. A goal looked likely but Neil Collins saw the danger and dived at McGowan's feet to block his drive. D.J. Kane swept up and sent the ball upfield where James McCartan shipped a couple of heavy tackles before releasing Blaney as he fell. The link-man carried forward and slipped the ball to Barry Breen who steadied and coolly lobbed over the bar left-footed from 30 yards. Five points in it when it could have been one.

The rest of the game was a procession. Carr hit a free, Linden and Mason got in on the act, Paul Higgins made up for his earlier miss with a point five minutes from time and wee James rounded off the entertainment.

Down had won personal battles in most positions, only McKernan and Deegan having the odd problem with Manus and Tony Boyle. John Kelly broke Donegal hearts all day long with timely interceptions while the tireless energy of Eamonn Burns was too much for three markers. Breen looked the part once again, Gary Mason came of age and Withnall caused problems for Sean Bonnar (replaced after eleven minutes) and Matt Gallagher. Greg Blaney was Man of the Match.

The previous Thursday I had found both captains in very different moods, Paddy O'Rourke relaxed and confident at Greg Blaney's wedding in Maghera and Charlie Mulgrew unsure of his team's chances and overly concerned about the word coming from Down.

'There's a feeling abroad that we're afraid of Down. I can assure you that that is not the case,' McEniff insisted, but Donegal do not like playing Down in the Championship. The Mourne county always have speedy forwards who like to go for goal, a Mickey Linden or a James McCartan. Donegal's revered defence felt uncomfortable in their presence, though at this stage they were without the pace of a Barry McGowan in the corners. Further up the field several forwards and the midfield did not seem to fancy the job.

To paint a true picture of Donegal that summer we must go back a few months to a defeat by Kildare in the semi-finals of the League. They went into the match as Ulster Champions with a creditable performance against Meath in the All-Ireland series behind them. Donegal looked well capable of reaching their first League final. They started brightly with a goal and eight points but crumbled to inexplicable defeat. Donegal were still the 'nearly men'.

Knives were well and truly sharpened for Brian McEniff after the defeat. Supporters phoned the offices of the *Donegal Democrat* in Ballyshannon on average every twenty-five minutes to have their complaints lodged with the manager.

Honest and frank as ever, McEniff accepted blame for the defeat. He admitted that changes had not worked but was experiencing the cruel side of football, 'you're an outcast if the changes don't work'.

Stories about Donegal players drinking 'to an extent that would affect their training' added fuel to the fire. McEniff kept angry fans at bay by announcing a ban on drinking between League and Championship.

And then there was the 'Padraig Brogan factor'. The towering Mayoman came to Bundoran to work and play for Brian McEniff in his quest for an All-Ireland medal. He was strong, useful and talented, but always remained an outsider, unable to win over players or supporters in his adopted county. Observers at the Kildare game claimed that Brogan was shunned by the rest of the team when in good positions.

Anthony Molloy was the local hero but in the Ulster final he stayed on the sideline, Brogan sent on ahead of him. Afterwards Molloy retired amid rumours of a split with the team manager.

McEniff argues that his captain was in no shape to play in an Ulster final, an opinion deduced from a lacklustre performance in the McKenna Cup final a fortnight before the Down game. Five points for Ardara against Aodh Ruadh of Ballyshannon the following weekend convinced Molloy but not McEniff.

Some people felt Donegal were nothing without Molloy, even half-fit, such was his status and respect within the county. He is one of those players who can lift a crowd and a team by entering the play. Another in this mould is Martin Shovlin from Dunkineely. Wiry, shaven-headed and modest, the number seven defies his physical frame to power through bigger men in the name of Donegal.

'He's the heart of our team, but in '91 he was not in the right mental state when it came to the championship crunch. In the few months beforehand Martin's wife had had a baby, he won a Railway Cup medal, went to Toronto as a replacement with the All Stars and his brother won a fortune in the Lotto. That's enough for anybody to take at once.'

McEniff had enjoyed the luck of the draw in the Ulster Championship but the easier passage did not work in their favour on this occasion. Cavan and Fermanagh offered token resistance while Down had a semi-final and a replay with Derry. Donegal had to hang around for five weeks while their opponents were sharpened by tough Championship battles.

The Donegal ship, already battered and unhappy, steered off-course. In contrast, there was a terrific atmosphere in Pete McGrath's squad, they did not need motivating. 'We have the players capable of measuring up to the best Donegal have to offer, we have made progress all year and it's all coming right.'

An All-Ireland semi-final with Kerry conjured up all sorts of nostalgia and magic memories for Down. In the sixties the Kingdom had been beaten in all three of Down's All-Ireland campaigns and in fact Down had never lost to Kerry in the Championship.

However on the Monday night after the Ulster final Pete McGrath told his players that the knock-on effect of their famous predecessors was negligible. Players like Conor Deegan had not even been born until the seventies. The manager also pointed out that tradition would not help their opponents, 'they're not the machine that won eight All-Irelands'. Jack O'Shea and Pat Spillane were still around, but it was to be Spillane's last time in the famous green and gold shirt. O'Shea was to retire the following year.

Both teams were untested in Championship fare at this level but McGrath believed that Down had the forwards to swing the verdict.

Peter Withnall did just that with two marvellous goals. Only two points scored in the Ulster Championship, yet in front of 41,666 people at Croke Park he shot past Charlie Nelligan with his left foot on ten minutes and his right on 58 minutes before being stretchered from the field with a damaged right foot. With his job done and the Hill alive with happy Down people, their hero grinned from ear to ear and gave the 'thumbs up' sign. Surely the happiest man ever carried off at Croke Park!

Withnall had taken Tom Spillane to the cleaners. Public opinion in Kerry had cried out for Spillane's call-up after 23 points had been conceded to Limerick in the Munster final. He was a triple All Star but the last of his awards was in 1987

Goal number one! Withnall shoots to the Kerry net. All-Ireland semi-final 1991.

and all of his awards were at centre-half-back. 'Who's Tom Spillane?' wondered the twenty-two-year-old from Down about to make a name for himself.

The first ten minutes of the game were simply electric with heart-stopping excitement and drama at both ends. Ross Carr opened with a point, and on five minutes Greg Blaney thundered the ball against the Kerry crossbar from only seven yards out. Two minutes later Linden was fouled by Nelligan for a Down penalty. Linden blasted the kick three yards wide.

Kerry raced down the field where Neil Collins' fingertips pushed Maurice Fitzgerald's shot onto the crossbar. Seconds later Collins was all at sea as Fitzgerald punched against the same crossbar.

Back came Down in the tenth minute with the high ball tactic. Mickey Linden slipped a pass to Withnall who drove left-footed low into the far corner of the Kerry net. Nelligan never moved. A whirlwind start, but Down only had 1-1 on the board and straight away Pat Spillane got Kerry's first score. Down's foot slipped off the pedal and by half-time Kerry led, 0-7 to 1-3, with four frees from Fitzgerald.

Down looked sound in defence with Higgins holding Pa Dennehy, Kane solid at centre-half-back, Deegan and Kelly on top of both Fitzgerald and O'Shea who swopped places. O'Shea had one clear sight of goal but Deegan did enough to put him off. Brendan McKernan followed Timmy Fleming into the middle of the field with some success. Otherwise, midfield had gone missing, and the attack had lost its early momentum.

Pete McGrath was furious as he stormed into the Down dressing-room after his players. 'I don't know what you're all sitting down for, you've been resting for the last fifteen minutes! Now get up and start thinking.' Neil Collins later described McGrath's outburst as 'one of the biggest rollickings he has ever given us, and he was right'.

The second period was extraordinary in that Kerry scored only once, a point from Pat Spillane in the 50th minute, and that Down managed just two points in the first 26 minutes. The strong wind made fluent play difficult as both sides huffed and puffed without blowing anything down.

For eight minutes after Spillane's score the teams were locked together. Paul Higgins snuffed out a Fitzgerald goal chance on 19 minutes and Liam Austin came on for Burns. Barry Breen looked like a midfielder in trouble with his injured chin supported by a bandage wrapped around his head.

Breen won a free on 48 minutes and passed to Mickey Linden. Speed and determination took the forward away from his man for a brilliant 40-yard point. Paddy O'Rourke watched from down the field: 'to see Mickey turn and punch the air said to all of us that we were going to win'.

It was the signal Down needed to break free from their slumber and within a minute Breen was again the provider. Another dropping ball into the centre of the Kerry defence escaped Linden and his marker but Peter Withnall was alert and alone. Running in from the right side this time he shot right-footed into the far corner of the Kerry net.

Tears of joy ran down County chairman Danny Murphy's face as he looked around Croke Park and saw 'those wonderful Down supporters' celebrate.

Ross Carr ran in to congratulate the goalscorer. 'Peter was coming out with his arm in the air, Mickey was dancing and I knew we had it won but as I looked to the line I received the solemn sign to get back out to my position. It was great to see the crowd in the Hogan Stand and on Hill 16 going delirious.'

Down were alive, Withnall added a point two minutes later and Breen another after a super seven-man move. Carr joined the party from a free after Withnall's exit. Ambrose Rodgers came on for the last three minutes.

The Down players knew what an achievement it had been for Rodgers to be there at all; the lonely figure at the other end of the training field all summer had battled to overcome serious injury in the hope of helping Down win the Sam Maguire.

Down had no time to look back. Pete McGrath was fully aware that they had just five weeks to get ready for the greatest event of their footballing lives. 'As I walked off the pitch my mind was already focused on how to prepare and indeed protect my players in the build-up to the county's first All-Ireland since the sixties.'

Ulster final 1991 and All-Ireland semi-final teams listed overleaf.

ULSTER FINAL 1991

DOWN 1-15 DONEGAL 0-10, 28 July at Clones: DOWN - Collins, McKernan, Deegan, Higgins, Kelly, O'Rourke, Kane, Breen, Burns, Carr, Blaney, Mason, Linden, Withnall, J. McCartan. *Subs* - M.Quinn for Higgins. DONEGAL - Walsh, Doherty, S. Bonnar, Matt Gallagher, Reid, Gavigan, McGowan, Murray, M. Gallagher, M. McHugh, Mulgrew, McMullan, D. Bonnar, T. Boyle, M. Boyle. *Subs:* Hegarty for S. Bonnar, Brogan for Murray, J. McHugh for Mulgrew. SCORERS - Down: Linden 1-1, Carr, Blaney, Mason 0-3, McCartan 0-2, Kane, Higgins, Breen 0-1. Donegal: D. Bonnar 0-4, T. Boyle 0-3, M. Boyle 0-2, Brogan 0-1.

ALL-IRELAND SEMI-FINAL

DOWN 2-9 KERRY 0-8 - 11 August, Croke Park: DOWN - Collins, McKernan, Deegan, Higgins, Kelly, Kane, O'Rourke, Breen, Burns, Carr, Blaney, Mason, Linden, Withnall, McCartan. *Subs* - Austin for Burns, Rodgers for Withnall. KERRY - Nelligan, Stack, T. Spillane, Murphy, Culhane, Burke, Nix, O'Mahoney, O'Donovan, Cronin, P. Spillane, O'Shea, Dennehy, Fitzgerald, Fleming. *Subs* - Lyne for Murphy, Farrell for Cronin. SCORERS - Down: Withnall 2-1, Carr 0-4, Linden, Mason 0-2. Kerry: Fitzgerald 0-5, P. Spillane 0-2, O'Donovan 0-1.

13

'We're the team that beat the team that couldn't be beaten'

'Meath are one of the greatest teams in the history of Gaelic football ... They must get the vote to crown a memorable season with the Sam Maguire Cup.' Paddy Downey, *Irish Times*

'Just how does any side contain the Meath attack for a full 70 minutes? Beggy, Dowd and Coyle provide the mobility, O'Rourke (if fit), Stafford and Flynn the awesome scoring power! Also, one feels the Meath defence will prove a greater stumbling block than Down have encountered so far this season, and that could have major bearing on this game.' Donal Keenan, *Irish Independent*

'Ever since Meath finally got rid of Dublin, winning this final became an obsession. Likely score? Meath 1-11, Down 0-11.' Martin Breheny, *Sunday Press*

The media had been enthralled by Meath all summer, reporting on nine games at Croke Park since the second of June. Four incredible marathons with Dublin, two more games with Wicklow, defeats of Offaly and Laois to win out in Leinster, and finally Roscommon in the All-Ireland semi-final. Nine games, nine times Meath had survived, frequently against all the odds. They were a team that simply could not be beaten.

The Dublin battles were played before packed houses on summer days with extra-time required three times and the referee collapsing with exhaustion on one occasion. In the fourth meeting Dublin led by three points with only seconds remaining. Then, a slick passing movement took Meath into the Dublin penalty area. Tommy Dowd slipped the ball across the edge of the square to Kevin Foley who had wandered up from half-back. Foley thumped the ball into the roof of the net and from the kick-out David Beggy tapped over a point in the most dramatic of endings to the most exciting series of contests you are likely to see.

Not permitted a breather, Meath stumbled their way through Leinster and in the All-Ireland semi-final Roscommon appeared to be defeating a tired team. Once again the Royal County raised their game by at least three gears to swing the contest, much like Kerry against Tyrone in the 1986 All-Ireland final. Meath looked destined to be champions again; they had shown tremendous character and steel to overcome mighty obstacles.

Down had been relegated in the National League in the spring and played four games fewer than Meath in the championship without suggesting they were in any way superhuman. Ordinary against Armagh, saved by a debatable late free-kick against Derry, impressive against an out-of-sorts Donegal and labouring to beat poor Munster champions. Occasionally brilliant, but only occasionally.

These are the reasons why the media were caught out by Down's win in the 1991 All-Ireland final. Meath had produced miraculous recoveries on their doorstep all summer while Down had been in Croke Park only once.

Pete McGrath had a different view of Meath after watching the semi-final with Roscommon: 'I was amazed at people commenting afterwards that we would have to be twice as good as Meath to win, such was the aura around them at the time. As I travelled home with Paddy O'Rourke I made the point that we *could* win the final despite the hype surrounding our opponents.'

Meath had been fortunate to beat Dublin; they had had difficulty in putting away moderate opposition and had been outplayed by Roscommon for most of their semi-final. They were vastly experienced (Colm O'Rourke's 51st Championship game) but were past their peak. As for his own team, McGrath felt they were underestimated, young and largely unproven but that with correct preparations and self-belief they could sustain their top form over longer periods than before.

No Ulster team had taken the Sam Maguire since 1968, and only two had made the final in the intervening period, but the last team to do it had been Down and there's no doubt the '91 team inherited some of the qualities of their predecessors.

Pete McGrath remembers listening to the radio in Mickey Cole's backyard in Rostrevor in 1960 when Down won their first title, and eight years later he was there to see his brother Hilary in the reserves as the third title was captured. Assistant John Murphy played in '68.

Past and present are connected in Down by 'the family' or the 'Corleones' as they are amusingly but respectfully referred to. They are the Down footballing elite, the O'Neills, McCartans, Kanes and Blaneys, all related in one way or another and known to offer the benefits of their tremendous experience. Former greats make quiet suggestions to the manager (he listens but makes up his own mind) while the current members on the team are more up-front. 'There's no back doors with them,' says Ross Carr, 'D.J. and Greg say it where it matters. If some players were not pulling their weight they would say it.'

Preparations began on the night of the Kerry game when County Chairman Danny Murphy asked the Activities Committee to abandon all club games involving county players in the five weeks to the final. Decisions could also be made by Board members where and when necessary, without having to call a full meeting. The Down Supporters Club took care of blazers, boots and the like.

A golf outing was organised for Warrenpoint on the Monday before the final by Larry Powell, substitute in '68. Present-day players rubbed shoulders with Down legends such as Sean O'Neill and Joe Lennon. International soccer legend Pat Jennings partnered 3 handicapper Conor Deegan.

All-Ireland fever swept the county. County PRO Seán Óg McAteer took a delivery of 200 jerseys at his Newry shop on a Saturday only to be sold out by Monday. The enthusiastic supporters were certain Down would win, though the basis of their reasoning had little to do with an analysis of the teams. They pointed out that Down always won titles in years 'with a one in them', the Ulster in 1961-'71-'81-'91 and the All-Ireland in 1961. In '61 Spurs won the FA Cup, Tipperary won the McCarthy Cup and the Cork Rose won in Tralee. Now, thirty years later, all three were waiting on Down to make up the foursome. Furthermore, Bob Beamon set a new world long-jump record in 1968 but, just like Ulster's barren run over the same period, it had been broken in 1991. How could Down lose?

Down training sessions were well attended, with many children following and inspiring their new idols. 'We did five or six nights each week at that time with great variety to the training. We sometimes went to the Park in Rostrevor in the summer evenings where kids ran after us, spurring us on and giving a new atmosphere each night,' recalls Ross Carr.

After the Kerry game Down took one night off and then trained very hard for seven or eight days. The ball was left to one side as the players put in vital stamina work to raise their level of fitness by another notch.

A quiet weekend was spent at the University of Ulster campus at Jordanstown near Belfast. No fancy hotels for Down, they were able to get a decent rest and could talk without interruption. Senior players like Paddy O'Rourke took younger members to one side to tell them that they might never play in another All-Ireland final.

Injury scares were few with the only real alarm caused by Peter Withnall arriving at training with a large white bandage wrapped around his foot. The joiner had leapt off a ladder at work onto a nail. It was not enough to keep him out of a vital confrontation with the Meath full-back.

'I wouldn't be surprised to hear that there are small boys in Dublin who believe that Mick Lyons is kept in a cage above in Summerhill and fed with raw meat ... there is no law where it says that Lyons should not be challenged inside a certain area but it seems that way,' wrote Con Houlihan.

Down selected an unchanged team though the manager had one major dilemma, whether to play Eamonn Burns or Liam Austin at midfield. 'Burns and Breen had formed a settled partnership and complemented one another while Liam Austin had been the number one midfielder at the start of the campaign and was bursting in training.' McGrath opted to leave well alone.

The manager pinpointed weaknesses in the opposition: a lack of pace in the full-back line, especially with the loss of Robbie O'Malley through injury, a tendency to concede plenty of scoring chances, and a certain inconsistency at midfield. Down had speedier and more accurate forwards than Meath had encountered to date.

Meath's full-forward line was their best but McGrath was happy with a defence that had conceded only one goal in five games. The half-backs picked their men in advance. John Kelly, 'the sort of man you could bet on if a ball was bounced seven yards from him and three yards from his opponent' (Ross Carr) would take Tommy Dowd. D.J. Kane added David Beggy to an impressive list of markers, Dermot McNicholl, Martin McHugh and Pat Spillane. Paddy O'Rourke was happy to mark Colm Coyle 'who wasn't a forward'.

Down were aware that Meath would put it up to them physically in the early stages but were prepared.

Those were the only tactics Down had, but they had confidence in each other to win their personal battles over the pitch and were ready for all eventualities. They were ready to withstand early physical pressure and for the guaranteed late comeback.

On the morning of 15 September the Down players woke up in their own homes, so following a Down tradition. Croke Park seemed very far away to Paddy O'Rourke in Burren but over in Clonduff Ross Carr was already there in spirit. 'There are more important things in life, and in Northern Ireland we are in no better place to realise that, but for nine months in 1991 and on that day in particular there was very little more important.'

The squad met at Newry and travelled by coach to the Country Club in Portmarnock for a light lunch, given a Garda escort from the border. Near their destination they caught a glimpse of the Meath players strolling along a beach. The morning papers had confirmed reports that Colm O'Rourke had a viral infection and would not start the game. Gerry McEntee was named at midfield with P.J. Gillic switching to the attack. Down talked about O'Rourke coming on as a substitute but they did not dwell on the matter. Paul Higgins was confident enough to handle the change of opponent.

By half-past two the Down dressing-room was a mill of people working through their private pre-match routines. Ross Carr observed: 'James McCartan had done nothing all year yet there he was walking around with no shirt on, like God Almighty. D.J. Kane was bouncing on his feet and muttering under his breath, "No bucks, No ball", while for a professional man I've never known anyone to swear as much as Greg Blaney when he's keyed up!

'Linden was a bit pale looking and quiet, as were the likes of Collins, Breen, Mason and Higgins, all going about their business without fuss, but just as inspirational as the others out on the field.'

The 'talkers' took their turn, the fluent Pete McGrath followed by big Ambrose Rodgers, 'a fantastic motivator' who could bring his big and powerful fists down on the table like sledgehammers. Last up was the captain. O'Rourke said 'I have one hand on the Sam Maguire, as has Liam Hayes. I'm going to swing the hardest. If you swing with me then I'll get both hands on it.'

At 12 minutes past three Paddy O'Rourke led his team out, three minutes before Meath. 'I was determined to enjoy the occasion though looking around Croke Park was nearly enough to make you turn and leave.' Pete McGrath was

Down captain Paddy O'Rourke and Meath's Liam Hayes.

last out but walked straight into the 'wall of sound'. He had reached the middle of the pitch when Meath came out: 'For three or four seconds it was deafening, like machine-gun rattle'.

The contrasting colours of red and black stood out starkly in the bright sunshine *(See colour photo section)*. During the parade Ross Carr looked up and tried to take it all in. 'I felt like God. We had to deliver because they had put their trust in us. We couldn't afford to lose.'

Down took a while to settle. Twenty minutes passed before their first point from play from Eamonn Burns but the score put Down ahead for the first time. Three vital frees from Mason and one from Carr had kept them in touch. Withnall and Linden were marked men but McCartan was not closed down so well, winning much of the ball fed out to the wings and fouled for the first two free-kicks. The only scare came on ten minutes when a slack clearance from Collins went astray but Stafford shot wide.

In this opening period Kevin Foley removed one of Mickey Linden's teeth and Liam Hayes body-checked Brendan McKernan, but the Northerners refused to succumb. The wounded men rose to their feet prepared to take more punishment if necessary, with the team captain always there to reassure them that the plan was still working, that Meath were getting rattled.

A Meath selector later revealed that they had thought their softest game all year would be against Down in the final. They could not believe the football Down produced against them.

Down's half-forwards buzzed around, blocking balls coming out, supporting their midfield and playing the early ball to the full-forwards. Free-kicks were won off the Meath defenders, and six converted to give a half-time lead of 0-8 to 0-4. Meath had not scored since the 18th minute.

Pete McGrath appealed to his players at half-time not to sit back. 'You have the most important 35 minutes of your footballing lives in front of you.' Sean Boylan had more reason to worry, as his team were again trailing. His full-back was injured and would not last to the finish, but Down certainly would.

One goal and six points they scored in the first 14 minutes of the second half, all but one from play. Meath were mesmerised by scintillating forward play from James McCartan in particular. The Down cornerman showed his resolve in responding to a hefty challenge from Mick Lyons to weave under several lunging tackles and curl over a brilliant left-footed point, four minutes into the half.

Down were in full flow, getting to the ball first and running at Meath. Carr and Linden added points before a sweeping movement through the right side of the Meath back division ended in a goal on 44 minutes. McCartan leapt among men six inches taller to catch a crossfield ball and gave a short pass to Withnall. He moved it along to Blaney who spotted Linden in a good position near the end line. Barry Breen had never scored a goal for Down but had drifted to the edge of the square unnoticed. 'I was standing there screaming at Mickey to pass but he seemed to take forever to see me. I needn't have worried as he drew the defender and the goalkeeper before lofting the perfect pass for me just to palm the ball into an empty net.' Down 1-11, Meath 0-5, 26 minutes left. 'Too early,' thought Pete McGrath.

Three minutes later Ross Carr had a free-kick fifty yards out and to the right of the Meath posts. Paddy O'Rourke had a word in his ear: 'I told Ross that we needed this free, that it was the kind of kick that won All-Irelands'. An almighty kick sailed over the bar. McCartan and Blaney made it 1-14 to 0-6 with 49 minutes played.

Pete McGrath replaced his goalscorer with Liam Austin. 'Gerry McEntee was playing extremely well in the middle of the field, as was Barry, but McEntee was playing better. They were allowing each other to play but Liam prevented McEntee from continuing to field and set up attacks.' But would the substitution and 11 points be enough?

Enter Colm O'Rourke and the Meath revival with four successive points from the 50th minute. Over the closing twenty minutes Meath tallied 1-8 to Down's 0-2, a complete turnaround. 'You could say we lost our way but we made the most of our opportunities when we were on top and Meath didn't. We ended up with more and that's what counts,' insists Ross Carr.

What also mattered was a vital point-blank block by Neil Collins from Bernie Flynn as the pressure mounted. Forays up the field allowed the defence to breathe and keep Meath at arm's length, something others had not managed to do. Eamonn Burns struck a lovely point off the outside of his right boot from Blaney's pass and with nine minutes left Austin and Withnall did the spadework for Gary Mason to strike Down's final point. D.J. Kane knew Down were going to win at that moment, six points in front, and a grimace on the face of his

The path to goal — *above,* James McCartan slips through the Meath defence. *Below:* Greg Blaney passes to Mickey Linden before the vital score.

All-Ireland Final 1991		
Minutes	Down	Meath
1 Stafford (F)	0-0	0-1
2 Flynn	0-0	0-2
4 Mason (F)	0-1	0-2
8 Mason (F)	0-2	0-2
10 Stafford	0-2	0-3
15 Mason (F)	0-3	0-3
18 Hayes	0-3	0-4
19 Carr (F)	0-4	0-4
20 Burns	0-5	0-4
24 McCartan	0-6	0-4
26 Carr (F)	0-7	0-4
34 Carr (F)	0-8	0-4
HALF-TIME		
37 Flynn	0-8	0-5
39 McCartan	0-9	0-5
41 Carr	0-10	0-5
42 Linden	0-11	0-5
44 Breen Goal	1-11	0-5
47 Carr (F)	1-12	0-5
48 Stafford	1-12	0-6
49 McCartan	1-13	0-6
49 Blaney	1-14	0-6
50 C. O'Rourke	1-14	0-7
51 Beggy	1-14	0-8
54 Stafford	1-14	0-9
56 Flynn	1-14	0-10
57 Burns	1-15	0-10
59 Hayes Goal	1-15	1-10
61 Mason	1-16	1-10
62 Flynn	1-16	1-11
65 Flynn	1-16	1-12
67 Flynn	1-16	1-13
69 Stafford (F)	1-16	1-14
FULL-TIME		

Up and over! Withnall coming to grips with Meath's Mick Lyons.

marker David Beggy showed that it was enough.

Still Meath chipped at Down's advantage with Flynn and O'Rourke causing most problems. Pete McGrath resisted the temptation to switch McKernan off Flynn or to put a bigger marker onto O'Rourke. 'If I had moved Breen into the defence or Higgins across to the right or even Paddy onto Colm O'Rourke it could have disrupted our shape, confidence and understanding.

'They were confident in one another and to suddenly find a different man behind or alongside you would have brought a little bit of doubt into their minds. I took a bit of a gamble on sticking with McKernan as Flynn scored three late points and I would have taken the blame if Meath had won but thankfully it paid off.'

The Down manager saw Tommy Dowd as one of the Meath play-makers in the closing stages and when that player won and took a quick free-kick to set up Liam Hayes for a goal eleven minutes from time, McGrath sprinted onto the field. John Kelly was told in no uncertain terms to re-tighten his grip on Dowd.

McGrath barely had time to get off the playing area when Mickey Linden was

Left: Side by side, Down's Brendan McKernan and Bernie Flynn of Meath. *Right:* Mickey Linden's miss in the last quarter of the final -- the ball skids off his boot and goes wide.

Overleaf, top: Paddy O'Rourke swamped on his way to collect the Sam Maguire Cup in 1991, and *below* with the Cup — triumphant!

presented with an open goal at the other end. Withnall flicked a high ball on for the kind of chance the Mayobridge man has for breakfast, but the ball skidded off the side of Linden's boot and went wide.

The excitement and noise in Croke Park was phenomenal. Working on a radio commentary I removed my headphones to talk to somebody behind me and was taken aback as the level of noise shot up. It had been cranked right down to allow the commentators to be heard!

Ambrose Rodgers came on for the last four minutes in place of the tiring Withnall, D.J. Kane hobbled on one leg, Flynn tacked on two more points and a Stafford free cut the lead to two points. Ross Carr was not overly concerned, 'I never thought Meath were going to catch us, never mind what the media said afterwards. If the match had lasted longer there was no way they could have kept that momentum going because every two or three attacks we were also having chances. If we had taken half the chances we missed in the second half there would have been about eight points in it.'

A desperate Meath punt forward broke to Paddy O'Rourke in the right-half-back position, near the Hogan Stand. Ninety seconds had passed since the referee had informed the Down captain that there was only a minute and a half to play so, quite deliberately, he belted the ball as high and far as he could into the crowd. The final whistle went, O'Rourke's hands shot into the air. He felt a sudden rush of emotion but the thought of making a winning speech immediately took over his mind.

Pete McGrath saw Sean Boylan about twenty yards across from him and as they met the Meath manager only had words of praise for the Down team. Some Down players made for Hill 16, climbing up on the railings to salute their supporters.

Above: 'Sam's for the Hills' Anthony Molloy watched by President Mary Robinson raises the Cup. Former Armagh captain Jimmy Smyth applauds from his commentators' box (top left)

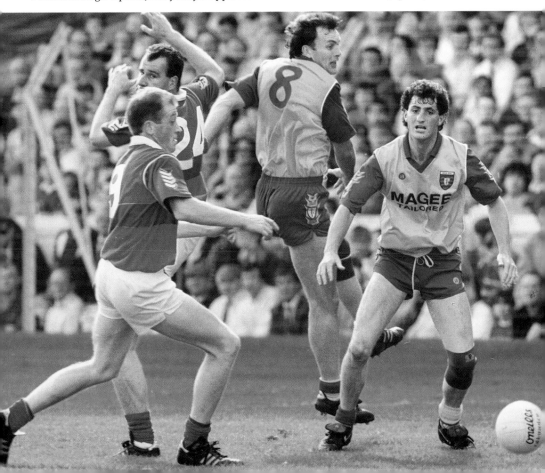

Above: Ger Houlihan, 'Player of the Championship' takes a pass before scoring a goal for Armagh against Donegal, Ulster Championship semi-final 1993. *Below:* Ace in the pack, Manus Boyle, nine-point hero in the All-Ireland final battling his way past Dublin's Mick Deegan with Tommy Sugrue well up with the play.

Above: Saved! All-Ireland semi-final 1992. Joyce McMullan's effort is stopped by Mayo goalkeeper Gabriel Irwin. Watching is Donegal's Brian Murray.
Below left: Fermanagh manager Hugh McCabe takes the blame on television for his team's collapse in the 1993 Ulster Championship replay against Armagh.
Below right: 'I've done it!' Ross Carr answers his critics and rescues Down in the 1991 championship against Derry.

Previous page overleaf: Action tableau as Mayo and Donegal meet in the All-Ireland semi-final 1992 — Padraig Brogan, Sean Maher, T.J. Kilgallen, Anthony Molloy and Noel Hegarty.
Overleaf: above, National League 1992 final: Plunkett Donaghy of Tyrone fends off John McGurk of Derry; *below left,* Gerry Sheridan of Cavan and Anthony Quigg of Derry in the 1989 National League quarter-final at Croke Park; *right:* Barry Cunningham, Donegal, on a solo run.

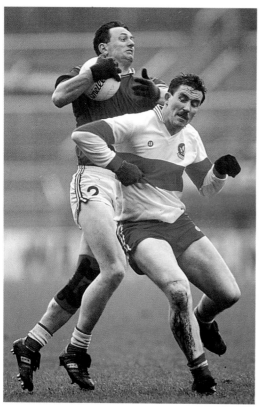

Above: Noel Donnelly supervises Gormley and Gormley as Derry's Enda and Tyrone's Brian challenge for the ball in the League final 1992.

Below: A long shot — the BBC's elevated camera shows Martin McHugh's free kick curling in from his left, over the Cavan crossbar in the 1992 Ulster Football Championship at Breffni Park.

Above: The Antrim bench celebrate their win over Offaly in the 1989 All-Ireland hurling semi-final.

Left: Down's Martin Mallon (left) and Chris Mageean celebrate a famous victory in the 1992/93 National League at Nowlan Park Kilkenny: former Down County Hurling Board Chairman, Joe McCrickard savours the moment.

Below: The 1989 All-Ireland hurling final: Antrim and Tipperary captains, Ciaran Barr and Bobby Ryan watch the toss by referee Pat Delaney.

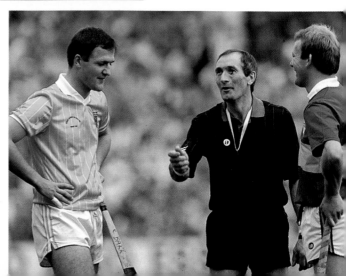

Above: Antrim's Dominic McKinley and Cork's Kevin Hennessey in the 1990 All-Ireland semi-final.

Above right: Down's Ger Coulter goes for a point in the National League against Kilkenny 1992/93.

Below: Jim Close of Antrim with the ball, tackled by Kilkenny's Joe Walsh in the 1993 All-Ireland semi-final.

'The Championship' studio, BBC 1991 with *from left* Jerome Quinn, Mark Robson, Sean McCague, Peter McGinnity and Jimmy Smyth.

The 1960 Down team who first brought Sam Maguire across the border. *Back, left to right:* James McCartan, Joe Lennon, Jarlath Carey, Leo Murphy, Dan McCartan, Seán O'Neill, Kevin O'Neill, Pat Rice. *Front:* Eamonn McKay, Patsy O'Hagan, Paddy Doherty, Kevin Mussen (captain), George Lavery, Tony Hadden, Brian Morgan.

One Down winner did not go to the rostrum to collect the cup. Instead, Ross Carr scrambled through the crowd, past the guards and over the seats in the Hogan Stand to see his mother and father. 'There had been a dream in our house for 28 years and that day it came true. They say the home never leaves you, well at that moment I never even saw my wife sitting beside my parents!

'For the first time I saw my dad crying and I knew it had meant more to him and my mum than to me. That was my outstanding memory from the whole day.'

Kevin O'Neill remembers being slightly puzzled at the sight of grown men crying after he had played on the 1960 Down team that won the county's first All-Ireland. Thirty-one years on, the wheel had turned full circle: 'I got a thrill I never believed I could get from seeing the underdogs beat the old enemy from Meath.'

Danny Murphy searched in his top pocket for Paddy O'Rourke's winning speech. Great care had been taken over the note, written on a piece of paper no bigger than a credit card and laminated to protect it. Fermanagh's Peter Quinn had the honour of presenting the Sam Maguire to an Ulsterman in his first year in the office as President of the GAA. 'Peter was keeping a straight face but I could tell he wanted to jump up and down,' recalls the winning captain.

Quinn later rated the Down triumph as greater than that of Donegal the following year. They were the first to break the mould of Southern domination and did it with a young team full of spirit, skill and discipline.

Mary Robinson, the Irish President, told O'Rourke she was 'delighted the North had won the cup'. Pete McGrath and the rest of the Down players watched as their leader lifted the solid silver Sam Maguire with ease above his head, as if it were as light as a teacup.

After a long and emotional speech the captain and manager were chaired across the pitch on a sea of Down fans until O'Rourke began to pass out. He was exhausted from the game, the heat and the whole occasion. Reaching the dressing-rooms he told reporters that he felt privileged to have the famous cup in his hands, 'Players with far more talent than me haven't had this. I'm a workhorse compared to Frank McGuigan and Eugene McKenna and boys like them, but I've got it!'

Danny Murphy visited an eerie Meath dressing-room to tell the losers that 'the Association owes an enormous debt to you and must feel sorrow after what you've gone through. Marathons are marathons but sometimes a lesser race can have the same prestige.'

Liam Hayes was unable to find words and later Paddy O'Rourke would find it difficult to understand his hurt; after all Hayes had won two All-Ireland medals. O'Rourke's memory flashed back to 1977 when as a Minor winner he saw Armagh's losing captain, Jimmy Smyth, in emotional mood. Paddy told himself he was lucky.

The last two men into the Down dressing-room were Pete McGrath and Ross Carr, the latter staying so long on the field signing autographs that the gates were locked. He had to get out through the Hogan Stand. McGrath satisfied the media and arrived after Carr. They were about to leave the room when they

Down 1991			
Player	Matches	Minutes	Score
Ross Carr	6	420	0-30
Neil Collins	6	420	---
D.J. Kane	6	420	0-3
John Kelly	6	420	---
James McCartan	6	420	0-6
Conor Deegan	6	419	---
Mickey Linden	6	415	2-8
Eamonn Burns	6	409	0-2
Barry Breen	6	404	1-1
Brendan McKernan	6	401	---
Greg Blaney	6	400	0-6
Peter Withnall	6	393	2-3
Gary Mason	6	385	0-12
Paddy O'Rourke	6	385	---
Paul Higgins	6	31	0-1
Liam Austin	4	167	0-1
Mark McCartan	2	25	---
Paul McCartan	1	25	0-1
Cathal Murray	1	10	---
Ambrose Rodgers	2	7	---
Michael Quinn	2	4	---

noticed a large, black object in the corner — the base of the Sam Maguire! Twenty-three years of waiting and they nearly forgot part of the cup.

On the victory trail around County Down that week the biggest cheer would come from the huge crowds when Pete McGrath would take to the microphone and introduce the All-Ireland champions: 'We're the team that beat the team they said couldn't be beaten!'

ALL-IRELAND FINAL 1991

DOWN 1-16, MEATH 1-14 Croke Park, 15 September: DOWN - Collins, McKernan, Deegan, Higgins, O'Rourke, Kane, Kelly, Breen, Burns, Carr, Blaney, Mason, Linden, Withnall, McCartan. *Subs* - Austin for Breen, Rodgers for Withnall. MEATH - McQuillan, Reilly, Lyons, Ferguson, Foley, Harnan, O'Connell, Hayes, McEntee, Beggy, Dowd, Coyle, Gillic, Stafford, Flynn. *Subs* - O'Rourke for Coyle, Browne for Lyons, McCabe for Gillic. SCORERS - Down: Carr 0-5, Mason 0-4, Breen 1-0, McCartan 0-3, Burns 0-2, Blaney, Linden 0-1. Meath: Flynn 0-6, Stafford 0-5, Hayes 1-1, Beggy, O'Rourke 0-1.

All-Ireland winners — the Down 1991 team. *Back, left to right:* Éamon Burns, Paul Higgins, Conor Deegan, Neil Collins, Barry Breen, Greg Blaney. *Front, left to right:* Ross Carr, James McCartan, Gary Mason, Brendan McKiernan, Mickey Linden, Paddy O'Rourke (captain), D.J. Kane, Peter Withnall, John Kelly.

14

The Morning After

7 o'clock on Tuesday morning after the All-Ireland final. Paddy O'Rourke has had enough. Thirty-eight unforgettable but exhausting hours after winning Sam, it's time to take leave of the celebrations at his Burren club and take the cup home.

Dozens of cars block the road, their owners still in party mood, so the Down captain improvises by taking the short-cut he had taken as a young boy, over Burren hill.

It was a most idyllic setting, dawn breaking over the beautiful Burren valley and rabbits scurrying for cover as the local hero climbed to the top of the hill. At the summit he paused for breath, turning and looking down at the clubrooms he had just left. Some happy faces caught sight of him, others were called to the windows and as they cheered, O'Rourke lifted the Cup and shook it vigorously above his head, as he had done at Croke Park.

'It all came home to me at that moment, twenty years of hard work to achieve the ultimate goal of bringing Sam Maguire to my county and my people.'

Maguire became a regular fixture on the O'Rourke kitchen sideboard over the next ten months. Wild nights were spent on loan but Oonagh O'Rourke and her family faithfully restored the silverware to its full beauty every time he returned. It was a sad day when Sam had to leave, though the passing of time did allow the O'Rourkes to return to normality.

'In the months after the final my life was a nightmare', recalls Oonagh, 'We were mobbed in shops and couldn't go out anywhere for a quiet drink. Everyone wanted to see Paddy and talk to him. He willingly travelled far and wide throughout the winter and we even went to a Down dinner in America, yet still had to turn down others. I wouldn't change it now but you would need to have spread it over ten years.'

The O'Rourkes joined Charlie Haughey at the top table of Fianna Fail's annual dinner, and other players and the manager attended dozens of functions across the North. Ross Carr, D.J. Kane, Greg Blaney, Liam Austin and James McCartan were the players most in demand. Martin Breheny hailed Down as 'Popular Champions', in tribute to their impeccable behaviour in victory and to the boost their rags to riches story gave to a province so deserving of Sam.

Some counties sent more invitations than others, Fermanagh, Antrim, Donegal, Cavan and Monaghan. The rest were notable by their lack of enthusiasm. 'Tyrone always feel they can beat us, Armagh are our neighbours and rivals, and Derry felt they should have beaten us' was the explanation from one Down player.

Down were now a team that people wanted to watch. Newry Town soccer fans joined the bandwagon for away trips and attendances at home games soared, even though the champions could only manage one win in five League games. Three were drawn.

Greg Blaney and Ross Carr missed the first game against Offaly at Newcastle. Blaney had been injured late in the All-Ireland final and Carr had troubles with his knee and ankle. D.J. Kane later went into hospital for a hernia operation.

Peter Withnall was fit enough to play for his hometown soccer club, Drumaness Mills, on the Saturday after the All-Ireland final. The centre-forward scored one goal in a 2-0 victory in the Steel and Sons Cup but his soccer loyalty would later cause a conflict of interest. In the autumn of 1992 Withnall played soccer the day before a National League game and was left off the team for 'not giving full commitment to the Down Senior team'.

Irish League clubs attempted to lure the unemployed joiner to sign for them. Disillusioned by sendings-off against Derry in the championship and in a League game with Westmeath only five minutes after coming on as a substitute, Withnall considered the offers.

Much of Pete McGrath's time was taken up with the young man who had shot to fame almost overnight. 'There had to be problems with adjustment. Peter did not come through the under-age system and did not share as many lows and disappointments as the rest. You have to work hard in the unsuccessful times but he took the easy way out.'

A compromise was reached. Withnall could continue to play for Drumaness in the Border Cup, a junior competition which ran until the end of December. There were temptations from elsewhere for Withnall. In the winter of 1991-92 he accepted an invitation to look at a job offer in Kildare.

All-Ireland winners sometimes expect their new status to work for them off the field and in Down's case a couple of players, in dead-end jobs, did complain that the County Board was not doing enough for them. They heard stories from Southern counties where jobs had been all but laid on for All-Ireland winners, but Northern Ireland is different. 'Only 40% of the population is Catholic, maybe 25% follow the game and even less are in positions of influence, whereas in the South all the companies want you to work for them,' realises Ross Carr.

Morale was shaken in the county when four Down players were named as 1991 All Stars. Only Offaly in 1971 and Dublin in 1983 had received as low an allocation after winning an All-Ireland. Meath got six awards, two more than Down and the first time the losing finalists got more than the winners. Dublin got just one fewer than the champions, despite going out in the first round.

Down's All-Stars, 1991 -- Conor Deegan (back), Ross Carr and Barry Breen (absent is Greg Blaney) with Bank of Ireland management, Colm Marley, Paddy Reel and Hugh McAlinney presenting the kits.

Obviously the Dublin media-dominated selection committee were swayed by the sensational Meath-Dublin series and Meath's defiant run to the final. But Down had won the All-Ireland!

More than that, Down had broken the Southern monopoly and opened the door to a new era for Ulster football. They did it with a young, exciting team who might have annihilated the team they said could not be beaten.

Over the years Ulster people had come to realise that by and large you win All Stars for performances on centre stage in the most important games of the year. Now, when the province had their first All-Ireland winners since the inception of the All Stars scheme, the goalposts were moved.

James McCartan was Man of the Match in the final and Neil Collins made a vital save from Bernie Flynn to add to earlier stops against Derry, Donegal and Kerry. D.J. Kane handled the best and was nominated in both wing-half-back

1991 Football All Stars		
	Martin McQuillan *(Meath)*	
Mick Deegan *(Dublin)*	Conor Deegan *(Down)*	Enon Gavin *(Roscommon)*
Tommy Carr *(Dublin)*	Keith Barr *(Dublin)*	Martin O'Connell *(Meath)*
Barry Breen *(Down)*		Martin Lynch *(Kildare)*
Ross Carr *(Down)*	Greg Blaney *(Down)*	Tommy Dowd *(Meath)*
Colm O'Rourke *(Meath)*	Brian Stafford *(Meath)*	Bernie Flynn *(Meath)*

Off to America in April 1992. Vice-captain John Kelly deputises for Paddy O'Rourke.

positions but lost out. Mickey Linden won a National Consistency Award but his goal misses against Kerry and Meath cost him dearly. Both corner-forwards were unfortunate to oppose quality performers in Flynn and Colm O'Rourke. Significantly, the selection rules altered the following year to accommodate outstanding candidates outside their usual position.

Fellow players appeared to sympathise with Down in a preview poll of the All Stars in a Dublin newspaper. John O'Leary and Tom Spillane gave Down the advantage by 5-4 on their selections, Damien O'Hagan made it five-all and Colm O'Rourke gave three each to Down, Meath and Dublin. Tony McManus fell heavily on Meath's side by 7-2.

'The Southern media were caught out,' says Ross Carr. 'Meath played nine games in Croke Park, we had only two. I feel the press did not come North enough. They're from the capital city, a cosmopolitan city, but this may be a necessary evil because I have seen them being unfair to Meath and Kerry as well. They made Meath out to be cocky yet they were probably the nicest players I'd ever met.'

Ross Carr was one of the lucky four to win an award though he points out that 'we all have All-Ireland winners medals and that's what really counts. The award didn't matter to me but it was the start of our trouble, we were beginning to bear grudges and weren't concentrating.'

In January the Down team and officials enjoyed a winter break in Tenerife, but the friction that had existed between some players and the County Board a year earlier raised its head again.

'There was a kick-up about girlfriends going on the trip and then another about spending money and accommodation,' recalls Liam Austin. 'We were told there was no money available, they were in the red because of the All-Ireland even though we had a good sponsor and a training fund. After all the business at the start of the Championship over the boots we felt we still had to go looking for things.'

Money had been made from the All-Ireland but was channelled to finance other areas of the Association in the county. Some players felt they had earned it and so were entitled to see more of it in one form or another. Some wanted to be covered for loss of wages and mortgage payments but this raises the grey area once again. How far can you go down the road of perks? Players are people and people will naturally test the limits, in this case, their amateur status, to see how much they can get for themselves.

'Ninety days drinking and one good holiday should have been enough,' maintains Ross Carr. 'We got too big for our boots, myself included, and we got too greedy. After Tenerife we had to go to America where we played games where they were just taking whacks at us.'

A game with the All Stars in the Toronto Skydome fell through when the sponsor pulled out, much to the annoyance of Down who lobbied Croke Park to part-fund a US tour. They felt it was important to bring their exciting new team to American cities with strong Irish populations. The GAA and the Bank of Ireland complied and a party of thirty-seven headed Stateside, the County Board hardly having to dip into its coffers.

The trip was fixed for Easter time, finishing just six weeks before the Championship. Paddy O'Rourke refused to go. He did not labour his objection, citing work as his excuse, but was worried that the priorities had become confused. His manager assured him there would be ample time until the Armagh game and anyway, the team deserved it.

O'Rourke argued that the overriding importance of winning another All-Ireland was being neglected. At other times he had been reluctant to become involved in making things happen off the pitch and this caused resentment among some players. 'In '91 they would have jumped if I had asked, but not in '92. I said to leave other matters to the Supporters Club but not everyone was thinking the same way. The camp was split and that's why we lost our title.' Some of the younger players fell into the trap of thinking that the good times were there to stay, that it should have been easier instead of harder to continue winning.

Despite everything the team

The brothers Grimm!
Armagh's Mark and John Grimley

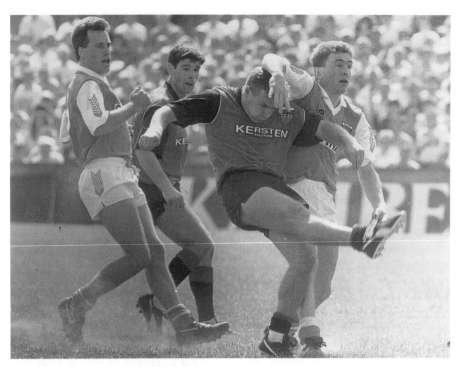

Above, James McCartan shoots to the Armagh net, Ulster Championship 1992. *Below*, DJ Kane of Down keeps his eye on the ball against Armagh as Ger Houlihan gets the elbow!

Ross Carr, Down and Gary Coleman of Derry.

that won the All-Ireland came together for the first time since September in a McKenna Cup game with Monaghan. Only just back from America, they played extremely well but days later a furious Pete McGrath left a club game where Barry Breen was one of four players sent off.

Down were still good enough to beat a poor Armagh team in the first round of the Championship on 7 June. Gary Mason settled a nasty affair with an exhibition of free-taking, despite a hamstring injury. Armagh tried various free-takers but all failed miserably. Mason's big-time experience proved a contrast to young Cathal O'Rourke who converted sixteen consecutive dead-balls in practice at the Athletic Grounds on the morning of the game but none in the afternoon.

Experience was the key. Armagh had five debut players and Down had their All-Ireland team. Also, Down were highly motivated, and they had targetted the defence of their title against their rivals as the game to win. In the first minute Mickey Linden uncharacteristically floored Jim McConville with a high tackle.

'Down roughed us up that day,' reflects Jarlath Burns. 'Neil Smyth got a broken nose, Mark McNeill was injured and Ciaran McGeeney had to come off after ten minutes. We were naive, neither reckless nor aggressive enough. James McCartan was allowed to saunter into the square, catch a high ball, turn and shoot to the net.'

Down did not realise that the next mountain would be more difficult to climb. Derry were underestimated, and reports of their League final and games with Monaghan did not cause sleepless nights. Derry though had set the game with Down as *their* target, from twelve months before when they had felt they were robbed.

Majestic midfielder Anthony Tohill launches another attack.

Pete McGrath's panel was broken up in the week after the Armagh game for Club Championship games. 'As many as eight players were hurt. Our momentum was broken irretrievably for the Derry game.'

The meeting of the All-Ireland champions and the National League champions was a milestone for Ulster football, with both national trophies displayed before a highly-charged full house at Casement Park. Still, Down tried to play it cool and travelled individually to the venue, not meeting for lunch.

Paddy O'Rourke got caught up in traffic coming into Belfast, arriving at the ground 40 minutes before the game. He must have been an unusual sight for fellow motorists, the All-Ireland captain in his own car with his family, shuffling about in his seat, anxious to get past.

James McCartan went into the match with an injury. He hurt his knee on landing after jumping over an iron gate at the family farm. 'When Derry defenders pushed down on him the knee flared up but he was worth keeping on,' viewed Pete McGrath. Ross Carr had been only sixty per cent fit for the Armagh game and maintained he was still not in peak condition as his young marker, Gary Coleman, held him scoreless: 'I hadn't done the power work which means that when you are knocked down you don't bounce up like I had been able to do in '91.' The rest of the team were in top physical condition but were not psychologically fit for Derry.

Every man on the winning team played out of his skin. The accurate Gormley and Cassidy made the most of their chances, midfield worked hard and the defence looked hungry and solid with Scullion and McKeever snuffing out the Down dangermen in the corners. Derry cut down the supply line to Linden and McCartan, a significant tactical victory. Down were outplayed.

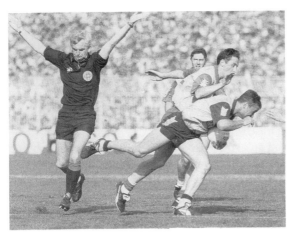

Above left, Up with play — referee Tommy Sugrue during the 1992 All-Ireland final. *Above right*, James McCartan sent off with Queen's University, 1993

To lose Barry Breen before the game with injury was a blow, and Paul Higgins was lost after just ten minutes when he fell awkwardly on his ankle. Six minutes into the second half Peter Withnall was sent off for kicking Dermot Heaney.

The fourteen men came back to within a point but Derry finished with a flourish for a deserved victory margin of three points. Damien Cassidy finished a flowing move to crown the dethronement in style. Conor Deegan summed up the feeling of losing an All-Ireland title when he said that he felt 'physically sick'.

It is not sour grapes on Pete McGrath's part, but in hindsight he contends that

John Toner of Armagh after being sent off in the 1993 Ulster Championship pleads his innocence to manager Jim McCorry.

the Ulster final proved he was right in his pre-match estimation of Derry: 'slow against Monaghan the first day and poor in the replay'. He maintains that Michael Greenan's refereeing ensured a 'stop-start type of game which suited Derry more than us. We rely on moving the ball quickly but too often play was hauled back.'

Supporters and players from both sides were critical of the referee's performance, arguing that Greenan had stolen centre stage on what was supposed to be a great occasion for Ulster football.

Peter Quinn says, 'We needed an experienced man for that particular job and if you analyse it again you will see that every decision he made was right. If others applied the rules the way he does then we would have no problems.'

Looking at the wider subject of refereeing, a frequent complaint is of inconsistency, right across the board from Croke Park to club games. One referee will let you 'bury a man' but another will put you off for a lesser offence; the application of the rules is different. For example, in 1992 head-high tackles escaped heavy punishment in the Down-Armagh and Derry-Tyrone games, with the latter setting the tone for the Championship until Greenan whistled to the letter of the law at Casement Park.

The message of uniformity is being hammered home to referees across the province but it is a slow process, sometimes agonisingly slow for frustrated administrators as well as players and managers. The GAA has made recruitment and training a priority in recent years.

Sean McCague is Chairman of the Games Administration Committee, which dispelled its 'jobs for the boys' image and began a grading system two years ago to streamline the best referees. They are now giving younger, fitter men opportunities to gain experience at the highest level, notably in the closing stages of this year's National League.

'One referee we picked was so up with play that he had to duck to avoid a shot at goal. The game is so fast that you have to be all over the park and the theory is that these younger fellas will in time improve technically.' Brian White from Wexford was slated by sections of the media for his performance in the League final but lauded by others for two justified sendings-off late in the game. He proved his courage in the replay by sending off Tommy Carr early on, after consulting with his team of umpires, and won over most of his critics. Tommy Sugrue shed two stones early in 1992 and took charge of the All-Ireland Final.

McCague suggests that his committee should take over the appointment of referees for provincial Championships from the four councils. He feels that this would improve uniformity of standards. 'Take the best sixteen referees for the sixteen first round games, the boundaries needn't come into it.'

Referees cannot take all the blame. Some responsibility lies with players who commit indiscretions and coaches who send their teams out. 'They know who the persistent violators are and should act to contain them,' argues Peter Quinn.

'Players learn how to tackle by instinct, learning by fouling instead of being coached properly. The tackle is clearly defined, you tackle the ball and not the man unless it is shoulder to shoulder with one foot on the ground, though I accept it is very difficult to dispossess in our game.'

Players often use their fist and sometimes more violent means to tackle the man with the ball. The GAC have led a crackdown recently, handing out longer suspension terms and impressing on referees the importance of protecting players.

'I would like to see forwards getting more protection. Skilful players like James McCartan and Stephen McGinnity take some sad abuse off and on the ball. Sometimes they end up being sent off for retaliating because of lack of protection. Coaches must take some responsibility here too,' orders McCague.

The referee's job is not helped by the unwelcome and growing practice of play-acting. Colm Donaghy of Tyrone, and Dominic Clarke and John Toner of Armagh all claimed they were innocent victims in this year's Ulster Championship. However, it appears to be more difficult to prove innocence than guilt as all three players received one-month suspension terms despite their protests.

Mistakes of course can be made and they are usually highlighted by the media. Antrim referee Gerry McClory looked on in horror when the television showed clearly that one of Monaghan's goals against Derry in their drawn game at Castleblaney in 1992 was illegal. 'The pace at the end of the game was terrific and I had one split second to make a decision. I couldn't say for sure and did not have the advantage of a television replay. It's an awful feeling to see your mistakes highlighted as they are now.' Who'd be a referee?

ULSTER SENIOR FOOTBALL CHAMPIONSHIP 1992. First Round
ARMAGH 0-9 DOWN 1-12 Athletic Grounds, 7 June: ARMAGH - Tierney, Rafferty, Clarke, McGeeney, McNeil, G. O'Neill, McQuillan, M. Grimley, Smyth, O'Rourke, Houlihan, McCabe, J. McConville, McGurk, Toye. *Subs* - Toner for McGeeney, Horisk for O'Rourke, Reid for Toye. DOWN - Collins, McKernan, Deegan, Higgins, Kelly, O'Rourke, Kane, Breen, Burns, Carr, Blaney, Mason, Linden, Withnall, McCartan. *Subs* - Austin for Breen, Smyth for Mason. SCORERS: *Armagh*: McCabe 0-4, McGurk 0-2, Houlihan, O'Neill, O'Rourke 0-1. *Down*: Mason 0-8, McCartan 1-0, Withnall 0-2, Blaney, Linden 0-1

ULSTER SEMI-FINAL
DERRY 0-15 DOWN 0-12. DERRY: McCusker, McKeever, Quinn, Scullion, J. McGurk, H. Downey, Coleman, McGilligan, Heaney, Tohill, McNicholl, Cassidy, Gormley, S. Downey, Bateson. DOWN: Collins, McKernan, Deegan, Higgins, Kelly, O'Rourke, Kane, Austin, Burns, Carr, Blaney, G. Mason, Linden, Withnall, McCartan. *Subs:* C. Mason for Higgins, Rodgers for Austin. SCORERS: *Derry:* Gormley 0-6, Cassidy, Tohill 0-3, Bateson, Coleman, Heaney 0-1. *Down:* G. Mason 0-7, Carr 0-3, Blaney, McCartan 0-1

15

The Power Shift

Derry City manager Roy Coyle was down for the match, the streets of Dublin were red and white for the day and an Ulster team was certain to win the National League. Unusual circumstances but a significant day for Ulster football, Derry and Tyrone on centre stage contesting the League final. 3 May, 1992.

Derry's only previous appearance in the decider had been way back in 1947. Tyrone were there for the first time. Between them they had lost just one game throughout the 1991-92 National League. Their progress was proof that the powerbase of Gaelic football had well and truly shifted northwards since Sam Maguire had gone in that direction seven months earlier.

The first, most clinical proof that Down's win had given instant hope and confidence to their neighbours came before Christmas when an exciting, youthful Tyrone team thumped four goals past Dublin in Croke Park, winning by 4-11 to 0-11.

Almost overnight the graveyard that was Croke Park became a happy hunting ground as Ulster teams lined up an unprecedented seven straight wins within a year, nine in-a-row if you include Down's earlier victories.

Tyrone had not won in Croke Park since their All-Ireland semi-final in 1986, Derry not since a National League semi-final in 1976 and Donegal not since 1972. Two Ulster wins in-a-row were unheard of, never mind ten. In the late eighties there was no sign of what was to come, with heavy defeats in the 1988-89 League. Down were trounced by Dublin 1-16 to 0-4, a miserable Derry lost by 2-9 to 1-5 to Cavan in a quarter-final, Donegal were beaten by Dublin by four points and Tyrone folded against Mayo in their 1989 All-Ireland semi-final.

Ulster in Croke Park, Aug 1991 to Oct 1992			
August 91	Down	bt	Kerry
September 91	Down	bt	Meath
November 91	Tyrone	bt	Dublin
April 92	Derry	bt	Meath
April 92	Tyrone	bt	Dublin
May 92	Derry	bt	Tyrone
August 92	Donegal	bt	Mayo
September 92	Donegal	bt	Dublin
October 92	Derry	bt	Dublin

Derry's All-Ireland football winning captains (from left): Dermot McNicholl, 1983 Minors; John McGurk 1991 Club Champions Lavey; Gary Coleman, 1989 Minors; Henry Downey, National League 1992, All-Ireland Senior 1993; Eamonn Burns, Hogan Cup 1990, St Pat's Maghera; Damien Barton, Vocationals, 1979; Tony Scullion, Railway Cup, 1991. [Kieran McKeever, not in photo, captained Derry to the 1984 All-Ireland Special Hurling title.]

As well as the inspiration from Down, the Ulster breakthrough came about because of years of endeavour throughout the province. Many champions were produced at under-age levels but the knock-on effect did not come, until now.

Derry had won All-Ireland Minor titles in 1983 and 1989, Donegal lifted the All-Ireland under-21 crown in '82 and '87 and Tyrone won it in 1991 and '92. The same three counties won six All-Ireland Vocational Schools titles from 1980-89 and you can add two Hogan Cups for St Pat's Maghera in 1989 and '90. Under former Derry player, Adrian McGuckin, the school reached an incredible 14 MacRory Cup finals from 1976-90.

The trend continues in third level education, mainly from the mid-eighties. Six Sigerson successes have been won by Queens, UUJ and St Mary's since 1986, five Ryan Cups since '85. Twelve of the last thirteen Freshers titles have been won by Queens or UUJ.

Three All-Ireland Club titles have come to Ulster since 1986, won by Burren and Lavey. The province has won the last three Railway Cups and three of the last four National League finals have featured Down, Derry-Tyrone and Donegal respectively.

Success everywhere, except in the All-Ireland Senior Championship. Derry, Monaghan, Tyrone and Donegal all lost in All-Ireland semi-finals from 1987-90, the first three with weak challenges. The great Kerry had departed the scene but Cork and Meath proved equally unbeatable.

Ulster Under-age and College Success				
	1960s	70s	80s	90s
All Ireland Minor	1	2	3	-
All Ireland Under-21	2	1	2	2
All Ireland Vocational	4	2	6	-
Hogan Cups	2	3	3	2
Sigerson Cups	1	1	4	3
Ryan Cups	-	-	4	1
Total	10	9	22	8

By 1992 Derry and Tyrone both had a mixture of new blood and maturing players who had experienced painful defeat at headquarters. The average age of the Derry team was twenty-four while Tyrone had only three players over twenty-three on from the start against Dublin in their League semi-final.

Tyrone reached that point by topping Division 1A and then beating Roscommon by five points in the quarter-finals, where Adrian Cush was unable

Top: Derry, Ulster Minor Champions, 1983. *Bottom*: Danny Ball and Ciaran Loughran celebrate Tyrone's Under-21 success in the 1990s.

to miss from within 45 yards. Derry had emphatic victories over Down and Cavan. Therefore the semi-final double bill on 19 April at Croke Park was Derry-Meath and Tyrone-Dublin.

The Southern 'big two' had not been going too well previously but neither had lost to an Ulster team at this level for the best part of a decade. Dublin were League champions and Meath the Leinster champions.

They had always been intimidating opposition for the nervous Northerners on the big day but the difference now was that the Ulster teams could handle the pressure. Derry had players who had won All-Ireland club and Minor titles in recent times, and they had conquered the All-Ireland champions a few months before. In the same winter Derry had twelve points to spare over Meath and had won in Killarney witout some regulars. Why should they fear Meath now?

Derry raced into a 0-5 to 0-0 lead, the domination continuing into the second-half when a superb sideline kick from Anthony Tohill made it 0-11 to 0-4. Gary McGill and Enda Gormley squandered excellent goal chances. Pat Spillane later incensed the Northern support by saying that a weakened Meath weren't trying, yet they fought back to 0-12 to 1-8 by the finish.

Tyrone and Dublin were neck-and-neck until a soft goal just before half-time put the Dubs in front by 1-5 to 0-7. Entering the closing stages of the game Dublin still led and Tyrone's 'old hands' were sent in, Kevin McCabe, Harry McClure and Plunkett Donaghy who had suffered a broken jaw in a club game only a month earlier.

Donaghy levelled matters at 0-12 to 1-9 and supplied Mattie McGleenan with possession out on the right. Big Mattie swung his left boot and put his team ahead with a marvellous score. Paul Bealin hit the Tyrone crossbar and Paul Clarke missed a scorable free-kick in the last moment of an exciting contest.

'A momentous day for Ulster football,' declared Tony Scullion, 'as important as winning the All-Ireland. I could see there was very little difference between teams from the North and South over the past few years. Now the belief is there and we're better than the Southern teams. We have two good teams in the League final, the rest of Ireland has to take Ulster seriously.'

It was also a triumph for both managers, Eamonn Coleman and John Donnelly. Just over a year after taking the Derry job, Coleman was half-way towards achieving his pre-stated ambition of winning the National League and All-Ireland. His team was still some way short of the finished article, but his basic principles of hard work, dedication and discipline in the dressing-room were being rewarded. Derry were in the middle of a fifteen-match unbeaten League run.

On coming into the job in February 1991, Coleman put his players through more than forty training sessions (under Eugene Young and Mickey Moran) before the start of the Ulster Championship in mid-May. Still, the manager admits Derry were lucky to catch Tyrone at the end of their opening game in Omagh.

John Donnelly bounced back with his 'new' Tyrone team in the 1991/92 League, with only a few players left over from the successful eighties and a cluster of exciting young footballers who won back-to-back All-Ireland under-21 titles in 1991 and '92.

In 1989 the Trillick schoolteacher accepted the 'job nobody wanted'. He knew it would take longer than three years for the team to mature but he would begin the rebuilding process. Like Eamonn Coleman, his philosophy was that every game had to be won.

'I set out to build a consistently good team in the League. Our under-21s needed to play with the best in Division One of the League so as to increase their confidence and belief. Donegal spent six years learning in Division One before they transferred this to the Championship.'

His successors took a different line in 1992-93, Art McCrory, a self-confessed 'Championship man', arguing that 'once you go for the League your Championship chances are definitely dimmed. Only the brilliant Kerry team managed to do both but even then the League was set up for them, as the top four teams qualified. It's harder to win now but still some managers will go for the League to cover themselves, like Mick O'Dwyer with Kildare in the last couple of years.'

McCrory's Tyrone unashamedly went for the Championship in 1993, dropping to Division Three in the process, while Donnelly's Tyrone unashamedly went for the League, winning Division Two in 1990-91 and reaching the final in 1992. 'To have won a National title would have had longer-term benefits and so was a bigger regret to me than the Championship defeats.'

Under Donnelly Tyrone failed to win one Championship game in three years, but fate was unkind. He gave five Championship debuts against Armagh in 1990 and lost by just a point after Raymond Munroe had a late goal disallowed by referee Damien Campbell. Damien Cassidy gave Derry victory in Omagh in the 1991 championship with a debated goal, Seanie Meyler penalised for over-carrying when Cassidy appeared to take as many steps in shooting into the Tyrone goal.

Exceptional circumstances surrounded Tyrone's preparations for the game against Derry in Omagh. The previous week some of their prize assets were busy winning national acclaim for their comprehensive 4-16 to 1-5 defeat of Kerry in the All-Ireland Under-21 final. Peter Canavan (2-5), Adrian Cush and Fay Devlin impressed Mick O'Dwyer so much that he told the Tyrone lads that if he had their talent to work with, they would have a Senior All-Ireland within two years.

Maybe, but just seven days later they had a Senior Championship date with Derry. 'A manager's nightmare,' sympathises Art McCrory. 'Only three first-choice men involved but their heads would have been up in the clouds. What is worse is the expectation on the terraces, probably worse than anywhere else in Ireland.' One or two of the older hands did not entirely appreciate the fresh-faced kids stealing the limelight, and one of the Under-21s recalled the difficulties of playing alongside a Senior member who had not congratulated them on their success.

Peter Canavan complained of a sore back and was doubtful up to the morning of the Derry match. John Donnelly left the decision to the player. Canavan was substituted and his marker Kieran McKeever awarded Man of the Match though

Confusion in the Tyrone goalmouth in the National League final gives away a first-half point.

the back problem was not used as an excuse.

In 1992 the Under-21s again came into conflict with the Senior team, despite an assurance from the County Board to the contrary. The day before a League quarter-final with Roscommon four first-teamers fought a bruising Ulster Under-21 semi-final with Donegal. Would Tyrone again be a victim of their own success?

It did not appear so in the opening stages of the League final as Tyrone raced into a 0-4 to 0-0 lead with two long-range points from McCaffrey in the first three minutes. Derry took 12 minutes to score but then levelled at 4 points-all as Tyrone failed to score for 15 minutes.

At the break Tyrone were in front 6 points to 5. Derry brought Seamus Downey and John McGurk into play but it was Ciaran Corr who sprinted through the Derry defence to point within 19 seconds of the restart. There was no doubt who had the upper hand. 'We outwitted their forwards, against the odds, and surprised them at midfield,' recalls the Tyrone manager.

Three points was Tyrone's advantage going into the closing stages, helped by an opportunist goal from Man of the Match Canavan from a McGleenan pass. Plunkett Donaghy felt his team should have been further in front: 'we attacked until we were blue in the face but couldn't score. We were playing against the famous swirling breeze in Croke Park but tried to shoot from all over the field and dropped an awful lot of balls short or wide.'

Derry kept in touch, showing all the resilience of a team which had not lost in the entire League. Declan Bateson's drive cannoned off McConnell's legs for a 45.

Anthony Tohill dropped his kick into the Tyrone square, Donaghy came to meet it but the ball slipped through his outstretched hands and into the net for the equalising score.

'I saw a Derry forward looking to get a flick on the high ball which was going to drop short. I came off the goal-line and called it but I lost my footing slightly in a divot and so lost the extra bit of height needed to catch the ball cleanly.'

In the absence of a Ciaran McGarvey figure in the square Donaghy took responsibility but his manager was furious. 'I told Plunkett at half-time and on previous occasions that the midfielder does not belong on the line. He should be marking his own man on the 14-yard line. We lost a point in the first half in similar fashion when he tried to take a ball that was Finbar's. To be honest, I felt Plunkett was going for glory, the big catch in the square in the last minute.'

An outstanding figure in Tyrone football in modern times, the man from the Moy has not had the best of fortune in Croke Park. In 1984 and 1986 he had been dispossessed for crucial goals, and now this. The goal only brought Derry level but Tyrone were stunned and Derry alive. Tohill and Heaney clinched victory, but the obvious focus point for the newspaper scribes was the Tohill goal.

'Tyrone undone by lucky goal' - *Irish Times*.

'Daylight robbery as Derry launch smash and grab' - *Irish News*.

'One slip is so costly', *Irish Press*.

Other reports took a different slant:

'Defeat is Tyrone's own fault' - *Irish Independent*.

'Tyrone rue misses as Derry win' - *Irish Times*.

Tyrone county chairman, Brendan Harkin, was gracious in defeat, 'you got more scores, you deserved to win', but voices in the Derry camp gave differing accounts.

'We were unbelievably lucky. It was the luckiest end result I have ever figured in, we were outplayed all over the field though I always felt we had a chance of delivering a sucker punch with the strong breeze and with our ability to keep going' - Derry forward Joe Brolly.

'We were starting to take over at the time of the goal, Enda Gormley and Bateson could have had goals and we still had to score two points to win the game. Besides, I felt their goal was a square ball' - Derry selector Harry Gribben.

Brolly was subsequently banned from giving interviews 'because he talks too much', but a year on Eamonn Coleman admitted that Derry were 'lucky to get the goal the way we got it. Tyrone were the better team on the day and we are a much better team twelve months down the road.'

NATIONAL FOOTBALL LEAGUE FINAL 1992

DERRY 1-10 TYRONE 1-8. 3 May, Croke Park: DERRY: D. McCusker, McKeever, Quinn, Scullion, H. Downey, C. Rafferty, Coleman, McGilligan, D. Heaney, Tohill, McNicholl, McGill, Brolly, F. McCusker, Gormley. *Subs:* S. Downey for McNicholl, McGurk for Rafferty, Bateson for McGill. TYRONE: McConnell, Meyler, E. Kilpatrick, C. Lawn, N. Donnelly, P. Donnelly, F. Devlin, Donaghy, Corr, Cush, McCaffrey, Gormley, McGleenan, O'Hagan, Canavan. *Subs* - P. Devlin for Meyler. SCORERS: *Derry:* Tohill 1-5, Brolly, Gormley, Heaney, McCusker, McGill 0-1. *Tyrone:* Canavan 1-2, McCaffrey 0-3, Cush, Corr, McGleenan 0-1.

16

Derry-Tyrone: Part Two

Jim Neilly stood at the side of the pitch, microphone in hand, telling the BBC's live television audience about the thrills and spills that were about to come their way from Celtic Park. The players already had their kickaround, had stood for the anthem and were now flexing themselves beside their markers, all thirty in position.

Usually the referee would start the game at this point but the BBC was working to a time slot. 'Eastenders' had only just finished and the referee had to wait for the opening titles of 'The Championship' to roll and for Neilly's introduction.

The crowd stirred impatiently, a rumble rising to an angry din.

Tension filled the air, pumping up the players even more than the incredible hype since their League final two weeks earlier. A lot had been said of that League final, winners and losers both with points to prove.

Eventually the ball was thrown-in and had barely come down from the sky when Dermot McNicholl lay prostrate on the floor. Damien O'Hagan and Danny Quinn jostled themselves to the ground and Tommy McDermott whistled furiously to restore order.

The game was played at breakneck speed with wild challenges the order of the day, mostly from Tyrone and only some punished with bookings. Stronger action was merited in more than one instance. Forty-nine frees were awarded and nine men booked. It was X-certificate entertainment for the thousands of supporters sitting in their homes and in clubs throughout the North, unable to get their hands on tickets for the match.

Then, a glimmer of quality play. Seamus Downey collected a ball in front of the Tyrone full-back and slipped it to the in-rushing Dermot Heaney. The midfielder steadied himself before drilling the ball low and hard into the right corner of Finbarr McConnell's net. It was a lead Derry would not lose, despite an own goal by Gary Coleman later in the first half. Derry thoroughly deserved the repeat success and this time there was no debate.

Tyrone's Plunkett Donaghy and Derry's Dermot McNicholl at Celtic Park.

Both managers felt that the team that won the first game would have the edge in the second, though John Donnelly kept his opinion from the players. 'I did not say this to the team but privately I knew there was not enough recovery time. Also, the motivation factor worked against Tyrone.'

Art McCrory agrees: 'Fate hit Tyrone an awful kick in the belly just when they were going along nicely. It was obvious from a distance that they were disappointed at the way they lost the League final and at Celtic Park they looked a jaded team.'

Top: Enda Gormley scores a point as Tyrone's Chris Lawn tries to block. *Left:* Adrian Cush of Tyrone outpaces Gary Coleman of Derry.

Derry had the comfort of the National League title under their belts but they were still highly-motivated for the game, thanks to the media, to Tyrone and to an address by Peter Quinn to both sets of players at a dinner in Croke Park after the League final.

'Peter Quinn briefly congratulated Derry but then praised Tyrone, talked about their Man of the Match Peter Canavan, said how unlucky Tyrone had been and how Derry had stolen the game. We had won our first League title in 45 years yet everyone, even the President, was saying that we shouldn't have won it,' remembers Harry Gribben.

The following Tuesday morning Eamonn Coleman found more useful after-match comment to keep the Derry pot boiling, this time courtesy of Mattie McGleenan on the back page of the *Irish News*.

'Revenge will be ours the next day. Derry know we are the better team and we know we can win in Celtic Park. We'll get the breaks and personally, I can't wait.' Mattie's article was pinned to the back of Derry's dressing-room door at Celtic Park.

Both managers censored their players from giving interviews. Having words put in your mouth was an unnecessary risk as the hype reached new levels for the rematch. In bars and on street corners, in schools and homes, the public chewed over the first game and debated who would do what this time.

Many focused on the Tyrone team selection, some questioning Damien O'Hagan's value after he disappointed at Croke Park. Under-21 manager Danny Ball argued for a young full-forward such as Adrian Kilpatrick 'to fit in better with the young men around him whom he knew well'.

Donnelly saw few alternatives for the number 14 shirt. 'McCabe was not a success the year before, Kilpatrick was not a success when tried there in the first game with Dublin in the League and the rest were either too small or inexperienced. Therefore I appealed to Damien O'Hagan's pride, we both knew he was on his last legs but he is a proud man and I told him he would have until half-time to improve on the first day.'

As it was, the only change was a straight switch at corner-back, Paul Devlin for Seanie Meyler. 'John's hands were tied,' defends Art McCrory. 'If the team you put out in a League final is your best, then it must still be your best two weeks later. All the pressure in the world is on you but the one mistake you can make in the Championship is to start experimenting.'

A certain amount of anxiety appeared to creep into the Tyrone camp with the players under pressure to put things right.

Adrian Cush personified the mood in a performance lacking in confidence, unable to find his range from dead-balls and caught in two minds in front of goal in the first-half, his weak shot trickling wide.

Derry had more room for improvement and had learnt their lessons well. Defence tightened up with Henry Downey now in the centre and Gary Coleman wrapping up Cush. Kieran McKeever had left Croke Park in a rage after Peter Canavan had scored 1-2 and taken the Man of the Match award; this time he would win the personal battle. Midfield insisted on taking on the Tyrone pair again, except this time they prevented Corr and Donaghy from catching cleanly. Man of the Match Dermot McNicholl was instructed to pounce on the breaking ball, so as to stifle Tyrone's free-flowing game. Enda Gormley turned possession into scores for Derry.

The away team's largely young, fast and mobile forwards were starved of good ball and, on a pitch not as wide as Croke Park, only one of them scored from play. O'Hagan and Brian Gormley were substituted. In the first half Tyrone were too often over-physical and reckless in their tackling; John Donnelly insists he did not advise his smaller team to 'mix it', but it is possible that the players felt they had to add something to their play and stand up to Derry.

Mind you, Derry refuted press talk that they were 'big and charmless'. Yes, they had McGilligan, Heaney, Quinn and Tohill but Henry Downey is 5'9" and he looks down on Coleman, McGurk and McKeever. Derry play honest, hard football, without a man sent off in the Championship since 1991. Five opposition men have got the line in that time.

Defeat of Tyrone meant a first round date for Derry with Monaghan in Castleblaney. This was a unique game, with Derry leading by ten points to no score after half an hour. The home team fought for their pride and pulled back to 0-14 to 0-7 going into the last ten minutes. Derry withdrew Dermot McNicholl and Seamus Downey, though the latter had just lobbed over a point.

A minute later Stephen McGinnity brought a bit of a sparkle to a dull occasion with a fine individual goal to narrow the gap. McGinnity shoved McKeever, took possession and rasped a shot against the Derry crossbar. Ray McCarron was on hand to finish to the net. One point in it with four minutes left.

Yet another high ball was lobbed into the Derry goalmouth and yet again the diminutive frame of McGinnity got to the ball first and punched a goal. Monaghan were two points ahead. The League champions were about to be dumped out of the Championship.

Derry stumbled forward, a loose ball was toe-poked by a Monaghan defender straight into the path of Declan Bateson, and from the edge of the square he goaled for Derry. Just time for another twist, Gerry Mone taking a short free and stroking over an equalising score. Full-time: 3-8 to 1-14.

Derry survived and played to form to win the replay but important question marks had been raised about their mental fitness and ability to go the distance. It had been a busy, demanding year but they would raise their game for the All-Ireland champions in the semi-finals. After that, Donegal would be waiting in Clones.

ULSTER SENIOR FOOTBALL CHAMPIONSHIP 1992. Preliminary Round.
DERRY 1-10 TYRONE 1-7, Celtic Park, 17 May: DERRY - McCusker, McKeever, Quinn, Scullion, McGurk, H. Downey, Coleman, McGilligan, Heaney, Tohill, McNicholl, F. McCusker, Brolly, S. Downey, Gormley. *Subs* - Bateson for Brolly, McGill for F McCusker. TYRONE - McConnell, P. Devlin, C. Lawn, P. Donnelly, N. Donnelly, E. Kilpatrick, F. Devlin, Corr, Donaghy, Cush, McCaffrey, Gormley, McGleenan, O'Hagan, Canavan. Subs - Munroe for Kilpatrick, McCabe for O'Hagan, McClure for Gormley. SCORERS: Derry: Heaney 1-1, Gormley 0-4, Tohill 0-2, S. Downey, McCusker, McGurk 0-1. Tyrone: Coleman (og) 1-0, Canavan, McCaffrey 0-3, Cush 0-1

First Round MONAGHAN 3-8 DERRY 1-14, 15 June, Castleblaney: MONAGHAN: O'Connor, B. Murray, Sherry, E. Murphy, Hoey, McGuirk, Tavey, Mone, F. McEneaney, King, McCarron, Byrne, McGinnity, Eamonn Murphy, E. McEneaney. Subs: Brendan Murray for E. McEneaney, Hughes for King, Marron for F. McEneaney. DERRY: McCusker, McKeever, Quinn, Scullion, H. Downey, Barton, Coleman, McGilligan, Heaney, Tohill, McNicholl, McCusker, Bateson, S. Downey, Gormley. Subs: E. Heaney for McNicholl, Cassidy for S. Downey. SCORERS: Monaghan: McCarron 1-5, McGinnity 2-1, Mone, Marron 0-1. Derry: Gormley, Tohill 0-5, Bateson 1-0, S. Downey 0-2, H. Downey, McCusker 0-1.

17

Donegal Bite Back

Half-time in the 1992 Ulster Final at Clones. On the steps to the dressing-rooms Brian McEniff protests to referee Jim Curran about the sending off of John Cunningham minutes earlier. The players are angry too, angry with themselves. A plastic bottle of water is propelled across the dressing-room. Voices are raised in argument and dismay, tormented souls mill around the room trying to make sense of their failings.

Donegal were not losing, the scores were level at five points apiece, but they needed to be in front. Five points was a paltry return after playing down the Clones slope and with the wind and sun on their backs. The last five minutes of the half had been disastrous, with Cunningham put off for an elbow tackle that narrowly missed Dermot McNicholl's jaw and Enda Gormley cancelling out Donegal's best efforts with a super kick from the sideline.

Now Derry had all the advantages and an extra man. It was almost too much for Donegal to take. Yet another day of woe looked unavoidable, and all this after they had vowed to bury the memories of exactly a year before when undignified defeat by Down had made them the subject of ridicule among their own people. Heads were bowed low in shame while the manager was left to ride the storm. A poll in a local newspaper came out three to two against him continuing.

Time after time this gifted group of players had travelled to the edge only to turn back at the vital moment. The water had looked too icy against Kildare in the League semi-finals of 1991, against Down in Clones later that summer and against Dublin at Breffni Park in the League quarter-finals in 1992.

Most of the squad had spent the best part of a decade striving to justify All-Ireland Under-21 titles in 1982 and 1987 at Senior level. The 1983 Ulster title marked an end instead of a beginning, seven years to the next Championship. By 1992, bones and limbs were weary, hearts and minds poised to settle for something short of greatness.

Against Dublin in Breffni, in the League quarter-final Donegal led by four points with two minutes remaining. Dublin scored two goals in ninety seconds and stole the match. It was another confidence-shattering experience but Brian McEniff appealed to their pride; they owed it to themselves not to be remembered in this way.

In the Championship Donegal returned to Breffni to survive a marvellous opening game with a spirited Cavan team. The visitors stayed in touch with a controversial goal, Tony Boyle appearing to touch Martin McHugh's lob into the net from inside the square. Television replays showed that Boyle did not contact the ball but did not clear up the latter point. With minutes left in the game, Damien O'Reilly struck the 'score of the Championship' with an improvised left-foot volley from an awkward angle. Just after, Martin McHugh curled over a wonderful free-kick from 50 yards before O'Reilly pointed again to force a replay *(See colour photo section)*.

No mistakes were made in the return at Ballybofey but in the semi-final Donegal were taken by surprise as Fermanagh chose to 'mix it'. There was

Brian McEniff 'in conversation' with Matt Gallagher, Ulster final 1992.

Donegal's Tommy Ryan eludes Derry full-back Danny Quinn.

nothing in it until early in the second half when Fermanagh were reduced to fourteen men. The sixteen-point winning margin flattered Donegal.

A fourth Ulster final beckoned but the manager and his players knew the performance had been sub-standard. They stayed behind for an hour after the game for another full, frank and sometimes heated inquest. The upshot was that the players realised they weren't fit enough and were prepared to do whatever Anthony Harkin demanded in the four weeks to Clones.

Yet another promise but something was missing. McEniff couldn't find it, either in Padraig Brogan or in the League or on the beach at Murvagh where they trained early in 1990 and '91. It rested within the team and finally, at half-time at Clones on July 19th, 1992, the Donegal players searched deep down into their souls and discovered it for themselves. Their patience snapped and Derry were made to pay.

Matt Gallagher described the commitment of the Donegal players in the second-half as 'bordering on madness. We threw ourselves at everything and defended with a passion'.

Once in possession Donegal played keep-ball. Attacks started from the corner-backs and flowed upfield, the ball only released to an overlapping runner. Positions meant nothing. Reid and Shovlin became attackers, Martin McHugh ran from deep at the Derry defence while Molloy and Murray began to carry the ball into the danger area. Bonnar and Ryan buzzed between the three full-backs, making light of the absence of Tony Boyle.

Boyle had been one of Donegal's ace cards but was injured in a challenge by Anthony Tohill. Ironically, the loss of Boyle and John Cunningham worked to Donegal's benefit. Midfield abandoned the high-ball tactic and Tommy Ryan

Anthony Molloy hoists the Anglo-Celt.

struck some lovely points off Danny Quinn where Boyle had laboured. Cunningham had problems containing Enda Gormley but new corner-back Barry McGowan slotted in perfectly, his speed to the breaking ball and natural attacking skills making him a permanent fixture.

Derry found Donegal's running game impossible to stop, and were forced to retreat and lose shape. 'Possession is nine-tenths of the law,' explained Martin McHugh afterwards.

Good fortune kept Derry in the contest. Martin McHugh had a point ruled out for over-carrying and Seamus Downey scrambled a goal to edge Derry in front after thirteen minutes of the half, 1-6 to 0-8. Within a minute Declan Bonnar brushed past Tony Scullion to equalise and McHugh made amends to put Donegal ahead.

Derry drew level three times but all the moves were coming from Donegal. McHugh was playing his best football in years and his fourth point was a telling one, bursting through several defenders on the left side to shoot across his right shoulder and over the bar. Minutes later Donegal were champions.

Brian McEniff danced onto the pitch. 'I'm overcome. This is the greatest display I've ever seen from a Donegal team. At half-time I told them we were Donegal people, we were proud and we had to carry the fight to Derry. That's what they did.'

'One of the toughest games I've ever played in,' admitted Anthony Molloy, the man McEniff had tempted out of retirement the previous winter. 'When the pressure was on the great closeness in our squad from years together and the work done with Anthony Harkin pulled us through.'

While Donegal celebrated, the losers crept quietly away, their 'double dream' of League and Championship brought to an abrupt end. Derry had gone into the final unbeaten in 12 months and with victories in 1992 over All-Ireland champions Down (twice), Cavan, Meath, Tyrone (twice) and Monaghan (replay).

Their previous three games had been played on successive Sundays but Derry refused to ease up in the three week break to the final, wary of breaking the momentum which had taken them thus far. After beating Down they took the Monday off but had 'a killing session at Kilrea on the Wednesday night'.

'By the week of the Ulster final we were mentally tired. At the time you think it is just nerves but it was tiredness from training and meeting nearly every night,' recalls Kieran McKeever.

The performance level at training suffered. 'I blame myself as much as anyone,' says Eamonn Coleman, 'we sat back and admired ourselves after beating the All-Ireland champions and I let it happen.'

One of the selectors, Harry Gribben, became concerned when he detected a definite mood of over-confidence. 'The players met in Garvagh one night to watch a video of the 1991 Ulster final. Donegal were so bad that one of our boys said we would beat them easy enough.'

A visit to Clones was arranged for the Tuesday before the final, a practice that had proved worthwhile before the semi-final at Casement. 'Everyone felt great that night in Belfast,' recalls Kieran McKeever, 'the pitch looked great, the organisers made us a cup of tea and were very helpful and efficient.

'But it was a waste of time going to Clones. The goals were fenced off with tape to protect the square so we could only practice in the middle of the field. The pitch was all humps and hollows and we didn't feel good about the whole thing.'

Clones was not Derry's favourite venue. They had lost to Donegal in both the 1989 and 1990 championships, as well as their last final in 1987 to Armagh. Five years on, a miscalculation on the morning of the game brought further unhappiness.

'We stopped at the Hillgrove on the way down but made sure to set off for the ground in good time to avoid getting stuck in the traffic. As it happened, we had a straight run and were in the park before the Minor game had even started. Players got fed up sitting around and the pressure started to build,' explains Harry Gribben.

Derry went into the game with injuries to corner-backs Kieran McKeever and Tony Scullion, their key men in the defeat of Down. McKeever had torn ankle ligaments late in that game and required constant treatment up to the final, able to train only twice. Scullion had hamstring trouble.

'Looking at it now Kieran should not have been on. He was carrying a bad injury but we didn't want to listen to any excuses, we thought he'd be alright,' recalls Gribben.

McKeever is not the type to complain. In 1986 he removed the plaster on a fractured wrist after just two weeks to play in the Ulster Minor final. 'I don't mind going in with a bit of pain but it was nearly unbearable against Donegal, especially when I went over on it after two minutes.'

Somehow he finished the 70 minutes, as did Scullion, which explains to some degree the freedom of Bonnar and company in the Donegal attack. McKeever thought about coming off but when he saw Anthony Tohill at half-time he was unwilling to add to Derry's headaches.

Tohill had hurt himself when an ill-timed swing of his boot at a loose ball had cracked into Tony Boyle's shin, resulting in both players retiring. 'We were banking on Anthony going to midfield,' recalls Gribben. 'He was our obvious change but when we went in at half-time he was sitting there in tears, our doctor Ben Clancy said he couldn't play on and everybody's heads dropped.' Damien Barton would replace Tohill and score a point but everyone knew he wasn't match fit.

Eamonn Coleman stood in the middle of the room, staring blankly into space. Muffled rantings from across the corridor could be heard above the Derry silence. Gradually the heads lifted, the players realising they had to get on with the job. The manager had found words to convince his team that things weren't that bad, that Derry were still going to win.

County Board officials had sent a message to the dressing-room for the players to 'be careful out there'. With a Donegal man put off, any reckless tackles might give the referee the opportunity to 'balance things up'. Compared to Donegal, Derry tip-toed back onto the pitch.

Derry did not take advantage of the extra man, as they had done in the semi-final with Down. Suggestions were passed to the manager, to give Johnny McGurk a free role or to move Danny Quinn to midfield. Nothing was done until near the end when John McErlean replaced Danny Quinn, 'It was obvious we had to do something but we did not do it,' admits Harry Gribben, 'We were not acting as a team on the line and got a little bit keyed up in the whole situation.'

Derry played like a team lacking in leadership on and off the field, going for goals when points were the easier option and throwing away valuable possession from short free-kicks. Four central positions were conceded, Henry Downey dragged out of position by Martin McHugh, Dermot McNicholl getting no change out of Martin Gavigan and at midfield McGilligan and Heaney were knocked out of their rhythm.

Afterwards, in the traffic-jam around Clones, the players saw pain on the faces of their supporters, the younger ones with tears in their eyes. It would be charitable to offer Derry the escape route that they 'played their Ulster final at Casement Park', that it was always going to be difficult replacing a desire as strong as they had that day, but they had fallen flat on their faces just three games short of winning everything. Better to store away the pain for next year.

ULSTER FINAL 1992

DERRY 1-9 DONEGAL 0-14, 19 July, Clones: DERRY - D. McCusker, McKeever, Quinn, Scullion, J. McGurk, H. Downey, Coleman, McGilligan, Heaney, Tohill, McNicholl, Cassidy, Gormley, S. Downey, Bateson. *Subs* - Barton for Tohill, McErlean for Quinn, Brolly for Bateson. DONEGAL - Walsh, J. Cunningham, Gallagher, Hegarty, Reid, Gavigan, Shovlin, Molloy, Murray, J. McHugh, Ryan, McMullan, M. McHugh, T. Boyle, Bonnar. *Subs* - McGowan for T. Boyle, Maguire for McMullan. SCORERS - Derry: Gormley 0-6, S. Downey 1-0, Barton, McNicholl, Tohill 0-1. Donegal: M. McHugh 0-4, Bonnar 0-3, J. McHugh, Ryan 0-2, Reid, Murray, T. Boyle 0-1.

18

'Time to get Manus on'

Patience was wearing thin in the Donegal dug-out. Chance after chance was being squandered on the field of play, not a single score since half-time. Mayo had been outplayed but were leading by two points, 0-8 to 0-6. James McHugh missed another free-kick.

'Time to get Manus on,' shouted John Cunningham from the bench, his message intended for the Donegal manager to hear as he paced back and forth. Manus Boyle punched the wall of the dug-out in frustration; he knew he was the man for the job even though he had not played in the Championship since the Ulster semi-finals.

Boyle is a man for the big occasion. He confesses that he 'loves crowds' and holds the unique record of winning the Man of the Match award at All-Ireland Under-21 and Senior finals. Conversely he is accused of not grafting enough when the stage is not as spectacular, but if you ever needed a forward to steady a sinking ship in an All-Ireland semi-final, then Manus is the man.

Donegal had many problems against Mayo but two specific weaknesses were identified by Pete McGrath in a television studio in Belfast and by Brian McEniff on the sideline at Croke Park. Wing-half-forwards Joyce McMullan and Tommy Ryan were off their game, so in came Manus Boyle for McMullan after 42 minutes and later, on 59 minutes, Barry Cunningham for Ryan. Brian Murray switched to right-half-forward to let Cunningham operate in midfield.

Neither substitute had played in the Ulster final. Boyle had not started a game since 24 May at Breffni Park against Cavan. They were unlikely heroes but would both play a major part in the winning of Sam. Boyle would score nine points against Dublin while Cunningham would boost midfield at a vital time. The difference was that everyone played well in the final but in the semi-final very few were on top of their game until these two came on.

Donegal were in serious danger of throwing away their best ever chance of making their first final. The burden of expectation weighed heavily on their shoulders and confidence visibly seeped away with every horrible wide (14

A man for the big occasion. Manus Boyle shoots for goal against Dublin in the All-Ireland final, 1992.

wides before Boyle came on, including three in as many minutes of the restart). Donegal became trapped within their short game, playing across the pitch and into blind alleys, unable to find a way out of the maze.

Boyle reminded his team-mates how to convert straight-forward chances and Cunningham's energy and pace demonstrated how much simpler and more productive it was to take the direct route to goal. The game took on a whole new meaning for Donegal, they *could* win after all.

Oddly enough, Boyle's impact was not immediate. 'My first free was to the left of the posts at the Canal End and I asked James McHugh which way the wind was blowing. He said "Aw, just hit it" so I did but it came back off the nearest post. Next time I aimed for the far post.'

Three free-kicks sailed over the Mayo crossbar from Boyle's boot in twelve minutes, as Donegal turned the 0-8 to 0-6 deficit into a 0-13 to 0-9 victory to reach the 1992 All-Ireland final. Manus Boyle had watched the previous All-Ireland final in a bar in New York with Charlie Redmond; now he had booked his place against Redmond's team. Continuing the American theme, it had been a Stateside phone call from Brian McEniff in the spring of '92 that persuaded the exiled Barry Cunningham to come home as midfield cover, now that Padraig Brogan had departed.

In 1987 Cunningham had played with Boyle on the All-Ireland under-21 team. Early season performances left some doubts but against Mayo he rediscovered

Right: A victory hug for Donal Reid. *Below:* Hands off! Donegal full-forward, Tony Boyle in the Mayo game.

the hunger and form which McEniff remembered. Cunningham carried the fight to Mayo, catching clean ball and setting off dynamically to enemy territory. One such raid produced a penalty for Donegal in the last minute, the substitute being illegally intercepted just as he swung his boot to shoot towards an empty net.

Martin McHugh gleefully tapped the penalty over the bar in the knowledge that it was the last kick of the game. A wave of relief spread over Croke Park with the realisation that Donegal were through to their first All-Ireland final at the fifth time of asking. The tears flowing down the cheeks of Mrs Tinney from Ballyshannon may have been highlighted by the television cameras but she was not alone.

'Little and large' — Donegal's Matt Gallagher with Mayo's Liam McHale.

Apart from the substitutes, there were two other sources of inspiration for Donegal in the second half. One was Tony Boyle, whose ability to collect balls in front of Peter Forde won free-kicks and scores. His was the first score of the half, fourteen minutes in. The second boost was the entrance of Padraig Brogan for Mayo. His former team-mates had not forgotten Brogan's comment on leaving Donegal that they were unlikely to get him an All-Ireland medal. The sight of Martin McHugh, one of the smallest men on the park, standing in the way of the giant frame of Brogan as he made his entrance, lifted Donegal just when needed.

Defensively, Donegal had few problems with Martin Gavigan outstanding and full-back Matt Gallagher winning a 'little and large' battle with the basketballer from Ballina, Liam McHale. Gallagher had wondered whether there was any point in turning up after reading newspaper previews though he realised that McHale was not happiest at full-forward.

The Bundoran pub-owner knew if he could win a few balls then his man might drift outfield, which is what eventually happened. Gallagher relinquished his duties only once in the first-half, when Brian Murray insisted on taking over the marking duties from a free-kick. The full-back watched with horror as McHale leapt to fist the ball powerfully against the Donegal crossbar.

Gallagher's stature as a full-back was now recognised by a wider audience. He had started the Championship season as the trusty corner-back he had been for years, but just twelve minutes into the first game with Cavan he took over from Paul Carr and made the position his own, telling reporters in the press box at the end of the replay that 'you can stop writing about the full-back problem now, boys!' By the end of the summer Gallagher had joined Gavigan as another general of the Donegal defence.

Relief and excitement were the main emotions in the winners' dressing-room after the triumph though Peter Forde, the Mayo captain, offered some level-headed advice to Donegal: 'You only get one chance. Ours was in 1989 and we didn't take it. Don't make the same mistake.'

Later that evening Jack Charlton phoned from Monaghan to tell his friend that Donegal's win had completed a profitable treble with Kilkenny hurlers and Nick Faldo in the British Open. The Republic of Ireland soccer manager asked whether he should bet on Donegal in the final ... and Brian McEniff told him 'to go ahead'.

ALL-IRELAND SEMI-FINAL 1992.
DONEGAL 0-13 MAYO 0-9, Croke Park 16 August: DONEGAL: Walsh, McGowan, Gallagher, Hegarty, Reid, Gavigan, Shovlin, Molloy, Murray, McMullan, M. McHugh, Ryan, Bonnar, T. Boyle, J. McHugh. *Subs:* M. Boyle for McMullan, B. Cunningham for Ryan. MAYO: Irwin, Beirne, Forde, Flannagan, McGarry, Tierney, Butler, Maher, Kilgallon, Jennings, Staunton, Morley, Dempsey, McHale, Finnerty. *Subs:* Durkin for Finnerty, Brogan for Maher.
SCORERS: *Donegal:* Bonnar 0-4, M.Boyle 0-3, T. Boyle, J. McHugh 0-2, M. McHugh, Murray 0-1. *Mayo:* Jennings 0-4, Dempsey 0-2, Finnerty, McHale, Maher 0-1.

ALL-IRELAND FINAL TEAM 1992

Back, left to right: Matt Gallagher, John Joe Doherty, Noel Hegarty, Gary Walsh, Brian Murray, Barry McGowan, Declan Bonner, Donal Reid. *Front:* Martin McHugh, Joyce McMullen, Manus Boyle, Tony Boyle, Anthony Molloy (captain), Martin Gavigan, James McHugh.

19

'Sam's for the Hills'

Anthony Molloy wrote a speech for himself just in case Donegal won the All-Ireland Senior Football Championship on 20 September 1992. But as he grabbed his bags to leave his Killybegs home the day before, the scribbled note was left behind.

It mattered little, for Molloy's delivery was one Donegal people will never forget. The captain paid tribute to all the relevant people, from Martin Shovlin to Brian McEniff, before dispensing with the formalities and roaring the immortal

The crowded pitch listen to Molloy's victory speech.

words, 'We've done it! Sam's for the Hills!'

The speech set off a whole winter of mad celebration. It also marked the successful completion of a mission, a journey which had begun the moment Martin McHugh scored the final point against Mayo. Fear and trepidation had inhibited the team going into the semi-final, but once freed from their ball and chain, the mission never looked impossible to Donegal.

Brian McEniff came into his own as an organiser and manager supreme, his diplomatic hotel skills fully employed. 'You always get complaints in business and have to deal with them in a nice way. You also need to run affairs well and it's the same with a team.' If a player has an off-the-field problem, McEniff will be there, helping in any way he can and regularly checking on their progress. When Brian Murray was unable to train, the manager brought his injured midfielder to Bundoran for the week before the final, to give him every chance of healing in time.

The same player was sent to a boxing gym after the 1991 championship. 'Brian had a problem with hanging back so we sent him to a former Donegal player called Ciaran McCreadie for sparring in a Dublin gym, over a period of a few months. It made him more aggressive and confident in match situations.' Murray was indeed a different player in '92, to the extent that Derry complained he had 'intimidated' Dermot Heaney in the Ulster final.

McEniff sought advice from Pete McGrath, Art McCrory, Paddy O'Hara, Larry Tompkins, Jack O'Shea, John Maughan via Martin Carney, and Ogie Moran who stayed in his hotel ten days before the final. If anything was to be learned about the whole occasion, or even about moves Dublin were trying in training, the Donegal manager knew about it. He would be in radio contact at Croke Park with Pauric McShea and Sean Ferriter in the Hogan Stand. In the pre-match kickaround he would be with his players, running among them, returning passes to make sure they were alert.

The manager had seen too many disappointments down the years to leave anything to chance. In 1952, McEniff the young boy was left at the train station as Donegal set off to play and lose their first League semi-final. Three more times in the League and five in the Championship, his county fell at the semi-final stage. In the early seventies, McEniff the player got off the team bus outside Bundoran to creep into his home by the back entrance after a heavy defeat by Leitrim. In 1976, his first spell as manager ended and left a sour taste after he made the mistake of appearing for Kerry against Donegal in the New York Championship. In 1986 he was sacked, and in 1991 it would have been easier to walk away.

The more McEniff studied the two teams, the more confident he became. Donegal had not done too much wrong against Dublin in their League quarter-final, apart from the late goals, and now he had a new full-back in Matt Gallagher, a quick corner-back in Barry McGowan and Declan Bonnar fully fit again.

The Dublin press all but handed the cup to the home team. Dublin supporters also anticipated a comfortable victory, so poor were Donegal against Mayo and so impressive was Vinny Murphy against Clare. But McEniff told his players that Dublin had done nothing to deserve being classed alongside former All-Ireland winning teams from the same county. They had enjoyed a relatively easy route to the final, beating Wexford, Louth, Offaly, Kildare and Clare. Maybe some of the Dublin players believed the press and their supporters, but the Donegal panel found their manager's version more plausible.

Only two of the Dublin team had won All-Ireland medals, John O'Leary and Gerry Hargan in 1983. The full-back was lured out of retirement but did not have the pace to stop a rampant Tony Boyle. Dublin's half-back trio of Curran, Barr and Heery were interviewed as one for television at their media night at Parnell Park. They were billed as an invincible barrier which would surely be the platform for a Dublin victory. After all, two of Donegal's half-forwards had been substituted in their previous game and the entire forward unit had managed only three points from play against Mayo.

Donegal were content in the knowledge that they had created a surplus of chances in the semi-final. Further heart was taken from Clare totalling 2-12 in their semi-final with Dublin, where the famed half-back-line appeared to be less than formidable when forced onto the back foot. Donegal's plan was to dull their attacking prowess by keeping the half-backs busy, with Martin McHugh primed to take short passes from Molloy and run at them. James McHugh pestered his man all afternoon, and I have a vivid memory of him chasing back a full forty yards to deny a clear shot at goal.

Dublin's forwards had only one ploy, to lob the high ball towards Vinny Murphy. Vinny could field with the best, but every time he landed, Matt Gallagher and his covering defenders surrounded him, giving him no room to swing his boot.

Competition for places on the Donegal team intensified. Training games were as near to real match situations as they could be, so much so that Declan Bonnar was concussed by an enthusiastic challenge by John Joe Doherty. The defender had not played all year but won a late call-up when Martin Shovlin withdrew. He looked the fittest player on the pitch.

On a visit to the county I was taken by two things. First, the excitement of the people on 'media day', crowds waiting for hours in towns such as Ardara for the cameras from RTE and the BBC to arrive. They stood in doorways to shelter from the rain but as I started an interview with Anthony Molloy on the main street the crowd crept quietly towards us. Within minutes we were surrounded and being listened to by about fifty people.

Secondly, there was the confidence of the Donegal players. Over in Kilcar James McHugh was a little bit tense but brother Martin was relaxed and happy as he declared that Donegal are going to win. 'Are you sure?' I pressed. 'Absolutely sure. We really believe ourselves that this team is good enough to win the All-Ireland. We've played Dublin a lot of times and we still believe we can beat anybody in the country when we play.'

Self-belief had always been a sticking point in Donegal, never quite confident enough to take the final, brave step. Listening to McHugh I sensed that the problem had been buried. He was 31 years old, one of eleven players from the final team aged 27 or more. The 'age factor' worked in Donegal's favour, and after years of setbacks this was to be their day.

No way! Matt Gallagher resists Dublin dangerman Vinny Murphy with a little bit of help from his friends.

Brian McEniff still had one blank on his team-sheet, at number 15. Manus Boyle or Tommy Ryan? The manager canvassed everyone's opinion, including the players themselves.

'Brian rang at half-past midnight on the Wednesday and asked me what I could offer,' recalls Manus Boyle. 'I said I was a different player to Tommy, I couldn't promise as much work but would produce the goods.' The next night at training, where the contenders were paired off for sprints, Manus exchanged notes with Tommy to discover that he had been phoned at 12.45 am, directly after the call to the Boyle house.

Manus got the nod mainly because a free-taker was needed from the left-side, though at a squad meeting on the Thursday before the game McEniff took Boyle and Declan Bonnar to one side to appeal to them to 'dig deep and perform on the day'. Bonnar was the joker in the pack, the self-declared 'Legend', and Boyle a bit of a maverick, but the manager warned that they 'could not hide'.

Anthony Molloy stole the show that night with a rousing, heartfelt speech to his team. When he finished, Martin McHugh declared that 'Molloy is the King of Donegal!' At 3.28 on Sunday afternoon, when the players gathered in a huddle, Molloy demanded one thing of his players, 'Sweat blood lads, sweat blood'.

Their captain was advised to stop playing in 1988 and had had operations on his left knee in 1980, '84 and '90. In 1991 he admitted that 'it would be nice to be able to walk in ten years time,' yet here he was asking their commitment. No wonder they responded.

Even before lifting Sam, Molloy was a folk hero in Donegal, not just because he had missed only one Championship game since 1983 but because everybody in the county loves the big man. 'You've met him,' explains Matt Gallagher. 'He's a lovely fella, doesn't brag about his achievements, he'll have a yarn with anyone who cares to stop him, and he won't have a bad word to say about anybody.' On the field Molloy looks heavy, with his head bowed between his broad shoulders, but he's quick to the ball and can deliver long, searching passes from his own half with a sweet left foot.

Donegal arrived at a top-class hotel in Lucan the day before the final, a hotel frequented by the national soccer and rugby teams. Brian McEniff had organised the room lay-out in advance so that the full-forward line would be in one room, the half-forwards in another, the goalkeeper and full-back together. Declan Bonnar, Manus Boyle and Tony Boyle considered putting their full-forward in the middle bed, just to be accurate.

Some spent the evening at Shelbourne Park, others played poker until 2 am and some watched 'Rambo' on video. Between Tony Boyle's nightmares and Bonnar's frequent trips to the bathroom during the night, they did get round to discussing how they would play together. At half-past seven Bonnar woke up the Boyles and the tomfoolery resumed, though a scam to get out of wearing ties was quashed when the manager appeared with all three, beautifully knotted.

Martin McHugh sat in a corner with a copy of the *Sunday Press*, mulling over an article by Liam Hayes. 'Meet Donegal's No.1 matchwinner. Meet the little man whom God created specifically to make life hell for Keith Barr. Alternatively, meet the most gifted player on the field, but a player who has grown tired and uncertain of his God-given talents.

'The Good Lord's timing has not been the best but if Martin McHugh can feast upon his magnificent talent, Donegal may have the All-Ireland title within their grasp for much of the seventy minutes. Though at the very end there is unlikely to be anything there.'

Sean O'Neill was even more direct; his advice to Brian McEniff usually was, be it in conversation or written messages. He challenged McHugh to 'look down the barrel of a gun', a taunt that irritated the player almost as much as the Hayes article.

Martin Shovlin's neck 'just went twang' in training in the week of the final

Molloy escorts President Mary Robinson as she greets the team.

and at half-past one on match day an inconsolable Shovlin cried off. Ninety minutes later the sight of the Donegal man wearing a track-suit and walking out despondently after the rest of the team drew a cry of despair from his wife up in the stands. The last Mary Shovlin had heard was that her husband was taking a fitness test. She was comforted by Matt Gallagher's wife, Cathie.

The rest of the team vowed to 'do it for Shov'. However, the call-up of John Joe Doherty for his first game since October 1991, caused some mumbling from John and Barry Cunningham. They had cases for being promoted from the substitutes but Brian McEniff wanted Doherty to mark Galvin. Seeing the discontent and worried that the upset might affect team morale, the manager shouted angrily, 'There are some players pulling against the grain. It's time they pulled together.'

One player he need not have worried about was Declan Bonnar. The perky character from the Rosses took his seat in the Hogan Stand for the Minor game, determined to enjoy the day. He spotted three Dublin players a few rows in front and called cheekily, 'How's the three boys!' The Dubs twisted round, a little bemused, to see a broad grin under Bonnar's bright orange hair.

Manus Boyle carried the playful mood into the line-up to meet President Mary Robinson. As Anthony Molloy turned to introduce his team he expected to see his goalkeeper first in line, but instead there was Manus with Gary Walsh at the far end, the team back-to-front.

Boyle remembers every single moment of the day clearly. During breaks in play he took the opportunity to have a good look round. 'I always wanted to see

The McHugh brothers torment Dublin. *Above:* Martin keeps his eye on the ball despite the attentions of Dublin's Jack Sheedy. *Below:* Sheedy grounded and Tommy Carr helpless as James solos clear.

All-Ireland Final 1992			
		Donegal	Dublin
2 mins	Redmond (F)	0-0	0-1
5 mins	Galvin	0-0	0-2
7 mins	M. McHugh	0-1	0-2
10 mins	Murphy	0-1	0-3
12 mins	J. McHugh	0-2	0-3
15 mins	Sheedy	0-2	0-4
18 mins	Bonnar (F)	0-3	0-4
19 mins	M.Boyle	0-4	0-4
20 mins	Sheedy	0-4	0-5
22 mins	M. McHugh	0-5	0-5
23 mins	Bonnar	0-6	0-5
25 mins	M. Boyle (F)	0-7	0-5
25 mins	T.Boyle	0-8	0-5
26 mins	Farrell	0-8	0-6
31 mins	M. Boyle	0-9	0-6
33 mins	Redmond (F)	0-9	0-7
34 mins	M. McHugh	0-10	0-7
HALF-TIME			
37 mins	Galvin	0-10	0-8
38 mins	M. Boyle (F)	0-11	0-8
44 mins	M. Boyle (F)	0-12	0-8
45 mins	M. Boyle (F)	0-13	0-8
48 mins	Guiden	0-13	0-9
50 mins	Bonnar (F)	0-14	0-9
58 mins	M. Boyle	0-15	0-9
60 mins	Clarke (F)	0-15	0-10
61 mins	Murphy	0-15	0-11
62 mins	Heery	0-15	0-12
64 mins	M. Boyle (F)	0-16	0-12
65 mins	Redmond (F)	0-16	0-13
66 mins	M. Boyle	0-17	0-13
68 mins	Clarke (F)	0-17	0-14
69 mins	Bonnar	0-18	0-14

from down the pitch how the Hill reacted to a Dublin score.' His manager shook his head in disgust but it could not be said that Manus lacked concentration at nine vital moments.

Molloy won the toss and decided to play into the Hill, to try and take the sting out of Dublin. 'Can you imagine if Redmond's penalty had been into their end?' asks the captain, who admits to throwing a glance at Martin McHugh when the penalty was awarded on nine minutes, as if to say 'here we are, the same old story'. Dublin were already 0-2 to 0-1 ahead and two minutes earlier James McHugh's shot had rebounded off Dublin's crossbar. Manus Boyle couldn't watch the penalty and asked Mick Deegan if Redmond had scored. 'Like hell he did.'

Donegal had looked in serious trouble in the first ten minutes, 'We started nervously,' admits Matt Gallagher. Dublin found lots of room and took scores with ease.

Directly after the penalty miss, Vinny Murphy collected cleanly from Sheedy's through-ball and put Dublin 0-3 to 0-1 in front. James McHugh and Sheedy exchanged points before Declan Bonnar rediscovered his shooting boots. Relieved of free-taking responsibilities after Mayo, he was surprised to be handed the ball by Martin McHugh. No time to think, Bonnar sent the first of his four points over the bar.

Bonnar's mood at that moment was indicative of the entire Donegal team. Everything fell into place, and almost without warning they totally changed tactics. They began to run at and beat their opponents. Whether the penalty miss lifted Donegal or the nerves disappeared, they settled into their game and were heartened by the changing scoreboard.

Dublin were torn apart at the seams, drawn in and left for dead by Donegal's slick short-passing game. In one sweeping move Molloy fisted the ball to Tony Boyle, Boyle slipped it across the goalmouth to his namesake and Manus's drive riocheted off the Dublin crossbar and over for a point. 4 points-all. The planned link-up between Molloy and McHugh began to function and McHugh struck a great point on 21 minutes. A minute later Bonnar put Donegal ahead, 6 points to 5. Dublin stopped competing and gave away a surplus of free-kick opportunities. Manus Boyle continued where he had left off in the semi-final, with two frees in a minute for 0-8 to 0-5.

By half-time the 0-2 to 0-1 deficit had been turned into a 0-10 to 0-7 advantage. The purple patch had shattered Dublin's morale but Brian McEniff urged his men on. 'Think of the 40,000 Donegal people in the crowd and the reception awaiting you in the Diamond in Donegal town tomorrow evening.'

Meanwhile, somewhere on the road from Bundoran to Dublin, the manager's wife was listening to the game on the radio. Between prayers, Cautie McEniff and some of their family tuned in for occasional updates.

The first free-kick of the second half fell to Manus Boyle. 'Better get this one,' whispered Martin McHugh, and he did. Dublin began to have some success at midfield where Paul Bealin had replaced Dave Foran. Molloy felt his knee for the first time in the championship and Murray's pre-match injuries flared up. The captain signalled to come off but when his partner had to be helped off, Molloy had to struggle on.

Manus Boyle waited over another free-kick as Barry Cunningham came into the play. Brian McEniff apologised on the way past for the delay but it didn't matter to Manus, another point for Donegal. In the next attack Cunningham was felled as he bore down on the Dublin goal *(see colour photo section.).* Another free, 0-12 to 0-8.

Dublin managed only two points in the first 25 minutes of the half and found themselves behind 15 points to 9 entering the last ten minutes of the game. In a desperate surge they clawed back three points in four minutes. Brian McEniff came screaming onto the pitch and Donegal, just like Down a year before, managed to take off on a pressure-relieving charge up the field. Boyle scored again from a free, 0-16 to 0-12. Redmond narrowed the gap again but from the kick-out Cunningham rose to win clean ball in the middle and picked out Manus Boyle for his ninth point, the fourth from play, and with it the Man of the Match award.

Dublin's options had dried up and Murphy's only glimpse of goal was instantly blocked by Gary Walsh. With 30 seconds of normal time remaining Donegal set off again, Joyce McMullan and James McHugh finding Bonnar on the right. He turned onto his favoured left side and drilled over the insurance point, giving a fisted salute to the cameras as he ran back 'because I knew that moment would go down in history!'

The same forward went down to a heavy challenge as the final whistle blew. He looked up to see Martin McHugh dashing towards him, not to help him up but to dive on the match ball. 'In the semi-final I ran away after kicking the last point but this time I was determined to get the ball.' As a matter of form it is the duty of the referee to present the match ball to the winning captain but nobody was going to argue and indeed in 1991 Paddy O'Rourke generously gave the ball to his fellow clubman and county chairman Danny Murphy.

Donegal had completed Ulster's first back-to-back since 1960-61 with a brilliant attacking display. Eleven points were scored from play, two of which could and should have been goals. Nobody played badly, a unique achievement for a team in its first final.

Paddy Cullen admitted his team had been 'played off the park in a sporting game'. Martin McHugh said it was 'the greatest day for our family ever': his brother said they had 'showed that wee men can win'. Brian McEniff declared his love for his county saying it had been 'all I ever dreamed of'. Matt Gallagher wanted to know where the Queen was.

This story goes back to the sixties when Donegal football was little more than a laughing stock. Others would tease, 'when you win the All-Ireland you have to kneel down in front of the Queen'. The gullible reply would protest that the Queen doesn't hand over the cup, thereby falling into the trap, 'she will by the time you win it!'

Meanwhile, Cautie McEniff stopped her car at a public house near Ashbourne. She thumped on the closed front door and shouted to the landlord to let her in to see the presentation of the cup on television. 'But I *am* Brian McEniff's wife,' she protested.

In Sydney, Australia, Nancy 'The Cope' Gallagher was one of thousands of Donegal exiles who gathered to listen to the match from afar. 'It was a very draining experience. The emotions ran from laughing and cheering

Donegal 1992			
Player	Matches	Minutes	Scores
Declan Bonnar	6	420	0-19
Tony Boyle	6	420	0-9
Matt Gallagher	6	420	0-1
Noel Hegarty	6	420	0-1
Anthony Molloy	6	420	0-2
Gary Walsh	6	420	---
Donal Reid	6	408	0-1
Martin McHugh	6	330	1-16
Martin Gavigan	5	350	---
James McHugh	5	350	1-9
Joyce McMullan	5	350	0-4
Brian Murray	5	350	0-5
Tommy Ryan	5	339	1-10
Barry McGowan	5	280	0-1
Barry Cunningham	5	220	0-2
Manus Boyle	5	200	0-16
Martin Shovlin	4	280	---
John Cunningham	4	240	---
Charlie Mulgrew	2	45	0-1
Michael Gallagher	2	75	---
Paul Carr	2	22	---
John Joe Doherty	1	70	---
Sylvester Maguire	1	1	---

to doubt to tears. We tried to follow the ball, one minute Dublin would get a point, the next Donegal would get one. It was probably the most rewarding experience we will ever have in our lifetime, because in our lifetime that was history.'

However there was one piece of news which put the party on hold. Brian McEniff had heard before the game from Bishop Seamus Hegarty of Raphoe that Joyce McMullan's brother Gerry, a leukemia sufferer and a great supporter of the team, was rumoured to have died back home in Donegal.

When the Bishop returned ten minutes after the match it appeared that the rumour had been confirmed. A room full of cheering, excited footballers, who had just achieved their lifetime ambition, fell silent as Joyce complained that 'it's a cruel world'.

The next minute Joyce's sister burst into the dressing-room and shouted 'He's not dead'. McEniff had had enough. He rushed up the steps of the Hogan Stand to Highland Radio's commentary point to phone Gerry McMullan for himself, to prove that it had all been a sick rumour.

From delight to despair to relief, the shaken Donegal camp staggered out of Croke Park and onto a special night of celebrations with Daniel O'Donnell and company at the Grand Hotel in Malahide. Sam Maguire began the first leg of his journey to the hills of Donegal.

ALL-IRELAND FINAL 1992
DONEGAL 0-18 DUBLIN 0-14. Croke Park, 20 September: DONEGAL: Walsh, McGowan, Gallagher, Hegarty, Reid, Gavigan, Doherty, Molloy, Murray, J. McHugh, M. McHugh, McMullan, Bonnar, T. Boyle, M. Boyle. *Sub:* B. Cunningham for Murray. DUBLIN: O'Leary, Deegan, Hargan, Carr, Curran, Barr, Heery, Clarke, Foran, Redmond, Sheedy, Guiden, Farrell, Murphy, Galvin. *Sub:* Bealin for Foran.
SCORERS: *Donegal:* M. Boyle 0-9, Bonnar, 0-4, M. McHugh 0-3, T. Boyle, J. McHugh 0-1. *Dublin:* Redmond 0-3, Clarke, Galvin, Murphy, Sheedy 0-2, Farrell, Guiden, Heery, 0-1.

Top: Donegal manager Brian McEniff at home in Donegal with 'Sam Maguire'.
Below: The King of Donegal, Anthony Molloy at Glengesh Pass near his home in Ardara.

20

A Magical Journey

4.37 pm on Monday, 21 September, 1992. The Sligo-bound train pulls out of Connolly Station in Dublin with the Donegal entourage and Sam Maguire on board, the start of a magical journey home to the hills.

A hundred people had gathered at Maynooth, two hundred at Mullingar, two thousand at Dromod village in Leitrim and ten thousand in Sligo where they arrived at 8.30 pm. 'I am a South Donegal man,' Brian McEniff proudly announced, 'as a small boy my father took me to Sligo to see some of my first football and I remember the days when Leitrim and ourselves fought to stay in Division Three. I hope your day will come as it has for me.'

83-year-old Elizabeth McEniff waited for her son in Bundoran, along with five thousand others. On the outskirts of the town the Bundrowse Bridge was lit with green and gold lights, and a large banner read 'Destination Donegal'. Bonfires marked the route of the champions; churches, schools and pubs were bedecked in their colours. At 11.15 pm Brian McEniff urged the coach driver to stop outside his hometown. He stepped off the victory bus and walked across the bridge with Sam Maguire firmly clenched in his hands. The last mile of the journey was savoured from the bonnet of his son's car, loud cheers and smiling faces greeting the man who had achieved his dream 33 years after first representing the county's minor team.

Finner Camp lit up the darkness along the three miles from Bundoran to Ballyshannon, and children stayed up to wave their flags in Ballintra. The journey to the Diamond in Donegal town took three hours to complete, but local radio stayed on the air and twenty-five thousand people waited patiently. As they caught sight of silver above Anthony Molloy's head, balloons were released and flags rippled in the night air to the cry of 'Ole, Ole, Ole'.

The heroes were presented on stage one by one, speeches shouted over the din and finally everyone joined in a rousing rendition of Tina Turner's hit song 'Simply the Best' belted out over the Diamond at 3 o'clock in the morning.

'That was my favourite moment,' says Martin McHugh, 'Even I shed a tear and I'm not the sort to do so easily.'

Nobody went home, they all wanted to touch Anthony Molloy and his cup. 'It was pure bedlam,' recalls the captain who was armlocked as he tried to get off the stage. 'I had eight police bodyguards to get me to the Abbey Hotel. Eventually they shepherded me upstairs to a room where we were locked in for an hour. They said it wasn't safe to go out.' Fear of the excited masses was tempered by good humour. Some of the guards joined in a drink and by morning there were bodies lying asleep all over the corridor.

First stop that day was the village of Pettigo on the border with Fermanagh. The evening took in Killybegs and Kilcar. Flares lit up the harbour in the fishing town while Kilcar was under torchlight. A children's band and a pipe band played the champions into the sloping main street of the McHughs' hometown. The tune filling the air was 'O'Donnell Abu', a rousing Donegal battle song written in the seventeenth century to celebrate the return of Chief Red Hugh O'Donnell and his warriors from far-off fields, still appropriate in 1992 for McEniff's army.

The night ended in Molloy's hometown of Ardara with beds found for most, others past caring. Next day, the tour moved on wearily to Glenties with the general disorganisation providing the unusual sight of Brian McEniff thumbing a lift to catch up with the rest.

Thursday was Gweedore, the Downings and Letterkenny at four o'clock in the morning, before the diehards finally went home to rest. Anthony Molloy's neighbours told him his phone had not stopped since Sunday and a sackful of letters waited to be opened. Thirty to forty letters arrived each day for the first six weeks, partly because the same neighbours had carried a banner with Molloy's address onto the pitch at Croke Park.

Well-wishers arrived at the house, whether it was seven o'clock in the morning or evening. Briege and Anthony Molloy were worried: 'they couldn't go into the house,' recalls Stephen McCahill, a family friend. 'I'm involved in marketing and they asked me to help. Their phone calls were diverted to me and I organised Anthony's life from then to Christmas.'

Molloy had sympathetic employers (ESB) who allowed a certain flexibility for a good six months to fulfil engagements. Five school visits a day were common, sometimes stretching to eight and reaching an overall total of 125. Other schools were covered by the rest of the squad, even remote schools with a dozen pupils or fewer.

Political parties were desperately keen to enlist the Donegal captain's stamp of approval for their campaigns in the autumn general election. 'I tried my best to protect Anthony from this but eventually agreed to take him to campaigning day in Letterkenny. The idea was that he would just happen to be there and would shake hands with both sides, but on the way into the crowded town the back door of the car opened and Anthony was dragged out. Next thing he was up on a stage being photographed and the media were on the phone wanting to know about his allegiance.'

The captain went Stateside several times, once making the round trip in barely two days. Invitations to functions came from expatriates though Molloy also has

In the Diamond, Donegal town on Monday night.

five brothers in America, including one with a pub in the Bronx, New York, called the 'Sam Maguire'. A year before, his form in the New York Championship suggested that retirement may have been premature, now he had won the same Championship with assistance from Tony Boyle, Declan Bonnar and Tommy Ryan, despite encountering several Derrymen on the Cavan team.

The itinerary for another week-long trip to the States gives an indication of the demand for first-time All-Ireland winners from a county with a particularly large emigration total. Molloy was accompanied by Martin McHugh, vice-captain.

> Thursday evening - Travel from the Faughanvale club in North Derry to the Donegal Association dinner in Navan, arriving at 12.30 am and getting to bed at 3 am.
> Friday - Up at 6 am to fly to Chicago for a dinner dance that evening, taking in a few pubs on the northside of the city en route.
> Saturday - More pubs on the southside and another dinner dance on the way to the airport to fly to New York.
> Sunday - Three dinner dances in different areas of the city.
> Monday - Function in mid-afternoon and two more in the evening.
> Tuesday - Upstate New York for a dinner-time function and drive to another in Boston.
> Wednesday - Drive from Boston to Philadelphia.
> Thursday - 2 am. Drive back to New York for flight home.

Demand outstripped availability with the captain and cup requested in several places at one time, though one double booking was satisfied by some clever diplomacy. The 'Old Sam' was borrowed from Croke Park for a local function while 'Young Sam' headed across the Atlantic; few were able to tell the difference.

But rumblings of discontent could be heard from some players left at home or at functions without the cup. Manus Boyle scored half of Donegal's scores in the

Mutual admiration — football's 'Sam Maguire' and boxing's Olympic silver medal.

All-Ireland final to secure the Sam Maguire but only had the prize in his possession for a day and a half.

'Financially there are gains to be made and those gains have gone to a few players. If you are able to take advantage, well and good, if not you are on your own. I thought that when we won we would put everything into a players' pool and when we started out we did, but boys who were getting a lot of money didn't like it.'

When Boyle's comments appeared in the *Irish Times* at the end of February, Brian McEniff faxed the article to him. Manus took his captain and Martin McHugh to one side to explain that he 'did not say half of the things'; he admitted he could have taken up more offers if he had wanted to, including some from the States. Publicly, Molloy played down the issue: 'some were busier than others but the lads are happy enough'.

Croke Park had been monitoring the situation from a distance. Donegal County Board officers were quizzed and at Congress GAA President Peter Quinn alluded to the subject. 'It is not feasible or acceptable for any GAA unit to assume that all should abide by the rules while a few conspire and collude in their subversion.'

Along with Molloy, Martin McHugh was most in demand. He accepts that grateful hosts were happy to pay for the privilege of having one of the Donegal heroes at their top table, but rejects the official train of thought. 'Why shouldn't we bring a few quid home for the wife after having driven to Carlow or gone to America? We were claiming no expenses from the GAA for travelling big distances. And why should money I get from putting myself out go into a fund? It's only a handful of players who do the bulk of the travelling to functions.'

Stephen McCahill insists that no functions were turned down because of money. 'Demands were not made for cash though some were disappointed when the captain could not attend. I had to hand him back to Brian McEniff after Christmas when 50-60 more invites were declined.' Most agree that the whole situation could have been handled better, the county secretary could have centralised bookings for the cup and so on, but Donegal were new to it.

A holiday in Tenerife was paid for by the County Board and sponsors but again there was friction over money. Some players, unable to stay both weeks, received spending money of £400 per couple, with half that amount given to those who enjoyed the full holiday, an arrangement all the players objected to.

Spirit in the Donegal camp remained good with straightforward league victories over Kildare, Carlow, Leitrim and Cavan, none by fewer than six points. Despite the late nights, Donegal looked the same as before, their fitness and confidence holding up while rival counties seemed almost to hold back, as if respecting the new status of their opponents.

December brought the presentation of the medals in Letterkenny when the players paid their own tribute to the manager, pooling together in excess of £500 to present McEniff with an All-Ireland medal. Later in the month, no fewer than seven of the team collected All Stars awards. Along with three for National League winners Derry, this doubled Ulster's best previous allocation.

1992 ALL STARS

Gary Walsh
(Donegal)

Seamus Clancy	Matt Gallagher	Tony Scullion
(Clare)	*(Donegal)*	*(Derry)*
Paul Curran	Martin Gavigan	Eamonn Heery
(Dublin)	*(Donegal)*	*(Dublin)*

Anthony Molloy   T.J. Kilgallon
(Donegal)   *(Mayo)*

Anthony Tohill	Martin McHugh	James McHugh
(Derry)	*(Donegal)*	*(Donegal)*
Tony Boyle	Vinny Murphy	Enda Gormley
(Donegal)	*(Dublin)*	*(Derry)*

The All Star selectors recognised the fact that Donegal had developed important team leaders throughout the year; six of the seven awards went to central players, including full-forward Tony Boyle selected in the corner. Matt Gallagher had started the year at corner-back but revelled in his new responsibility, Martin McHugh was the pivot of the attack and Boyle was as good as any number 14 around. On the wings, Declan Bonnar was unlucky not to get an award while Barry McGowan was the Donegal Player of the Year.

Before the League restarted in February the team delighted the many Donegal immigrants in Glasgow by playing and beating Mayo in a challenge game there. In March, another ecstatic welcome greeted McEniff and his men in London after more League victories on the home front over Tipperary, Cork and Longford.

'A lot of beer has to be sweated out,' confessed the manager before his team came through the biggest test, against Cork, though with Derry out for revenge in their quarter-final at Breffni Park in April, most expected the celebrating to finally catch up with the champions.

'We've waited six months for this,' gestured Dermot McNicholl with fists clenched to Donegal players before the start of the quarter-final, but Derry were unable to channel their aggression once things started to go wrong. One journalist described their mood as 'belligerent'. Early goals from Heaney and McNicholl gave them a half-time lead of 2-2 to 0-4 points, but when Murray and Molloy upped their game at midfield to overwhelm the previously dominant Tohill, Derry folded.

Derry scored only one point in the second half and only one substitution was made, Joe Brolly for Collie McGurk in the corner, as Donegal clawed back the deficit and edged ahead with a Tony Boyle free, curled in from the left side. Donegal had refused to panic when behind, and Derry's frustration culminated in the dismissal of Kieran McKeever following an incident which left Tommy Ryan with a broken jaw.

Indiscipline off the field raised its ugly head at the final whistle when a Derry official had to be restrained. Brian McEniff was refused entry to the losers' dressing-room and it's clear that he was the subject of Derry's anger and frustration. They felt that the Donegal manager had provoked McKeever's sending-off by rushing onto the pitch and remonstrating with the umpires, though McEniff argued that all he did was ask the officials if they had seen the incident. The umpires told him they would answer only to the referee.

'The Donegal chairman was not refused permission to our dressing-room but we suggested that Brian McEniff would not be very welcome,' explained Harry Chivers, Derry county chairman. 'Sadly a number of incidents involving McEniff over the last few months have not endeared him to many Derry GAA folk.'

The Derry-Donegal problem stretches back to a challenge game played at Feeney in North Derry before the 1992 National League final. Donegal were on top when McGilligan and Molloy squared up to one another in the middle of the park, and Manus Boyle appeared on the scene along with his marker Kieran McKeever. The end result was that Boyle required stitches to a head wound and the contest was not completed.

At the Ulster final in Clones in July Boyle came off the substitutes' bench at

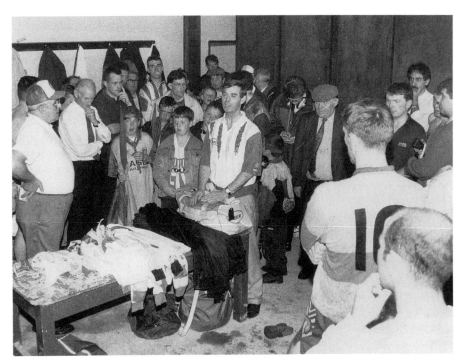

Donegal manager Brian McEniff in the Derry dressing-room after the 1993 Ulster final.

the end of the game to make for McKeever but was fended off by players on both sides. At the All Stars banquet Boyle apologised for the incident and in the League game at Breffni there was no bother until Boyle was replaced by Ryan. Derry argue that Ryan provoked McKeever into retaliation.

They also feel that McKeever has been neglected by the Railway Cup manager over the years and in one case was not drafted in when a corner-back position became vacant. McEniff had reasoned on the day, along with his assistant Art McCrory, that Matt Gallagher was more suited to what was a heavy pitch. Donegal folk will tell you that their manager does them no favours in Railway Cup selection, Gary Walsh for example not winning a call-up until recently. Then there was the Glasgow trip: Derry revealed that they and Tyrone had initially been suggested as opponents for Donegal. McEniff bypassed both to pick Mayo, not wanting to meet another Ulster team at that stage.

In March, Derry were delighted to defeat Donegal in a McKenna Cup game in front of a crowd of three thousand in Ballybofey. But again they were annoyed at on-field incursions by Brian McEniff, and later, at Breffni and Clones, they were only too aware of the tactic. In the League game Danny Quinn followed Declan Bonnar into a private head-to-head with his manager in the first-half. When McEniff told Quinn to scarper, he claims a right hook was thrown in reply; the Derry player says it was more of a 'pushing match'.

At Clones in July, Anthony Tohill and Eamonn Coleman confronted McEniff as he ran towards an end-of match melee. There was a more serious incident after the final whistle when one Derry supporter allegedly struck the Donegal manager over the head with an umbrella and another attempted to punch him. McEniff was quickly ushered to the safety of the dressing-rooms, where he shrugged off the incident and made for the Derry dressing-room. 'I make little apology for what's happened in the past. If I have to run on the pitch or get at the referee for some extra-time then so be it. I'm a competitor, we all want to win and will do what we have to do to win,' but McEniff added that he had no gripes with Derry and would support them in Croke Park. He also shook the hand of the official involved at the end of the game in Breffni, and laid the issue to rest. On his way through the Clones rain to a television interview he borrowed a red and white umbrella from Sean O'Neill and partook in good-humoured banter from Derry supporters. In August, Donegal offered their services for a challenge with the All-Ireland finalists, Derry, and McEniff assisted Eamonn Coleman in his match preparations. 'We've always been friends,' insisted Coleman throughout the summer. 'There's never been a problem between us.'

Back in April, Barry Cunningham's goal had kept the Donegal bandwagon rolling towards their first National League final with a win over Clare, stretching the unbeaten run in League and Championship to fifteen games. Ulster was now on the verge of a fourth successive National title, but Dublin were looking to avenge defeat in the 1992 All-Ireland final.

Donegal started slowly in the National League final and needed a thrilling second-half rally to force a draw. McEniff admitted a 'dreadful mistake' in playing flu victim Martin Gavigan, but it was his replacement, Noel Hegarty, who burst through the Dublin defence for the equalising point right at the death. Two Dublin players, Charlie Redmond and Keith Barr, were sent off within 90 seconds by Brian White.

'Referee does no favours as Boys in Blue lose two,' the *Irish Press* contested. 'Time and again he angered Dublin supporters as he ignored fouls, gave Donegal the benefit of the doubt, and whistled for needless frees.' The frees count was tipped heavily in Donegal's favour by 35-12 though White did disallow a Donegal goal, and as another referee pointed out, 'if there's 35 fouls, then there's going to be 35 frees.' Perhaps it is a counter-product of Donegal's possession game for there is a definite trend in their games to win more frees than the opposition. In the quarter-final with Derry the count was 28-13 and in the first championship game with Armagh in June it was 34-14.

Much of the time Ulster teams do get a fair hearing and showing, with some professed admirers of Ulster football, such as Liam Hayes and David Walsh. But there are instances which defeat the charge of Northern paranoia, and now especially, with four National titles coming to the province in the space of twenty-four months, there is extra weight behind the argument.

One theory is that Ulster's success in recent times has stolen the thunder of counties 'nearer to home', so that the first scent of a Southern revival sends the media bandwagon into overdrive. For example, Dublin were elevated to an unreal status before the 1992 All-Ireland final and in July this year the hype that followed Dublin's defeat of Meath lived on through the week. Monday morning's excited headlines celebrated Jack Sheedy's dramatic winner but the day after we were treated to more interviews reliving the tale and a photograph of the same Jack holding a pair of boots. A little bit of the same endeavour might have avoided an amusing headline the previous week when two changes were reported on the Down hurling team for the Ulster final. 'McRickard and Oprey', should have read 'McCrickard and O'Prey'.

The counter argument to the charge of favouritism is that there are something like 1.3 million potential readers in the metropolitan area, and that competition from Northern dailies makes for a fairly small market for the Dublin-based papers. In other words, the cold facts of business, yet the rest of the nation rightly expects balanced reporting.

Meanwhile, Donegal's unbeaten run was about to come to an abrupt end in May. Four minutes into the League final replay with Dublin, Brian White sent Tommy Carr to the line for a kick on Brian Murray, behind the referee's back but caught by the cameras and reported by his linesman and umpires. Dublin made light of Carr's absence and led by eight points before Donegal's first score in injury time at the end of the half.

Dublin manager Pat O'Neill had done his homework well as his team became the first to figure out how to negate the confident, fluent champions. They closed down Donegal's short game coming out of defence, and their defence hunted in packs. Dermot Deasy proved a match for the previously untouchable Tony Boyle, Jack Sheedy outpaced Molloy in the middle, Paul Clarke was accurate from frees and Dublin no longer relied solely on the high ball into Murphy.

There were signs that the wheels were starting to wobble in the Donegal camp. Martin Gavigan was absent, Declan Bonnar was still not himself after a heavy challenge at the end of the Clare game and Martin McHugh had cried off before the game with flu. His value in knitting the attack together was underlined as Donegal lost their shape, running down blind alleys instead of using the extra man. Dublin only scored two second-half points but the difference was too great and Brian McEniff conceded that his players had not been hungry enough. Eight months of undiluted and uninterrupted bliss, on and off the field, had come to an end. The magical journey was over.

NATIONAL FOOTBALL LEAGUE QUARTER-FINAL 1993
DONEGAL 0-10 DERRY 2-3, Breffni Park, 11 April: DONEGAL: Walsh, Doherty, Gallagher, McGowan, Reid, Carr, Shovlin, Molloy, Murray, J. McHugh, B. Cunningham, M. McHugh, Bonnar, T. Boyle, M. Boyle. *Subs:* Ryan for M. McHugh, M. Boyle for Ryan. DERRY: D. McCusker, McKeever, Quinn, McErlean, Diamond, H. Downey, Coleman, McGilligan, Tohill, Ferris, Barton, McNicholl, C. McGurk, Heaney, Gormley. *Subs:* Brolly for McGurk. SCORERS: *Donegal:* Bonnar 0-5, T. Boyle, M. Boyle 0-2, Cunningham 0-1. *Derry:* Gormley 0-3, McNicholl, Heaney 1-0.
NATIONAL FOOTBALL LEAGUE FINAL 1993
DONEGAL 0-9 DUBLIN 0-9, Croke Park, 2 May. DONEGAL: Walsh, Doherty, Gallagher, McGowan, Reid, Gavigan, Shovlin, Molloy, Murray, J. McHugh, M. McHugh, B. Cunningham, Bonnar, T. Boyle, M. Boyle. *Sub:* N. Hegarty for Gavigan. DUBLIN: O'Leary, Walsh, Deasy, Calvert, Moran, Curran, Deegan, Bealin, Sheedy, Heery, Carr, Guiden, Doran, Murphy, Redmond. *Subs:* Barr for Calvert, Galvin for Doran. SCORERS: *Donegal:* M. Boyle 0-4, Bonnar 0-2, McGowan, M. McHugh, Hegarty 0-1. *Dublin:* Murphy 0-4, Redmond 0-3, Bealin, Guiden 0-1.
REPLAY - DONEGAL 0-6 DUBLIN 0-10, Croke Park, 9 May, 1993. *Replay Changes:* DONEGAL: Hegarty for Gavigan, McMullan for M. McHugh. *Subs:* Maguire for McMullan, Gavigan for Shovlin, M. McHugh for Cunningham. SCORERS: M. Boyle 0-3, Cunningham, Molloy, J. McHugh 0-1. DUBLIN: Gavin for Calvert, Clarke for Redmond. SCORERS: Clarke 0-5, Guiden, Murphy 0-2, Gavin 0-1.
NB: Record National League attendance at replay; 59,703. The first game was watched by 51,400.

21

All-Time Football Selections

1. EAMONN COLEMAN, Derry

John Somers
(Derry)

Tom O'Hare	Bermard Brady	Tony Scullion
(Down)	*(Donegal)*	*(Derry)*
Brian McEniff	Anthony McGurk	Jim Reilly
(Donegal)	*(Derry)*	*(Cavan)*

Jim McKeever   Eugene McKenna
(Derry)   *(Tyrone)*

Colm McAlarney	Frank McGuigan	Mickey Niblock
(Down)	*(Tyrone)*	*(Derry)*
Sean O'Connell	Sean O'Neill	Martin McHugh
(Derry)	*(Down)*	*(Donegal)*

Eamonn's reasons — 'My team is filled mainly with players I either played with or looked up to, or both. Jim McKeever is the best example, he was my boyhood hero whom I was lucky enough to play alongside in a county final with Ballymaguigan when I was only 14 years old. Jim was an exceptional fielder and played between the two 14-yard lines. He captains my team.

Mickey Niblock played on the same Minor and Under-21 teams as myself in the sixties, before making a name for himself on the national scene in the early seventies. What he lacked in pace he made up for in brains, and I recall him scoring two goals in the 1971 Ulster final against Down.

In 1976, Anthony McGurk was the outstanding character in the Ulster final and replay with Cavan. He read the game well and gave it everything. In goals, John

Somers was a super shot-stopper while Sean O'Connell was a brilliant score-taker. The game has changed much in twenty years, but Sean would fit into today's game perfectly. He was strong at 6' 2", had pace and was always two moves ahead of everyone else.

Tony Scullion would be on any team from the last ten years or so. He must be a nightmare to play against, with his great anticipation and speed. That's six Derrymen, for which I make no apologies, and only one from the current side. I wouldn't say the men I have picked are better than the '93 team, and certainly players such as Henry Downey are as good as any, but I have mainly gone for players who I grew up with and admired along the way.

Tom O'Hare was ahead of his time, a marvellous corner-back, though I have accommodated him outside his normal position on the left. Bernard Brady won Railway Cup medals with Ulster in the sixties though he had quite a short career. He was a big man, safe in the air and used the ball well. Brian McEniff, from the same town as Bernard, was very quick and a good attacking wing-back.

Eugene McKenna was the best midfielder in the early eighties, able to field and use the ball equally well. Colm McAlarney was another superb all-rounder and was comfortable anywhere from the midfield up.

I played with Frank McGuigan in Works tournaments and in one particular game he scored the best goal I have ever seen. He caught the ball under his own crossbar and set off up the field, supporting a four-man move which ended in Frank shooting left-footed into the top of the net.

In the Railway Cup I played wing-half-forward on the same team as Sean O'Neill. He was such an intelligent player that all you had to do was drop the ball into him and run on for the return, which you knew you would get. Finally, I rate Martin McHugh as the best ever of the "small man" players. He's fearless, skilful and I feel he's been at his best in recent times in the centre of the Donegal attack.'

2. BRIAN McENIFF, Donegal

Brian McAlinden
(Armagh)

| Nudie Hughes (Monaghan) | Pauric McShea (Donegal) | Tony Scullion (Derry) |
| Anthony McGurk (Derry) | Paddy Moriarty (Armagh) | Jim Reilly (Cavan) |

Frank McGuigan
(Tyrone)

Colm McAlarney
(Down)

| Peter McGinnity (Fermanagh) | Eugene McKenna (Tyrone) | Greg Blaney (Down) |
| Martin McHugh (Donegal) | Sean O'Neill (Down) | James McCartan (Down) |

Brian's reasons: 'The first thing I must say is that I found this an impossible task, probably made more difficult by my involvement with the Railway Cup and my close study of Ulster football over a long period.

One of the easier tasks was to pick the goalkeeper, Brian McAlinden, who was like an extra defender on the team.

Gabriel Kelly was a rock solid right-corner-back but Nudie Hughes edges the vote. Nothing was impossible to Nudie, if you asked him to climb Everest he would do it. A fabulous character to have around any team. Similarly, Tom O'Hare was a two-sided, creative defender while Tony Scullion's value to Derry down the years has been underlined in 1993. Full-back is my old friend Pauric McShea, again for great service to Donegal and Ulster. He was strong under the high ball and an exciting full-back who was one of the first to carry the ball out of defence, even going on to take a return pass. Unheard of in those days!

My own position of right-half-back goes to Anthony McGurk, just ahead of his fellow county-man, Mickey Moran. The inspirational Paddy Moriarty is in the middle and Jim Reilly on the left, players with years of service behind them.

Ray Carolan and Jim McKeever could easily go into midfield though I didn't see enough of McKeever to pick him. Colm McAlarney won an All-Ireland medal in 1968 and played right through the seventies. Frank McGuigan's career was not as long but a fabulous player for Tyrone who were fortunate enough to have another outstanding footballer in the same era, that being Eugene McKenna.

Peter McGinnity was a special Ulster captain and he carried Fermanagh to the 1982 Ulster final. Greg Blaney is another of my favourite Railway Cup men. Of course he has also given great service to Down. Martin McHugh staked a claim for the number 11 shirt but gets in the corner, again a consistent and excellent servant. In time Tony Boyle could earn the full-forward position but for now it has to be Sean O'Neill, winner of eight Railway Cup medals. Jim McCartan was my boyhood hero and I'm delighted to include his son James, a special young player.

Mickey Niblock, Andy McCallin, Joe Kernan, Paddy Doherty and Charlie Gallagher are in the subs!'

3. PETE McGRATH, Down

Brian McAlinden
(Armagh)

Tony Scullion	Conor Deegan	Tom O'Hare
(Derry)	*(Down)*	*(Down)*
Ciaran Murray	Paddy Moriarty	Enda McGowan
(Monaghan)	*(Armagh)*	*(Cavan)*

Frank McGuigan   Colm McAlarney
(Tyrone)   *(Down)*

Peter McGinnity	Eugene McKenna	Greg Blaney
(Fermanagh)	*(Tyrone)*	*(Down)*
Martin McHugh	Sean O'Neill	James McCartan
(Donegal)	*(Down)*	*(Down)*

Peter's reasons: 'My selection is post-1968 because that is when I began to be properly conscious of county football. It also marks Down's last All-Ireland win in the sixties, which goes some way towards explaining the five Down men on the team.

Furthermore, there is an abundance of flair and attacking possibilities, even in defence. This team might lose on a high score but would enjoy playing together and would play Gaelic football the way I like to see it played. Imagine Paddy Moriarty and James McCartan on the one pitch, the sleek brilliance of Frank McGuigan, the strides of McAlarney up and down the pitch, and the athleticism of Deegan and Murray in defence.

Nudie Hughes would also have slotted in perfectly but he loses out to two quality corner-backs in Tony Scullion and Tom O'Hare. Tony gets the job done and at the end of Derry games you have to ask "What did Tony's man do?" He did a job for his county at full-back this year but he is at his best on the wing, albeit the right wing.

I simply could not move Tom O'Hare from the left corner, perhaps because I have his number four etched in my memory from his masterly performance in the 1968 All-Ireland semi-final against Galway. Tom always seemed to have time on the ball and swept up so well. Conor Deegan is a complete footballer who had the confidence to have an excellent All-Ireland final on Brian Stafford in 1991.

In the half-backs Ciaran Murray was a thinker who used the ball well. Henry Downey was in the running for the middle but I have always admired Paddy Moriarty's style of play. I played with him at university where his approach and dedication impressed me. Not tall and not the most creative but mobile, good in the air and he got the job done. You always need one "Enda McGowan" on every team, a teak-tough, tight marker as I can verify from experience.

Midfield is my dream partnership, Frank McGuigan's fielding and vision allied to Colm McAlarney's running power.

In attack, Peter McGinnity was a Rolls Royce of a player, almost effortless in his movements, a good free-taker from the right and would maybe have played here with a stronger county. Eugene McKenna was a great fielder, even from a standing position and very strong in possession. He could suck defenders in and release the ball to others at the right moment, a dramatic focal point of any attack. Greg Blaney matured into a central position but played on the left in the 1983 League final and is worth his place for creativity, vision and sheer power. Not a prolific scorer but a great provider and has presence.

Martin McHugh is an artist with speed, courage, scoring ability and is a tremendous carrier of the ball. Sean O'Neill was one of the two greatest Gaelic footballers I have seen, the other being Pat

Spillane. Sean had leadership, courage and vision. In the modern game James McCartan is simply the player with the most menace in front of goal. Very few Ulster players got to All-Ireland finals in the period I am looking at, but James did and he was superlative in it. He had to be included if only for that alone.'

4. ART McCRORY, Tyrone

Thady Turbett
(Tyrone)

Nudie Hughes	Ciaran McGarvey	Tom O'Hare
(Monaghan)	*(Tyrone)*	*(Down)*
Brian McEniff	Paddy Corey	Jim McDonnell
(Donegal)	*(Tyrone)*	*(Cavan)*

Jim McKeever
(Derry)

Eugene McKenna
(Tyrone)

Peter McGinnity	Frank McGuigan	Paddy Doherty
(Fermanagh)	*(Tyrone)*	*(Down)*
Martin McHugh	Sean O'Neill	Iggy Jones
(Donegal)	*(Down)*	*(Tyrone)*

Art's reasons: 'You may accuse me of Tyrone bias for having six of my fellow county men on the team and you would be absolutely right. I make no apologies for including six of the best I have seen and I go back to the first Tyrone team to win an Ulster title in 1956.

To an impressionable young fella like myself Thady Turbett was just a colossus in the Tyrone goals, a big man who had to withstand more physical pressure from incoming forwards than goalkeepers today. He was there to stop the ball and get rid of it, though he did not have to take the kick-outs.

Nudie Hughes' best position was in the corner of the defence as he read the game and swept up so well. Tom O'Hare was another great back, while in the middle big McGarvey stands out as the best full-back in the modern game. He could take the high ball under pressure from big full-forwards and yet was mobile enough to deal with smaller, fast opponents. He developed into a magnificent full-back and it could be said that he has yet to be replaced.

Brian McEniff was the first of the attacking half-backs but Jim McDonnell was a different breed. He stayed in his position and was a tower of strength, just getting my vote over Sean Quinn of Armagh. The great Sean Purcell of Galway proclaimed Paddy Corey to be his hardest and toughest opponent from the 1956 All-Ireland semi-final with Tyrone. Corey was a direct, strong defender, the kind that made the crowd rise when he got the ball.

Jim McKeever had a tremendous work-rate as well as being a great leaper while Eugene's strength became his leadership. He led by example from midfield which was his best position. Eugene and Frank are talents that come along once every fifty years, so Tyrone were lucky to have them at the one time. Frank was a ball-winner who could create from nothing, and his performance in the 1984 Ulster final was incredible. I could only stand with my mouth open.

Peter McGinnity was a natural footballer and Paddy Doherty a scoring machine. Paddy was so accurate with that left foot that he sickened opponents. Martin McHugh has done well in recent times but was at his peak in the early eighties when his pace, athleticism and accuracy made him almost a one-man team.

Sean O'Neill had a great brain allied with toughness, he took a lot of abuse but came away with the ball. Finally, from my own club, Dungannon Clarkes, Iggy Jones: in 1946 he scored three goals for St Pat's Armagh in a Hogan Cup final and impressed observers with his toe-tapping skills. When I played with him later he was a man apart, a small man but with the skill and technique to stand out anywhere on a team.'

5. JIMMY SMYTH, Armagh

Brian McAlinden
(Armagh)

Tom O'Hare   Tom Quinn   Tony Scullion
(Down)   *(Derry)*   *(Derry)*
Paddy Moriarty   Malachy McAfee   Jim Reilly
(Armagh)   *(Derry)*   *(Cavan)*

Colm McKinstry   Colm McAlarney
(Armagh)   *(Down)*

Greg Blaney   Joe Kernan   Peter McGinnity
(Down)   *(Armagh)*   *(Fermanagh)*
Frank McGuigan   Sean O'Neill   Nudie Hughes
(Tyrone)   *(Down)*   *(Monaghan)*

Jimmy's reasons: 'A strong Derry, Down and Armagh connection here making up eleven of my selection. Most are from the seventies with four of our 1977 All-Ireland final team.

McAlinden was telepathic, his kick-outs always finding one of his own men. Paddy Mo liked to solo forward but was restrained in the middle; he would have been an even better wing-half-back.

McKinstry was underrated at midfield where his catching ability excited crowds — in fact on a trip to Nemo once they wanted to give him a job to hold onto him! Big Joe Kernan was strong going through with the ball, give it to him 25 yards out and he'd put it in the net, as in the '77 final.

In the middle of my defence are two Derry men who excelled at St Columb's and at the Ranch where I got to know them well. Tom Quinn was laid-back but tall and safe, McAfee big, brainy and with two good feet. Tony Scullion came later with great speed and anticipation. Also in defence Tom O'Hare was very hard as well as inventive while Jim Reilly copied the attacking style of Brian McEniff.

More Down men up the field with Colm McAlarney, a supreme catcher who could carry a ball and score, and Greg Blaney who was involved in Down's major scores in the 1991 campaign. A great linkman, Greg set up the goals in the Ulster and All-Ireland finals.

Peter McGinnity was a class act who could play all over the place while Frank McGuigan was talked of as an all-time great at the age of 17 when his club, Ardboe, came to play mine, Clann na Gael. He had beautiful balance and could do everything.

Sean O'Neill was fast and fearless with good reactions — remember his goal in the 1968 All-Ireland final? Finally Nudie put his knowledge as a corner-back to good use as a corner-forward, drawing in defenders to create or win frees. Best of all, he played with a smile which is something we don't see very often these days.'

6. PETER McGINNITY, Fermanagh

Brian McAlinden
(Armagh)

Finian Ward   Tommy McGovern   Tony Scullion
(Donegal)   *(Down)*   *(Derry)*
Kevin McCabe   Paddy Moriarty   Jim Reilly
(Tyrone)   *(Armagh)*   *(Cavan)*

John McKiernan   Liam Austin
(Antrim)   *(Down)*

Eugene McKenna   Joe Kernan   Colm McAlarney
(Tyrone)   *(Armagh)*   *(Down)*
Nudie Hughes   Eugene Young   Greg Blaney
(Monaghan)   *(Derry)*   *(Down)*

Peter's reasons: 'I played alongside ten of this selection in the 1980 Railway Cup winning team and all but two of them won medals in the glory period of 1979-84 when Ulster lifted the interprovincial title four times. They are players I liked to play with, maybe at the expense of better-known names but I maintain that this team would have been fit for anyone.

Its strength comes from its compatibility. Sean O'Neill was the first to introduce the idea that the best fifteen players in Ulster do not necessarily make up the best Ulster team. What use are the three best full-backs in your full-back line? We became a squad, all in it together. Frank McGuigan was a great player but he only came into the squad really for 1984 and as for Sean himself, I did not play much with him either.

My favourite position was midfield so I would have to include myself as first sub should Austie or John McKiernan have to come off. Either of them would have suited me, they were both good, dependable fielders who would mind the house while I disappeared off into the attack. John won a Hogan medal with St Mary's, Belfast and made a name at Queen's and with Antrim over the years.

In defence, Tommy, Paddy and Tony epitomise the dependable defender, not spectacular but prepared to give everything when you are behind with ten minutes to go. The others liked to play a bit, Reilly, McCabe and Finian Ward who was not afraid to go forward, much in the mould of Barry McGowan today.

McCabe was the best right-half-back in Ireland for a short time. He was strong, fast, a brilliant tackler who could go forward but who took his defensive responsibilities seriously. That was until he started to believe he was the best in Ireland and became more attack-minded!

McKenna and McAlarney had to get in somewhere, the former a player's player who made scores and the latter with a fantastic work-rate. I felt it was an honour to play with Colm, he had such an aura about him. Joe Kernan's bustling style always caused problems while Eugene Young was the ideal target man, big, rangy and with good hands.

We spent more time slagging Nudie off the pitch but he bounced back with interest and was the same on the field, cheeky, inventive and totally irrepressible. Greg Blaney won us the 1983 Railway Cup in extra-time over Matt Connor's Leinster at Breffni Park, driving forward with such power, riding tackles and laying the ball off at the right moment.'

NB - Peter McGinnity was a Railway Cup winning captain in 1983 and 1984.

7. SEAN McCAGUE, Monaghan

Brian McAlinden
(Armagh)

Gabriel Kelly	Gerry McCarville	Tony Scullion
(Cavan)	(Monaghan)	(Derry)
Brian McEniff	John Rice	Jim McDonnell
(Donegal)	(Monaghan)	(Cavan)

Colm McAlarney   Jim McKeever
(Down)   (Derry)

Martin McHugh	Frank McGuigan	Paddy Doherty
(Donegal)	(Tyrone)	(Down)
Tony Hadden	Sean O'Neill	Nudie Hughes
(Down)	(Down)	(Monaghan)

Sean's reasons: 'Since my first All-Ireland final was in 1960 when I was young and impressionable my selection includes a fair amount of players from the sixties era. Three are from Down's marvellous forward unit, Sean O'Neill an automatic choice, Paddy Doherty so accurate from frees and play, and Tony Hadden one of the most underrated corner-forwards I have ever seen, as good as Sheehy and Egan.

I have three from my own county but from different eras. John Rice was a strong man and a great fielder from the fifties; Gerry McCarville a Railway Cup full-back who gets in ahead of Leo Murphy for his strength and long service, and Nudie was simply the best Monaghan player I've ever seen.

Brian McAlinden was more than a goalkeeper, his accurate kick-outs setting up moves for Armagh, able to place the ball into space for his half-forwards and half-backs. Gabriel Kelly had all-round ability, while Tony Scullion is a model player, he has handled the best and will give the same even when you're ten points down. Matt Gallagher was my second choice.

Brian McEniff edges out Donal Reid while Jim McDonnell was another excellent wing-back; he was Cavan's best player for ten years though his style of play would maybe not suit nowadays.

At midfield the choice of Jim McKeever was an easy one for his legendary fielding and use of the ball while Colm McAlarney was the first "mobile" midfielder, the style later perfected by Jack O'Shea.

Martin McHugh's contribution to Donegal over the years has been immense, his importance underlined by his absence from this year's National League final replay. Frank McGuigan was simply class and had he not gone to the States Frank would certainly have been the "wonder boy" of Gaelic football.

Very difficult to pick a team from different generations, with the changing styles in our game. For example, Sean O'Neill would be more a right-half-forward these days with Tony Boyle the full-forward. Players were individuals in the old days, but now it's more of a team performance.

In the subs, Jackie Taggart, Iggy Jones, Frankie Donnelly, Jim McCartan, Greg Blaney, Peter McGinnity, Brian McGilligan, Eugene McKenna, Ray Carolan, John Burns of Antrim, Jimmy Whan, Jimmy Smyth and Henry Downey though he's only been on the scene a few years.'

8. JIM REILLY, Cavan

Brian McAlinden
(*Armagh*)

Gabriel Kelly	Gerry McCarville	Tom O'Hare
(*Cavan*)	(*Monaghan*)	(*Down*)
Kevin McCabe	Anthony McGurk	Jim McDonnell
(*Tyrone*)	(*Derry*)	(*Cavan*)

Brian McGilligan
(*Derry*)

Peter McGinnity
(*Fermanagh*)

Nudie Hughes	Greg Blaney	Charlie Gallagher
(*Monaghan*)	(*Down*)	(*Cavan*)
Sean O'Neill	Frank McGuigan	Eugene McKenna
(*Down*)	(*Tyrone*)	(*Tyrone*)

Jim's reasons: 'Quite a few of my selection were team-mates in the Railway Cup, mainly in the eighties. Others are true greats whom I either saw in the twilight of their careers or simply heard so much about.

Brian McAlinden always told you before a game what he was going to do, where he was going to put the ball. Gabriel Kelly was a brilliant player whose very name commanded respect, notably when he became Cavan team manager. Gerry McCarville was totally committed and handled "the Bomber" Liston in his prime. Tom O'Hare deserves to get in if only for his majestic display in the 1968 All-Ireland

final.

In the half-backs Kevin McCabe was very pacy and just got the nod over Martin McQuillan while Anthony McGurk had a fabulous game in the 1976 Ulster final for Derry against Cavan. Jim McDonnell is another of the Cavan greats.

Brian McGilligan's strength, work-rate and fielding ability give him a place in the middle beside the intelligent Peter McGinnity, a good scorer and accurate distributor of the ball.

Nudie Hughes was gifted, cheeky and a wonderful ball-player, and Greg Blaney gets in for his consistency for Down, Ulster or Ireland. Charlie Gallagher was simply a god in Cavan football.

My favourite line is the full-forward line, with three superb footballers. Sean O'Neill was also an impressive Railway Cup manager who could tell you what your opponent had for breakfast. Eugene McKenna had the ability to win ball no matter how you played it into him and could always get you a score when it was most needed. Frank McGuigan "almost" scored the best goal I've ever seen, in the Centenary Cup final. He won the ball on the sideline, beat three defenders, shuffled this way and that, tapping the ball with either foot, and cracked the ball against the post. No goal, but pure genius.'

9. PADDY O'HARA, Antrim

Brian McAlinden
(Armagh)

Gabriel Kelly	Jim McCullough	Tom O'Hare
(Cavan)	*(Armagh)*	*(Down)*
P.J. Duke	John Joe O'Reilly	Sean Quinn
(Cavan)	*(Cavan)*	*(Armagh)*

Frank McGuigan   Eugene McKenna
(Tyrone)   *(Tyrone)*

Kevin Armstrong	Mick Higgins	Alf Murray
(Antrim)	*(Cavan)*	*(Armagh)*
Colm McAlarney	Sean O'Neill	Paddy Doherty
(Down)	*(Down)*	*(Down)*

Paddy's reasons: 'Fifty years of playing and watching Gaelic football have gone into my selection and in that time I have seen huge changes in the game, from the speed it is played at to the sad neglect of the finer, basic skills. Ironically these trends are related, with skills at a minimum because the game has speeded up so much.

Physical fitness is more important these days with games played at a hundred miles an hour but going nowhere. They say the older generation of player would not have lived in this modern game, that they did not have the speed. My argument is that the older players did not need to have the same speed but if required then they could have become as quick.

They also had better basic football skills than players have today. For example, every man on my team could catch a ball whereas today if a player catches a ball during a game he stands out. It's an indictment of the modern game rather than the players but the end result is less refined talent than in my day.

When selecting a footballer, sound character, intelligence and anticipation are high on my list of considerations, with the ability to think quickly and make that extra yard of space. Players today are billed as "stars" by the media after only one or two good performances but I have chosen men who proved themselves over many games and years to have real star quality.

I would love to have seen my forward six play together, all hand-picked to suit one another's style of play with half-forwards who could run and create, draw defenders and handpass perfectly. I saw Alf Murray handpass the ball over the bar from between the 14 and 21-yard lines.

Colm McAlarney came thirty years after the rest but he would have fitted in so well, a mobile, fast and accurate player. A rare asset today is coolness under pressure but Sean O'Neill had it and more — intelligence, positioning and a playmaker. Paddy Doherty is simply the greatest scoring forward I have had the privilege to see, capable of getting scores from half-chances and no-chances, and crafty with it!

My midfielders were two of the best fetchers of a ball you could hope to find; McKenna was a classical fielder and he used the ball well while McGuigan had marvellous touch and a smooth kicking style which looked effortless. He could have been the greatest footballer of all time.

Six tough men in my defence, from Gabriel Kelly to the powerful John Joe O'Reilly who was the cornerstone of some of Cavan's great All-Ireland teams. Jim McCullough was another hard defender, tall, rangy, a great exponent of the high catch and revered on Ulster teams.

Corner-backs are very important and there was none better than Tom O'Hare at getting in front of his man, yet fast enough to get back and cover his full-back. Sean Quinn at left-half-back was small but tough and could use the ball well, while on the right I have P.J. Duke. P.J. died in his early twenties but was a joy to watch — fast, tough and another fine catcher.

Brian McAlinden is my choice in goals for his consistency and intelligence with the ball.'

Combined All-time Ulster Football Team

Brian McAlinden
(Armagh)

Gabriel Kelly
(Cavan)
Brian McEniff
(Donegal)

Tony Scullion
(Derry)
Paddy Moriarty
(Armagh)

Tom O'Hare
(Down)
Jim Reilly
(Cavan)

Eugene McKenna
(Tyrone)

Colm McAlarney
(Down)

Peter McGinnity
(Fermanagh)
Martin McHugh
(Donegal)

Frank McGuigan
(Tyrone)
Sean O'Neill
(Down)

Greg Blaney
(Down)
Nudie Hughes
(Monaghan)

Players Nominated

8. Sean O'Neill, Frank McGuigan.
7. Brian McAlinden, Colm McAlarney, Eugene McKenna
6. Tom O'Hare, Nudie Hughes, Tony Scullion
5. Greg Blaney, Peter McGinnity, Martin McHugh.
4. Paddy Moriarty, Jim Reilly.
3. Paddy Doherty, Gabriel Kelly, Jim McDonnell, Brian McEniff, Anthony McGurk, Jim McKeever.
2. Joe Kernan, Ciaran Murray, James McCartan, Gerry McCarville.

NB - Brian McAlinden and Sean O'Neill are the clearest winners for one position, seven votes for full-forward and goalkeeper respectively. Frank McGuigan, Nudie Hughes, Eugene McKenna and Greg Blaney were all named in four different positions. McGuigan still managed to win most votes for centre-half-forward while the other three tied and then won their selected positions on the strength of more overall votes.

Hughes takes the left corner of the attack from James McCartan, McKenna's combined votes give him a midfield place ahead of Jim McKeever, and Blaney edges out Paddy Doherty.

McKenna's midfield partner is Colm McAlarney who is in fact the most popular choice for the department. So too, Peter McGinnity and Martin McHugh in the right side of the attack.

In defence, Tony Scullion is positioned at full-back despite defeating Tom O'Hare by 5-4 for the left corner. O'Hare has two more votes for the right corner and Scullion one, making it 6 votes each. The argument is settled by the Derryman moving across to the central position in which he excelled this year. Both men out-voted the leading full-back, Gerry McCarville, who was one of eight different players named for the number three shirt.

All of the half-back line are clear winners in their positions though Anthony McGurk and Jim McDonnell are unfortunate to miss out. Both men have the same number of votes as Brian McEniff but McGurk's three votes are split between two positions while McDonnell lost a straight fight with Jim Reilly.

22

Antrim 1984-89

John Joseph McGuinness and Jim Nelson have a lot in common. They have the same postcode, Belfast 11, they have both managed Antrim hurling teams and they are proud, dedicated men of working-class origins and from the same generation. John became 'Sean' so that he would stand a better chance of getting a job at the shipyard, while Jim left his hometown for Chicago through the sixties.

Nelson and McGuinness have raised families in the heart of the Troubles of West Belfast for 24 years, more aware than most of the Saracen blocking the main road and the soldier crouched in the corner with a rifle. They express themselves through hurling, it is an identification. 'For some of us hurling is more important than work. It is how we live and explains what we want out of life,' says Nelson. Both men journey out of West Belfast for much of their identification, Nelson to the Glens of Antrim and McGuinness to the Ards Peninsula.

Eighteen-year-old Jim Nelson made his senior county debut against Kilkenny at Casement Park in the late fifties. A few years earlier he played in an All-Ireland Minor semi-final against Tipperary with a cracked thumb, an injury picked up in a challenge game three days earlier. On returning to the hospital on Monday morning, minus the plaster, he was shown the door. The experience did not deter the young man, and his association with the county would span four decades.

Sean McGuinness caught the hurling bug when his father took him to the 1952 All-Ireland hurling final between Cork and Dublin. He confesses to not being a great hurler or footballer though a bad leg injury curtailed any promise. His influences were Brother Greene from Clare, Fran McCann, Davy Rice and his father. Today all things Gaelic are passed on to five girls and three boys while his wife Eileen directs Irish dancing lessons at Sean's beloved Sarsfields club. He led their senior team to the Antrim title in 1974.

Nelson is a St Paul's man, formerly St John's, and his son Hugh has been on the county panel. There are no pictures of Antrim teams adorning the walls of his

Jim Nelson, Antrim's hurling manager.

home, instead pride of place goes to a painting presented by the P3 and P4 pupils of St Colman's, Lambeg. The artwork is sketchy but the effort is there for all to see, and most importantly it reflects their memories of a landmark in Antrim hurling. It was the day promotion to Division One was secured by victory over Dublin in Casement Park in 1988. 'Hurling to me is about giving it back to the people. You could write a book about the little people who play the game, they turn up in their overalls, grab a hurl and away they go. They may never play for the county, may not ever be interested in doing so, but it's their game.'

In the seventies McGuinness and Nelson sat together on coaching courses and have been dedicated to spreading the word ever since, although they feel they could do with some help. 'Munster have twenty full-time coaches, we could do with half that,' pleads Nelson, who is currently a Games Development Officer. 'They have top hurling colleges giving a flow of young players into the system whereas we don't even have a Minor League. After 1989 we should have been in the schools hammering away at the hurling message'. McGuinness points out that there are 'not enough good people going forward. Too many armchair viewers'.

You'll still find Jim Nelson with the St Paul's under-10s on a Saturday morning, and Sean McGuinness at Sarsfields. They hate to lose; McGuinness was once booked for over-zealous comments directed at a referee at an Under-12 game and was visibly distressed earlier this year at the injustice of a League defeat by Tipperary.

And how do they rate as managers? Ciaran Barr has played under both: 'Sean is more aggressive and will also use as much psychology as he can to motivate

Seán McGuinness, Down's hurling manager

you. He has worked from less in the Down job so that is the more spectacular achievement.

'Jim is more low-key, he takes care of his players and their problems, he has had more to play with but he gave Antrim a lot of push when they needed it. Both men have a vital missing link in that they do not have All-Ireland winning experience.'

Barr gives McGuinness credit for kick-starting Antrim from 1984-86, though Nelson was involved in All-Ireland B Championship wins in 1979-81. Those successes promoted the county to Senior status but the step-up was a shock to the system. In the 1983 All-Ireland quarter-finals Galway beat Antrim by 3-22 to 1-5, and the next year Cork won by 3-26 to 2-5 in the semi-finals. 'What are Antrim doing in a match of this kind? It is a waste of time,' concluded one match report.

Sean McGuinness replaced Neilly Patterson soon after, a city man for a Glens man. Their origin is not an insignificant detail, but reflects a north-south division. Players travelled with club-mates, played cards and ate together.

Sean McGuinness had a bit of a reputation in the county, earned on and off the pitch. 'At my club we call a spade a spade. We retaliate first, which doesn't always go down too well! Therefore when I got the job and was invited to a dinner in Cushendall you can understand the apprehension. Most of those present had fought with me at one time or another!' The new manager insisted on taking a seat in the middle of the hall rather than at the top table, 'in case they would be talking about me'. Cold glances were thrown in McGuinness's direction but he broke the ice by joking that he half-expected to have been on the plate instead of eating from it.

Even with this strength of character, and his coaching credentials, McGuinness saw the need to enlist Eddie Donnelly, 'a god in Antrim hurling', to add credence to the new set-up. At his first squad session he told the players, 'You might not know me or even like me but things are going to be done my way for the next year'. One or two points had to be sorted out at selection meetings as well, for example, that a player could be considered even if he had not been to Mass that morning!

Players responded to his passion and enthusiasm. McGuinness will clear out the hangers-on in the dressing-room to get down to basics, and he'll make sure that players stay in the best hotels. Antrim revealed a hitherto unseen spirit to beat Laois in the Centenary Cup, when Niall Patterson flung himself into a ruck of flying boots to save on the goal-line and one McNaughton yelled to another to 'get up and face the ball'. Never mind the open cut on his forehead.

They had talent, Dessie Donnelly and young Paul McKillen to name two, and now they had spirit and a growing self-belief. After losing a challenge game in Offaly by close on sixty points McGuinness insisted that they could beat the same opposition the next time they met. The coach had noted how Offaly 'worked' and could devise a plan for the return at Armagh in the All-Ireland series of 1985. He even travelled to Birr and climbed over a wall to spy on an Offaly training session, to learn how their forwards worked. Antrim lost the game by fourteen points but were on the right road.

Cork was the next target, in 1986. McGuinness rented a holiday house in Cushendall to be near his players; he told them where Cork were weak, how Antrim could beat the 1984 All-Ireland champions. Olcan Laverty had been in poor form but McGuinness put his head on the block to have him in the corner-forward position. 'I knew he'd die for me that day and he did. The three full-forwards were great.' Antrim amassed 24 points and forced Ger Cunningham into several saves before two late Jimmy Barry Murphy goals killed them off. After the game most of the players were in tears, so convinced had they been that their day had come.

McGuinness had battles off the field, like trying to win confidence and support for the team. Only 300 attended the Cork game, many Northern cars driving past Croke Park on the way to Thurles to watch the other semi-final. The Sunday before, his county fixed a football replay despite a request for a free date.

He remembers waiting with his Belfast players for more than two hours for a lift to Dublin on a Saturday afternoon.

'We were second-class to the footballers, not even allowed to train on Casement Park. One day I noticed a cupboard full of Antrim kit bags covered in dust, being kept for the football lads. I rang an official to ask if there was any chance of getting bags for my players. He said there weren't any available, I replied that there was a room full of them and I was taking them.'

On November 6th, 1986, Sean McGuinness resigned as team manager. Irregularities at his Sarsfields club had led to individuals being suspended for life and when the club asked the county executive to act in similar fashion they refused to do so. A week later one of those concerned was made a football selector.

The Donnellys from Ballycastle — *above*, Eddie (left) in 1984 and *below*, his sons Brian and Dessie in 1989.

Hurling board chairman Jim Nelson spent a couple of hours trying to persuade him not to resign but McGuinness was caught between club and county. How could he continue with the county when they had defied his club? 'It broke my heart to make the decision to quit and my club did not want me to, but on principle it was the only decision I could make.'

Strong words were exchanged and not forgotten. To this day the division between some sections of the Antrim hierarchy and McGuinness is as wide as ever. At one point McGuinness was enticed by a friend to coach the county's Under-21 hurlers, his presence ensuring a turn-out of 29 players. But when he walked out behind the team at Casement Park, officialdom blocked his way. He was offered the chance to apologise to a Board meeting for comments he made two years before. Later, when he was manager of Down, a motion to Congress from Antrim called for 'outside coaches' to be banned, a move that was seen within hurling circles as a cynical exercise to undermine McGuinness.

Always an Antrim man at heart, McGuinness had tears in his eyes when they beat Offaly in 1989 and remains a firm favourite with the players. Some will whisper that they might have won the All-Ireland with him.

Nelson's first game in charge was a League game in Trim which Antrim won by 3-13 to 1-4. Still unbeaten by January, he was elected manager at county convention. Targets were set, promotion to Division One and an All-Ireland final. The latter objective came close to being achieved in double-quick time when Antrim led Kilkenny at Dundalk by five points in 1987. Nelson's team stumbled within sight of the finishing line, taken apart by substitute Harry Ryan and Christy Heffernan in the last ten minutes.

A little bit wiser in 1988, Antrim appeared to have the beating of Tipperary. Ciaran Barr was in top form, 'one of those days when the ball is like a football and just sticks to your hand'. But, when Brendan Laverty presented Barr with a goal chance, his drive towards Ken Hogan's goals cracked against the crossbar. Tipp went upfield immediately to score and win by eight points.

Antrim's consolation was their first hurling All Star, Ciaran Barr, and a winter of hurling in Division One. They were also enjoying a new profile: 'up to the league defeat of Dublin, hurling had been low-key but it just avalanched after that. Ulster Television came to our next game.'

Five defeats out of six left Antrim in danger of a swift return to Division Two but a late winner from Olcan 'Klute' McFetridge in Offaly forced a three-way play-off. Steamrolled by Wexford, 3-21 to 2-9, Antrim were left in a straight scrap for survival with Offaly at Dundalk. An epic battle saw Antrim lead by nine points, trail by one and eventually come good after extra-time by 3-15 to 2-16. Two wins over Offaly augured well for later that summer.

Jim Nelson fretted more over the semi-final than the final, because he knew it was the best chance Antrim had ever had of reaching their first final in 46 years. He was still worried at half-time when Antrim trailed by four points, but a goal from McFetridge on 47 minutes gave Antrim a lead they would not lose. McFetridge and Aidan McCarry rattled three more glorious goals to the Offaly net. 'I said Olcan would win Goal of the Year and he did. He was half on his knees, half in mid-air when he caught and struck the ball to the net. No-one else

in Ireland could have done that, not even Nicky English.'

The Offaly players afforded their victors a marvellous tribute by forming a guard of honour as they left the pitch though Nelson's favourite memory came after all the fuss had died down.

'I was the last one into the dressing-rooms and when I came out of the shower my four-year-old grandson Paul was waiting there. He's mad-keen on hurling

Top: Antrim team which beat Offaly, 1989; front: Terence McNaughton, Olcan McFetridge, Ciaran Barr, Donal Armstrong, Gary O'Kane, Leonard McKeegan, Aidan McCarry; back: Brian Donnelly, Dessie Donnelly, Dominic McKinley, Niall Patterson, Terry Donnelly, Paul McKillen, Dominic McMullan, James McNaughton. *Below*: Olcan McFetridge of Antrim.

and he said "Hi Jim, well done". His was the best face I could have seen.' Ciaran Barr was busy elsewhere, lambasting the Southern press 'for giving no credit to Antrim' on RTE Radio before the second semi-final between Galway and Tipperary. Nelson wandered up to the Hogan Stand to see that game, ticket in hand, but was turned away because someone was on his seat. Eventually, his daughter saw him and gave up her seat.

There are many pitfalls waiting for a county preparing for their first All-Ireland final in nearly half a century, and Antrim fell into most of them. Organisation had not improved since McGuinness's days and Nelson found that he and his county chairman Oliver Kelly were snowed under. 'The phones never stopped after the Offaly game. We had to organise suits, equipment, accommodation and so on. I went down to Oliver's house one morning and didn't leave until the afternoon. We had no idea where to start.'

In Southern counties a massive publicity and fund-raising machine automatically rolls into motion for such an event. In Offaly, organisers of a function once laid on a plane to bring the Antrim manager south, and then a car when it became too windy to fly. Local businesses get behind the team whereas in the North, and especially in Belfast, public backing is much more difficult to come by.

Nelson could have sought advice from his friend Cyril Farrell but chose to stand proud and alone. 'I felt it had to come from within, we had got that far and we would go all the way. The problem was Cork and Tipperary had generations of All-Ireland experience to pass on, we tried to learn it all in four weeks.'

Every newspaper in Ireland seemed to have a representative at the press nights in Loughgiel, their presence and the novelty of the situation contributing to a party atmosphere. In hindsight, it was a mistake to have two open nights as the players were distracted and training disrupted. 'I told the players to arrive for training at 6.30 so that we could get the work done before the press turned up. They were usually late anyway, but as I got out of my car there was Martin Breheny and half of the Dublin media waiting for us.'

Players came under pressure to get tickets for the big day, a pressure transferred onto the manager. An allocation of five each was increased to ten but it still wasn't enough, 'people thought I got a hundred for myself which just isn't the case'. One night before training Nelson yelled at a couple of players who were moaning about not getting tickets to get out on the field.

Peter Finn had prepared the squad for the Offaly game. A 400 metres Irish Universities champion and a lecturer at St Mary's Teacher Training College in Belfast, he brought a scientific approach to Antrim, methodically organising routines to prime the players into peak physical and mental condition on match day. The weekend before the game was spent at Murlough House in Dundrum, developing tactics and working hard. Finn's plan worked perfectly but unfortunately for Nelson, his trainer then got married and missed two weeks, so burdening the already pressurised manager with training. 'I remember conducting a session with four press men standing around me, all firing questions. It was like a tunnel for me, there was no way out and things just had to be done.'

When Finn returned from honeymoon, he found that the players had been away making a record, 'Jim Nelson's Men', featuring Niall Patterson on lead vocals. Worse still, the fine tuning on the training field had been overdone. A repeat trip to Murlough House had been organised but this time it was not necessary. A light session with plenty of rest would have been sufficient with just a week to go to the final but the players left Dundrum weary and leaden-footed. Furthermore, Danny McNaughton aggravated an injury he had had from the semi-final, so depriving Antrim of much-needed quality and experience.

On final day Antrim were propelled through the streets of Dublin at such speed that they arrived too early and were left at a loose end: 'should we take our seats in the stand or wait in the dressing-rooms?' Tipperary knew what to do, they had been there the previous year. 'You need one All-Ireland to break you in,' commented Nicky English. Ciaran Barr contends that Antrim fell into a supporting role as Tipp exorcised their ghost of the seventies. They had not won an All-Ireland since 1971.

'We lost our focus on the game and instead became wrapped up in the whole event,' says Barr. Jim Nelson was aware that the world was looking in and stressed to his players and supporters the importance of conveying a healthy image. But naivety became respect and respect became regret. 'Losing dismantles

Niall Patterson, Antrim goalkeeper.

that respect, our only regret afterwards was not having done ourselves justice. You only get one bite.' Tipperary selector Donnie Nealon said 'Antrim did not draw a dirty stroke.' Theo English added that the losers had hurled 'like first-class gentlemen'. Such comments raised the hackles of some Antrim observers who would rather their team had gone in with a 'nothing to lose' attitude.

Paul McKillen talked later of the nerves that afflict a team in its first All-Ireland. 'On the way out of the tunnel at the start I noticed that other players were shaking. Then I realised that I was shaking as well.' Jim Nelson called his players into a huddle before the wonderfully-coloured Antrim support on Hill 16 to remind them of the job in hand. 'Tipp will try to put us away in the first fifteen minutes,' he warned. On 16 minutes a McFetridge point kept Antrim in touch at 0-1 to 1-4 but soon after Niall Patterson misjudged a weak lob from Declan Ryan and a gift goal was given away.

With a little more experience of the situation, Brian Donnelly might have shot below the bar instead of over it from a half-chance minutes later. Instead, Tipp cut loose and raced into a 1-13 to 0-5 half-time lead, with seven singles from Nicky English who was proving a handful for young Gary O'Kane in the corner. Some had favoured putting Leonard McKeegan on the five-time All Star, but Nelson and his assistant Brother O'Grady agreed during the week that O'Kane was ready. 'He was flying and was the right man for the job though maybe he froze a bit and could have been more aggressive,' assesses Nelson who ignored advice to make a switch early on, the message sent via walkie-talkie from the Brother in the Hogan Stand.

'Our problems were further out the field. Tipp were all over us at midfield and the supply was coming from there to English. It didn't matter who was on him. We had the forwards to score 3-9 but our problems were at midfield and half-back.' McCarry, Brian Donnelly and Donal Armstrong all goaled in the second half but the margin never came within ten points. English's personal tally of 2-12 matched Antrim's total of 3-9, and the talented cornerman fittingly wrapped up the 4-24 to 3-9 with an elegant running stroke to the net in the last minute.

Nelson kept the newspaper men out of the Antrim dressing-room but words failed him as he attempted to talk to his players. The horror of losing struck an exhausted manager, and a week later he went on holidays but wasn't much company. He slept the whole time.

Hindsight is a wonderful thing but it is clear that 1989 marked both an end and a beginning for Antrim. The team was a patchwork of players like Patterson and the Donnellys who had been around for ten years, and young fellas like O'Kane just starting out. The former group had been rewarded for a lifetime's work but before long Antrim would have to rebuild. Much of the squad nearly made another All-Ireland final two years later but by 1993 only five of the '89 team would play in the Ulster final.

Perhaps if the League breakthrough had come a year earlier the extra experience of mixing with the big boys in Division One would have better prepared Antrim for Tipperary. They lacked what Nelson refers to as 'field craft', the cuteness to survive in tricky situations and the first touch, so important when the ball comes at you at speed.

Antrim made mistakes in '89. They were bound to, and even without the mistakes they would probably not have beaten Tipperary anyway. Still, it was a landmark to reach the final, and the future was full of possibilities.

ALL-IRELAND HURLING SEMI-FINAL 1989

ANTRIM 4-15 OFFALY 1-15. Croke Park, 6 August: ANTRIM: Patterson, O'Kane, T. Donnelly, D. Donnelly, J. McNaughton, D. McKinley, McKeegan, McKillen, D. McMullan, B. Donnelly, McCarry, McFetridge, Armstrong, Barr, T. McNaughton. *Sub:* D. McNaughton for McMullan. OFFALY: Troy, Fogarty, E. Coughlan, Hanamy, Mannion, Delaney, G.Coughlan, Kelly, J.Pilkington, Dooley, Regan, M. Corrigan, Teehan, Duignan, D. Pilkington. *Subs:* P.Corrigan for Teehan, Owens for M. Corrigan, Cahill for D. Pilkington. SCORERS: Antrim: McCarry 2-4, McFetridge 2-3, B. Donnelly, T. McNaughton 0-2, Armstrong, Barr, McKillen, McKinley 0-1. Offaly: M.Corrigan, Delaney, Dooley 0-3, Teehan 1-0, Kelly 0-2, Mannion, D. Pilkington, J. Pilkington, Regan 0-1.

ALL-IRELAND HURLING FINAL 1989

ANTRIM 3-9 TIPPERARY 4-24. Croke Park, 3 September: ANTRIM: Patterson, O'Kane, T. Donnelly, D. Donnelly, J. McNaughton, D. McKinley, McKeegan, McKillen, D. McMullan, Barr, McCarry, McFetridge, Armstrong, B. Donnelly, T. McNaughton. *Subs:* D. McNaughton for McMullan, D. McKillop for O'Kane, M. Sullivan for McKinley. TIPPERARY: Hogan, Heffernan, O'Donovan, Sheehy, Conal Bonnar, Ryan, Kennedy, Colm Bonnar, Carr, Leahy, D. Ryan, Cleary, Fox, Cormac Bonnar, English. *Subs:* Hayes for Cormac Bonnar, O'Connell for Leahy, A. Ryan for Cleary. SCORERS: Antrim: B. Donnelly 1-1, Armstrong 1-0, McCarry 1-0, McFetridge, T. McNaughton 0-3, McKeegan, McKillen 0-1. Tipperary: English 2-12, D.Ryan 1-3, Fox 1-2, Leahy 0-3, Carr, Cleary 0-2

23

1989-93: Down on the Up

'I thought you had a bit of sense, McGuinness,' shouted Hugh Dorrian of Ballygalget to the new Down Senior Hurling team manager after hearing of his appointment in the autumn of 1989.

It was a dead-end job; you only had 50-60 senior players to pick from and you were duty-bound to give Antrim little more than match practice each summer.

Just four days before his first League game McGuinness was beginning to wonder if he had any sense. His squad was reduced to thirteen players when representatives from the county champions Portaferry declared that they wanted to save themselves for the Ulster Club Championship. Their club manager doubled as a county selector and had earlier given McGuinness a guarantee that his players would be available. 'You're not a selector any more,' scorned the Belfast man, 'we'll get players from somewhere else.'

A return phone call renewed the guarantee but McGuinness had already picked his team: 'they can come along but tell them to be there at 2 o'clock and they'll be in the subs'. At 2.10 pm on Sunday one of the four turned up, and the rest at ten minutes to three when the manager was delivering his team talk. As they began to get changed an irate McGuinness ordered them to stop and leave the dressing-room. 'When I say 2 o'clock, I mean 2 o'clock. Don't try to make a monkey out of me.' The three outcasts, all Ulster players, bowed their heads in shame while the county chairman desperately tried to calm the raving lunatic he had appointed only weeks before!

Down nearly won the match, caught by a few late goals, but McGuinness had made a stand and within a week the problem was thrashed out at a meeting with the club, never to raise its head again. Discipline and respect are qualities high on McGuinness' agenda. He strives to be first at training and has never had a player sent off with Antrim or Down. Respect he wins from standing by his players. He'll make sure they are put up in the best hotels, he'll support them as long as they 'play the shirts off their backs' in return.

For years Down hurlers had ambled along, yo-yoing between Divisions Two and Three of the League. A total of three seasons had been spent in the higher division with only one point collected, leaving them very much in the shadow of the county's footballers. Now they were being afforded the same status and shown the way to reach the same plateau. 'You don't want to go back to places like Monaghan, Carlow and Mayo through the winter. All it needs is more effort. If you train, you'll win.'

They gathered in the dark of winter at Portaferry, Ballycran or Ballygalget, the three Ards clubs taking turns to host the county team. It's 'hurling only' country, with all the clubs within a seven-mile radius and the members as fanatical as Loughgiel or Ballycastle.

As McGuinness had broken down barriers in Antrim, so he did in Down. 'At the start, players from the three clubs would take a wall each in the dressing-room, leaving the fourth wall to me!'

Sean McGuinness was appointed Down manager in 1989 after meeting with county officials in Downpatrick. He wondered why on earth they wanted him and in return, they wondered what his targets might be. He said survival in Division Two was the least of the possibilities. McGuinness insisted on a one-year contract: 'if you aren't happy after 12 months then you have the option of kicking me out'. One further condition was that he would leave the moment there was any interference from officials in the running of the team. 'There's no point buying a dog and barking yourself.'

The new man needn't have worried, as his new 'bosses' awarded him every respect and courtesy, from ending their leagues whenever he wished, to encouraging Mr and Mrs McGuinness to take themselves off to Thurles for the weekend if there was anything that could be learned from the game at Semple Stadium on Sunday afternoon.

Two wins out of seven in the National League of 1989-90 were just enough to reach McGuinness' first target. In the championship Down lost by two goals to Antrim, a margin that narrowed to just a point in the 1990-91 League. It was one of only two defeats as Down made the play-offs and found themselves in a restructured Division One. Down were on the up.

Beating Laois that winter was like winning an All-Ireland to Down, while in February they won the first Royal Liver Hurling Merit Award after a win over Kerry at Ballycran by 1-14 to 1-12 and a history-making eclipse of Offaly in Tullamore by 1-14 to 1-9. Greg Blaney was carried off the pitch that day, enjoying a new lease of life with the hurlers, and Sam Maguire was never further from his mind. 'Eggy (Blaney) gave us an unbelievable lift, especially when he came back after winning an All-Ireland medal. Our big problem was lack of belief but playing alongside an All Star rubbed off. He didn't say much off the pitch but on it he encouraged them and was as strong as a horse, driving the ball on.'

If Blaney was a motivator on the field, then McGuinness is the inspiration off it. His method is one of simple and clever psychology; he challenges his players' 'pride in the jersey'. On one occasion McGuinness reminded his team of a suggestion by Declan Carr of Tipperary that Down should be in a special section. Before the 1992 Ulster final he appealed to their basic instincts: 'in thirty years time you'll be able to tell your grandchildren that you were on the first Down team to win the Ulster title'. In 1993 he hammered home the point before games with Tipperary and Kilkenny that the Leagues had been restructured so that the big boys would walk over the smaller counties.

McGuinness struck up a rapport with the men from the Ards, his jovial manner making the training ground a happy place to be. The 'city boy' could poke fun at the local dialect without causing offence, once he realised that a pitch 'in gutters' is a wet field, that a 'starving day' is a cold one and that when someone is 'across the water' it doesn't mean that they are in England. In return, they imitated his broad Belfast accent — 'Buy that man a Bass' they would say (from a television advertisement). Pranksters were allowed to 'plant' jerseys in kit bags to cause a stir. The 'collector of jerseys' took his job very seriously, from taking a shirt from a player being carried off to hospital, to climbing into a back garden to remove another from a clothes line.

Results came, and with them came greater team spirit. They drew strength from their familiarity within a close-knit community. McGuinness remembers being fourteen men short at training one night because of a local wake. Twelve of the team that started the Ulster final this year work locally, as butchers, electricians, bricklayers and joiners. Only three were white collar workers. Still, the manager would like to see development outside the Ards 'for the future' and made no bones about going across the water to fetch Jerome and Pearse McCrickard from the Leitrim Fontenoys for his team.

Down's next target was Antrim and their Ulster title. In 1991, they failed in dramatic circumstances without the suspended Greg Blaney. Despite having goals from Pearse McCrickard and Chris Mageean disallowed, Antrim only won the game in the last two minutes with a Paul McKillen point from a 65 and a late goal from Aidan McCarry, 3-14 to 3-10.

Warning bells sounded for Antrim. Down were neck and neck, but the champions weren't listening. They balanced Blaney's loss with their own; they were without four Dunloy players and Sambo McNaughton (banned for six months after a row with a county official). Anyway, they still had that little bit extra to pull away from Down. At the end of the year Sean McGuinness told his county executive that Down had learned from the experience of '91 and that they would be back, fitter and more determined than ever, to take the title.

Antrim had entered a transitional period under Jim Nelson soon after their All-Ireland final appearance in 1989. The expected follow-up did not materialise, and instead there was a feeling of anti-climax and the need for new faces became evident. League re-organisation placed them in a lower section for 1991-92, so they took the opportunity to begin the search for a nucleus for a new team, embracing no fewer than thirty-three players.

Ironically, Antrim had come closest to scaling the heights once again in their 1991 All-Ireland semi-final with Kilkenny. They led by six points in the second half, then trailed by two, and were level with four minutes to go when Sambo McNaughton, who won an All Star for an outstanding performance, drilled over a super point from near the touchline. A late burst from Christy Heffernan finally killed off the Northerners on a scoreline of 2-18 to 1-19. Had Olcan McFetridge been fit, and had the team not been deprived of four Dunloy players because of a much-publicised split with the county, then Antrim may well have made the final where they would surely have given Tipperary a rougher ride than before.

County captain Seamus McMullan, top scorers in the League Jarlath and Alistair Elliott, and Nigel Eliott, were dropped from the panel nine days before the Ulster final. They had opted to play for their club on the same night as county training. Nelson met the Dunloy players after the Ulster final, along with their club chairman and secretary. 'They offered to return the players to training but they were telling me *when* they could train with the county. I said no individual was bigger than the county and that they could only come back with the consent of the players.'

Some said Antrim needed the Dunloy players but others threatened to leave if they were allowed back. 'We did not take a vote but consented that the answer was no. I said anyone who wanted to, could walk out, but nobody did.' Dunloy were bitterly disappointed, they argued that the Hurling Board had refused to switch their fixture, and that their players had shown loyalty earlier in the year when playing for the county seven days before an All-Ireland club semi-final. They also felt that the transfer of responsibility to the players was a dangerous precedent.

A club official later phoned the manager urging a re-think but he was steadfast, 'how could I have instilled discipline later if I had let them back? They had missed tough stamina work and it would have made a mockery of the whole thing. Anyway it made us stronger in the long run, the Dunloy lads realised they took the wrong road, they returned for the League and one of them later became team captain.'

Nelson does not regret his stand though he acknowledges that Antrim might have beaten Kilkenny with the Dunloy players. The stress of the very public affair took him to the verge of quitting. 'I got a lot of bad press, probably because I stuck by a decision to remain silent on the issue. Someone seemed to be stirring the situation and feeding the *Irish News* which referred to the issue as the Dunloy Five, a phrase which I felt had political undertones. Everywhere I travelled in my job as a sales representative I was pulled up in the matter. It does get to you, and your family, which is why I wondered if it was worth staying on.'

He made up his mind before the Kilkenny game to resign and intended telling the players after dinner in Dunleer that evening. His team captain and county chairman talked him out of it. They told him his record was good and defeat had not been his fault. Seven weeks later Nelson bowed to advice from his club and support from players to remain in the job.

His problems were not over. The Down ship was sailing merrily on through a winter of top-class hurling in Division One while Antrim trudged through Division Two. The tables had turned from the day only three years earlier when Antrim made their debut in Division One and Down played in front of a handful of people in Division Three against Mayo. Antrim did win promotion in the spring but Down's reflexes were sharper from playing in a higher division. 'Lack of competitive play at the top level brought about our downfall in the Championship. You need to be in with the top sides to hurl at speed, to react in less space and less time on the ball. We went on a training week to Portugal and

Sean McGuinness looks forward to Croke Park. A downcast Jim Nelson reflects on what went wrong.

did a lot of work but couldn't get that sharpness back.'

Still, the prospect of defeat did not dawn on Antrim until it was too late. 'Until you're beaten you never expect it,' says Ciaran Barr. Greg Blaney warned Jim Nelson, with a smile, that Down were going to catch Antrim 'when you're not on a full tank' but the champions always felt that their superior skills would tell against Down's direct style. 'We felt we had the players to beat Down, no matter what. In fact, we genuinely believed we would beat Cork in the semi-finals! We focused on them which meant we were only seventy per cent fit for the Ulster final.'

Sean McGuinness had his team believe that Antrim were not that good, that Down were the Division One team and that their day was finally to arrive. 'We were very cocky and had a plan, helped by Antrim's team selection. We surprised them with switches over the field.'

Dermot Woods was one of those switches. A relative unknown, he had to be persuaded to join the Down panel and in the semi-final with Derry the watching Antrim players saw him play at full-back. On Ulster final day Woods unexpectedly moved out to put the clampers on John Carson while Paul McMullan did well on Ciaran Barr. The Antrim full-forward had one clear chance in the second half when he drove the ball to Noel Keith's left side. The Down goalkeeper guessed correctly and Jim Nelson whispered to one of his selectors, 'We're losing this,' the first time defeat crossed his mind.

Antrim had been outplayed from the start, managing only three points from play in the first half and staying in the contest because of poor finishing by Down (24 wides). Danny Hughes and Gary Savage dominated midfield and up front, Gerard McGrattan from Portaferry tormented James McNaughton. In only his second Senior game the unknown twenty-year-old turned in a breathtaking display of skilful running with the ball and score-taking. Ten minutes into the second half, Down led 0-12 to 0-8 when Dominic McKinley was sent off for head-butting. It was the beginning of the end for Antrim as Paul Coulter finished a rebound from a Hughes shot to the net and Bailie added another for 2-16 to 0-11.

Sean McGuinness had no regrets at beating his home county. 'As a coach you try to train and discipline your team to a certain level and will obviously want them to win. You cannot have divided loyalties.' The Belfast man thoroughly enjoyed the festivities on the Ards that evening, a cavalcade of about a hundred cars crawling through Kircubbin with the heroes waving from the back of a lorry. Next stop was Portaferry where the Liam Harvey Cup found its new home with Noel Sands.

Down had an All-Ireland semi-final with Cork to look forward to, the press

Above: Sean McGuinness with Greg Blaney relishing the cup. *Below*: Down captain Noel Sands carried shoulder high by his team manager after their historic win over Antrim in the Ulster final, 1992.

Hurling craft at its best: Down's Gerard McGrattan on a solo run.

night for which was held on a bright August evening at Ballycran, a new experience for much of the media. The roar of Sean McGuinness's hearty laugh erupted occasionally as the interviewers were supplied with ample material for their match previews. 'Have Down got any chance?' wondered Adrian Logan of UTV. 'Has the Queen got soldiers?' came the reply. 'Cork have more mentors than we have and dozens more clubs than us but it won't make any difference. Some say it'll be over in ten minutes but there's no way that will happen. They live for hurling down here and are proud to be representing their area. The rest of Ireland wouldn't know the colour of our jerseys but for the footballers but we'll enjoy the day and have a go.'

New track-suits arrived and a new route was taken on the journey to Dublin, through football country where they were pleasantly surprised to be afforded a warm send-off in decorated villages and towns. The new personalities also noticed the benefits of the McGuinness 'school of quotes' as their names and pictures dominated press sports pages. No longer were they in Antrim's shadow.

Down's challenge lasted much longer than had been predicted as they won over the Croke Park crowd with a gutsy, enterprising performance. A goal from Martin Bailie in the second-half even suggested a sensation was possible but before the television replays had ended the ball was in the net at the other end. Cork had enough in reserve, and some argue that they were only on 'half-steam', but weaknesses were exposed by the 'new boys'.

Gerard McGrattan left three markers for dead, while the highly-rated Cork corner-forwards were shackled by a mean defence. 'Egan and Manley were their runners in the Munster final but we didn't give them a sniff of the ball. Cork replaced them with older players for the final but missed their running power. Because of that I would contend that we cost Cork the All-Ireland,' says

Beaten by Cork at Croke Park, but Down manager Sean McGuinness had an All Star in the making in Gerard McGrattan.

McGuinness.

'Humiliation' best describes the feeling in Antrim throughout that summer, tempered only by the reassurance that they would put matters right in the last League game before Christmas at Casement Park. But the harshness of winter was no place for their skills to shine and they again adopted naive tactics of going for goals and roughing up their opponents.

Down were only too willing to wage war, albeit a controlled one, and indicated so when they paused in the corridors before the game.

Tipperary referee Willie Barrett said he had never seen a game like it in twenty years but some of the Southern press were not so impressed, reporting a 'nasty, physical affair with too much pulling'. Ciaran Barr senses a lack of consistency: 'Ulster games are supposed to be the roughest but look at the ugly scenes at the end of the Tipperary-Cork League game earlier this year. They did not get much bad press for that.'

Down's Gerard McGrattan suffered a serious injury, though there are different accounts of the incident which resulted in the player being taken to hospital. Jim Nelson went to the trouble of writing to McGrattan to say that his name had not been mentioned in their team-talk but Sean McGuinness was incensed that his 'star attraction' had been singled out: 'I saw him being struck across the kidneys off-the-ball'.

McGrattan recovered to collect his All Star award a few weeks later, though his county was again angered when Noel Sands and Martin Bailie were the only other Down men nominated, and none of their defenders or midfield were even in the frame. The most glaring omission was that of goalkeeper Noel Keith; the three nominated goalkeepers came from Limerick, Cork and Kilkenny.

'The Ulster GAA Writers' Hurler of the Year was Noel Keith and judged over the whole year he deserved it,' offers McGuinness while county chairman Danny Murphy demands that questions be asked about how the people responsible saw the game of hurling.

'The standard reached by our county was not getting due recognition. The previous year we beat Offaly twice and were unlucky in the Ulster final but got no nominations. Now we were Ulster Champions, still in Division One and we gave Cork a good game in Croke Park. It is again obvious that you must be seen at headquarters, as our only All Star dazzled there for seventy minutes.'

1991 ALL-IRELAND SEMI-FINAL

ANTRIM 1-19 KILKENNY 2-18. Croke Park, 4 August: ANTRIM: Gallagher, O'Kane, McKinley, Rogan, McKillop, J. McNaughton, Jennings, McKillen, T. McNaughton, Carson, Barr, Armstrong, D. Donnelly, McCarry, Close. KILKENNY: M. Walsh, O'Connor, Henderson, Simpson, L.Walsh, Dwyer, Hennessy, R. Power, Phelan, Ronan, J. Power, D.J. Carey, Morrissey, Heffernan, McCarthy. *Subs:* Brophy for Henderson, Fennelly for Ronan. SCORERS: *Antrim:* Carson 0-7, T. McNaughton 0-4, McCarry 0-3, Donnelly 1-0, Barr 0-2, Close, McKillen, J.McNaughton 0-1. *Kilkenny:* Morrissey 2-4, Carey 0-8, McCarthy 0-3, Dwyer, Fennelly, Heffernan 0-1.

1992 ULSTER HURLING CHAMPIONSHIP FINAL

DOWN 2-16 ANTRIM 0-11. Casement Park, 12 July: DOWN: Keith, K. Coulter, G. Coulter, Branniff, Mallon, McMullan, Woods, Hughes, G. Savage, McGrattan, G. Blaney, P. Coulter, M. Blaney, Bailie, Sands. *Subs:* Mageean for M. Blaney, P. Savage for P. Coulter. ANTRIM: Patterson, R. Donnelly, McKinley, J. McNaughton, D. McKillop, Gary O'Kane, Jennings, McKillen, T. McNaughton, S.P. McKillop, McCarry, Armstrong, A. Elliott, Barr, Close. *Subs:* S. McMullan for Jennings, Carson for T. McNaughton, D. Donnelly for Armstrong. Scorers: *Down:* Bailie 1-3, P. Coulter 1-1, Sands 0-4, McGrattan 0-4, G. Savage 0-2, K. Coulter, Hughes 0-1. *Antrim:* Elliott 0-6, Carson 0-2, Close, McKillen, S.P. McKillop 0-1

DOWN 1-11 CORK 2-17. Croke Park, 9 August: DOWN: Keith, K. Coulter, G. Coulter, Branniff, Mallon, McMullan, Woods, Hughes, G. Savage, Mageean, G. Blaney, McGrattan, P. Coulter, Bailie, Sands. *Subs:* P. Savage for P. Coulter, M. Blaney for Mageean. CORK: Cunningham, Corcoran, D. Mulcahy, O'Gorman, Casey, Walsh, Kelleher, Buckley, S. McCarthy, T. Mulcahy, O'Sullivan, Fitzgerald, Hennessy, Manley. *Subs:* McGuckian for D. Mulcahy, T. McCarthy for Egan. SCORERS: *Down:* Sands 1-3, McGrattan 0-5, K. Coulter, Hughes, Bailie 0-1. *Cork:* O'Sullivan 0-5, Hennessy 1-2, T. Mulcahy 0-4, Fitzgerald 1-0, Manley, S. McCarthy 0-2, Buckley, T. McCarthy 0-1.

24

1993: The cup is back where it belongs

Kilkenny v Down, Nowlan Park in Kilkenny on 21 March 1993 in the final round of Division One of the National Hurling League. Relegation awaited the losers, the quarter-finals the winners. 'At the business end of the league Kilkenny are wheeling out the high-rollers' explained the *Sunday Press* as the All-Ireland champions paraded their strongest team since the previous September. 'Despite Down's progress it would be a major shock if they win today,' was the pay-off line.

Just after half-time the Cats led by 1-7 to 1-4. Down pointed twice and won a penalty on 42 minutes but the golden opportunity was not taken. Kilkenny scored immediately afterwards, and on 44 minutes the referee spotted an infringement as Chris Mageean's 65 entered the Kilkenny net. Minutes later, Noel Sands was brilliantly denied, but Down kept going.

Full-back Ger Coulter switched to full-forward. Three minutes to go, three points in it. Bang, bang, bang. The sides were level with time up on the watch. Chris Mageean grabbed the ball, burst through and belted a glorious winner for Down, 1-12 to 1-11.

Kilkenny were relegated, Down remained in Division One for the third year in-a-row and qualified for the League quarter-finals for the first time. Unquestionably, this was Down's and Sean McGuinness's finest hour.

'I'm at the top of the stand but I can't feel my feet. I'm walking on air!' he joked to Des Cahill on RTE Radio before being carried shoulder-high as the small but fanatical Down support vented their emotions.

'All my hurling days were worth today,' declared veteran goalkeeper Noel Keith, 'I never thought we'd beat an All-Ireland winner.' Beating Antrim was important but this was something more, a prestigious victory which put Down on the hurling map (*see colour photo section*).

'Down pack a heavy punch these days,' admitted the reporter who had doubted them. Their first touch may not have been terribly impressive but it was that 'heavy punch', Down's full-blooded determination, that had forced Kilkenny into submission. 'It's all about commitment and self-belief,' explained McGuinness, 'the lads were dying for it. Danny Hughes was the hero in midfield but they've never played better as a team.'

Two weeks earlier Down had narrowly lost at home to Tipperary when a dubious refereeing decision and the intervention of one Nicholas English in the last ten minutes turned the game. On

National League Division One 1992-93		
	Games	Points
Tipperary	5	10
Down	5	6
Antrim	5	5
Limerick	5	5
Kilkenny	5	4
Offaly	5	0

Limerick beat Antrim in a play-off for the quarter-finals. The top four qualified for the new eight-team Division One.

the same day Kilkenny rattled twenty points over the Offaly crossbar. But Down were hungry, had much improved through the winter and, more important, they had lost any inhibitions about playing the major teams.

Support for the reconstruction of the League had supplied their motivation. Effectively, the League was adapted to a top division of eight teams with three to be relegated, making survival of the weaker counties extremely difficult.

The system won a substantial vote but not from Peter Quinn who told Congress that 'the League should not be used just to find out who is the best team in any division. We should use our competitive structures to make progress, to give games against teams who are of a slightly higher standard. The football League worked in 1992-93 because the smaller counties were given the chance to test themselves against the bigger ones. They could compare and see how to improve.'

The irony of relegating the All-Ireland champions was not lost on Down. Nor was the fact that Antrim had also made the cut, so ensuring there would be two Ulster teams in Division One for the first time, one more than the Leinster representation. Antrim's vital point earned in Limerick told a similar tale to Down's in Nowlan Park, with four points scored in the last five minutes to draw level with the League champions.

Limerick had just begun training three nights a week but Antrim and Down were already a step ahead. From the start of the League to the Ulster final in July, Antrim met 73 times, while Down had been training with near championship intensity since the second week in January. 'We have to train all year to catch the Southern teams cold,' admits McGuinness. 'Teams like Cork and Tipperary improve by forty per cent for the championship. It's like they inject them with something!'

Down and Antrim came from nowhere in the past decade by upping their workload from almost nothing to intense, hard training. The benefits of this and of good organisation are bearing fruit. One Kilkenny reporter observed in March that counties like Down 'put a lot of advance planning into their game whereas some Southern counties just hope that everything will be alright on the day'.

Conversely, Down eased up for the League quarter-final with Cork and lost heavily. The defence of the Ulster Championship was the next objective but when 4 July came round, Antrim were emphatic victors by 0-24 to 0-11. Surprisingly, the fire and passion of previous battles was not in evidence as

1993 'Back where it belongs': Antrim captain Dominic McMullan holds aloft the Ulster hurling trophy amid jubilant supporters.

Antrim strolled through the 70 minutes. Their gameplan was to avoid a physical confrontation, to let their stickwork tell and to take their points. Hours of practice on long-range shooting paid off with eighteen points from play to Down's three. The Antrim forwards took a new form, with Ciaran Barr absent from the edge of the square (transferred to Dublin) and Olcan McFetridge on the long-term injury list. Five of them switched position at the start, Terence McNaughton tormented Marty Mallon and Gary O'Kane's performance gave the Antrim manager particular satisfaction: 'they said I was mad when I moved him from defence to attack'.

Three points was the difference at half-time, 0-10 to 0-7, and Sean McGuinness told his players they were lucky it wasn't ten. The second-half was almost an exhibition with Paul McKillen the main attraction, eclipsing Danny Hughes who had outshone the Ballycastle midfielder a year earlier. James McNaughton was another to regain lost face by winning his personal duel, with Gerard McGrattan. 'Pride was our sole motivation,' admitted Terence McNaughton.

The Antrim faithful were happy again; 'the cup is back where it belongs', they proclaimed. Jim Nelson knew why: 'we did our homework for Down this time and our stickwork carried us away from them. I'll always go for a player with good stickwork.' The manager deserved his moment of glory; he had been under considerable pressure and dismissal was more than a possibility if Antrim had lost. 'It was very important for the next few years that the younger lads came of age today. Now we really have something to build on.'

Sean McGuinness was not so optimistic for the future of Down hurling. Before the final he told me that 'another year might do me as manager. There's only so much you can do with a team, especially where the resources are limited.' His squad has changed little in four years, save for Gerard McGrattan and a couple of others, and many of the regulars have been there for a long time. 'The boys are weary, Sean,' said Noel Keith as they sat in an empty dressing-room, the goalkeeper waiting to have fourteen stitches inserted to a head wound. In four years they had given everything but now they were physically and mentally burnt-out.

Down bore no animosity to the champions, though McGuinness was saddened by abuse coming from a couple of women in the band and from some of the Antrim support at the end of the game. He had also been angered by the three-month suspension which kept Chris Mageean out of the contest. The player had been sent off in the Antrim leagues and disciplined by that county, though Down argued that one month would have been appropriate for the offence. In the event, Ulster Council upheld the suspension and the matter had no bearing on the result.

Both counties were unhappy that the provincial final was knocked off centre stage because of the Ulster Council decision to fix the football replay between Donegal and Armagh for the same afternoon. Within Antrim, Jim Nelson then found himself embroiled in a battle to free his players from club commitments before the All-Ireland quarter-final with Meath. The battle was lost and Cushendall played Dunloy in the championship just seven days prior to the Meath game, with many county men involved. A counter opinion is that club games maintain players' sharpness better than county training.

After the Ulster final, Sean McGuinness contended that 'Antrim aren't that great, yet' and certainly they learnt a lesson against Meath, conceding four goals and trailing at half-time by two points, 2-9 to 2-7. Once Nelson hammered home the message 'take your points', Antrim assumed total control in the second half. With Olcan McFetridge returned from injury and scoring two goals ('he'll never be one hundred per cent but his percentage is enough'), the Ulster Champions ran out easy winners.

Jim Nelson had great hopes for his new-look team in the All-Ireland semi-finals. 'We can win,' he declared on Kilkenny Radio the day before Antrim took on the reigning champions. At half-time, his team led by 1-8 to 1-5, with wind advantage, and a marvellous goal from Terence McNaughton contrasted sharply with the overall standard of finishing. Midfield supplied four of the first five Antrim points as their light forwards were easily contained. Some of the 'new boys' froze while the heart of the team, 'Sambo' McNaughton, may have been more effective in the centre, though he carried a hand injury into the game.

'Their backs were getting it too comfortably,' complained Dominic McKinley as Kilkenny went on the offensive in the second half. A defence that coped well in the first half now crumbled under the incessant pressure and took too long to get the ball away.

Twelve minutes in, Ronan Donnelly caught a good ball out on the right but with nowhere to turn and no support, he lost possession. Aidrian Ronan floated a high ball towards Pat Gallagher's crossbar, the Antrim goalkeeper prevented a point but the in-running PJ Delaney flashed the loose ball to the net.

It was the beginning of the end. The scores had been level before the goal but by full-time there were eighteen points between the sides, 4-18 to 1-9. Antrim managed only one point in the second period to Kilkenny's 3-13. 'Our heads went down after that killer goal and we collapsed,' said a bemused Jim Nelson. 'It's as if the players didn't believe they could win, even when we were in front. I'm very disappointed and will have to think about my future.'

This was Antrim's heaviest Championship semi-final defeat since 1984, and a setback to the splendid work that had been done in the nine years since. It had been only two years since they ran Kilkenny to two points but the Cats of '93 were much-improved while Antrim still had some quite revealing shortcomings in their play; they struggled to lift sideline cuts and succumbed to the speed and slickness of their opponents when the heat was turned on in the second half, as if lacking in match fitness.

Antrim's remoteness remains a major disadvantage. Considerable planning is required to take the squad to Galway or Tipperary for worthwhile challenge matches. Southern counties sharpen their high skill-levels in regular tests against one another. They also have superior club structures and competitions of a higher standard. This is why Division One status is so important to the Ulster teams.

'It is more important to stay in the Division One than to keep the Ulster title,' Sean McGuinness insisted early in the year. 'We'll get seven good games and you can only improve from playing the best.' But the heavy defeat of Antrim Minors by Kilkenny was possibly more depressing to Northern fans than the Senior loss. Is an All-Ireland Senior title any more realistic than it was five years ago? Is enough being done in Ulster to help the game?

Antrim have some young hurlers coming through but the under-age set-up is a long way from the conveyor belts churning out fresh talent in places like Cork. It appears that a lot of work has to be done between Under-14 and Under-21 levels, a vital time for enlisting players for the future. Ten years ago, Ciaran Barr was in this age grouping but was more intent on playing water polo. Only the encouragement of the Hamill brothers at Rossa, Aidan and Eamonn, kept Barr out of the water though he admits that he 'fell into hurling almost by accident' .

Down captain Noel Sands has even more cause for concern than Antrim, despite his county's revival. 'Hurling is falling behind football. Down and Donegal have won All-Ireland football titles and the game has really taken off in Ulster. Every kid wants to play football now and it's much harder to get them to pick up a stick and train with a hurling club.'

It may not be too dramatic to project that Down may not win another Ulster title for ten years, unless progress is made outside the Ards. The former hurling hotbeds of Leitrim and Kilclief are striving to promote the game but Jerome McCrickard was the only non-Ards player on the Ulster final team in 1993. Teams have been entered in Division Two of the Antrim Leagues and Down's Junior team is selected only from non-Ards players, but the gap is still a yawning one. There is a development policy and a schools programme but only one secondary school for hurling, St Columba's of Portaferry. Jim Nelson feels Down should consider ultimately withdrawing from the Antrim Leagues and persevere in building a structure within their own county, Sean McGuinness prefers to see work beginning with the Under-12s and some of the smaller clubs combining. Both men call for outside expertise to help in some way. McGuinness remembers the instant respect Brother Greene from Clare commanded in his early days, while Brother O'Grady was a major psychological help to Antrim in 1989.

Elsewhere, the withdrawal of Derry from the Senior Championship is hopefully a temporary measure. Only five years ago they jostled with Down in the B Championship before football success by Lavey and Derry took from their small pool. They have under-age Leagues in operation and a few of their good Minor teams combined at Under-21 level (coached by Jim McKeever) to reach an All Ireland semi-final in 1993. Fermanagh has also caught Sean McGuinness's eye as he looks around for another challenge, though 'it's a pity it's so far away'.

Jim Nelson completes seven years as Antrim manager in November 1993. However, only a month short of this milestone, he was reported to have resigned from the position when only four players turned up for the county's first training session since the Kilkenny defeat. Around the same time, Terence McNaughton was suspended for eighteen months by the County Board. In all, four players were banned after disgraceful scenes at the end of the county final between Ballycastle and Cushendall.

To make matters worse, details of the suspension were leaked to the media before the players were informed. McNaughton learned his fate as he sat in a work lorry listening to the radio. Nelson received the news from a cryptic message from a reporter on his answering machine.

'I was annoyed about that, but there were other problems which myself and the players were unhappy with,' states Nelson. 'I stayed on as manager on the condition that certain basic requests were looked at seriously by the County Executive.'

'The players and the manager are now happy, and that's the most important thing. We have a good young team and with the support of the whole county, we can get over the Kilkenny defeat and keep Antrim firmly on the hurling map.'

NATIONAL LEAGUE 1992-93

DOWN 1-12 KILKENNY 1-11. Nowlan Park, 21 March. DOWN: Keith, K. Coulter, G. Coulter, Branniff, Mallon, P.McMullan, Woods, Hughes, O'Prey, McGrattan, Mageean, Sands, M.Blaney, Bailie, L. McMullan. *Subs:* Dorrian for L. McMullan, McCarthy for Bailie. KILKENNY: M.Walsh, O'Connor, Dwyer, Simpson, J. Walsh, O'Neill, Hennessy, Phelan, Brennan, Heffernan, Power, D.J. Carey, Morrissey, McCarthy, P.J. Delaney. *Subs:* Ronan for Morrissey, Murphy for J. Walsh, Prendergast for Heffernan.
SCORERS: *Down:* Mageean 0-7, Blaney 1-0, Hughes 0-2, G. Coulter, McGrattan, Sands 0-1.
Kilkenny: Power 1-1, Carey 0-3, Brennan, Delaney, Heffernan 0-2, Phelan 0-1.

ULSTER SENIOR CHAMPIONSHIP FINAL 1993

ANTRIM 0-24 DOWN 0-11. Casement Park, 4 July. ANTRIM: Gallagher, S. McMullan, D. McMullan (c), McCloskey, R. Donnelly, McKinley, J. McNaughton, McKillen, Jennings, Elliott, Gary O'Kane, McKillop, Close, T. McNaughton, Gregory O'Kane. DOWN: Keith, McAree, G. Coulter, Branniff, Mallon, P.McMullan, Woods, Hughes, Savage, McGrattan, Bailie (c), O'Prey, Blaney, McCrickard, Sands. *Sub:* B. Coulter for McCrickard.

SCORERS: Antrim: Gregory O'Kane 0-7, McKillen 0-5, McKillop 0-3, R. Donnelly, Elliott, Jennings, T. McNaughton 0-2, Close 0-1. *Down:* McCrickard 0-6, Savage 0-2, Bailie, Hughes, McGrattan 0-1.

ALL-IRELAND SEMI-FINAL 1993

ANTRIM 1-9 KILKENNY 4-18. Croke Park, 8 August. ANTRIM: Gallagher, S. McMullan, D. McMullan, McCloskey, R. Donnelly, McKinley, J. McNaughton, Jennings, McKillen, Close, Gary O'Kane, T. McNaughton, Gregory O'Kane, McFetridge, Elliott. *Subs:* Carson for Close, McKillop for McFetridge. KILKENNY: M.Walsh, E. O'Connor, Simpson, J. Walsh, Keoghan, O'Neill, W. O'Connor, Phelan, Hennessy, McCarthy, Power, D.J. Carey, Morrissey, P.J. Delaney, Ronan. *Subs:* Prendergast for Phelan, Lawlor for Carey, Brennan for Delaney.

SCORERS: *Antrim:* T. McNaughton1-0, Elliott, Jennings, McKillen 0-2, Close, McFetridge, Gregory O'Kane 0-1. *Kilkenny:* Carey 2-5, Delaney 1-2, Morrissey 1-1, Ronan 0-3, Lawlor 0-2, Hennessy, McCarthy, O'Neill, Phelan, Power 0-1.

25

Hurling Selections

1. JIM NELSON ANTRIM SELECTION 1956-76

	Johnny Coyle	
Robbie Elliott	Kevin Donnelly	Frank Ward
Niall Wheeler	Sean Collins	Sean Burns
Paddy Morgan		Seamus McDonnell
Brendan McGarry	Eddie Donnelly	Seamus Richmond
Aidan Hamill	Randal McDonnell	Peter Boyle

Jim's reasons: 'I picked two teams because hurling has changed so much since the fifties when I started. There wasn't much running though the game did flow with the ball played in the air more often. Nowadays there's more handling, tactics and physical fitness. Present-day players do ten times more than the fifties players did.

The first time I joined the Antrim Senior panel was on the Sunday of a game when, to my surprise, I was handed the number ten shirt because somebody failed to turn up. The only tactic was to play the ball first time on the ground for the first ten minutes and stand up to your opponent. After that you were allowed to play a bit.

We regularly lost by 25 and 30 points but had a few players who could mix with the best, such as Seamus "Stout" McDonnell from Rossa who was selected on a Rest of Ireland team in the late fifties. Stout was one of those who guldered and roared on the field, a leader with courage and strength. In midfield I have with him Paddy Morgan from Loughgiel who never reached his full potential but had a good hand and was a great stickman. Players like Morgan had natural skills, there was no coaching in those days.

Goalkeeper Johnny Coyle played for Antrim into his forties, a great servant who passed on his considerable knowledge to Niall Patterson. Robbie Elliott was so versatile he could have played anywhere; he retired in the late fifties.

At full-back Kevin Donnelly from Ballycastle won nine out of ten balls in the square and was never dispossessed coming out. He had great physical strength and got the vote over Brendan "The Bear" Donnelly on superior skill. In the corner, Frank Ward from Glenarm was probably the first Antrim captain from a junior club. Frank was first to training and the last to leave, an example to the rest, which is why I broke with the tradition of taking a captain from the county champions.

The half-backs are all tremendous stick players, the classy Niall Wheeler from Glenariffe, Sean Collins (Rossa) a super athlete and an artist on the pitch, great from dead-balls, and on the left one of the all-time skill players, Sean Burns of St John's, never sent off or booked.

Brendan McGarry of Loughgiel was one of the most prolific scorers Antrim ever had. He had a great first touch, could run with the ball and usually came inside to take scores. You couldn't budge Eddie Donnelly under a dropping ball, he could hold you off with one hand and catch with his free hand. Once in possession you couldn't get the ball off Eddie, such was his power.

Seamus Richmond from Loughgiel had a good hand and gave long service, his height often an advantage at full-forward. Rossa's Aidan Hamill was a smaller man but had great heart and loved to carry the ball. He was equally good at football and one of the first "thinkers in hurling.

Nobody has ever hit a ball harder than Randal McDonnell from Glenariffe. Once at Corrigan Park in a game with Leinster Randal struck a penalty to the net before the three men on the line moved an inch.

Peter Boyle didn't so much run with the ball, he glided along and always had that extra second on the ball. In 1989 he was still only in his early thirties and I tried unsuccessfully to lure him back from America for the All-Ireland semi-final.

2. JIM NELSON ULSTER SELECTION 1986-93

Niall Patterson
(Antrim)

| Seamus McMullan *(Antrim)* | Terence Donnelly *(Antrim)* | Paddy Branniff *(Down)* |

| Martin Mallon *(Down)* | Leonard McKeegan *(Antrim)* | James McNaughton *(Antrim)* |

Paul McKillen *(Antrim)*   Danny Hughes *(Down)*

| Olcan McFetridge *(Antrim)* | Aidan McCarry *(Antrim)* | Terence McNaughton *(Antrim)* |

| Dessie Donnelly *(Antrim)* | Ciaran Barr *(Antrim)* | Noel Sands *(Down)* |

Jim's reasons: 'This selection is based on my term as manager of Antrim, and as the highlight of that period is of course the 1989 All-Ireland final, I suppose it's not surprising that I have picked ten of that team. Seamus McMullan and four Down men make up the rest. In time, the likes of Gary O'Kane and Alistair Elliott would get on this selection but I had a difficult enough time in juggling around to get some favourites in.

As I said after this year's Ulster final I will always go for players with good stickwork and that is a shining quality throughout this team.

Big Niall in goals could have been the greatest keeper in Ireland if he had got down to sixteen stone. Great reflexes, a brilliant hand, a long puck and years of service. In front of him, "Hippy" Donnelly took care of all the big names. Nicky English rated him very highly while another Tipperary man, Cormac Bonnar, rarely got a score off Terence.

"Mushy" McMullan was Antrim captain at 21 and this year took our penalties despite being a corner-back. Never gets hooked or blocked and has good pace.

Paddy Branniff has been a top-class defender for Down for many years and is deserving of the left corner. Marty Mallon is a lovely hurler and another must, though his inclusion meant James McNaughton switched wings. James is a good blocker and an excellent reader of the game.

Leonard McKeegan completes the half-back-line, a fantastic hurler and the most gifted we have had, outside of Olcan McFetridge. Leonard could have won an All Star but is a reserved character and probably didn't realise how good he was.

Paul McKillen deserved an All Star in 1991 along with Terence McNaughton, so well did he play against Kilkenny. I rate Danny Hughes an excellent midfielder and one of the reasons for Down's successes in recent times.

Three All Stars in the forwards though none in the positions they got their awards, that's what I mean about juggling. "Sambo" McNaughton won his at midfield but I've made room for him in the half-forwards. He likes to hustle but has great skills, a good hand and a fine ground stroke.

Dessie Donnelly won an All Star at corner-back but played most of his career in the forwards, scoring some great goals. Remember the piledriver against Kilkenny in '91? Dessie made up for a lack of pace with a good reading of the game. Ciaran Barr has a tremendous hand but doesn't have a high skill level. Strength, courage and will-to-win are his hallmarks. A good target man who, as he says himself, manufactures frees. Very precise and a leader.

"Cloot" McFetridge and "Beaver" McCarry tore Offaly apart in 1989 with sensational goals. Nobody else in Ireland could have scored Olcan's "Goal of the Year", while McCarry hits the ball so hard. Before the final that year he was positively dangerous in training, and we had to make him shoot from further out. Aidan is also the best overhead player I have seen, with a great eye and superb timing.

Noel Sands has great stickwork and the courage to match. Very dangerous when he heads for goal but I feel he has a bit more to offer yet. If anyone is going to win another All Star for Down, it's him.'

3. SEAN McGUINNESS ULSTER SELECTION 1984-93

Noel Keith *(Down)*

Kevin Coulter *(Down)*   Sean McNaughton *(Antrim)*   Paddy Braniff *(Down)*

Martin Mallon *(Down)*   Gerard Coulter *(Down)*   Terence McNaughton *(Antrim)*

Paul McKillen *(Antrim)*   Danny Hughes *(Down)*

Danny McNaughton *(Antrim)*   Brian Donnelly *(Antrim)*   Tony McGrath *(Antrim)*

Peter Boyle *(Antrim)*   Dessie Donnelly *(Antrim)*   Noel Sands *(Down)*

Sean's reasons: 'I have selected only from players I have worked with since 1984 in Antrim and Down. The breakdown is seven from Down and eight from Antrim.

In recent times the Down defence has been as good as any in Ireland so I have four of them included along with Noel Keith in goal who has been so consistent over the years. I felt he should at least have been nominated for an All Star in 1992 but his typically modest reaction was that the three nominated were "far better than me". I don't agree!

Paddy Braniff is the sort of man who would die for you in the square, a terrific defender, while Martin Mallon is one of the most skilful defenders I have ever seen, and powerful with it. Gerard Coulter is another with no fear, tremendous strength and determination, being used at full-back these days but at his peak a great centre-half-back. Kevin Coulter gets a very close vote over Dominic "Woody" McKinley.

Of the Antrim defenders Sean McNaughton gets in for his drive and determination. I'll never forget his contribution to the win over Laois in 1985 which was to prove a real watershed in Antrim hurling. To me, Sambo was always a wing-half-back. He reminds me of Dan McCartan of Down who used to catch the ball in the square, bounce it once on the 14 yard-line and boot it from the 21-yard-line

way down the field, so strong and inspirational. I played Paul McKillen as a 17-year-old and still rate him a classy hurler and a worker who likes to deliver the long ball. Four times he's been nominated for an All Star, once taken as a replacement but deserving of the full award. Paul would have complemented Danny Hughes, a terrific runner with the ball.

Two Donnellys in attack — big Brian had everything, another good runner and powerful, while Dessie was one of the hardest hitters of the sliothair I have ever seen. He was top scorer in the National League one year with me and struck some unstoppable goals.

On his day Danny McNaughton was as good as anything around. He could play anywhere in attack while on the other wing Tony McGrath had fabulous skills. He could strike the ball accurately on either side and had a trick where he could pretend to throw the ball to strike but then catch it and go another way. Always on my Antrim teams.

Peter Boyle had skill, speed and could read the game. Noel Sands is a wee tiger, or as I like to call him, an angel with a dirty face! Loves to score and win — captain of Down. It was difficult picking only one Down forward on my team but three of them would have been among the first subs — Gerard McGrattan, Martin Bailie and Chris Mageean. What a bench!'

ULSTER STATISTICS
Football and Hurling 1884-1993

Abbreviations: R (Replay); WO (Walk over); (C) (Captain); aet (After extra time); Obj (Objection); Abd (Abandoned); P (Protest); Apd (Appealed)

FOOTBALL

1. ULSTER SENIOR FOOTBALL CHAMPIONSHIP FINALS 1888-1993

1888	Monaghan 0-3	Cavan 0-1 (R)
1889	No Championship	
1890	Armagh 2-8	Tyrone 1-2
1891	Cavan 1-11	Armagh 0-0
1892-99	No Championship.	
1900	Antrim walk over.	
1901	Antrim 3-5	Armagh 2-5
1902	Armagh 0-8	Antrim 0-7
1903	Cavan 0-8	Armagh 0-4 (2nd Replay)
1904	Cavan 0-7	Monaghan 0-4
1905	Cavan 0-7	Monaghan 0-3
1906	Monaghan 2-10	Antrim 1-2
1907	No records.	
1908	Antrim 1-8	Cavan 0-4
1909	Antrim 1-9	Cavan 0-4
1910	Antrim 3-4	Cavan 0-1
1911	Antrim 2-8	Cavan 0-4
1912	Antrim 2-2	Armagh 0-1
1913	Antrim 2-1	Monaghan 1-2
1914	Monaghan 2-4	Fermanagh 0-2
1915	Cavan 0-4	Monaghan 0-3 (R)
1916	Monaghan 2-3	Antrim 0-2
1917	Monaghan 4-2	Armagh 0-4
1918	Cavan 3-2	Antrim 0-0
1919	Cavan 5-6	Antrim 0-2
1920	Cavan 4-6	Armagh 1-4
1921	Monaghan 2-2	Derry 0-1
1922	Cavan 3-4	Monaghan 3-3 (R)
1923	Cavan 5-10	Monaghan 1-1
1924	Cavan 2-3	Monaghan 1-3 (R)
1925	Cavan 3-6	Antrim 0-1 (R)
1926	Cavan 5-3	Antrim 0-6
1927	Monaghan 3-5	Armagh 2-5
1928	Cavan 2-6	Armagh 1-4
1929	Monaghan 1-10	Cavan 0-7 (R)
1930	Monaghan 4-3	Cavan 1-5
1931	Cavan 0-8	Armagh 2-1
1932	Cavan 2-4	Armagh 0-1
1933	Cavan 6-13	Tyrone 1-2
1934	Cavan 3-8	Armagh 0-2
1935	Cavan 2-6	Fermanagh 2-1
1936	Cavan 1-7	Monaghan 0-7
1937	Cavan 0-13	Armagh 0-3
1938	Monaghan 2-5	Armagh 2-2
1939	Cavan 2-3	Armagh 1-4 (R)
1940	Cavan 4-10	Down 1-5
1941	Cavan 3-9	Tyrone 0-5
1942	Cavan 5-11	Down 1-3
1943	Cavan 2-3	Monaghan 0-5
1944	Cavan 1-9	Monaghan 0-5
1945	Cavan 4-10	Fermanagh 1-4
1946	Antrim 2-8	Cavan 1-7
1947	Cavan 3-4	Antrim 1-6
1948	Cavan 2-12	Antrim 2-4
1949	Cavan 1-7	Armagh 1-6

1950	Armagh 1-11	Cavan 1-7
1951	Antrim 1-7	Cavan 2-3
1952	Cavan 1-8	Monaghan 0-8
1953	Armagh 1-6	Cavan 0-5
1954	Cavan 2-10	Armagh 2-5
1955	Cavan 0-11	Derry 0-8
1956	Tyrone 3-5	Cavan 0-4
1957	Tyrone 1-9	Derry 0-10
1958	Derry 1-11	Down 2-4
1959	Down 2-16	Cavan 0-7
1960	Down 3-7	Cavan 1-8
1961	Down 2-10	Armagh 1-10
1962	Cavan 3-6	Down 0-5
1963	Down 2-11	Donegal 1-4
1964	Cavan 2-10	Down 1-10
1965	Down 3-5	Cavan 1-8
1966	Down 1-7	Donegal 0-8
1967	Cavan 2-12	Down 0-8
1968	Down 0-16	Cavan 1-8
1969	Cavan 2-13	Down 2-6
1970	Derry 2-13	Antrim 1-12
1971	Down 4-15	Derry 4-11
1972	Donegal 2-13	Tyrone 1-11
1973	Tyrone 3-13	Down 1-11
1974	Donegal 3-9	Down 1-12 (R 1-14 2-11)
1975	Derry 1-16	Down 2-6
1976	Derry 0-22	Cavan 1-16 aet. (R 1-8 1-8)
1977	Armagh 3-10	Derry 1-5
1978	Down 2-19	Cavan 2-12
1979	Monaghan 1-15	Donegal 0-11
1980	Armagh 4-10	Tyrone 4-7
1981	Down 3-12	Armagh 1-10
1982	Armagh 0-10	Fermanagh 1-4
1983	Donegal 1-14	Cavan 1-11
1984	Tyrone 0-15	Armagh 1-7
1985	Monaghan 2-9	Derry 0-8
1986	Tyrone 1-11	Down 0-10
1987	Derry 0-11	Armagh 0-9
1988	Monaghan 1-10	Tyrone 0-11
1989	Tyrone 2-13	Donegal 0-7 (R 0-11 0-11)
1990	Donegal 0-15	Armagh 0-14
1991	Down 1-15	Donegal 0-10
1992	Donegal 0-14	Derry 1-9
1993	Derry 0-8	Donegal 0-6

ROLL OF HONOUR
Cavan 38; Monaghan 13; Down 11; Antrim 10;
Armagh 7; Derry, Tyrone 6; Donegal 5. TOTAL - 96.

Final appearances
Cavan 58; Armagh 28; Monaghan 24; Down 22;
Antrim 20; Derry 13; Tyrone 12; Donegal 11;
Fermanagh 4.

2. ALL RESULTS IN ULSTER SENIOR FOOTBALL CHAMPIONSHIP 1888-1993

1888	Monaghan 0-3	Cavan 0-1 (R: 0-2 0-2)
1889	No Championship.	
1890	Armagh 3-17	Antrim 0-0
	Armagh 2-8	Tyrone 1-2
1891	Cavan 1-11	Armagh 0-0 (R)
1892-99	No Championships.	
1900	Antrim Walk Over.	
1901	Antrim 3-5	Armagh 2-5
1902	Tyrone 0-3	Armagh 1-6
		(R: 0-2 0-3 abandoned)
	Armagh 2-2	Antrim 0-7
1903	Down 0-1	Armagh 2-9
	Monaghan 0-3	Cavan 1-8
	Armagh 7-4	Tyrone 0-1
		(0-12 0-3, appealed)
	Cavan 0-8	Armagh 0-4
		(Rs: 0-5 0-5, 0-5 0-5)
1904	Down 0-1	Armagh 2-9
	Monaghan w.o.	Derry
	Monaghan 1-13	Armagh 1-2
	Cavan 0-7	Monaghan 0-4
1905	Down 1-1	Antrim 1-11
	Cavan 0-7	Monaghan 0-3
1906	Tyrone 0-2	Derry 1-3
	Down 1-5	Armagh 0-4
	Donegal 0-2	Derry 0-18
	Monaghan w.o.	Derry
	Antrim 1-8	Down 0-9
	Monaghan 2-4	Cavan 0-5
	Monaghan 2-10	Antrim 1-2
1907	Antrim 0-9	Down 0-5
	Monaghan w.o.	Derry
1908	Armagh 0-3	Cavan 1-5
	Antrim 1-8	Cavan 0-4
1909	Monaghan 1-7	Armagh 0-3
	Fermanagh 2-4	Tyrone 1-6
	Monaghan 0-6	Antrim 0-10
	Antrim 1-9	Cavan 0-5
1910	Armagh 0-2	Monaghan 1-6 (R)
	Tyrone 1-4	Cavan 1-9
	Monaghan 0-3	Antrim 1-2 (R: 1-3 1-4 Obj)
	Antrim 3-4	Cavan 0-1
1911	Armagh 1-3	Monaghan 0-0
	Antrim 2-8	Cavan 0-4
1912	Armagh 1-1	Cavan 1-2 Obj. (R: 0-1 0-1)
	Monaghan 0-3	Antrim 3-1
	Antrim 2-2	Armagh 0-1
1913	Fermanagh bt	Armagh
	Antrim bt	Tyrone
	Monaghan 0-3	Cavan 0-2 (R: 2-0 0-6)
	Antrim bt	Down
	Antrim bt	Fermanagh
	Antrim 3-1	Monaghan 1-2
1914	Down 0-3	Armagh 0-10
	Monaghan 3-2	Derry 0-2
	Cavan bt	Antrim
	Tyrone 1-2	Fermanagh 2-4
	Armagh 0-2	Monaghan 1-1 (R: 0-0 0-0)
	Fermanagh bt	Cavan
	Monaghan 2-4	Fermanagh 0-2
1915	Down 1-3	Armagh 1-7
	Monaghan 5-2	Fermanagh 2-0
		(R: 1-1 1-2 Obj)
	Armagh 0-4	Cavan 1-6 (R: Obj)
	Cavan 0-4	Monaghan 0-3 (R: 3-2 2-5)
1916	Antrim bt	Down
	Monaghan 2-5	Derry 0-1
	Cavan bt	Fermanagh
	Antrim bt	Armagh
	Monaghan 4-3	Cavan 1-5
	Monaghan 2-3	Antrim 0-2
1917	Armagh 2-3	Tyrone 1-3
	Cavan bt	Derry
	Monaghan 0-5	Fermanagh 0-3
	Antrim 0-22	Down 0-4
	Cavan 0-2	Monaghan 3-1
	Armagh 0-5	Antrim 0-3 (R: Obj)
	Monaghan 4-2	Armagh 0-4
1918	Monaghan 4-4	Tyrone 1-0
	Antrim bt	Derry
	Cavan bt	Fermanagh
	Armagh bt	Down
	Monaghan 0-3	Antrim 0-5
	Cavan 2-4	Armagh 0-0
	Cavan 3-2	Antrim 0-0
1919	Derry 2-4	Fermanagh 0-3
	Monaghan 0-3	Armagh 0-4
	Tyrone 0-3	Donegal 0-16
	Cavan 0-10	Down 0-3
	Antrim 1-4	Derry 1-1
	Donegal 0-8	Cavan 0-17
	Antrim 0-10	Armagh 0-7
	Cavan 5-6	Antrim 0-2
1920	Tyrone 0-0	Armagh 2-1
	Down 0-10	Antrim 0-5
	Derry 0-11	Donegal 1-2
	Monaghan 1-3	Cavan 2-2
	Cavan bt	Fermanagh
	Armagh 0-4	Down 0-3
	Cavan bt	Derry
	Cavan 4-6	Armagh 1-4
1921	Antrim 1-5	Down 1-2
	Cavan bt	Fermanagh
	Monaghan 0-3	Armagh 0-1
	Derry 2-1	Donegal 0-3
	Monaghan 2-1	Cavan 0-2 (R: 2-1 2-1)
	Derry bt	Antrim
	Monaghan 2-2	Derry 0-1
1922	Down 0-1	Armagh 2-4
	Monaghan 1-4	Antrim 1-3
	Donegal 1-1	Cavan 0-8
	Armagh 0-2	Monaghan 2-9
	Cavan bt	Derry
	Cavan 3-4	Monaghan 3-3 (R: 2-3 2-3)
1923	Tyrone w.o.	Down
	Monaghan 2-6	Tyrone 0-3
	Cavan bt	Antrim
	Derry 0-6	Donegal 1-2 (Protest)
	Monaghan 4-1	Armagh 1-4
	Donegal 3-1	Cavan 4-10
	Monaghan 2-6	Tyrone 0-3
	Cavan 5-10	Monaghan 1-1
1924	Donegal 0-1	Tyrone 0-2
	Cavan bt	Armagh
	Monaghan 4-6	Fermanagh 2-1
	Antrim 1-6	Down 1-2
	Cavan 1-6	Tyrone 0-7
	Monaghan 1-4	Antrim 1-1 (R: 1-5 1-4 Obj)
	Cavan 2-3	Monaghan 1-3 (R: 1-3 1-3)
1925	Tyrone 1-3	Cavan 1-5
	Donegal 3-6	Fermanagh 0-1

	Monaghan 2-2	Armagh 1-4 (R: 1-3 0-5, appealed)
	Antrim 3-6	Down 0-1
	Cavan 6-0	Donegal 0-2
	Monaghan 0-4	Antrim 2-5
	Cavan 3-6	Antrim 0-1 (R)
1926	Tyrone 3-8	Fermanagh 2-1
	Monaghan 0-4	Down 0-1
	Cavan 4-7	Donegal 1-5
	Antrim bt	Armagh
	Tyrone 3-2	Derry 1-3
	Monaghan 1-3	Cavan 0-7 (R: 0-7 0-7)
	Tyrone 0-3	Antrim 2-5
	Cavan 5-3	Antrim 0-6
1927	Armagh 0-8	Donegal 1-1
	Antrim 1-9	Tyrone 0-11
	Cavan bt	Derry
	Monaghan 2-5	Down 1-2
	Armagh 3-6	Antrim 0-4
	Monaghan 2-6	Cavan 1-6
	Monaghan 3-5	Armagh 2-5
1928	Monaghan 3-5	Down 1-3
	Tyrone 7-3	Derry 2-3
	Donegal 1-4	Armagh 1-8
	Monaghan 6-3	Fermanagh 1-7
	Tyrone 0-3	Cavan 4-3
	Monaghan 0-1	Armagh 0-4
	Cavan 2-6	Armagh 1-4
1929	Fermanagh 0-2	Tyrone 0-8
	Donegal 0-1	Monaghan 2-8
	Cavan bt	Antrim
	Down 3-2	Armagh 5-4
	Monaghan 3-7	Tyrone 1-2
	Cavan 4-10	Armagh 0-2
	Monaghan 1-10	Cavan 0-7 (R: 1-4 1-4)
1930	Armagh 1-8	Tyrone 1-3 (R: 1-6 2-3)
	Antrim bt	Fermanagh (Obj)
	Monaghan 7-8	Down 1-6
	Cavan bt	Fermanagh
	Armagh 0-5	Monaghan 2-2
	Monaghan 4-3	Cavan 1-5
1931	Tyrone 1-3	Monaghan 3-9
	Down 0-4	Armagh 0-6
	Donegal 2-4	Antrim 0-2 (Protest)
	Monaghan 0-4	Armagh 1-9
	Cavan bt	Antrim
	Cavan 0-8	Armagh 2-1
1932	Armagh 1-5	Tyrone 1-4
	Antrim 4-10	Down 0-1
	Cavan 8-7	Donegal 2-6
	Monaghan 1-7	Fermanagh 1-3
	Antrim 0-6	Armagh 2-6
	Cavan 8-8	Monaghan 2-6
	Cavan 2-4	Armagh 0-1
1933	Tyrone 1-8	Antrim 1-2 (Rs: 0-3 0-3, 3-5 3-5)
	Down 1-3	Armagh 1-4
	Monaghan 0-3	Fermanagh 2-3
	Cavan 1-8	Armagh 0-2
	Tyrone 1-4	Fermanagh 1-3
	Cavan 6-13	Tyrone 1-2
1934	Tyrone 2-4	Cavan 2-5
	Monaghan 4-7	Down 2-6
	Donegal 1-3	Fermanagh 2-5
	Armagh 1-6	Monaghan 1-3
	Cavan bt	Fermanagh
	Cavan 3-8	Armagh 0-2
1935	Fermanagh 1-11	Tyrone 2-6 (R: 0-5 1-2)
	Armagh 2-4	Down 0-5
	Monaghan 3-8	Antrim 2-2
	Donegal 1-9	Cavan 1-11
	Armagh 2-2	Fermanagh 3-4 (R: 1-6 1-6)
	Cavan 2-12	Monaghan 0-1
	Cavan 2-6	Fermanagh 2-1
1936	Down 4-5	Tyrone 2-3
	Antrim 2-1	Armagh 0-11
	Fermanagh 0-7	Donegal 1-8
	Down 0-4	Monaghan 4-8 (R: 2-8 3-5)
	Armagh 2-1	Cavan 1-8
	Monaghan 2-8	Donegal 0-11
	Cavan 1-7	Monaghan 0-7
1937	Donegal 3-8	Antrim 0-7
	Armagh 4-14	Down 2-7
	Fermanagh 2-6	Cavan 3-11
	Tyrone 0-8	Monaghan 3-12
	Cavan 2-12	Donegal 1-4
	Monaghan 1-3	Armagh 2-12
	Cavan 0-13	Armagh 0-3
1938	Tyrone 0-6	Monaghan 3-3
	Antrim 1-4	Armagh 2-5
	Cavan 3-10	Fermanagh 1-4
	Donegal 0-6	Monaghan 0-7
	Armagh 2-7	Cavan 1-4
	Monaghan 2-5	Armagh 2-2
1939	Antrim 1-5	Down 1-6
	Tyrone 1-2	Cavan 4-11
	Donegal 0-6	Down 1-1
	Armagh 1-6	Monaghan 0-2 (R: 1-6 1-6)
	Cavan 5-12	Donegal 0-4
	Cavan 2-3	Armagh 1-4 (R: 2-6 2-4)
1940	Antrim 3-3	Cavan 0-12
	Armagh 0-5	Donegal 0-6
	Down 4-4	Tyrone 2-5
	Cavan 4-13	Antrim 0-4
	Down 0-8	Monaghan 1-3 (R: 2-3 2-3)
	Donegal 2-4	Cavan 0-12
	Cavan 4-10	Down 1-5
1941	Tyrone 3-13	Armagh 0-1
	Cavan 3-7	Monaghan 3-2
	Antrim 0-4	Down 5-4
	Donegal 0-7	Cavan 1-6
	Down 1-7	Tyrone 1-10
	Cavan 3-9	Tyrone 0-5
1942	Armagh 3-4	Tyrone 0-0
	Monaghan 0-6	Cavan 1-6
	Down 2-11	Antrim 1-5 (R: 4-4 3-7)
	Cavan 7-10	Donegal 4-6
	Down 1-12	Armagh 2-5
		(R: 0-7 0-6, abandoned)
	Cavan 5-11	Down 1-3
1943	Tyrone 1-8	Donegal 0-7
	Antrim 0-13	Down 1-8
	Monaghan 3-8	Armagh 3-4
	Cavan 4-10	Tyrone 1-3
	Monaghan 1-10	Antrim 1-5
	Cavan 2-3	Monaghan 0-5
1944	Antrim 1-2	Cavan 1-4
	Monaghan 3-7	Armagh 3-3
	Down 3-4	Tyrone 0-4
	Cavan 5-9	Donegal 2-3
	Monaghan 1-5	Down 1-4
	Cavan 1-9	Monaghan 0-5
1945	Donegal 3-7	Derry 2-3
	Cavan 2-11	Antrim 3-3
	Armagh 3-13	Tyrone 0-2
	Fermanagh 4-13	Monaghan 0-5
	Cavan 0-14	Down 1-3
	Armagh 1-6	Fermanagh 2-4

	Cavan 6-12	Donegal 2-4
	Cavan 4-10	Fermanagh 1-4
1946	Derry 4-6	Fermanagh 0-4
	Tyrone 3-2	Cavan 8-13
	Monaghan 1-9	Donegal 4-5
	Down 0-4	Armagh 1-10
	Antrim 1-11	Derry 0-10
	Cavan 5-8	Donegal 0-3
	Armagh 0-6	Antrim 1-12
	Antrim 2-8	Cavan 1-7
1947	Tyrone 3-5	Fermanagh 2-6 (R: 1-4 0-7)
	Donegal 0-3	Antrim 3-8
	Down 2-11	Derry 2-5
	Monaghan 1-9	Cavan 1-11 (R: 1-6 0-9)
	Tyrone 2-5	Armagh 1-4 (R: 1-6 1-6)
	Antrim 3-13	Down 1-8
	Tyrone 0-2	Cavan 4-5
	Cavan 3-4	Antrim 1-6
1948	Monaghan 2-9	Derry 2-6
	Antrim 4-5	Donegal 1-4 (R: 1-3 0-1 Abd)
	Tyrone 5-9	Fermanagh 0-4
	Down 4-10	Armagh 2-3
	Antrim 0-12	Tyrone 1-3
	Cavan 2-9	Down 2-4
	Cavan 1-9	Monaghan 0-7
	Cavan 2-12	Antrim 2-4
1949	Derry 1-6	Antrim 5-9
	Armagh 3-6	Monaghan 1-8
	Donegal 2-6	Down 0-8
	Cavan 7-10	Tyrone 1-7
	Antrim 2-6	Cavan 3-7
	Donegal 1-4	Armagh 0-14
	Cavan 1-7	Armagh 1-6
1950	Donegal 1-7	Down 4-3 (R: 3-5 2-8)
	Antrim 5-10	Derry 0-5
	Tyrone 0-3	Cavan 8-7
	Armagh 0-14	Monaghan 0-5
	Cavan 1-12	Antrim 2-6
	Armagh 1-8	Down 1-7
	Armagh 1-11	Cavan 1-7
1951	Armagh 1-13	Tyrone 2-3
	Derry 1-3	Monaghan 0-5
	Antrim 1-6	Donegal 1-5 (R: 2-7 2-7)
	Cavan 2-9	Down 0-7
	Armagh 0-5	Antrim 1-8
	Cavan 1-6	Derry 1-4
	Antrim 1-7	Cavan 2-3
1952	Monaghan 2-12	Derry 0-12
	Tyrone 1-6	Armagh 1-8
	Antrim 1-7	Donegal 2-3
	Cavan 3-10	Down 1-3
	Monaghan 1-8	Armagh 1-5
	Cavan 0-8	Antrim 0-2
	Cavan 1-8	Monaghan 0-8
1953	Donegal 0-6	Tyrone 0-12
	Monaghan 0-2	Cavan 2-7
	Armagh 1-8	Antrim 1-4
	Derry 1-11	Down 2-5
	Cavan 2-10	Tyrone 2-4
	Armagh 4-11	Derry 1-5
	Armagh 1-6	Cavan 0-5
1954	Tyrone 1-7	Donegal 1-5
	Cavan 3-8	Monaghan 2-5
	Antrim 1-6	Armagh 1-8
	Derry 4-11	Down 3-4
	Cavan 3-10	Tyrone 2-10
	Armagh 1-12	Derry 1-6
	Cavan 2-10	Armagh 2-5
1955	Derry 0-13	Tyrone 1-5

	Armagh 1-8	Down 0-5
	Donegal 3-6	Monaghan 2-8
	Antrim 0-4	Derry 2-7
	Cavan 2-5	Donegal 1-6
	Derry 3-4	Armagh 0-2
	Cavan 0-11	Derry 0-8
1956	Tyrone 3-7	Derry 2-4
	Monaghan 1-14	Donegal 1-5
	Cavan 3-15	Antrim 2-4
	Down 0-6	Armagh 2-5
	Tyrone 2-9	Monaghan 0-7
	Cavan 1-9	Armagh 1-5
	Tyrone 3-5	Cavan 0-4
1957	Armagh 3-5	Tyrone 2-9
	Derry 4-14	Antrim 0-8
	Derry 4-14	Antrim 0-8
	Donegal 3-2	Down 0-3
	Monaghan 1-5	Cavan 1-12
	Derry 1-10	Cavan 1-9
	Tyrone 3-5	Donegal 2-3
	Tyrone 1-9	Derry 0-10
1958	Antrim 0-5	Derry 0-8
	Cavan 0-14	Monaghan 1-6
		(R: 0-7 0-7, 1-5 1-5)
	Tyrone 1-9	Armagh 0-10
	Down 3-11	Donegal 3-5
	Derry 3-7	Cavan 3-6
	Down 1-9	Tyrone 0-2
	Derry 1-11	Down 2-4
1959	Donegal 0-4	Cavan 2-9
	Armagh 1-6	Derry 0-5
	Down 4-9	Antrim 1-5
	Tyrone 1-9	Monaghan 0-7
	Cavan 1-9	Armagh 1-7 (R: 0-13 2-7)
	Down 1-12	Tyrone 0-4 (R: 1-6 1-6)
	Down 2-16	Cavan 0-7
1960	Cavan 3-9	Fermanagh 2-2 (R: 3-4 2-7)
	Down 0-14	Antrim 1-4
	Tyrone 3-6	Monaghan 3-11
	Cavan 1-10	Donegal 1-0
	Derry 3-10	Armagh 1-9
	Down 2-11	Monaghan 0-7
	Cavan 3-6	Derry 0-5
	Down 3-7	Cavan 1-8
1961	Derry 2-10	Donegal 0-4
	Armagh 2-7	Cavan 0-8
	Monaghan 1-10	Antrim 0-6
	Down 0-12	Fermanagh 0-7
	Derry 1-9	Tyrone 0-10
	Armagh 5-9	Monaghan 0-5
	Down 2-12	Derry 1-10
	Down 2-10	Armagh 1-10
1962	Derry 2-10	Donegal 2-7
	Cavan 3-8	Armagh 2-2
	Antrim 2-7	Monaghan 0-2
	Fermanagh 1-3	Down 4-10
	Tyrone 1-9	Derry 2-2
	Cavan 1-6	Antrim 1-5
	Down 1-12	Tyrone 1-6
	Cavan 3-6	Down 0-5
1963	Antrim 2-9	Tyrone 0-3
	Down 6-11	Monaghan 1-3
	Cavan 3-9	Derry 2-8
	Donegal 2-12	Fermanagh 1-6
	Armagh 1-8	Antrim 2-3
	Cavan 0-6	Donegal 4-5
	Down 0-9	Armagh 0-5
	Down 2-11	Donegal 1-4
1964	Tyrone 0-8	Antrim 1-9

	Monaghan 1-6	Down 2-9	
	Cavan 3-9	Derry 2-3	
	Donegal 1-10	Fermanagh 0-7	
	Antrim 2-6	Armagh 1-8	
	Donegal 0-7	Cavan 1-9	1973
	Down 2-8	Antrim 1-9	
	Cavan 2-10	Down 1-10	
1965	Monaghan 2-12	Fermanagh 1-5	
	Derry 1-6	Antrim 2-9	
	Down 3-13	Tyrone 1-6	
	Cavan 0-9	Donegal 0-8	
		(R: 1-8 1-8, 1-11 0-14)	1974
	Armagh 3-7	Monaghan 1-9	
	Down 0-10	Antrim 1-5	
	Cavan 1-10	Armagh 0-4	
	Down 3-5	Cavan 1-8	
1966	Monaghan 0-12	Fermanagh 3-8	
	Antrim 2-7	Derry 0-6	
	Tyrone 0-4	Down 2-9	
	Cavan 1-11	Donegal 5-6	1975
	Fermanagh 3-8	Armagh 0-8	
	Down 0-9	Antrim 0-5	
	Donegal 4-17	Fermanagh 1-8	
	Down 1-7	Donegal 0-8	
1967	Tyrone 0-13	Fermanagh 3-2	
	Armagh 1-8	Donegal 2-13	
	Down 3-9	Derry 1-10	
	Cavan 2-12	Antrim 2-8	
	Tyrone 1-13	Monaghan 1-7	
	Down 2-8	Donegal 2-5	1976
	Cavan 1-13	Tyrone 3-3	
	Cavan 2-12	Down 0-8	
1968	Fermanagh 2-8	Tyrone 0-8	
	Donegal 2-10	Armagh 1-3	
	Derry 1-6	Down 1-8	
	Cavan 5-9	Antrim 1-12	
	Monaghan 2-12	Fermanagh 2-5	
		(R: 0-12 1-9)	1977
	Down 2-14	Donegal 0-8	
	Cavan 1-11	Monaghan 0-5	
	Down 0-16	Cavan 1-8	
1969	Antrim 2-10	Donegal 0-14	
	Tyrone 0-8	Derry 2-8	
	Cavan 1-9	Fermanagh 2-4	
	Armagh 0-8	Monaghan 1-9	
	Down 0-8	Antrim 0-4	1978
	Cavan 1-8	Derry 0-6 (R: 2-3 0-9)	
	Down 2-15	Monaghan 1-7	
	Cavan 2-13	Down 2-6	
1970	Donegal 2-6	Antrim 3-8	
	Derry 3-12	Tyrone 0-7	
	Cavan 3-13	Fermanagh 1-3	
	Monaghan 3-7	Armagh 1-7	
	Antrim 2-9	Down 1-6	1979
	Cavan 1-5	Derry 1-8	
	Antrim 2-10	Monaghan 1-8	
	Derry 2-13	Antrim 1-12	
1971	Derry 4-10	Fermanagh 1-10	
	Armagh 4-9	Tyrone 2-10	
	Monaghan 1-12	Cavan 2-10	
	Down 3-14	Donegal 3-6	
	Derry 0-8	Antrim 0-4	1980
	Down 0-11	Cavan 2-3	
	Derry 3-12	Armagh 1-10	
	Down 4-15	Derry 4-11	
1972	Fermanagh 0-7	Derry 5-7	
	Tyrone 0-13	Armagh 1-7	
	Cavan 3-9	Monaghan 0-6	
	Donegal 1-8	Down 0-8	

Right-hand columns:

	Derry 2-9	Antrim 2-5
	Donegal 2-11	Cavan 1-9 (R: 0-12 2-6)
	Tyrone 1-8	Derry 0-9
	Donegal 2-13	Tyrone 1-11
1973	Down 2-10	Armagh 2-9
	Fermanagh 3-9	Antrim 4-4
	Derry 1-7	Monaghan 0-5
	Donegal 1-7	Tyrone 0-12
	Cavan 0-8	Down 1-7
	Tyrone 1-15	Fermanagh 0-11
	Down 1-12	Derry 0-9
	Tyrone 3-13	Down 1-11
1974	Armagh 0-6	Down 1-10
	Antrim 2-7	Fermanagh 1-8
	Monaghan 0-8	Derry 3-6
	Tyrone 0-8	Donegal 1-9
	Down 2-8	Cavan 0-12
	Donegal 5-9	Antrim 1-7
	Down 1-12	Derry 0-7
	Donegal 3-9	Down 1-12 (R: 1-14 2-11)
1975	Fermanagh 0-10	Armagh 4-6
	Monaghan 0-13	Tyrone 1-5
	Donegal 0-13	Cavan 0-15
	Down 3-12	Antrim 0-7
	Derry 2-15	Armagh 1-7
	Down 1-13	Cavan 1-10
	Derry 0-14	Monaghan 1-6
		(R: 1-11 1-11)
	Derry 1-16	Down 2-6
1976	Armagh 1-13	Fermanagh 1-12
	Tyrone 2-10	Monaghan 1-10
	Cavan 1-9	Donegal 0-8
	Antrim 2-6	Down 0-14
	Armagh 2-1	Derry 1-19
	Cavan 1-18	Down 0-11
	Derry 0-10	Tyrone 0-8
	Derry 0-22	Cavan 1-16 aet. (R: 1-8 1-8)
1977	Donegal 0-12	Derry 1-12
	Monaghan 0-10	Antrim 0-6
	Down 3-9	Fermanagh 0-7
	Armagh 2-14	Cavan 1-12
	Derry 3-10	Tyrone 1-11
	Armagh 2-12	Monaghan 3-5
	Derry 0-10	Down 0-8
	Armagh 3-10	Derry 1-5
1978	Derry 3-12	Donegal 0-7
	Antrim 4-6	Monaghan 2-4
	Fermanagh 2-7	Down 0-14
	Cavan 0-16	Armagh 0-9
	Tyrone 0-9	Derry 3-11
	Cavan 2-13	Antrim 1-10
	Down 1-14	Derry 2-8
	Down 2-19	Cavan 2-12
1979	Tyrone 2-9	Antrim 2-5
	Monaghan 0-14	Down 0-10
	Armagh 5-3	Fermanagh 1-7
	Derry 2-12	Cavan 1-13
	Donegal 1-11	Tyrone 1-9
	Monaghan 2-10	Armagh 2-8
	Donegal 2-9	Derry 0-14
	Monaghan 1-15	Donegal 0-11
1980	Antrim 1-7	Tyrone 1-8
	Down 1-4	Monaghan 0-13
	Fermanagh 1-4	Armagh 3-8
	Cavan 2-9	Derry 2-7
	Tyrone 1-17	Donegal 0-9
	Armagh 0-12	Monaghan 0-5
	Tyrone 2-12	Cavan 1-9
	Armagh 4-10	Tyrone 4-7

1981	Monaghan 2-9	Tyrone 0-6	Donegal 0-6	Armagh 1-8
	Antrim 2-13	Cavan 2-12	Derry 2-11	Cavan 2-8 (R: 2-7 1-10)
	Armagh 2-15	Donegal 0-13	Armagh 5-9	Tyrone 1-9
	Derry 0-12	Fermanagh 0-10	Derry 0-11	Armagh 0-9
	Down 3-4	Monaghan 1-9	1988 Fermanagh 1-13	Armagh 2-12
		(R: 0-10 0-10)	Monaghan 0-16	Cavan 0-14
	Armagh 4-7	Antrim 1-3	Derry 0-7	Down 1-11
	Down 0-12	Derry 0-9	Tyrone 3-13	Antrim 2-4
	Down 3-12	Armagh 1-10	Armagh 2-10	Donegal 0-8
1982	Tyrone 1-9	Monaghan 0-9	Monaghan 1-11	Down 0-9
	Cavan 0-8	Antrim 1-7	Tyrone 0-15	Armagh 1-8
	Donegal 0-13	Armagh 1-11	Monaghan 1-10	Tyrone 0-11
	Fermanagh 1-9	Derry 1-8	1989 Antrim 0-5	Monaghan 0-8
	Down 0-11	Tyrone 1-12	Cavan 0-14	Donegal 3-12
	Armagh 1-20	Antrim 1-6	Fermanagh 1-7	Derry 4-15
	Fermanagh 1-8	Tyrone 0-10	Tyrone 1-11	Armagh 2-7
	Armagh 0-10	Fermanagh 1-4	Monaghan 0-9	Down 1-14
1983	Derry 0-11	Cavan 1-12	Donegal 2-8	Derry 1-9
	Monaghan 2-18	Antrim 0-4	Tyrone 1-12	Down 1-7
	Donegal 1-10	Armagh 0-7	Tyrone 2-13	Donegal 0-7
	Fermanagh 0-10	Down 0-8		(R: 0-11 0-11)
	Cavan 0-11	Tyrone 0-10	1990 Monaghan 3-17	Antrim 0-8
	Donegal 1-14	Monaghan 1-9	Donegal 0-13	Cavan 0-9
	Cavan 2-12	Fermanagh 1-7	Derry 4-14	Fermanagh 1-7
	Donegal 1-14	Cavan 1-11	Armagh 0-12	Tyrone 0-11
1984	Cavan 0-14	Derry 1-13	Down 3-11	Monaghan 1-12
	Antrim 1-6	Monaghan 2-17	Donegal 1-15	Derry 0-8
	Armagh 1-10	Donegal 0-12	Armagh 2-7	Down 0-12 (R: 1-13 2-10)
	Down 3-6	Fermanagh 0-8	Donegal 0-15	Armagh 0-14
	Derry 3-4	Tyrone 1-13	1991 Tyrone 1-8	Derry 1-9
	Armagh 2-8	Monaghan 0-9	Donegal 2-14	Cavan 0-12
	Tyrone 0-10	Down 0-5	Antrim 1-8	Fermanagh 3-12
	Tyrone 0-15	Armagh 1-7	Down 1-7	Armagh 0-8
1985	Donegal 2-12	Down 2-8	Derry 0-13	Monaghan 0-8
	Antrim 0-5	Cavan 0-9	Donegal 1-18	Fermanagh 0-13
	Derry 1-9	Tyrone 1-8	Down 0-14	Derry 0-9 (R: 0-13 1-10)
	Armagh 2-13	Fermanagh 0-5	Down 1-15	Donegal 0-10
	Monaghan 1-14	Donegal 0-7	1992 Derry 1-10	Tyrone 1-7
	Derry 0-11	Cavan 0-7	Donegal 0-20	Cavan 1-6 (R: 1-15 1-15)
	Armagh 2-7	Monaghan 1-11	Fermanagh 1-9	Antrim 1-8
		(R: 0-10 0-10)	Armagh 0-9	Down 1-12
	Monaghan 2-11	Derry 0-8	Derry 2-9	Monaghan 0-7 (R: 1-14 3-8)
1986	Down 2-8	Donegal 1-10	Donegal 2-17	Fermanagh 0-7
	Cavan 1-8	Antrim 0-7	Derry 0-15	Down 0-12
	Tyrone 2-6	Derry 1-7	Donegal 0-14	Derry 1-9
	Fermanagh 0-7	Armagh 1-11	1993 Armagh 4-8	Fermanagh 1-16
	Down 2-11	Monaghan 0-11		(R: 1-9 1-9)
		(R: 1-10 0-13)	Monaghan 3-10	Cavan 2-9 (R: 2-9 0-15)
	Tyrone 2-16	Cavan 1-12	Down 0-9	Derry 3-11
	Armagh 0-12	Down 3-7	Donegal 0-12	Antrim 0-9
	Tyrone 1-11	Down 0-10	Armagh 2-8	Tyrone 0-12 (R: 0-13 1-10)
1987	Fermanagh 0-9	Armagh 2-9	Derry 0-19	Monaghan 0-11
	Cavan 0-12	Monaghan 0-10	Donegal 2-16	Armagh 1-7 (R: 0-15 1-12)
	Down 2-7	Derry 1-12	Derry 0-8	Donegal 0-6
	Tyrone 2-6	Antrim 2-5 (R: 0-9 0-9)		

3. TEAMS IN ULSTER FINALS 1951-93

(Note: If a Christian name is not given, it can be found under a previous appearance by the player.)

1951 ANTRIM: Mickey Darragh, Jimmy Roe, Paddy Duggan, Joe Hurley, Brian O'Kane, Ray Beirne, Paddy Murray, Peter O'Hara, Sean Gallagher, Harry O'Neill, Kevin Armstrong (c), Tony Best, Paddy O'Hara, Donough Forde, Joe McCallin. Sub: Bobby Cunningham.
CAVAN: Seamus Morris, Paul Fitzsimmons, Phil "The Gunner" Brady, James McCabe, Paddy Carolan, John Joe O'Reilly (c), Dessie Maguire, Victor Sherlock, Liam Maguire, Tony Tighe, Mick Higgins, Peadar Doyle, John Joe Cassidy, Peter Donohue, Edwin Carolan.

1952 CAVAN: S.Morris, J.McCabe, P.Brady, P.Fitzsimmons, Tom Hardy, L.Maguire, D.Maguire, V.Sherlock, P.Carolan, Seamus Hetherton, M.Higgins (c), Brian Gallagher, JJ Cassidy, T.Tighe, E.Carolan.
MONAGHAN: Percy McCooey, Pat McQuaid, Ollie O'Rourke, Mickey McCaffrey, Brendan O'Duffy, John Rice (c), Mackie Moyna, Tommy Moyna, Tony

Prunty, Hughie McKearney, Joe Smith, Paddy O'Rourke, Pat Clarke, Jimmy Brannigan, Eamonn McCooey.

1953 ARMAGH: Eamon McMahon, Eugene Morgan, Jack Bratten, John McKnight, Frank Kernan, Pat O'Neill, Sean Quinn (c), Mick O'Hanlon, Malachy McAvoy, Joe Cunningham, Brian Seeley, Bill McCorry, Pat Campbell, Art O'Hagan, Gerry O'Neill. Sub: Joe O'Hare for Campbell.
CAVAN - S.Morris, P.Fitzsimons, L.Maguire, D.Maguire, P.Carolan, T.Hardy, Noel O'Reilly, Brendan Maguire, V.Sherlock, S.Hetherton, E.Carolan, B.Gallagher, Johnny Cusack, Simon Deignan, M.Higgins (c). Sub: Gerry Keyes for Deignan.

1954 CAVAN: S.Morris, P.Fitzsimmons, P.Brady, J.McCabe, J.Cusack, T.Hardy, B.Reilly, Tom Maguire, V.Sherlock, B.Gallagher, P.Carolan, Gerry Keyes, S.Hetherton, S.Deignan (c), Brian Deignan.
ARMAGH: Brian Daly, Mickey McKnight, J.Bratten, J.McKnight, F.Kernan, P.O'Neill, S.Quinn, M.O'Hanlon (c), M.McAvoy, John McBreen, Patsy Kieran, B.McCorry, P.Campbell, A.O'Hagan, John Hanratty.

1955 CAVAN: S.Morris, P.Fitzsimons, P.Brady (c), N.O'Reilly, Hubert Gaffney, P.Carolan, Jim McDonnell, V.Sherlock, T.Maguire, B.Gallagher, T.Hardy, Colm Smith, J.Cusack, P.Donohue, E.Carolan.
DERRY: John Murphy, Eddie Kealey, Hugh Francis Gribben, Tommy Doherty, Mickey Gribben, Harry Cassidy, Frank Stinson, Jim McKeever, Patsy Breen, Francie Niblock, Tommy J.Doherty, Emmett Fullen, Charlie Higgins, Roddy Gribben (c), Colm Mulholland.

1956 TYRONE: Thady Turbett, Brian McSorley, Jim Devlin, Pat Donaghy, Sean Donnelly, Paddy Corey, JJ O'Hagan, Jody O'Neill (c), Pat Devlin, Iggy Jones, Jackie Taggart, Frankie Donnelly, Mickey Kerr, Frank Higgins, Donal Donnelly. *Sub*: Hughie Kelly for Kerr.
CAVAN: S.Morris, N.O'Reilly, P.Brady (c), B.Reilly, H.Gaffney, J.McDonnell, Donal Kelly, Con Smith, B.Gallagher, T.Hardy, P.Carolan, Charlie Gallagher, Sean Keogan, V.Sherlock, Tommy White. Subs: G.Keyes for Smith, James Brady for White.

1957 TYRONE: T.Turbett, B.McSorley, J.Devlin, P.Donaghy, Pat Devlin, Eddie Devlin (c), Joe O'Hagan, J.O'Neill, Mick Cushanan, D.Donnelly, J.Taggart, Mick McIlkenny, S.Donnelly, F.Higgins, F.Donnelly.
DERRY: Patsy Gormley, Patsy McLarnon, H.F.Gribben, T.Doherty, Gabriel Muldoon, J.McKeever (c), Peter Smith, P.Breen, Owen Gribben, Sean O'Connell, R.Gribben, E.Fullen, Willie Cassidy, T.J.Doherty, Seamus Young.

1958 DERRY: P.Gormley, P.McLarnon, H.F.Gribben, T.Doherty, P.Breen, C.Mulholland, P.Smith, J.McKeever (c), Phil Stuart, S.O'Connell, Brendan Murray, Denis McKeever, Leo O'Neill, O.Gribben, C.Higgins.
DOWN: Eamon McKay, Kevin O'Neill, Leo Murphy, Pat Rice, Patsy O'Hagan, Jim McCartan, Kevin Mussen (c), Jarlath Carey, Tony Hadden, Kieran Denvir, Paddy Doherty, Ronnie Moore, Sean Fearon, Jim Fitzpatrick.

1959 DOWN: E.McKay, George Lavery, L.Murphy, P.Rice, K.Mussen (c), J.McCartan, K.O'Neill, Joe Lennon, P.O'Hagan, Sean O'Neill, J.Carey, P.Doherty, K.Denvir, T.Hadden, Brian Morgan.
Subs - Dan McCartan for S.O'Neill, S.O'Neill for Denvir.
CAVAN: Brian O'Reilly, N.O'Reilly, Gabriel Kelly, Mickey Brady, H.Gaffney, T.Maguire (c), J.McDonnell, Hugh Barney O'Donoghue, Kieran McIntyre, Con Smith, B.Gallagher, Seamus Conaty, Jimmy Sheridan, C.Gallagher, J.Brady. Subs: Jimmy Meehan for N.O'Reilly, Tommy Galligan for Maguire, Maguire for Galligan.

1960 DOWN: E.McKay, G.Lavery, L.Murphy, P.Rice, K.Mussen (c), D.McCartan, K.O'Neill, P.J.McElroy, J.Lennon, S.O'Neill, J.McCartan, P.Doherty, T.Hadden, P.O'Hagan, B.Morgan.
Subs: J.Carey for McElroy, Eamon Lundy for Lennon.
CAVAN: B.O'Reilly, J.Meehan, D.Kelly, M.Brady, H.Gaffney, T.Maguire, T.Galligan, H.B.O'Donoghue, J.McDonnell (c), J.Sheridan, Mal Shiels, Con Smith, S.Conaty, J.Brady, C.Gallagher. Sub: P.Carolan for Sheridan.

1961 DOWN: E.McKay, G.Lavery, L.Murphy, P.Rice, K.Mussen (c), D.McCartan, John Smith, P.J.McElroy, J.Lennon, S.O'Neill, J.Carey, P.Doherty, T.Hadden, P.O'Hagan, B.Morgan.
Sub: J.McCartan for Mussen, K. O'Neill for Lavery.
ARMAGH: Eamon McMahon, Hughie Casey, Felix McKnight, Brendan Donaghy, Des Harney, Dan Kelly, Harry Hoy (c), John McGeary, Gene Larkin, Jimmy Whan, Danny McRory, Kevin Halfpenny, Bertie Watson, Pat Campbell, Harry Loughran.
Subs: John McKnight for Harney, Pat McKenna for Campbell, Campbell for Loughran.

1962 CAVAN: Sean Og Flood, G.Kelly, P.J.McCaffrey, M.Brady, Tony Morris, T.Maguire, J.McDonnell (c), Ray Carolan, Tom Lynch, C.Smith, H.B.O'Donoghue, Jimmy Stafford, Seamus McMahon, C.Gallagher, J.Brady. Sub: P.J.O'Gorman for Kelly.
DOWN: E.McKay, G.Lavery, L.Murphy, P.Rice, Pat Hamill, D.McCartan, P.O'Hagan, J.Carey, J.Lennon, S.O'Neill, J.McCartan, P.Doherty (c), T.Hadden, P.J.McElroy, B.Morgan.
Subs: Gerry McCashin for McKay, K.O'Neill for Hamill, K.Mussen for Carey.

1963 DOWN: Patsy McAlinden, G.Lavery (c), L.Murphy, P.Rice, P.O'Hagan, D.McCartan, J.Smith, J.Lennon, T.Hadden, S.O'Neill, J.McCartan, P.Doherty, B.Morgan, B.Johnston, Val Kane. *Subs:* Jackie Fitzsimons for Morgan, K. O'Neill for Doherty.
DONEGAL: Seamus Hoare, Finn Gallagher, Bernard Brady, Brendan McFeely, Sean O'Donnell, John Hannigan, Paul Kelly, Frankie McFeely, P.J.Flood, Donal Breslin, Sean Ferriter (c), Des Houlihan, Cormac Breslin, Mick Griffen, Harry Laverty. Sub: Paddy Ward.

1964 CAVAN: P.J.Gorman, G.Kelly, P.J.McCaffrey, T.Morris, Frank Kennedy, T.Maguire (c), J.McDonnell, R.Carolan, T.Lynch, J.J.O'Reilly, H.B.O'Donoghue, C.Gallagher, Mattie Cahill, Jimmy O'Donnell, J.Stafford. Sub: Peter Pritchard.
DOWN: P.McAlinden, G.Lavery (c), L.Murphy, K.O'Neill, P.O'Hagan, Tom O'Hare, P.Hamill, Larry Powell, D.McCartan, B.Johnston, J.Lennon, P.Doherty, S.O'Neill, J.McCartan, V.Kane.
Subs: J.Fitzsimons for Lavery, B.Morgan for O'Hare.

1965 DOWN: P.McAlinden, Seamus Doyle, L.Murphy, T.O'Hare, J.Lennon, D.McCartan, P.O'Hagan, George Glynn, L.Powell, Felix Quigley, V.Kane, P.Doherty, J.Fitzsimmons, S.O'Neill (c), B.Johnston. Sub: Colm Curtis for Powell.
CAVAN: John Reilly, G.Kelly, Tony Keyes, T.Morris, Brian Kennedy, T.Maguire (c), Donal O'Grady, R.Carolan, T.Lynch, John Joe O'Reilly, J.O'Donnell, C.Gallagher, S.McMahon, Danny Brady, Phil Murray.

1966 DOWN: P.McAlinden, S.Doyle, L.Murphy, T.O'Hare, Tom Morgan, D.McCartan (c), J.Lennon. F.Quigley, G.Glynn, J.Fitzsimmons, L.Powell, B.Johnston, P.Doherty, J.McCartan, S.O'Neill. Subs: Colm McAlarney for Quigley, Francie Doherty for Fitzsimmons,
DONEGAL: S.Hoare, F.Gallagher, B.Brady, P.Kelly, S.O'Donnell, P.J.Flood, Anton Carroll, Declan O'Carroll, Sean Ferriter, Mickey McLoone (c), F.McFeely, M.Griffen, D.Houlihan, J.Hannigan, Pauric McShea. Subs: B.McFeely for Gallagher, Brian McEniff for O'Donnell.

1967 CAVAN: Seamus Gallagher, Andy McCabe, G.Kelly, P.Pritchard, Pat Tinnelly, R.Carolan, Brendan Murtagh, Brendan Donoghue, T.Lynch, Steve Duggan, J.J.O'Reilly, Michael Greenan, J.O'Donnell, C.Gallagher (c), P.Murray.
DOWN: P.McAlinden, Brendan Sloan, L.Murphy, T.O'Hare, Ray McConville, D.McCartan (c), L.Powell, G.Glynn, J.Lennon, John Murphy, C.McAlarney, John Purdy, J.McCartan, S.O'Neill, V.Kane. Subs: Ray Carville for Murphy, J.Fitzsimmons for Kane, Brian McVeigh for Sloan.

1968 DOWN: Danny Kelly, B.Sloan, D.McCartan, T.O'Hare, R.McConville, Willie Doyle, J.Lennon (c), C.McAlarney, Jim Milligan, Mickey Cole, Dickie Murphy, J.Murphy, P.Doherty, S.O'Neill, J.Purdy.
CAVAN: Pat Lyons, G.Kelly, B.Donoghue, P.Pritchard, P.Tinnelly, T.Lynch, A.McCabe, Fergus McCauley, Hugh Newman, M.Greenan, J.J.O'Reilly, P.Murray, J.O'Donnell, C.Gallagher (c), S.Duggan. Sub: B.Murtagh for Newman.

1969 CAVAN: Paddy Lyons, G.Kelly, B.Donoghue, A.McCabe, P.Tinnelly, T.Lynch, Enda McGowan, R.Carolan, H.Newman, S.Duggan, J.J.O'Reilly, Hugh McInerney, Gene Cusack, Declan Coyle, C.Gallagher (c).
DOWN: D.Kelly, B.Sloan, D.McCartan, T.O'Hare, R.McConville, W.Doyle, J.Lennon, C.McAlarney, J.Milligan, M.Cole, J.Murphy, J.Fitzsimons, Peter Rooney, S.O'Neill (c), P.Doherty. Sub: James Morgan.

1970 DERRY: Seamus Hasson, Mick McGuckin, Henry Diamond, Tom Quinn, Malachy McAfee, Colm Mullan, Gerry O'Loughlin, Larry Diamond, Seamus Lagan, S.O'Connell (c), Mickey Niblock, Eamonn Coleman, Adrian McGuckin, Brian Devlin, Hugh Niblock. Subs: Anthony McGurk for Mullan, Seamus Gribben for H.Niblock.
ANTRIM: Ray McIlroy, Eamonn Grieve, John Burns, Jimmy Ward, Seamus Killough, Billy Millar, Des McNeill, Tony McAtamney (c), Frank Fitzsimmons, Gerry McCann, Gerry McCrory, Terry Dunlop, Andy McCallin, Owen Ruddy, Aidan Hamill. Subs: Alistair Scullion for Killough, Gerry Dillon for Millar.

1971 DOWN: D.Kelly, B.Sloan, D.McCartan, T.O'Hare, R.McConville, Maurice Denvir, Cecil Ward, Dan Connolly, Donal Gordon, J.Murphy,

C.McAlarney (c), J.Morgan, Mickey Cunningham, S.O'Neill, Donal Davey. Sub: M.Cole for Morgan.
DERRY: S.Hasson, M.McGuckin, H.Diamond, T.Quinn, Peter Stevenson, H.Niblock, G.O'Loughlin, L.Diamond, S.Gribben, S.O'Connell (c), A.McGurk, Johnnie O'Leary, A.McGuckin, M.Niblock, E.Coleman. Subs: M.McAfee for H.Niblock, Mickey P.Kelly for Quinn, Tom McGuinness for S.Gribben.

1972 DONEGAL: Alan Kane, Donal Monaghan, P.McShea, John Boyce, B.McEniff, Anthony Gallagher, A.Carroll, Seamus Bonner, F.McFeely (c), Martin Carney, Mick McMenamin, D.O'Carroll, Seamie Granaghan, Mick Sweeney, Joe Winston. *Subs:* J.Hannigan for O'Carroll, Andy Curran for Boyce.
TYRONE: Kieran Harte, Ollie Nugent, Peter Mulgrew (c), Jackie Duffy, Michael John Forbes, Gerry Taggart, Mickey Hughes, Brendan Dolan, Seamus Donaghy, Patsy Hetherington, Sean McElhatton, Paddy McMahon, Hugh Crawford, Kevin Teague, John Early. Subs: Paddy Parke for Teague, Frank McGuigan for Crawford.

1973 TYRONE: Liam Turbett, G.Taggart, P.Mulgrew, Barney McAnespie, Joe McElroy, Michael Jordan, M.Hughes, F.McGuigan (c), Aidan McMahon, S.Donaghy, Pat King, P.Hetherington, S.McElhatton, Brendan Donnelly, K.Teague. Subs: J.Early for McMahon, P.McMahon for Early, H.Crawford for Donaghy.
DOWN: Macartan Bryce, Peter Hamill, D.McCartan, T.O'Hare, John Brown, W.Doyle, R.McConville, C.McAlarney, D.Gordon, D.Davey, P.Rooney, M.Cole (c), Eugene Cole, S.O'Neill, Willie Walsh. Subs: J.Murphy for M.Cole, Colm Shields for Walsh, B.Sloan for Gordon.

1974 DONEGAL: A.Kane, D.Monaghan, P.McShea (c), A.Curran, B.McEniff, A.Gallagher, Finian Ward, Michael Lafferty, M.Carney, S.Granaghan, Hugh McClafferty, Neilly Gallagher, J.Winston, S.Bonner, Kieran Keeney. Subs: Paul McGettigan for Keeney, Michael Carr for Granaghan, PJ McGowan for Lafferty.
DOWN: Joe O'Hare, B.Sloan, D.McCartan, P.Hamill, Cathal Digney, Mark Turley, Martin Slevin, Clem Stewart, P.Rooney (c), C.McAlarney, M.Cunningham, C.Ward, Peter McGrath, S.O'Neill, W.Walsh. Subs: Bill Gardner for Stewart, Eugene Grant for Walsh.
Replay Changes: Donegal: Noel McCole for Kane, M. Carr for Keeney. Subs: P.McGettigan for Lafferty, Gerry McElwee for McClafferty, K.Keeney for Carr. Down: D.Gordon for C.Stewart. Subs: B.Gardner for Walsh, E.Grant for McGrath, C.Stewart for McAlarney.

1975 DERRY: John Somers, M.McAfee, T.Quinn, Gabriel Bradley, P.Stevenson (c), A.McGurk, G.O'Loughlin, Eugene Laverty, T.McGuinness, Brendan Kelly, Mickey Lynch, Gerry McElhinney, J.O'Leary, S.O'Connell, Mickey Moran. Subs: Seamus Lagan for McAfee, Kevin Teague for Lagan, H.Niblock for McElhinney.
DOWN: Lawrence McAlinden, B.Sloan, D.McCartan, Paddy Galbraith, P.Hamill, C.Digney, M.Slevin, C.McAlarney, Dan Connolly, J.Murphy, P.Rooney, J.Morgan, M.Cunningham (c), S.O'Neill, W.Walsh. Subs: M.Turley for Walsh, D.Gordon for Connolly, Barry Fitzsimmons for Digney.

1976 DERRY: J.Somers, Liam Murphy, T.Quinn,

P.Stevenson (c), G.O'Loughlin, A.McGurk, M.Moran, T.McGuinness, Colm McGuigan, B.Kelly, M.Lynch, J.O'Leary, Fintan McCluskey, A.McGuckin, G.McElhinney. Subs: L.Diamond for McGuigan, Christy Grieve for McCloskey.
CAVAN: Aidan Elliott, P.Tinnelly (c), Dermot Dalton, E.McGowan, Sean Leddy, Frankie Dolan, Pat McGill, Ollie Leddy, Donal Meade, Noel Smith, Ollie Brady, Owen Martin, G.Cusack, Kieran O'Keeffe, S.Duggan. Sub: Adge King for Smith.
Replay changes: Derry: L.Diamond for McGuigan, Grieve for McGuckin. Subs: E.Laverty for Diamond, S.O'Connell for Grieve, G.Bradley for O'Loughlin.
Cavan: E.McGowan (c), John Dwyer for Smith. Subs: Garrett O'Reilly for Dalton, John Joe Martin for McGill, Jimmy Carroll for S.Leddy, Adge King for Cusack.
1977 ARMAGH: Brian McAlinden, Denis Stevenson, Jim Finnegan, Jim McKerr, Kevin Rafferty, Tom McCreesh, Joey Donnelly, Colm McKinstry, Joe Kernan, Larry Kearns, Jimmy Smyth (c), Noel Marley, Peter Loughran, Paddy Moriarty, Peter Trainor. Subs: Eamon O'Neill for Trainor, Sean Daly for Marley, Frank Toman for Rafferty.
DERRY: J.Somers, L.Murphy, Frank Trainor, Gerry Forrest, G.O'Loughlin, A.McGurk (c), G.Bradley, E.Laverty, C.McGuigan, T.McGuinness, M.Lynch, Terence McWilliams, Gerry Keane, G.McElhinney, P.Stevenson.
1978 DOWN: Martin McCabe, B.Sloan, M.Turley, Michael Sands, C.Digney, Brendan Toner, John McCartan, C.McAlarney (c), Liam Austin, B.Gardner, M.Cunningham, Ronnie Matthews, Joe Byrne, P.Rooney, Jarlath Digney. Subs: Emmett McGivern for Matthews, Tommy McGovern for Toner, Pat Murtagh for McCartan.
CAVAN: A.Elliott, F.Dolan, D.Dalton, J.J.Martin, D.Meade, O.Brady, E.McGowan (c), A.King, O.Martin, Tony Brady, Paddy McNamee, Ray Cullivan, O.Leddy, Donal Donohue, Mark Goldrick. Subs: K.O'Keeffe for King, S.Leddy for Cullivan.
1979 - MONAGHAN: Paddy Linden, Nudie Hughes, Sean Hughes, Fergus Caulfield, Paddy Kerr, Sean McCarville, Eamonn Tavey, Gerry McCarville, Hugo Clerkin, Gene Finnegan, Dessie Mulligan, Kevin Trainor, Kieran Finlay, Tom Moyna, Brendan Brady (c). Subs: Anthony McArdle for Finnegan, PJ Finlay for Trainor.
DONEGAL: N.McCole, Michael Heuston, Martin Griffen, Sandy Harper, M.Carr, F.Ward (c), Martin Sweeney, M.Lafferty, Michael Gallagher, K.Keeney, S.Bonnar, Brendan Dunleavy, Jim Brennan, Fionn McDonnell, Seamus Flynn. Subs: Eugene Sharkey for Dunleavy, H.McCafferty for Gallagher, Seamus Reilly for Brennan.
1980 ARMAGH: B.McAlinden, Brian Canavan, J.McKerr, K.Rafferty, P.Moriarty (c), Jim McCorry, J.Donnelly, C.McKinstry, J.Kernan, N.Marley, J.Smyth, Fran McMahon, Sean Devlin, Brian Hughes, P.Loughran. Subs: Hank Kernan for Devlin, Denis McCoy for Marley.
TYRONE: Barry Campbell, Ciaran McGarvey, Frank Rafferty, Kieran McRory, Kevin McCabe (c), Sean Donnelly, P.King, Patsy Kerlin, Kevin Toner, P.Hetherington, G.Taggart, Damien O'Hagan, Paul Donnelly, Eugene McKenna, Mickey Harte. Subs: Seamus Daly for P.Donnelly, Willie McKenna for Toner.

1981 DOWN: Pat Donnan, Adrian McAulfield, Paddy Kennedy, T.McGovern (c), Ned King, B.Toner, M.Turley, L.Austin, Paddy O'Rourke, Damien Morgan, Ambrose Rodgers, Greg Blaney, Brendan McGovern, John McCartan, Jim McCartan. Subs: C.McAlarney for Jim McCartan, Ned Toner for McAlarney.
ARMAGH: B.McAlinden, Denis Stevenson, J.McKerr, Joe Murphy, P.Moriarty, Des Mackin, J.Donnelly, C.McKinstry (c), F.McMahon, S.Devlin, J.Smyth, Peter Rafferty, Jim Loughran, B.Hughes, P.Loughran. Subs: J.McCorry for Murphy, Martin Murphy for Devlin, J.Kernan for Mackin.
1982 ARMAGH: B.McAlinden, D.Stevenson, J.McKerr, J.Murphy, N. Marley, P.Moriarty, P.Rafferty, C.McKinstry (c), F.McMahon, Dermot Dowling, B.Hughes, Aidan Short, S.Devlin, John Corvan, Mickey McDonald. Subs: J.Donnelly for Murphy, J.Kernan for McDonald, P.Loughran for Short.
FERMANAGH: Peter Greene, Donald Fee, Ciaran Campbell, Niall Corrigan, John Mohan, Pat McCann, Michael Sheridan, Peter McGinnity, Philip Courtney, Arthur McCaffrey (c), Aidan Jones, Brendan O'Reilly, Paul McKenna, Dominic Corrigan, Arthur Mulligan. Subs: Gerry McIlroy for Mulligan, Ken McPartland for O'Reilly.
1983 DONEGAL: N.McCole, Des Newton, M.Griffen, Tommy McDermott, B.Dunleavy, M.Lafferty (c), M.Carr, P.McGettigan, Anthony Molloy, Donal Reid, Martin McHugh, Joyce McMullan, Pauric Carr, S.Bonnar, K.Keeney. Sub: Frank Rushe for McHugh.
CAVAN: Damien O'Reilly, Eugene Kiernan, Jim McAweeney, F.Dolan, T.Brady, Joe Dillon, Jim Reilly (c), A.King, Danny Finnegan, D.Donohue, Michael Faulkner, R.Cullivan, Martin Lynch, Derek McDonnell, P.McNamee. Subs: Brian O'Grady for Brady, Stephen King for A.King.
1984 TYRONE: Aidan Skelton, F.Rafferty, C.McGarvey, S.Donnelly, K.McCabe, Hugh O'Hagan, Noel McGinn, E.McKenna (c), Plunkett Donaghy, Colm Donaghy, D.O'Hagan, P.Kerlin, S.Daly, F.McGuigan, Paddy O'Neill. Sub: John Lynch for C.Donaghy.
ARMAGH: B.McAlinden, J.Donnelly, Thomas Cassidy, J.McCorry, Kieran McNally, Colin Harney, B.Canavan, C.McKinstry, F.McMahon, Tommy Coleman, J.Kernan, Ger Houlihan, J.Corvan, P.Moriarty (c), P.Rafferty. Subs: J.McKerr for McKinstry, D.Stevenson for Cassidy, B.Hughes for Rafferty.
1985 MONAGHAN: P.Linden, Gene Sherry (c), G.McCarville, F.Caulfield, Brendan Murray, Ciaran Murray, Declan Flanagan, David Byrne, H.Clerkin, Ray McCarron, Michael O'Dowd, B.Brady, Eamon McEneaney, Eamonn Murphy, N.Hughes.
DERRY: John Mackle (c), Ciaran Keenan, Tony Scullion, Hugh Martin McGurk, Paddy Mackle, Brendan McPeake, Joe Irwin, Plunkett Murphy, Damien Barton, Dermot McNicholl, Eddie McElhinney, Declan McNicholl, Damien Cassidy, Brian Kealey, Terence McGuckian.
Subs: Tom Doherty for McElhinney, Eunan Rafferty for Cassidy, Paul McCormack for Declan McNicholl.
1986 TYRONE: A.Skelton, S.Donnelly, C.McGarvey, J.Lynch, K.McCabe, N.McGinn, Joe Mallon, P.Donaghy, Harry McClure, Mickey McClure,

E.McKenna (c), Sean McNally, Stephen Rice, D.O'Hagan, Mickey Mallon. Subs: Pat McKeown for Donnelly, Stephen Conway for Lynch, Enda Kilpatrick for Rice.

DOWN: P.Donnan, A.McAulfield, P.Kennedy, Barry Breen, Peter Walsh, P.O'Rourke, Ross Carr, L.Austin (c), John McCartan, Mickey Linden, G.Blaney, Tony McArdle, John Traenor, A.Rodgers, Brendan Mason. Subs: Brian Conlon for McArdle, Francie McKibben for Traenor, John Trainor for O'Rourke.

1987 DERRY: Damien McCusker, H.M.McGurk, Danny Quinn, T.Scullion, P.McCormack, J.Irwin, Paul McCann, P.Murphy (c), Brian McGilligan, Enda Gormley, Dermot McNicholl, D.Barton, D.Cassidy, B.Kealey, Kevin McWilliams. Sub: John McGurk for McWilliams.

ARMAGH: B.McAlinden (c), Vinny Loughran, T.Cassidy, J.McCorry, B.Canavan, K.McNally, A.Short, Kieran McGurk, Martin McQuillan, Neil Smyth, Paul Grimley, G.Houlihan, Shane Skelton, Denis Seeley, Jim McConville. Subs: J.McKerr for Grimley, D.McCoy for Smyth, J.Kernan for Seeley.

1988 MONAGHAN: P.Linden, Gerard Hoey, G.Sherry, Brendan Murray, C.Murray (c), Declan Loughman, D.Flanagan, Bernie Murray, D.Byrne, R.McCarron, G.McCarville, Owen Hamilton, N.Hughes, E.McEneaney. Sub: E.Murphy for Hamilton.

TYRONE: A.Skelton, S.Donnelly, C.McGarvey, Raymond Munroe, J.Lynch, N.McGinn, Paddy Ball, P.Donaghy (c), H.McClure, K.McCabe, E.McKenna, S.Conway, D.O'Hagan, P.Kerlin, Paudge Quinn. Subs: Paul Byrne for Munroe, S.McNally for Quinn, M.McClure for Kerlin.

1989 TYRONE: A.Skelton, J.Mallon, C.McGarvey, R.Munroe, Seanie Meyler, E.Kilpatrick, John McGoldrick, P.Donaghy (c), H.McClure, Ciaran Corr, D.O'Hagan, S.Conway, K.McCabe, E.McKenna, P.Quinn. Subs: N.McGinn for Meyler, M.McClure for Quinn, P.Kerlin for McCabe.

DONEGAL: Gary Walsh, John Joe Doherty, John Connors, Brian Tuohy, D.Reid, Martin Gavigan, Martin Shovlin, A.Molloy (c), Michael Gallagher, Charlie Mulgrew, M.McHugh, J.McMullan, Tommy Ryan, Brian Murray, Marty Carlin. Sub: Leslie McGettigan for Carlin.

Replay Changes: Tyrone: S.McNally for McCabe, S.Donnelly for Quinn (Meyler switched to forwards). Subs: K.McCabe for Conway, P.Ball for Mallon.

Donegal: B.Dunleavy for JJ Doherty. Subs: L.McGettigan for Carlin, Paddy Gavigan for Murray.

1990 - DONEGAL: G.Walsh, J.J.Doherty, M.Gavigan, Matt Gallagher, D.Reid, John Cunningham, M.Shovlin, A.Molloy (c), B.Murray, James McHugh, M.McHugh, J.McMullan, Declan Bonnar, T.Ryan, Manus Boyle. Subs: Tony Boyle for Ryan, John Ban Gallagher for Murray, Barry McGowan for Bonnar.

ARMAGH: B.McAlinden, Padraig O'Neill, Gareth O'Neill, B.Canavan (c), Leo McGeary, John Grimley, A.Short, Mark Grimley, N.Smyth, Ollie Reel, John Toner, Martin Toye, J.McConville, K.McGurk, G.Houlihan. Sub: Shane Skelton for Toye.

1991 DOWN: Neil Collins, Brendan McKernan, Conor Deegan, Paul Higgins, John Kelly, P.O'Rourke (c), DJ Kane, B.Breen, Eamonn Burns, R.Carr, G.Blaney, Gary Mason, M.Linden, Peter Withnall, James McCartan. Sub: Michael Quinn for Higgins.

DONEGAL: G.Walsh, J.J.Doherty, Sean Bonnar, Matt Gallagher, D.Reid, M.Gavigan, B.McGowan, B.Murray, Michael Gallagher, M.McHugh, C.Mulgrew (c), J.McMullan, D.Bonnar, T.Boyle, M.Boyle. Subs: Noel Hegarty for S.Bonnar, Pauric Brogan for Murray, J.McHugh for Mulgrew.

1992 DONEGAL: G.Walsh, J.Cunningham, Matt Gallagher, N.Hegarty, D.Reid, M.Gavigan, M.Shovlin, A.Molloy (c), B.Murray, J.McHugh, T.Ryan, J.McMullan, M.McHugh, T.Boyle, D.Bonnar. Sub: B.McGowan for Boyle, Sylvester Maguire for McMullan.

DERRY: D.McCusker, Kieran McKeever, D.Quinn, T.Scullion, J.McGurk, Henry Downey (c), Gary Coleman, B.McGilligan, Dermot Heaney, Anthony Tohill, Dermot McNicholl, D.Cassidy, Declan Bateson, Seamus Downey, E.Gormley. Subs: D.Barton for Tohill, John McErlean for Quinn, Joe Brolly for Bateson.

1993 DERRY: D.McCusker, K.McKeever, T.Scullion, J.McGurk, Fergal McCusker, H.Downey (c), G.Coleman, A.Tohill, B.McGilligan, Brian McCormack, D.Barton, D.Cassidy, Stephen Mulvenna, D.Heaney, E.Gormley. Subs: Dermot McNicholl for Heaney, J.Brolly for Mulvenna, Karl Diamond for McNicholl.

DONEGAL: G.Walsh, J.J.Doherty, Matt Gallagher, B.McGowan, Mark Crossan, Paul Carr, M.Shovlin, Michael Gallagher, B.Murray, J.McHugh, M.McHugh (c), J.McMullan, D.Bonnar, M.Boyle, John Duffy. Subs: Mark McShane for Bonnar, A.Molloy for J.McHugh, M.Gavigan for Michael Gallagher.

Note: Sean O'Neill and Dan McCartan played in fifteen Ulster finals between 1959-75.

4. TOP SCORERS IN ULSTER SENIOR FOOTBALL CHAMPIONSHIPS 1967-93

Year	Player	Score		Year	Player	Score
1967	Charlie Gallagher (Cavan)	0-27			Donal Donohue (Cavan)	0-12
1968	Paddy Doherty (Down)	1-17		1979	Kieran Finlay (Monaghan)	1-18
1969	Gene Cusack (Cavan)	4-6		1980	Patsy Hetherington(Tyrone)	1-11
1970	Andy McCallin (Antrim)	3-14		1981	Eamon McEneaney (Monaghan)	1-17
1971	Sean O'Connell (Derry)	1-18			Brendan McGovern (Down)	1-17
1972	Joe Winston (Donegal)	0-26		1982	John Corvan (Armagh)	1-9
1973	Patsy Hetherington(Tyrone)	0-17			Peter McGinnity(Fermanagh)	1-9
1974	Seamus Bonnar (Donegal)	7-3		1983	Derek McDonnell (Cavan)	4-12
1975	Sean Daly (Armagh)	3-7		1984	Frank McGuigan (Tyrone)	0-19
1976	Brendan Kelly (Derry)	0-25		1985	Eamon McEneaney (Monaghan)	3-16
	Steve Duggan (Cavan)	1-22		1986	Brendan Mason (Down)	3-18
1977	Brendan Kelly (Derry)	2-11		1987	Enda Gormley (Derry)	0-20
1978	Gerry Keane (Derry)	1-9		1988	Stephen Conway (Tyrone)	0-17

1989	Martin McHugh (Donegal)	2-16
1990	Manus Boyle (Donegal)	1-16
1991	Ross Carr (Down)	0-21
1992	Enda Gormley (Derry)	0-26
1993	John Toner (Armagh)	0-23

NB: Paddy Doherty totalled 7-99 (106 points) from 24 games in 1961. He made the Top Five National Charts eight times. Charlie Gallagher topped 100 points in seasons 1965/67, Sean O'Neill did the same in 1968.

5. ULSTER IN THE ALL-IRELAND CHAMPIONSHIP 1911-93

(Semi-final except where marked)

1911	FINAL Antrim 1-2	Cork 6-6	
1912	FINAL Antrim 1-2	Louth 1-7	
1923	Cavan 1-2	Kerry 1-3	
1924	Cavan 1-1	Dublin 0-6	
1925	Cavan 2-3	Kerry 1-7	
1926	Cavan 0-1	Kerry 1-6	
1927	Monaghan 0-2	Kildare 1-7	
1928	Cavan 2-5	Sligo 0-4	
	FINAL Cavan 2-5	Kildare 2-6	
1929	Monaghan 0-1	Kildare 0-9	
1930	Monaghan 1-6	Kildare 1-4	
	FINAL Monaghan 0-2	Kerry 3-11	
1931	Cavan 1-5	Kildare 0-10	
1932	Cavan 0-8	Mayo 2-4	
1933	Cavan 1-5	Kerry 0-5	
	FINAL CAVAN 2-5	Galway 1-4	
1934	Cavan 0-8	Galway 1-8	
1935	Cavan 1-7	Tipperary 0-8	
	FINAL CAVAN 3-6	Kildare 2-5	
1936	Cavan 1-5	Laois 2-6	
1937	Cavan 2-5	Mayo 1-7	
	FINAL Cavan 1-7	Kerry 4-4	
		(R: 1-8 2-5)	
1938	Monaghan 2-3	Galway 2-10	
1939	Cavan 1-1	Meath 1-9	
1940	Cavan 0-8	Kerry 3-4	
1941	Cavan 1-4	Galway 1-12	
1942	Cavan 1-3	Dublin 1-6	
1943	Cavan 1-8	Cork 1-7	
	FINAL Cavan 2-2	Roscommon 2-7	
1944	Cavan 1-3	Roscommon 5-8	
1945	Cavan 1-4	Wexford 0-5	
	FINAL Cavan 0-7	Cork 2-5	
1946	Antrim 0-10	Kerry 2-7	
1947	Cavan 2-4	Roscommon 0-6	
	FINAL CAVAN 2-11	Kerry 2-7	
1948	Cavan 1-14	Louth 4-2	
	FINAL CAVAN 4-5	Mayo 4-4	
1949	Cavan 1-9	Cork 2-3	
	FINAL Cavan 1-6	Meath 1-10	
1950	Armagh 0-6	Mayo 3-9	
1951	Antrim 1-7	Meath 2-6	
1952	Cavan 0-10	Cork 2-3	
	FINAL CAVAN 0-9	Meath 0-5	
1953	Armagh 0-8	Roscommon 0-7	
	FINAL Armagh 1-6	Kerry 0-13	
1954	Cavan 0-7	Meath 1-5	
1955	Cavan 0-5	Kerry 4-7	
		(R: 1-13 2-10)	
1956	Tyrone 0-6	Galway 0-8	

1957	Tyrone 0-7	Louth 0-13	
1958	Derry 2-6	Kerry 2-5	
	FINAL Derry 1-9	Dublin 2-12	
1959	Down 1-4	Galway 1-11	
1960	Down 1-7	Offaly 1-5	
		(R: 1-10 2-7)	
	FINAL DOWN 2-10	Kerry 0-8	
1961	Down 1-12	Kerry 0-9	
	FINAL DOWN 3-6	Offaly 2-8	
1962	Cavan 1-6	Roscommon 1-8	
1963	Down 0-7	Dublin 2-11	
1964	Cavan 0-6	Kerry 2-12	
1965	Down 0-7	Galway 0-10	
1966	Down 1-9	Meath 2-16	
1967	Cavan 0-12	Cork 2-7	
1968	Down 2-10	Galway 2-8	
	FINAL DOWN 2-12	Kerry 1-13	
1969	Cavan 1-10	Offaly 3-18	
		(R: 1-9 0-12)	
1970	Derry 0-10	Kerry 0-23	
1971	Down 2-7	Galway 3-11	
1972	Donegal 2-10	Offaly 1-17	
1973	Tyrone 2-4	Cork 5-10	
1974	Donegal 1-14	Galway 3-13	
1975	Derry 3-8	Dublin 3-13	
1976	Derry 1-10	Kerry 5-14	
1977	Armagh 0-15	Roscommon 0-14	
		(R: 3-9 2-12)	
	FINAL Armagh 3-6	Dublin 5-12	
1978	Down 0-8	Dublin 1-16	
1979	Monaghan 0-7	Kerry 5-14	
1980	Armagh 3-11	Roscommon 2-20	
1981	Down 0-6	Offaly 0-12	
1982	Armagh 1-11	Kerry 3-15	
1983	Donegal 1-11	Galway 1-12	
1984	Tyrone 0-8	Dublin 2-11	
1985	Monaghan 0-10	Kerry 2-9	
		(R: 2-9 1-12)	
1986	Tyrone 1-12	Galway 1-9	
	FINAL Tyrone 1-10	Kerry 2-15	
1987	Derry 0-8	Meath 0-15	
1988	Monaghan 0-6	Cork 1-14	
1989	Tyrone 1-6	Mayo 0-12	
1990	Donegal 1-7	Meath 3-9	
1991	Down 2-9	Kerry 0-8	
	FINAL DOWN 1-16	Meath 1-14	
1992	Donegal 0-13	Mayo 0-9	
	FINAL DONEGAL 0-18	Dublin 0-14	
1993	Derry 0-15	Dublin 0-14	
	FINAL DERRY 1-14	Cork 2-8	

ALL-IRELAND ROLL OF HONOUR

Kerry - 30	Dublin - 21	Galway - 7
Cork - 6	Cavan, Meath, Wexford - 5	Down, Kildare, Tipperary - 4
Louth, Mayo, Offaly - 3	Limerick, Roscommon - 2	Derry, Donegal - 1

Ulster have been in 23 of the 106 finals, winning 11. The attendance of the 1961 final was the biggest ever for a sports event in Ireland: 90,556. Other final attendances were *1960* 87,768; *1968* 71,294; *1977* 66,542; *1986* 68,628; *1991* 65,000; *1992* 64,547, *1993* 64,500.

6. ULSTER TEAMS IN ALL-IRELAND FINALS 1911-93

1911 ANTRIM: Harry Sheehan (c), Hugh Kane, J.Murphy, Paddy Barnes, J.Mulvihill, P.Moylan, P.L.Kelly, J.M.Darby, C.McCurry, J.Fegan, J.Mullan, E.Gorman, J.Healy, John Coburn, W.Manning, P.Meany, W.Williams.

1912 ANTRIM: J.Coburn (c), J.Monaghan, P.Moylan, T.Meany, H.Sheehan, P.L.Kelly, W.Manning, J.Murphy, W.Goggins, L.Waters, J.Mulvihill, E.Ward, J.Mullan, E.Gorman, P.Barnes, M.Maguire, Joe Gallagher.

1928 CAVAN: J.D.Morgan, George Malcolmson, Tom Campbell, Herbie Clegg, Harry Mulvanny, Patsy Lynch, Jack Clarke, Jim Smith (c), Hughie O'Reilly, Willie Higgins, Packie Devlin, James Murphy, Andy Conlon, Willie Young, Sean Farrelly. Sub: Tom Crowe.

1930 MONAGHAN: Paddy Kilroy (c), Tommy Bradley, Tom Shevlin, Joe Farrell, Peter Duffy, Paddy Heeran, Jimmy Duffy, Peter Lambe, Billy Mason, Mickey McAleer, Christy Fisher, Sean O'Carroll, Peter McConnon, Jimmy Sexton, Jim Brannigan. Subs: P.J.Duffy, Joe Finnegan, Pat McGrane.

1933 CAVAN: W.Young, Willie Connolly, P.Lynch, Mick Dinneny, Terry Coyle, J.Smith (c), Packie Phair, H.O'Reilly, Tom O'Reilly, Donal Morgan, P.Devlin, Jack Smallhorn, Vincent McGovern, Louis Blessing, M.J.(Sonny) Magee.

1935 CAVAN: W.Young, W.Connolly, J.Smith, M.Dinneny, Terry Dolan, T.O'Reilly, P.Phair, H.O'Reilly (c), Tom O'Reilly (Mullahoran), D.Morgan, P.Devlin, J.Smallhorn, Paddy Boylan, L.Blessing, M.J.Magee.

1937 CAVAN: W.Young, Eugene Finnegan, J.Smith, M.Denneny, Dan Kerrigan, T.O'Reilly (c), J.J.O'Reilly, Vincent White, Paddy Smith, D.Morgan, P.Devlin, J.Smallhorn, P.Boylan, L.Blessing, M.J.Magee.

1943 CAVAN: Dessie Benson, E.Finnegan, Barney Cully, Peter Paul Galligan, Gerry Smith, T.O'Reilly (c), John Joe O'Reilly, Simon Deignan, T.P.O'Reilly, D.Morgan, P.Smith, Mick Higgins, P.Boylan, Joe Stafford, Harry Rodgers.

1945 CAVAN: Brendan Kelly, T.O'Reilly (c), B.Cully, P.P.Galligan, John Wilson, J.J.O'Reilly, P.Smith, Tony Tighe, S.Deignan, Jack Boylan, Fonsie Cummiskey, T.P.O'Reilly, J.Stafford, Peter Donohue, P.J.Duke.

1947 CAVAN: Val Gannon, Willie Doonan, Brian Reilly, Paddy Smith (Pullamore), J.Wilson, J.J.O'Reilly (c), S.Deignan, P.J.Duke, Phil Brady, T.Tighe, M.Higgins, Columba McDyer, J.Stafford, P.Donohue, T.P.O'Reilly.

1948 CAVAN: D.Benson, W.Doonan, B.Reilly, P.Smith, P.J.Duke, J.J.O'Reilly (c), S.Deignan, P.Brady, Victor Sherlock, T.Tighe, M.Higgins, John Joe Cassidy, J.Stafford, P.Donohue, Edwin Carolan.

1949 CAVAN: Seamus Morris, James McCabe, P.Smith, Owen Roe McGovern, P.J.Duke, J.J.O'Reilly (c), S.Deignan, P.Brady, V.Sherlock, T.Tighe, M.Higgins, J.J.Cassidy, J.Stafford, P.Donohue, E.Carolan.

1952 CAVAN: S.Morris, J.McCabe, P.Brady, Dessie Maguire, Paddy Carolan, Liam Maguire, B.Reilly, V.Sherlock, Tom Hardy, Seamus Hetherton, M.Higgins (c), E.Carolan, J.J.Cassidy, T.Tighe, Johnny Cusack.

1953 ARMAGH: Eamon McMahon, Eugene Morgan, Jack Bratten, John McKnight, Frank Kernan, Pat O'Neill, Sean Quinn (c), Mick O'Hanlon, Malachy McEvoy, Joe Cunningham, Brian Seeley, Bill McCorry, Pat Campbell, Art O'Hagan, Gerry O'Neill. Subs: Gerry Wilson for McMahon, Gerry Murphy for Wilson, Joe O'Hare for Quinn.

1958 DERRY: Patsy Gormley, Patsy McLarnon, Hugh Francis Gribben, Tommy Doherty, Patsy Breen, Colm Mulholland, Peter Smith, Jim McKeever (c), Phil Stuart, Sean O'Connell, Brendan Murray, Denis McKeever, Brian Mullan, Owen Gribben, Charlie Higgins. Subs: Roddy Gribben for Higgins, Leo O'Neill for Mullan, Colm O'Neill for Breen.

1960 DOWN: Eamon McKay, George Lavery, Leo Murphy, Pat Rice, Kevin Mussen (c), Dan McCartan, Kevin O'Neill, Joe Lennon and Jarlath Carey, Sean O'Neill, Jim McCartan, Paddy Doherty, Tony Hadden, Patsy O'Hagan, Brian Morgan. Sub: Kieran Denvir for Lennon.

1961 DOWN: E.McKay, G.Lavery, L.Murphy, P.Rice, P.O'Hagan, D.McCartan, John Smith, J.Carey, J.Lennon, S.O'Neill, J.McCartan, P.Doherty (c), T.Hadden, P.J.McElroy, B.Morgan. Subs: K.O'Neill for Rice and Rice for Lavery.

1968 DOWN: Danny Kelly, Brendan Sloan, D.McCartan, Tom O'Hare, Ray McConville, Willie Doyle, J.Lennon (c), Jim Milligan, Colm McAlarney, Mickey Cole, P.Doherty, John Murphy, Peter Rooney, S.O'Neill, John Purdy. Subs: Larry Powell for Lennon, George Glynn for Powell.

1977 ARMAGH: Brian McAlinden, Denis Stevenson, Tom McCreesh, Jim McKerr, Kevin Rafferty, Paddy Moriarty, Joey Donnelly, Joe Kernan and Colm McKinstry, Larry Kearns, Jimmy Smyth (c), Noel Marley, Sean Devlin, Peter Trainor, Peter Loughran. Subs: Jim Loughran for Donnelly, Sean Daly for Marley, Frank Toman for McKerr.

1986 TYRONE: Aiden Skelton, Joe Mallon, Ciaran McGarvey, John Lynch, Kevin McCabe, Noel McGinn, Paddy Ball, Plunkett Donaghy and Harry McClure, Mickey McClure, Eugene McKenna (c), Sean McNally, Mickey Mallon, Damien O'Hagan, Paudge Quinn. Subs: Stephen Conway for Lynch, Stephen Rice for McKenna, Aidan O'Hagan for Mickey Mallon.

1991 DOWN: Neil Collins, Brendan McKernan, Conor Deegan, Paul Higgins, John Kelly, Paddy O'Rourke (c), DJ Kane, Barry Breen and Eamonn Burns, Ross Carr, Greg Blaney, Gary Mason, Mickey Linden, Peter Withnall, James McCartan. Subs: Liam Austin for Breen, Ambrose Rodgers for Withnall.

1992 DONEGAL: Gary Walsh, Barry McGowan, Matt Gallagher, Noel Hegarty, Donal Reid, Martin Gavigan, John Joe Doherty, Anthony Molloy (c) and Brian Murray, Joyce McMullen, Martin McHugh, James McHugh, Declan Bonnar, Tony Boyle, Manus Boyle. Sub: Barry Cunningham for Murray.

1993 DERRY: Damien McCusker, Kieran McKeever, Tony Scullion, Fergal McCusker, John McGurk, Henry Downey (c), Gary Coleman, Anthony Tohill,

Brian McGilligan, Dermot Heaney, Damien Barton, Damien Cassidy, Joe Brolly, Seamus Downey, Enda Gormley. Subs: Dermot McNicholl for Cassidy, Eamon Burns for S. Downey.

NATIONAL LEAGUE

7. ULSTER IN NATIONAL LEAGUE FINALS 1931-1993

1931	Cavan 1-2	Kerry 1-3	1970	Down 0-10	Mayo 4-7
1933	Cavan 1-6	Meath 0-10	1976	Derry 0-15	Dublin 2-10
1947	DERRY 2-9	Clare 2-5	1983	DOWN 1-8	Armagh 0-8
1948	CAVAN 5-9	Cork 2-8	1985	MONAGHAN 1-11	Armagh 0-9
		(R: 2-11 3-8)	1986	Monaghan 2-5	Laois 2-6
1950	Cavan 0-12	New York 2-8	1990	Down 0-11	Meath 2-7
	Home Final Cavan 2-8	Meath 1-6	1992	DERRY 1-10	Tyrone 1-8
1953	Cavan 0-9	Dublin 4-6	1993	Donegal 0-6	Dublin 0-10
1959	Derry 1-9	Kerry 2-8			(R: 0-9 0-9)
1960	DOWN 0-12	Cavan 0-9			
1961	Derry 1-5	Kerry 4-16		**ROLL OF HONOUR**	
1962	DOWN 2-5	Dublin 1-7		Kerry 14; Mayo 10; Dublin 8; Meath 6; Galway 5;	
1963	Home Final Down 1-5	Kerry 0-9		Down, Cork - 4; New York 3; Derry, Laois - 2;	
1964	Home Final Down 0-7	Dublin 2-9		Cavan, Longford, Monaghan, Roscommon - 1.	
1968	DOWN 2-14	Kildare 2-11		ULSTER TOTAL - 8 from 62.	

8. WINNING ULSTER TEAMS IN NATIONAL LEAGUE FINALS

1947 DERRY: Charlie Moran, Seamus Keenan, Jack Convery, Joe Hurley, John Murphy, Matt (Sonny) McCann, Thomas Ed.McCloskey, Mickey McNaught, Roddy Gribben, Pat Keenan (c), Francis Niblock, Larry Higgins, Paddy McErlean, John Eddie Mullan, Jimmy Cassidy.

1948 CAVAN: D.Benson, W.Doonan, B.Reilly, P.Smith, O.R.McGovern, J.J.O'Reilly (c), S.Deignan, P.J.Duke, P.Brady, T.Tighe, M.Higgins, J.J.Cassidy, J.Stafford, P.Donohue, E.Carolan.

1960 DOWN: E.McKay, G.Lavery, L.Murphy, P.Rice, K.Mussen (c), D.McCartan, K.O'Neill, PJ McElroy, P.O'Hagan, S.O'Neill, J.Carey, P.Doherty, T.Hadden, J.McCartan, B.Morgan. Subs: K.Denvir for Carey, Eamon Lundy for Murphy, Lundy for Hadden.

1962 DOWN: E.McKay, G.Lavery (c), L.Murphy, P.Rice, K.Mussen, P.O'Hagan, K.O'Neill, J.Carey, J.Lennon, S.O'Neill, J.McCartan, P.Doherty, T.Hadden, D.McCartan, B.Morgan. Sub: Pat Hamill for K.O'Neill.

1968 DOWN: D.Kelly, B.Sloan, D.McCartan, T.O'Hare, R.McConville, L.Powell, J.Lennon (c),

J.Milligan, C.McAlarney, M.Cole, P.Doherty, J.Murphy, P.Rooney, S.O'Neill, J.Purdy. Sub: Dickey Murphy for Powell.

1983 DOWN: John McAleavey, Ned King, Tommy McGovern, Mark Turley (c), Paddy Kennedy, Paddy O'Rourke, Brendan McGovern, Liam Austin, Brendan Toner, John McCartan, Donal Bell, Greg Blaney, Mickey Linden, Ambrose Rodgers, Brendan Mason.

1985 MONAGHAN: Paddy Linden, Gene Sherry (c), Gerry McCarville, Fergus Caulfield, Gerard Hoey, Ciaran Murray, Brendan Murray, Hugo Clerkin, David Byrne, Declan Flanagan, Eamonn McEneaney, Bernie Murray, Ray McCarron, Eamonn Murphy, Nudie Hughes.

1992 DERRY: Damien McCusker, Kieran McKeever, Danny Quinn, Tony Scullion, Henry Downey (c), Colm Rafferty, Gary Coleman, Brian McGilligan, Dermot Heaney, Anthony Tohill, Dermot McNicholl, Gary McGill, Joe Brolly, Fergal McCusker, Enda Gormley. Subs: Seamus Downey for McNicholl, John McGurk for Rafferty, Declan Bateson for McGill.

9. ULSTER ALL STARS

1971 Andy McCallin (Antrim), Sean O'Neill (Down).
1972 Brian McEniff (Donegal), Sean O'Neill (Down), Paddy Moriarty (Armagh).
1973 Anthony McGurk (Derry).
1974 Donal Monaghan (Donegal).
1975 Peter Stevenson, Anthony McGurk, Gerry McElhinney (Derry), Colm McAlarney (Down).
1976 None.
1977 Paddy Moriarty, Joe Kernan, Jimmy Smyth (Armagh).
1978 Ollie Brady (Cavan), Colm McAlarney (Down).
1979 Nudie Hughes (Monaghan).

1980 Kevin McCabe (Tyrone), Colm McKinstry (Armagh).
1981 Paddy Kennedy (Down).
1982 Peter McGinnity (Fermanagh), Joe Kernan (Armagh).
1983 Liam Austin, Greg Blaney (Down), Martin McHugh (Donegal).
1984 Eugene McKenna, Frank McGuigan (Tyrone), Dermot McNicholl (Derry).
1985 Ciaran Murray, Nudie Hughes (Monaghan).
1986 John Lynch, Plunkett Donaghy, Eugene McKenna, Damien O'Hagan (Tyrone), Ray McCarron (Monaghan).

1987 Tony Scullion, Brian McGilligan (Derry).
1988 Paddy Linden, Nudie Hughes (Monaghan).
1989 Eugene McKenna (Tyrone).
1990 Joyce McMullen (Donegal),
     James McCartan (Down).
1991 Conor Deegan, Barry Breen, Ross Carr,
     Greg Blaney (Down).
1992 Gary Walsh, Matt Gallagher, Martin Gavigan,
     Anthony Molloy, Martin McHugh,
     James McHugh, Tony Boyle (Donegal),
     Tony Scullion, Anthony Tohill,
     Enda Gormley (Derry).

ALL STAR AWARDS ROLL OF HONOUR
Kerry 74; Dublin 53; Cork 40; Offaly 29; Meath 26;
Galway 18; Roscommon 14; DOWN 12; DONEGAL,
Mayo - 11; DERRY 10; TYRONE 8; ARMAGH, MON-
AGHAN - 6; Kildare, Laois, Sligo - 2;
ANTRIM, CAVAN, Clare, FERMANAGH, Leitrim,
Wicklow - 1.
PROVINCIAL BREAKDOWN - Munster 115;
Leinster 113; ULSTER 56; Connacht 46.
Note: All 9 Ulster counties have had at least one rep-
resentative, only Connacht can also say that. In 1992,
a rule change allowed two outstanding candidates
for one position to both be selected, for example,
Tony Boyle named in the right corner. John Lynch
captained the All Stars in Chicago in 1987. Dermot
McNicholl was the youngest Ulster All Star at the
age of 19 years and 65 days, James McCartan and
Paddy Moriarty were both 20 when they won their
awards. Frank McGuigan was an All Star replacement in 1973 aged 18.

GOALKEEPERS
Paddy Linden
Gary Walsh

RIGHT-CORNER-BACK	FULL-BACK	LEFT-CORNER-BACK
Donal Monaghan	Paddy Kennedy	John Lynch
Nudie Hughes	Conor Deegan	Tony Scullion (2)
	Matt Gallagher	

RIGHT-HALF-BACK	CENTRE-HALF-BACK	LEFT-HALF-BACK
Brian McEniff	Anthony McGurk	None
Peter Stevenson	Paddy Moriarty	
Kevin McCabe	Ollie Brady	
	Ciaran Murray	
	Martin Gavigan	

MIDFIELD	MIDFIELD
Colm McAlarney (2)	Plunkett Donaghy
Joe Kernan	Brian McGilligan
Colm McKinstry	Barry Breen
Liam Austin	Anthony Molloy
Eugene McKenna	

RIGHT-HALF-FORWARD	CENTRE-HALF-FORWARD	LEFT-HALF-FORWARD
Gerry McElhinney	Jimmy Smyth	Greg Blaney
Peter McGinnity	Joe Kernan	Joyce McMullen
Ray McCarron	Eugene McKenna	James McHugh
Ross Carr	Greg Blaney	
Anthony Tohill	Martin McHugh	

RIGHT-CORNER-FORWARD	FULL-FORWARD	LEFT-CORNER-FORWARD
Andy McCallin	Sean O'Neill (2)	Paddy Moriarty
Martin McHugh	Frank McGuigan	Anthony McGurk
Tony Boyle	Eugene McKenna	Dermot McNicholl
	Damien O'Hagan	James McCartan
		Enda Gormley
		Nudie Hughes (2)

10. ALL STAR REPLACEMENTS FROM ULSTER

(Year given is year of tour.)
1972 Brian McEniff, Eamonn Coleman.
1973 Donal Monaghan, Anthony McGurk,
     Frank McGuigan.
1974 Pauric McShea, Brian McEniff,
     Frank McGuigan, Sean O'Neill.
1975 Seamus Bonner, Peter McGinnity,
     Colm McAlarney.
1976 Brendan Sloan, Martin Carney, Sean O'Connell.
1977 John Somers, Anthony McGurk, Ollie Brady,
     Steve Duggan, Frank McGuigan,
     Colm McAlarney.
1978 Brian McAlinden, Enda McGowan,
     Mickey Moran, Peter McGinnity.
1979 Brendan Donnelly, Tommy McGovern,
     Finian Ward.
1980 Patsy Kerlin.
1982 Fran McMahon.
1983 Brian McAlinden, Denis Stevenson,
     John Corvan, Paddy O'Rourke, John McCartan,
     Eugene McKenna, Frank McGuigan,
     Martin McHugh.
1985 Plunkett Donaghy, Joe Kernan, Jim Reilly,
     Eamonn McEneaney.
1987 Ambrose Rodgers, Brian McGilligan.
1988 Jim Reilly, Brendan Mason, Ciaran McGurk,

Nudie Hughes.
1990 Martin McHugh, Donal Reid, Mickey Linden, Jim McConville.
1991 Conor Deegan, Martin Gavigan, Martin Shovlin, John Grimley, Ciaran McGurk, Tony Scullion.

Note: In 1970 an Irish All Stars team was selected through Central Council to play All-Ireland champions Kerry in San Francisco. It was chosen from nine counties. Seven Ulster players were selected - Andy McCabe and Ray Carolan (Cavan), Seamus Lagan (Derry), Sean O'Neill and Colm McAlarney (Down), Brian McEniff and Declan O'Carroll (Donegal). Ulster All Stars Managers - Gerry Fagan (Armagh) 1978, Fr Sean Hegarty (Armagh) 1988, Brian McEniff (Donegal) 1991.

ALL-TIME ALL STAR AWARDS FOR ULSTER

1983 - Jim McCullagh (Armagh)

1986 - Alf Murray (Armagh)

11. AUSTRALIAN TRIPS

1986 - Ulster players - Brian McAlinden, Ciaran Murray, Plunkett Donaghy, Greg Blaney, Eamonn Murphy, Dermot McNicholl, Damien O'Hagan, Brian McGilligan. Jim McDonnell of Cavan was Tour Manager.

1990 - Martin Gavigan, John Grimley, Mark Grimley, James McCartan, Tony Scullion. Sean McCague was Assistant Team Manager.

12. TEXACO FOOTBALLER OF THE YEAR

1958 - Jim McKeever
1960 - Jim McCartan
1961 - Jim McCartan

1968 - Sean O'Neill
1992 - Martin McHugh

13. SENIOR COUNTY TEAM MANAGERS (Some dates are approximate)

ANTRIM - Paddy O'Hara (Player-manager) 1956-57, Sean Gallagher, Harry O'Neill 1960s, Jimmy Ward, Kevin Armstrong, Br Joe McKeever 1970s, Br Laurence Ennis 1980-82, Phil Stuart 1982-83, Frank Fitzsimmons 1983-86, Eamonn Grieve 1986-90, Hugh Murphy 1990-92, PJ O'Hare 1992-

ARMAGH - John Vallely 1953-54, Malachy McEvoy 1955-62, John McBreen 1963, Paddy O'Hara 1965-66, Jimmy Whan 1967-69, Gerry O'Neill 1970-72, Peter Makem, Gerry O'Neill, Fr Sean Hegarty, John Morrison 1974, Gerry O'Neill 1975-81, Peter Makem 1982-83, Fr Sean Hegarty (with Eamonn Coleman) 1983-88, Paddy Moriarty 1988-91, Jim McCorry 1991-

CAVAN - Hughie O'Reilly 1945-57, Simon Deignan 1958-61, Mick Higgins 1962-69, Jim McDonnell 1970-72, Fr Benny Maguire 1973-78, PJ Carroll 1979, Gabriel Kelly 1980-83, Eugene McGee 1983-88, Gabriel Kelly 1988-90, Eamonn Curley 1990-92, PJ Carroll 1992-

DERRY - John L.Fay 1947, Roddy Gribben 1958-59, Jim McKeever 1968-71, Paddy O'Hara 1971-2, Harry Cassidy 1972-74, Frank Kearney 1975-79, Mickey Moran 1980-84, Tom Scullion 1985, Tom Scullion, Jim McKeever and Phil Stuart 1986-88, Tommy Diamond 1989-90, Fr Sean Hegarty 1990, Eamonn Coleman 1991-

DONEGAL - Paddy O'Hara 1960s, Brian McEniff (Player-manager) 1972-76, John Hannigan 1976-77, Sean O'Donnell 1977-80, Brian McEniff 1980-86, Tom Conaghan 1986-89, Brian McEniff 1989-

DOWN - Barney Carr 1959-63, Kevin Mussen, Brian Denvir 1963-64, Paddy O'Hara 1964-65, Gerry Brown 1968, Jackie Fitzsimons 1972- 73, Sean Smith 1973-76, Jackie Fitzsimons 1976-77, James McCartan 1977-79, Gerry Brown 1979-80, Joe Lennon 1980-82, James McCartan 1982-84, Sean Smith 1984-87, Jackie McManus 1987-89, Peter McGrath 1989-

FERMANAGH - Paddy O'Hara 1958-59, John Vesey 1970s, John Donnelly 1974-75, John McElroy 1976-86, Peter McGinnity (Player-manager) 1986-87, Peter Greene 1988-89, PJ McGowan 1990-91, John Vesey 1991, Hugh McCabe 1992-

MONAGHAN - Sean McCague 1977-80, Tony Loughman 1980-83, Sean McCague 1983-86, Fr. McQuaid 1986-87, Sean McCague 1988-89, Paddy Kerr 1990-91, Liam Stirrat 1992, Selection Committee with Sean McCague 1993.

TYRONE - Jody O'Neill 1970-76, Tom McKeagney 1976-78, Jody O'Neill 1978-79, Art McCrory 1980-87, Donal Donnelly 1987-89, John Donnelly 1989-92, Eugene McKenna, Art McCrory, Dessie Ryan 1992-

NB - Most county teams were looked after by a committee of officials up to about 1970.

14. ULSTER IN RAILWAY CUP FINALS

1928	Ulster 2-4	Leinster 1-8		1968	ULSTER 1-10	Leinster 0-8
1936	Ulster 2-3	Connacht 3-11		1970	ULSTER 2-11	Connacht 0-10
1939	Ulster 3-3	Leinster 3-8		1971	ULSTER 3-11	Connacht 2-11
1942	ULSTER 1-10	Munster 1-5		1975	Ulster 0-15	Munster 6-7
1943	ULSTER 3-7	Leinster 2-9		1978	Ulster 0-19	Munster 4-12
1944	Ulster 1-3	Leinster 1-10		1979	ULSTER 1-7	Munster 0-6
1947	ULSTER 1-6	Leinster 0-3		1980	ULSTER 2-10	Munster 1-9
1948	Ulster 2-6	Munster 4-5		1983	ULSTER 0-24	Leinster 2-10 (aet)
1950	ULSTER 4-11	Leinster 1-7		1984	ULSTER 1-11	Connacht 1-7
1956	ULSTER 0-12	Munster 0-4		1988	Ulster 0-12	Leinster 2-9
1960	ULSTER 2-12	Munster 3-8		1989	ULSTER 1-11	Munster 1-8
1962	Ulster 0-11	Leinster 1-11		1990	No Competition	
1963	ULSTER 2-8	Leinster 1-9		1991	ULSTER 1-11	Munster 1-8
1964	ULSTER 0-12	Leinster 1-6		1992	ULSTER 2-7	Munster 0-8
1965	ULSTER 0-19	Connacht 0-15				
1966	ULSTER 2-5	Munster 1-5				
1967	Ulster 0-11	Connacht 1-9				

ROLL OF HONOUR Leinster 22; Ulster 20; Munster 13; Connacht 9; Universities 1.

15. ULSTER RAILWAY CUP WINNING TEAMS

(Note: Christian names and counties can be found under previous appearance.)

1942 Brendan Kelly (Cavan), Eddie McLoughlin (Armagh), Barney Cully, Big Tom O'Reilly, Gerry Smith (Cavan), Jim McCullagh (Armagh), Vincent O'Duffy (Monaghan), Columba McDyer (Donegal), John Joe O'Reilly (Cavan) (c), Kevin Armstrong (Antrim), Alf Murray (Armagh), T.P.O'Reilly (Cavan), Brian Cullen (Tyrone), Simon Deignan (Cavan), Hughie Gallagher (Donegal).

1943 Dessie Benson (Cavan), E.McLoughlin, B.Cully, T.O'Reilly, G.Smith, J.McCullagh, V.O'Duffy, J.J.O'Reilly (c), C.McDyer, K.Armstrong, A.Murray, Paddy Maguire (Derry), Peter McCarney (Monaghan), S.Deignan, H.Gallagher. Sub: Tom McCann (Down).

1947 John O'Hare (Down), Billy Feeney, George Watterson (Antrim), J.McCullagh, Eugene McDonnell (Monaghan), J.J.O'Reilly, S.Deignan, Harry O'Neill, Sean Gallagher, K.Armstrong (Antrim) (c), Mick Higgins (Cavan), Frank Niblock (Derry), Sean Gibson, Brian McAteer, Joe McCallin (Antrim). Sub: Harry Brown (Down).

1950 J.O'Hare, J.J.O'Reilly (c), Mickey Moyna (Monaghan), Paddy Smith, P.J.Duke (Cavan), Pat O'Neill, Sean Quinn (Armagh), Phil Brady (Cavan), Bill McCorry (Armagh), Tony Tighe, M.Higgins, Victor Sherlock (Cavan), K.Armstrong, Peter Donohue (Cavan), Hughie McKearney (Monaghan). Sub: Sean Gallagher (Antrim) for Sherlock.

1956 Seamus Morris, Noel O'Reilly (Cavan), Jack Bratten, John McKnight (Armagh), Kevin Mussen (Down), John Rice (Monaghan), Jim McDonnell (Cavan), Jim McKeever (Derry), Tom Maguire (Cavan) (c), Kieran Denvir (Down), Jackie Taggart (Tyrone), John Cunningham, Pat Campbell (Armagh), V.Sherlock, Roddy Gribben (Derry). Subs: George Lavery, Paddy Doherty (Down).

1960 Thady Turbett (Tyrone), Gabriel Kelly (Cavan), Hugh Francis Gribben (Derry), Pat Rice (Down), Patsy Breen (Derry), T.Maguire, J.McDonnell, Joe Lennon (Down), Jody O'Neill (Tyrone), Sean O'Neill (Down) (c), J.McKeever, P.Doherty, Jimmy Whan (Armagh), James Brady (Cavan), Tony Hadden (Down). Subs: K.Mussen, Patsy O'Hagan (Down).

1963 T.Turbett, G.Kelly, Leo Murphy, P.Rice (Down), P.J.Flood (Donegal), T.Maguire, J.McDonnell (c), Sean Ferriter (Donegal), Ray Carolan (Cavan), S.O'Neill, Frank McFeeley (Donegal), P.Doherty (Down), J.Whan (Armagh), P.T.Treacy (Fermanagh), Brian Morgan (Down). Subs: J.O'Neill, Jim McCartan (Down).

1964 Seamus Hoare (Donegal), G.Kelly, L.Murphy, Bernard Brady (Donegal), Dan McCartan (Down), T.Maguire, J.McDonnell, J.Lennon, S.Ferriter, S.O'Neill, J.McCartan, P.Doherty (c), J.Whan, P.T.Treacy, Frankie Donnelly (Tyrone). Subs: Charlie Gallagher (Cavan), J.O'Neill.

1965 S.Hoare, G.Kelly, B.Brady, Tony Morris (Cavan), D.McCartan, T.Maguire, Paul Kelly, S.Ferriter (Donegal), R.Carolan, Sean O'Connell (Derry), J.O'Neill, P.Doherty, C.Gallagher (c), S.O'Neill, P.T.Treacy. Sub: Joe Carroll (Monaghan).

1966 S.Hoare, P.Kelly, Tom McCreesh (Armagh), Tom O'Hare, Patsy O'Hagan, D.McCartan (Down), P.J.Flood (Donegal), R.Carolan, J.O'Neill, J.Lennon, J.McCartan (c), P.Doherty, C.Gallagher, S.O'Neill, P.T.Treacy. Subs: Tony Morris (Cavan), S.O'Connell.

1968 S.Hoare, G.Kelly, B.Brady, T.O'Hare, J.Lennon (c), D.McCartan, Peter Pritchard, R.Carolan (Cavan), Colm McAlarney (Down), Mickey Niblock (Derry), John J.O'Reilly (Cavan), Neilly Gallagher (Donegal), S.O'Connell, S.O'Neill, C.Gallagher. Sub: Declan O'Carroll (Donegal).

1970 Anthony Gallagher (Tyrone), Andy McCabe (Cavan), T.McCreesh, T.O'Hare, Brian McEniff (Donegal), Malachy McAfee (Derry), Enda McGowan, R.Carolan (Cavan) (c), Tony McAtamney (Antrim), John Murphy (Down), M.Niblock, Steve Duggan, Gene Cusack (Cavan), S.O'Neill, S.O'Connell.

1971 Paul McCarthy (Monaghan), John Burns (Antrim), Henry Diamond (Derry), A.McCabe, B.McEniff, M.McAfee, E.McGowan, R.Carolan, Frank Fitzsimmons (Antrim), S.O'Connell (c), C.McAlarney, M.Niblock, G.Cusack, S.O'Neill, Andy McCallin (Antrim). Subs: Eamonn Coleman (Derry), J.Murphy.

1979 Brian McAlinden, Denis Stevenson (Armagh),

Tommy McGovern (Down), Finian Ward (Donegal), Kevin McCabe (Tyrone), Paddy Moriarty (Armagh), Mickey Moran (Derry), Peter McGinnity (Fermanagh), Liam Austin, C.McAlarney (Down) (c), Joe Kernan (Armagh), Brendan Donnelly (Tyrone), Peter Loughran (Armagh), Peter Rooney (Down), Sean Devlin (Armagh). Subs: Cathal Digney (Down) for Moran, Paddy McNamee (Cavan) for Loughran, Jimmy Smyth (Armagh) for Donnelly.

1980 B.McAlinden, Nudie Hughes (Monaghan), T.McGovern, F.Ward, K.McCabe, P.Moriarty, Sean McCarville (Monaghan), P.McGinnity(c), L.Austin, C.McAlarney, J.Kernan, Eugene Young (Derry), P.McNamee, P.Rooney, P.Loughran. Sub: M.Moran for Loughran.

1983 B.McAlinden, Paddy Kennedy (Down), Gerry McCarville (Monaghan), Joe Irwin (Derry), N.Hughes, P.Moriarty, Jim Reilly (Cavan), L.Austin, Fran McMahon (Armagh), P.McGinnity (c), Greg Blaney, John McCartan (Down), John Corvan (Armagh), Eugene McKenna (Tyrone), Martin McHugh (Donegal). Subs: Paddy O'Rourke (Down) for McCarville, P.McNamee for McCartan, Denis Stevenson (Armagh) for Hughes, McCarville for McHugh.

1984 B.McAlinden, P.Kennedy, G.McCarville, J.Irwin, Michael Carr, Michael Lafferty (Donegal), J.Reilly, L.Austin, E.McKenna (c), P.McGinnity, J.Kernan, G.Blaney, M.McHugh, Frank McGuigan (Tyrone), N.Hughes. Subs: Tommy McDermott (Donegal) for Irwin, F.McMahon for Austin, P.O'Rourke for Carr.

1989 Paddy Linden (Monaghan), Ciaran Hamill (Antrim), Gene Sherry (Monaghan), Tony Scullion, Martin McQuillan (Armagh), Declan Loughman (Monaghan), J.Reilly (c), Plunkett Donaghy (Tyrone), Mark Grimley (Armagh), M.McHugh, E.McKenna, G.Blaney, Joyce McMullan (Donegal), Damien O'Hagan (Tyrone), Jim McConville (Armagh). Subs:

Paul McErlean (Antrim) for McMullan, Anthony Molloy for Donaghy.

1991 Gary Walsh, John Joe Doherty (Donegal), Conor Deegan (Down), T.Scullion (c), M.McQuillan, D.Loughman, Martin Shovlin (Donegal), Brian McGilligan (Derry), P.Donaghy, Adrian Cush (Tyrone), Neil Smyth (Armagh), Declan Bonnar (Donegal), Peter Canavan (Tyrone), G.Blaney, James McCartan (Down). Subs: Dermot McNicholl (Derry) for Cush, Enda Kilpatrick (Tyrone) for Deegan, Ciaran McGurk (Armagh) for Bonnar.

1992 Neil Collins (Down), Matt Gallagher (Donegal), C.Deegan, T.Scullion, M.McQuillan (c), E.Kilpatrick, Barry Breen (Down), Stephen King (Cavan), Pauric Brogan (Donegal), Ross Carr (Down), N.Smyth, A.Cush, Mickey Linden (Down), Tony Boyle (Donegal), Ronan Carolan (Cavan). Subs: B.McGilligan for Brogan, M.McHugh for Cush.

Note: Ulster's most successful period was 1960-71 with eight Railway Cup wins from 11 finals. The first treble came in 1965 when Paddy Doherty scored 11 points in the final. In 1966 Ulster won again with Doherty scoring all of Ulster's 8 points, seven of them from frees. In 1968 three goals from Sean O'Neill and 1-2 by Sean O'Connell secured another title. O'Neill won his eighth winners medal in 1971 and played for Ulster 26 times. Ray Carolan has six winners medals; Jody O'Neill, Paddy Doherty, Tom Maguire and Greg Blaney have five. Colm McAlarney won medals in three different decades. In 1989 Jim McConville of Armagh scored 4-3 in a 4-8 to 0-7 semi-final victory over Connacht. Frank O'Neill, Alf Murray, Barney Carr, Mick Higgins and Jody O'Neill managed Ulster before Sean O'Neill took over from 1976-81. Brian McEniff has been in charge since 1982, the last two managers have been assisted by Art McCrory.

16. Dr McKENNA CUP FINALS 1927-93

Year	Winner	Runner-up	Year	Winner	Runner-up
1927	Monaghan 2-7	Donegal 2-3	1953	Cavan 2-9	Tyrone 1-5
1928	Monaghan 3-6	Antrim 0-6	1954	Derry 1-8	Armagh 2-4
1929	Armagh 4-4	Monaghan 2-7	1955	Cavan 3-6	Derry 0-9
1930	Fermanagh 2-7	Derry 0-3	1956	Cavan 1-9	Donegal 0-9
1931	Armagh 0-9	Fermanagh 0-3	1957	Tyrone 3-12	Derry 1-10
1932	Monaghan 0-7	Armagh 0-3	1958	Derry 2-10	Armagh 0-1
1934	Fermanagh 2-5	Monaghan 1-7	1959	Down 1-7	Monaghan 1-5
1935	Monaghan 1-6	Armagh 1-5	1960	Derry 2-5	Cavan 1-5
1936	Monaghan 2-7	Cavan 1-7	1961	Down 2-10	Monaghan 1-6
1936	Cavan 3-9	Monaghan 0-4	1962	Cavan 0-9	Armagh 0-2
1937	Monaghan 2-8	Armagh 1-9	1963	Donegal 2-8	Cavan 0-5
1938	Armagh 2-8	Cavan 1-1	1964	Down 1-12	Derry 0-2
1939	Armagh 3-8	Antrim 0-4	1965	Donegal w.o.	Cavan
1940	Cavan 3-5	Tyrone 1-4	1966	Antrim 1-10	Tyrone 1-6
1941	Antrim 3-7	Tyrone 2-6 (R, aet)	1967	Donegal 0-12	Down 1-7
1942	Antrim 3-8	Fermanagh 0-8	1968	Cavan 1-10	Down 1-9
1943	Cavan 4-8	Armagh 3-4	1969	Derry 0-14	Tyrone 0-8
1944	Down 2-9	Tyrone 1-2	1970	Derry 0-10	Down 1-4
1945	Antrim 1-10	Down 1-5	1971	Derry 3-6	Down 1-8
1946	Antrim 2-11	Down 2-4	1972	Down 2-13	Derry 1-6
1947	Derry 6-1	Armagh 2-7	1973	Tyrone 0-13	Down 0-5
1948	Monaghan 5-9	Down 0-10	1974	Derry 4-5	Monaghan 2-10
1949	Armagh 1-9	Monaghan 0-3	1975	Donegal 0-14	Derry 2-7
1950	Armagh 2-10	Antrim 1-3	1976	Monaghan 2-11	Armagh 0-8
1951	Cavan 3-5	Antrim 1-8	1977	Fermanagh 1-8	Donegal 1-7
1952	Monaghan 2-7	Armagh 0-7	1978	Tyrone 3-7	Fermanagh 0-15

1979	Monaghan 1-7	Armagh 1-6	1988	Cavan 0-14	Derry 1-8
1980	Monaghan 1-8	Cavan 0-7	1989	Down 3-9	Derry 1-11
1981	Antrim 3-5	Armagh 0-7	1990	Armagh 1-11	Tyrone 0-13
1982	Tyrone 1-7	Cavan 0-8	1991	Donegal	Tyrone
1983	Monaghan 0-9	Down 0-4	1992	Down 1-11	Cavan 0-7
1984	Tyrone 3-7	Donegal 1-4	1993	Derry 2-6	Down 0-7
1985	Donegal 0-13	Cavan 0-8			

ROLL OF HONOUR

1986	Armagh 3-7	Antrim 1-8	Monaghan 12; Cavan 10; Derry 9; Armagh, Down - 8;
1987	Down 2-9	Cavan 1-10	Antrim, Donegal - 6; Tyrone 5; Fermanagh 3.

CLUB FOOTBALL

17. ULSTER CLUB FINALS

1917	Castleblaney 2-5	Derry Sarsfields 2-1	1980	Scotstown 1-4	St Johns 1-3
1968	Bellaghy 0-8	St Josephs, Ballyshannon/Bundoran 0-5	1981	Ballinderry 2-3	Burren 0-5
			1982	St Galls, Belfast 0-15	Roslea 2-5
1969	Bryansford 1-10	Crosserlough 1-9	1983	Burren 1-4	St Galls 0-5
1970	Bryansford 0-6	Newbridge 0-3	1984	Burren 0-10	St Johns 2-2
1971	Bellaghy 1-11	Clann na Gael, Lurgan 0-5	1985	Burren 0-6	Scotstown 1-2
1972	Clann na Gael 0-8	Ardboe 1-3	1986	Castleblaney 0-4	Burren 0-3
1973	Clann na Gael 1-10	St Josephs 0-3	1987	Burren 0-8	Kingscourt 0-6
1974	Clann na Gael 1-7	Trillick 1-4	1988	Burren 0-8	Pearse Og 0-3
1975	St Josephs 3-6	Castleblaney 1-8	1989	Scotstown 2-9	Coalisland 0-5
1976	Ballerin 2-8	Clann na Gael 2-3	1990	Lavey 2-10	Kingscourt 0-4
1977	St Johns, Belfast 2-10	Cavan Gaels 2-2	1991	Castleblaney 0-8	Killybegs 0-6
1978	Scotstown 1-8	St Johns 1-4	1992	Lavey 0-11	Burren 1-5 (R: 0-10 0-10)
1979	Scotstown 0-9	Carrickcruppin 0-8			

18. ULSTER IN ALL-IRELAND CLUB FINALS

1971	Bryansford 2-7	East Kerry 5-9	1979	Scotstown 1-3	Nemo Rangers (Cork) 2-9
1972	Bellaghy 0-15	UCC 1-11	1986	Burren 1-10	Desmonds (Kerry) 1-6
1974	Clann na Gael 1-4	UCD 0-14 (Replay)	1988	Burren 1-9	Clann na Gael (Roscommon) 0-8
	Clann na Gael 1-6	UCD 1-6			
1977	Ballerin 2-7	Austin Stacks (Kerry) 1-13	1990	Lavey 2-9	Salthill (Galway) 0-10
1978	St Johns 1-3	Thomond College, Limerick 2-14			

19. ALL-IRELAND CLUB WINNING TEAMS FROM ULSTER

1972 Bellaghy: Paddy McTaggart, Tom Scullion, Austin Mulholland, Frankie Cassidy, Tommy Diamond, Hugh McGoldrick, Chris Browne, Larry Diamond (c), Peter Doherty, Francis Downey, Brendan Cassidy, Frankie O'Loane, Hugh Donnelly, Tom Quinn, Kevin Cassidy.

1986 Burren: Declan Murdock, Brendan McKernan, Aidan Murdock, Malachy Murdock, Ciaran McConville, Willie McMahon, Brendan McGovern, Tommy McGovern (c), Paddy O'Rourke, Larry Fitzpatrick, John Traenor, Pat McKay, Jim McGreevy, Vincent McGovern, Tony McArdle. Sub: Charlie Doyle.

1988 Burren: D.Murdock, B.McKernan, A.Murdock, M.Murdock, C.McConville, L.Fitzpatrick, B.McGovern, Brian Laverty, T.McGovern, T.McArdle, J.Traenor, P.McKay, Ronan Fitzpatrick, V.McGovern (c), Tom Fegan. Sub: Paul Fegan.

1990 Lavey: Brendan Regan, Damien Doherty, Anthony Scullion, Brian Scullion, John McGurk (c), Henry Downey, Ciaran McGurk, Damien O'Boyle, James Chivers, Fergal Rafferty, Brian McCormack, Hugh Martin McGurk, Don Mulholland, Seamus Downey, Collie McGurk. Sub: Anthony McGurk for Collie McGurk.

MINOR FOOTBALL

20. ULSTER MINOR CHAMPIONSHIP 1930-93

1930	Armagh 3-4	Monaghan 0-10	1938	Cavan 2-7	Armagh 2-4
1931	Tyrone 0-7	Armagh 0-4	1939	Monaghan 1-8	Cavan 1-7
1932	Antrim 2-7	Tyrone 1-2	1940	Monaghan 0-8	Antrim 0-4
1933	Antrim 2-7	Armagh 1-2	1941	Antrim 4-7	Cavan 1-8
1934	Tyrone 1-4	Down 1-3	1942-44		Abandoned.
1935	Void		1945	Monaghan 1-7	Down 0-7
1936	Antrim 2-7	Tyrone 2-4	1946	Tyrone 1-4	Monaghan 0-5
1937	Cavan 1-10	Armagh 0-3	1947	Tyrone 3-6	Armagh 2-3

1948 Tyrone 5-6	Monaghan 2-3	1973 Tyrone 1-13	Down 0-9
1949 Armagh 4-6	Donegal 1-4	1974 Cavan 2-9	Derry 1-4
1950 Antrim 1-9	Armagh 1-1	1975 Tyrone 0-10	Cavan 0-7
1951 Armagh 3-1	Cavan 1-5	1976 Tyrone 5-7	Cavan 1-9
1952 Cavan 1-5	Down 1-3	1977 Down 0-11	Armagh 1-6
1953 Armagh 2-15	Tyrone 3-2	1978 Tyrone 3-11	Monaghan 2-9
1954 Armagh 2-8	Down 0-9	1979 Down 1-5	Tyrone 0-2
1955 Antrim 4-3	Cavan 2-6	1980 Derry 3-14	Armagh 1-2
1956 Donegal 2-5	Armagh 0-6	1981 Derry 0-11	Armagh 1-2
1957 Armagh 3-6	Donegal 0-10	1982 Antrim 2-9	Down 3-5
1958 Down 3-9	Cavan 3-1	1983 Derry 3-9	Monaghan 0-4
1959 Cavan 2-11	Antrim 2-7	1984 Derry 1-14	Armagh 0-3
1960 Down 2-7	Monaghan 1-4	1985 Donegal 2-11	Cavan 1-3
1961 Armagh 3-8	Monaghan 1-4	1986 Derry 1-12	Down 0-10
1962 Down 2-5	Armagh 0-8	1987 Down 1-7	Armagh 0-4
1963 Down 4-6	Donegal 2-11	1988 Tyrone 2-7	Cavan 0-3
1964 Antrim 2-10	Cavan 0-6	1989 Derry 2-15	Armagh 2-3
1965 Derry 3-11	Cavan 2-4	1990 Derry 2-10	Down 2-8
1966 Down 1-12	Derry 1-9	1991 Donegal 1-10	Tyrone 1-9
1967 Tyrone 0-16	Fermanagh 2-5	1992 Armagh 0-13	Donegal 0-9
1968 Armagh 4-8	Derry 1-7	1993 Tyrone 1-9	Derry 1-5
1969 Derry 0-9	Tyrone 0-5		
1970 Derry 1-14	Fermanagh 0-11	**ROLL OF HONOUR**	
1971 Tyrone 0-19	Fermanagh 0-7	Tyrone 14; Derry 10; Armagh 9; Antrim, Down - 8;	
1972 Tyrone 3-6	Cavan 1-6	Cavan 5; Donegal, Monaghan - 3; Fermanagh - 0.	

21. ULSTER IN ALL-IRELAND MINOR FINALS

1937	CAVAN 1-11	Wexford 1-5	1975	Tyrone 0-4	Kerry 1-10
1938	CAVAN 3-3	Kerry 0-8	1977	DOWN 2-6	Meath 0-4
1939	Monaghan 1-7	Roscommon 1-9	1980	Derry 0-11	Kerry 3-12
1947	TYRONE 4-4	Mayo 4-3	1981	Derry 2-7	Cork 4-9
1948	TYRONE 0-11	Dublin 1-5	1983	DERRY 0-8	Cork 1-3
1949	ARMAGH 1-7	Kerry 1-5	1987	DOWN 1-12	Cork 1-5
1951	Armagh 1-5	Roscommon 2-7	1988	Tyrone 0-10	Kerry 1-8
1952	Cavan 1-6	Galway 2-9	1989	DERRY 3-9	Offaly 1-6
1957	Armagh 0-4	Meath 3-9	1992	Armagh 0-10	Meath 2-5
1959	Cavan 1-4	Dublin 0-11			
1965	DERRY 2-8	Kerry 2-4	**ROLL OF HONOUR**		
1966	Down 1-8	Mayo 1-12	Dublin, Kerry - 10; Cork 8; Mayo 6; Galway 5;		
1969	Derry 0-11	Cork 2-7	DERRY, Meath, Roscommon, TYRONE - 3; CAVAN,		
1972	Tyrone 2-11	Cork 3-11	DOWN, Louth - 2; ARMAGH, Clare, Offaly,		
1973	TYRONE 2-11	Kildare 1-6	Tipperary - 1.		

22. ALL-IRELAND MINOR WINNING TEAMS FROM ULSTER

1937 CAVAN: John Joe Brady, Mick Argue, Barney Cully, Tom Cully, Patsy Fay, Patsy Clarke, Mickie O'Reilly, Donal Brady, T.P.O'Reilly, Paddy Conaty, Micheal Farrell, Harry Bouchier (c), P.A. O'Reilly, Patsy McDonnell, Jim McCormack.

1938 CAVAN: Dessie Benson, Willie Doonan, B.Cully, Peter Paul Galligan, M.Reilly, Paddy Coyle, Simon Deignan, Seamus Maguire, Jim McCormack, Kevin O'Reilly, P.Conaty (c), Michael Fitzsimons, Felim Coyle, John Johnson, Peadar Doyle.

1947 TYRONE: Michael Bradley, Liam Campbell, Robert McNulty, Vincent Cullen, Michael Vaughan, Eddie Devlin (c), Mick Cushnahan, Sean McGrath, Jack Poyntz, Harry Hartop, Malachy Dargan, Jackie McConnell, Dan McCaffrey, Tom Sullivan, Paddy Donnelly.

1948 TYRONE: Jimmy McGahern, D.Donnelly, Mal Connolly, Eddie Knox, Louis Campbell, E.Devlin (c), Pat O'Hanlon, S.McGrath, H.Hartop, John O'Reilly, M.Dargan, Barney Eastwood, Leo Devlin, John Joe O'Hagan, Jack Twomey. Sub: Sean Donnelly.

1949 ARMAGH: Liam McCorry, Eddie McCann,

Jack Bratten, John McKnight, Frank Kernan, Brendan O'Neill, Thomas McConville, Eugene Mee, Sean Collins, Tony Connolly, Sean Blaney (c), Joe Cunningham, Sean Smith, Paddy Joe McKeever, Brian McGrane.

Sub: Mickey McKnight.

1965 DERRY: Eugene McCall, Anthony Burke, Tom Quinn, Michael P.Kelly, Colum Mullan, Malachy McAfee, Adrian McGuckin, Tommy Diamond (c), Seamus Lagan, Brendan Mullan, Mickey Niblock, Eamonn Coleman, John Joe Kearney, Seamus McCloskey, Phil Friel.

1973 TYRONE: Barry Campbell, Gerry Goodwin, Martin Lennon, Hugh Mooney, Seamus Gormley, Colm McAleer, Justin O'Doherty, Patsy Kerlin, Dessie McKenna (c), Sean O'Kane, Eugene McKenna, Joe Cunningham, Mickey Quinn, Bosco O'Neill, Kieran Currie. Sub: Seamus Coyne.

1977 DOWN: Pat Donnan, Sean McNulty, Adrian McAulfield, Shane Brunker, Paddy O'Rourke, Michael Sands, Brendan McGovern, John McCartan (c), Paddy Kennedy, Eamonn Toner, Ambrose

Rodgers, Martin McCann, Tommy Bradley, Brendan Loughran, Jarlath Digney. Subs: Emmett McGivern, Francis Rooney.

1983 DERRY: Don Kelly, Patrick O'Donnell, Paul Bradley, Raymond Conway, John McGurk, Brian Kealey, Niall Mullan, Peter Young, Ciaran Barton, Dermot McNicholl (c), Eddie McElhinney, Damien Cassidy, Cathal McNicholl, Eamonn Lynch, Tony McKiernan.

1987 DOWN: Dermot Hawkins, Neil Caulfield, Larry Duggan, Martin McGivern, Mark Quinn (c), Conor Deegan, Collie Mason, Brian McCartan, Pat Hannaway, Cathal Murray, Raphael Haughian. Geoffrey Breen, Ronan Fitzpatrick, Tom Fegan, James McCartan.

1989 DERRY: Martin O'Connor, Jarleth Martin, Paddy McAllister, Gregory Simpson, Barry McGonigle, Gary Coleman (c), Roderick Skelly, John Mulholland, Anthony Tohill, Rory McEldowney, James Lynn, Eamonn Burns, Eunan O'Kane, Dermot Heaney, Declan Bateson. Subs: Karl Diamond and Ryan Murphy.

UNDER-21 FOOTBALL

23. ULSTER UNDER-21 FINALS 1963-93

1963	Donegal 3-6	Cavan 1-3	1981	Monaghan 0-8	Donegal 0-6
1964	Donegal 2-14	Monaghan 0-4	1982	Donegal 0-10	Derry 1-5
1965	Down 0-9	Cavan 1-2	1983	Derry 3-13	Donegal 1-3
1966	Donegal 1-11	Monaghan 1-4	1984	Down 1-10	Antrim 1-8
1967	Derry 1-11	Monaghan 1-4	1985	Down 3-7	Tyrone 0-7
1968	Derry 4-9	Monaghan 2-4	1986	Derry 4-7	Donegal 0-6
1969	Antrim 2-8	Down 1-9	1987	Donegal 1-11	Monaghan 0-8 (R: 0-7 1-4)
1970	Fermanagh 0-13	Cavan 0-8	1988	Cavan 3-10	Antrim 0-6
1971	Fermanagh 2-12	Tyrone 1-8	1989	Antrim 1-6	Down 1-5?
1972	Tyrone 3-13	Derry 1-6 (R: 1-7 1-7)	1990	Tyrone 2-8	Down 0-11
1973	Tyrone 2-14	Monaghan 2-5	1991	Tyrone 3-10	Down 0-8
1974	Antrim 2-6	Tyrone 1-8	1992	Tyrone 0-14	Monaghan 2-6
1975	Antrim 2-7	Tyrone 0-7	1993	Derry 1-9	Down 1-8
1976	Derry 1-6	Down 1-4			
1977	Down 3-5	Cavan 0-10	**ROLL OF HONOUR**		
1978	Down 0-11	Cavan 1-6	Derry, Down, Tyrone - 6; Donegal 5; Antrim 4;		
1979	Down 1-9	Tyrone 0-5	Fermanagh 2; Cavan, Monaghan - 1.		
1980	Tyrone 4-4	Down 2-5			

24. ULSTER IN ALL-IRELAND UNDER-21 FINALS

1968	DERRY 3-9	Offaly 1-9	1983	Derry 1-5	Mayo 1-8 (R: 1-8 2-5)
1969	ANTRIM 1-8	Roscommon 0-10	1985	Derry 1-8	Cork 0-14
1970	Fermanagh 0-9	Cork 2-11	1987	DONEGAL 1-12	Kerry 2-4 (R: 1-7 0-10)
1971	Fermanagh 0-3	Cork 3-10	1988	Cavan 0-9	Offaly 0-11
1974	Antrim 2-8	Mayo 2-10 (R: 0-9 0-9)	1990	Tyrone 2-11	Kerry 5-12
1977	Down 1-5	Kerry 1-11	1991	TYRONE 4-16	Kerry 1-5
1979	DOWN 1-9	Cork 0-7	1992	TYRONE 1-10	Galway 1-7
1982	DONEGAL 0-8	Roscommon 0-5			

25. ALL-IRELAND UNDER-21 WINNING TEAMS FROM ULSTER

1968 DERRY: John Somers, Matt Trolan, Tom Quinn, Michael P.Kelly, Tommy Diamond (c), Malachy McAfee, Gerry O'Loughlin, Tom McGuiness, Seamus Lagan, Eamonn Coleman, Mickey Niblock, John Joe Kearney, Adrian McGuckin, Seamus McCloskey, Kevin Teague.

1969 ANTRIM: Ray McIlroy, Donal Burns, Seamus Killough, Martin McGranaghan, Jim Mullan, Billy Millar (c), Mick Colbert, Liam Boyle, Terry Dunlop, Aidan Hamill, Gerry McCann, Gerry Nellis, Andy McCallin, Gerry Dillon, Din Joe McBrogan. Subs: Gerry Pollock for Colbert.

1979 DOWN: Pat Donnan, Ned King (c), Adrian McAulfield, Michael Sands, Gerry Murdock, Paddy O'Rourke, Brendan McGovern, Paddy Kennedy, Liam Austin, John McCartan, Malachy Burns, Greg Blaney, Peter Donnan, Gervase O'Hare, Jarlath Digney. Sub: Martin McCann for O'Hare.

1982 DONEGAL: Michael Kelly, Michael McBrearty, Sean Bonner, Matt Gallagher, Eunan McIntyre, Tommy McDermott, Brian Tuohy (c), Anthony Molloy, Donal Reid, Martin McHugh, Charlie Mulgrew, Joyce McMullan, Patrick McGroarty. Subs: Pauric Gallagher for Bonner, Sylvester Maguire for McGroarty.

1987 DONEGAL: Danny Gallagher, John Joe Doherty, John Connors, Thomas Maguire, Diarmuid Keon, John Cunningham (c), Paul Carr, Barry Cunningham, John Ban Gallagher, Paddy Hegarty, Tommy Ryan, Barry McGowan, Dermot Ward, Manus Boyle, Luke Gavigan. Subs: Conor White, Joey McDermott. Replay Sub: Seamus Ward.

1991 TYRONE: Cathal Blee, Damien Hagan, Chris Lawn, Fay Devlin, Paul Donnelly, Barry McGinn, Terence O'Neill, Adrian Kilpatrick, Danny Barr, Adrian Cush, Eamonn McCaffrey, Peter Canavan (c),

Ciaran Loughran, Ciaran McBride, Brian Gormley. Subs: Stephen Lawn for Donnelly, Joe Cassidy for Blee.

1992 TYRONE: Brian McConnell, Eamonn Martin, C.Lawn, F.Devlin, S.Lawn, Jody Gormley, Ciaran Hughes, A.Kilpatrick, Seamus McCallin, E.McCaffrey, Colm Donnelly, P.Canavan (c), C.Loughran, C.McBride, B.Gormley. Sub: Michael Slevin for C.Lawn

Note: Peter Canavan scored 2-3 in the 1990 final, 2-5 in the 1991 final and 0-7 in the 1992 final.

JUNIOR FOOTBALL

26. ULSTER JUNIOR FINALS

1915	Cavan 2-3	Antrim 1-3	1952	Donegal 4-5	Tyrone 1-8
1916	Cavan 0-7	Monaghan 0-0	1953	Derry 3-6	Cavan 1-5
1923	Antrim 1-3	Cavan 1-2	1954	Donegal 1-7	Tyrone 0-8
1924	Cavan 3-7	Antrim 2-0	1955	Derry 0-13	Down 0-6
1925	Armagh 2-3	Cavan 2-1	1956	Monaghan 0-10	Cavan 0-2
1926	Armagh 0-3	Tyrone 0-2	1957	Cavan 3-6	Donegal 2-2
1927	Cavan 4-8	Armagh 1-2	1958	Down 0-10	Antrim 2-5
1929	Armagh 3-14	Derry 1-2	1959	Fermanagh 2-13	Antrim 1-4
1930	Donegal (Walk over)		1960	Antrim 1-7	Derry 1-6
1931	Down 1-3	Cavan 0-5	1961	Monaghan 2-8	Antrim 1-6
1932	Cavan 2-5	Down 1-1	1962	Cavan 0-8	Down 0-7
1935	Armagh 3-6	Derry 3-2	1963	Antrim 5-8	Donegal 1-3
1936	Cavan 4-7	Down 4-2	1964	Derry 2-13	Antrim 0-8
1937	Antrim 2-6	Tyrone 1-6	1965	Down 3-8	Derry 2-8
1938	Cavan 2-3	Armagh 2-1	1966	Down 2-6	Monaghan 0-8
1939	Donegal 2-8	Cavan 3-4	1967	Derry 2-8	Cavan 0-4
1940	Cavan 3-5	Antrim 1-6	1968	Tyrone 2-6	Armagh 0-3
1941	Cavan 2-7	Armagh 1-8	1969	Derry 4-9	Down 2-5
1942	Antrim 3-10	Fermanagh 1-6	1970	Antrim 3-8	Donegal 3-5
1943	Fermanagh 3-8	Antrim 2-6	1971	Down 3-10	Fermanagh 1-1
1944	Cavan 0-10	Donegal 0-5	1972	Antrim 3-8	Monaghan 1-6
1945	Derry 4-2	Armagh 0-6	1973-82	Competition Abandoned	
1946	Down 2-5	Donegal 0-7	1983	Tyrone 5-7	Monaghan 1-8
1947	Down 5-4	Derry 0-7	1984	Cavan 2-7	Tyrone 0-10
1948	Armagh 1-12	Antrim 3-2	1985	Armagh	
1949	Down 2-4	Fermanagh 1-3	1986	Tyrone 1-7	Monaghan 0-4
1950	Derry 2-7	Antrim 1-4		Competition abandoned again.	
1951	Armagh 3-6	Down 0-6			

27. ALL-IRELAND JUNIOR FINALS

1926	Armagh 4-11	Dublin 0-4	1955	Derry 1-7	Cork 3-10
1927	Cavan 4-1	Britain 1-1	1956	Monaghan 3-7	London 2-6
1941	Cavan 0-4	Kerry 0-9	1959	Fermanagh 1-11	London 2-4
1946	Down 2-10	Warwickshire 1-9	1969	Tyrone 3-8	London 0-7
1949	Down 3-5	Kerry 3-11			

COLLEGE FOOTBALL

28. SIGERSON CUP FINALS

1959	Queens 0-10	UCD 0-9 (R: 2-7 2-7)	1987	UUJ 0-6	UCC 0-4
1964	Queens 3-5	UCD 0-8	1989	St Marys, Belfast 3-13	UCC 1-5
1971	Queens 0-7	UCC 0-6	1990	Queens 3-8	St Marys 1-9
1982	Queens 0-12	UCG 1-7	1991	UUJ 0-7	UCG 0-6
1986	UUJ 1-8	UCC 1-5	1993	Queens 1-12	St Marys 0-4

29. SIGERSON CUP WINNING TEAMS

1959 QUEENS: John O'Neill (Fermanagh), Christy Mallon (Tyrone), Mick Brewster (Fermanagh), Charlie Murphy (Antrim), Leo O'Neill (Derry), Brendan Donaghy (Armagh), Peter Smith, Phil Stuart (Derry), Hugh O'Kane (Antrim) (c), Tom Scullion (Derry), Frank Higgins (Tyrone), Sean O'Neill (Down), Barney McNally (Antrim), Seamus Mallon, Kevin Halfpenny (Armagh).

1964 QUEENS: Des Sharkey (Antrim) (c), Pat Loughran, Leonard McEvoy (Armagh), Niall McEnhill (Fermanagh), Paddy Diamond (Antrim), James McKinney (Down), Phil McCotter (Derry), Terry Gilmore (Antrim), Jimmy Hughes (Tyrone), Oliver McDonald (Armagh), Gerry McCrory

(Antrim), Jackie Fitzsimmons (Down), Jimmy Beggs (Tyrone), Sean O'Neill (Down), Eamonn Flannigan (Fermanagh). Subs: Pat Catney (Antrim), Austin Cunningham (Armagh), Tom Savage (Louth).

1971 QUEENS: Ciaran Lewis (Armagh), Liam Murphy (Derry), Seamus Killough, Malachy Duffin, Donal Laverty (Antrim), Maurice Denvir (Down), Kevin Stevenson (Armagh), J.J.O'Reilly (Fermanagh), Pat Turley (Down), Paddy Park (c), Kevin Teague (Tyrone), Fionn Sherry (Fermanagh), Martin McAleese (Antrim), Anthony McGurk (Derry), John Rainey (Antrim).

1982 QUEENS: Paddy Mahon (Down), Joe Fearon, Sean Gordon (Armagh), Donagh O'Kane, Gerard Rodgers (Down), Joey Donnelly (Armagh), Martin Small, John McAleenan (Down), Sean McAuley (Antrim), Brian MrErlean (Derry), Dermot Dowling, Aidan Short (Armagh), Seamus Leonard (Fermanagh), Greg Blaney (Down), Donal Armstrong (Antrim). Subs: Eamonn Larkin (Down), Seamus Boyd (Antrim) (c), John Mackle (Derry).

1986 UUJ: Fergal Harney (Armagh), DJ Kane (Down), Martin Lennon (Armagh), Paul Mahon (Down), Barry Young (Derry), Colin Harney (Armagh) (c), Barry Breen (Down), Cahal Glass (Derry), Stephen Conway (Tyrone), Dermot McNicholl (Derry), Ger Houlihan (Armagh), Enda Gormley (Derry), Stephen Rice (Tyrone), Donal Durkan (Down), Cathal McNicholl (Derry). Subs: Mal O'Hare, Mark Bohill (Down), Donal Armstrong (Antrim).

1987 UUJ: Cathal Canavan (Armagh), DJ Kane (c), Padraig O'Neill (Armagh), Seanie Meyler (Tyrone), B.Young, B.Breen, Gary McConville, S.Conway, C.Glass, D.McNicholl, E.Gormley, Declan Canavan (Armagh), Thomas Maguire (Fermanagh), C.McNicholl, Rory Scullion (Derry). Subs: M.Bohill, Peter Young (Derry), Conal Heatley (Antrim).

1989 ST MARYS: Benny Tierney (Armagh), Malachy O'Rourke (Fermanagh), Martin McNally (Antrim), Pascal Canavan (Tyrone), John Rafferty (Armagh), Danny Quinn (Derry), Cathal Murray (Down), John Reihill (Fermanagh) (c) and Jarlath Burns (Armagh), Seamus Downey (Derry), Olly Reel (Armagh), Paddy Barton (Derry), Martin Houlihan (Armagh), Fergal McCann (Fermanagh), Iggy Gallagher (Tyrone). Subs: Conrad McGuigan (Derry)

for Gallagher, Eamonn Shannon (Fermanagh) for Houlihan.

1990 QUEENS: Eamonn Connolly (Down), Shane O'Neill (Armagh), Paul O'Neill (Tyrone), Mark McNeill (Armagh), Fergal Logan (Tyrone) (c), Colm Hanratty (Armagh), Mickey Quinn (Down), Danny Barr (Tyrone), Liam Conneely (Clare), Collie McGurk (Derry), Paul McErlean (Antrim), Damien Devine (Tyrone), Hugh Tohill (Derry), Tony McMahon, James McCartan (Down). Subs: Declan Conlon (Down), Iggy McGowan (Fermanagh), Keith Quigley, Neil Smyth (Armagh).

1991 UUJ: Hugh Fitzpatrick (Fermanagh), Aidan Morris (Tyrone), Gareth O'Neill, P.O'Neill (Armagh), Gary Lyons (Down), Noel Donnelly (Tyrone) (c), Paddy Tinnelly (Down), D.McNicholl, Gerard Colgan (Down), Laurence Strain (Tyrone), Gary Mason, Conor Burns (Down), Brian Carty (Fermanagh), Alan Downey, Collie Burns (Down). Subs: Mark Gallagher (Fermanagh) for Strain, Niall McGuinness (Tyrone) for Downey.

1993 QUEENS: E.Connolly, Gary McGirr (Tyrone), Paddy McGuinness (Fermanagh), Paddy McGeary (Armagh), Stephen Walls (Derry), Ciaran McGeeney (Armagh), Paul Brewster (Fermanagh) (c), Anthony Tohill (Derry), Cathal O'Rourke, Paddy McGeeney (Armagh), Brian McCormack (Derry), Paul McGrane (Armagh), Dennis Holywood (Armagh), Paul Greene (Fermanagh), J.McCartan. Subs: John Hanna (Fermanagh) for Holywood, Paul Burns for McGrane.

Note: Before 1987 the Sigerson Cup was for Universities only. The rules then allowed Division One College teams into the competition, which is when St Marys joined. UUJ first entered in 1985 after they became a University.

SIGERSON MANAGERS: Paddy O'Hara (1958 and 1964), Jimmy Beggs (1971), Sean O'Neill (1982), Charlie Sweeney and Eamonn Coleman (1986-87), Jim McKeever and Peter Finn (1989), Dessie Ryan (1990), Val Kane and DJ Kane (1991), Dermot Dowling (1993).

RYAN CUP winners: Queens 1985/1992. UUJ 1987-89.

SCHOOLS FOOTBALL

30. MacRORY CUP FINALS

1917	St Pats, Armagh		
1919	St Pats, Armagh		
1920-23	None		
1924	St Pats, Armagh 2-4	St Macartans, 1-3 Monaghan	
1925	Unfinished		
1926	St Pats, Armagh 2-2	St Macartans, 0-4 Monaghan	
1927	St Pats, Armagh 3-9	St Macartans, 0-3 Monaghan	
1928	St Pats, Armagh 1-11	St Colman's, Newry 2-2	
1929	St Malachys, Belfast		
1930	St Macartans, Monaghan		
1931	St Pats, Armagh 3-3	St Macartans, 0-2 Monaghan	
1932	St Macartans, Monaghan		
1933	St Macartans, Monaghan		
1934	St Macartans, St Pats Armagh (joint)		
1935	St Pats, Cavan 7-11	Monaghan CBS 0-0	
1936	St Pats, Cavan 3-3	St Pats, Armagh 1-7	
1937	St Pats, Cavan bt	St Marys, Dundalk	
1938	St Marys, Dundalk		
1939	St Pats, Cavan 2-7	St Marys, Dundalk 1-1	
1940	St Macartans, bt	St Marys, Dundalk (R) Monaghan	
1941	St Marys, Dundalk		
1942	St Macartans, Monaghan		
1943	St Pats, Cavan 2-12	St Pats, Armagh 1-3	
1944	St Pats, Armagh		
1945	St Pats, Armagh		
1946	St Pats, Armagh		
1947	St Pats, Armagh		

1948	St Pats, Cavan 7-8	St Malachys, Belfast 1-7	
1949	St Colmans, 2-5 Newry	St Malachys, Belfast 0-7	
1950	St Colmans, 2-11 Newry	St Pats, Armagh 3-7	
1951	St Pats, Cavan bt	St Macartans, Monaghan	
1952	St Macartans, Monaghan		
1953	St Pats, Armagh 2-10	St Macartans, 1-6 Monaghan	
1954	Abbey CBS 0-11	St Pats, Cavan 1-3	
1955	St Pats, Cavan 2-8	St Malachy's, Belfast 0-2	
1956	St Macartans, 2-7 Monaghan	St Eunans Letterkenny 2-6	
1957	St Colmans, 0-8 Newry	St Pats, Armagh 1-2	
1958	St Colmans, 4-11 Newry	St Pats, Cavan 1-1	
1959	Abbey CBS 3-7	St Eunans Letterkenny 1-3	
1960	St Colmans, 2-6 Newry	St Pats, Cavan 0-4	
1961	St Pats, Cavan 1-13	St Eunans Letterkenny 0-5	
1962	St Pats, Cavan 2-11	Abbey CBS 2-6	
1963	St Colmans, 2-8 Newry	St Pats, Cavan 0-2	
1964	Abbey CBS 3-8	St Pats Cavan 2-5	
1965	St Columbs, 1-13 Derry	St Michaels Enniskillen 0-4	
1966	St Columbs, 3-5 Derry	De La Salle Downpatrick 3-3	
1967	St Colmans, 2-10 Newry	St Pats, Armagh 1-4	
1968	St Colmans, 6-4 Newry	St Michaels, 1-3 Enniskillen	
1969	St Colmans, 1-9 Newry	St Michaels, 1-6 Enniskillen	
1970	St Malachys, 2-6 Belfast	St Michaels, 0-6 Enniskillen	
1971	St Marys CBS, 1-11 Belfast	Abbey CBS 1-7	
1972	St Pats, Cavan 1-9	Abbey CBS 2-4	
1973	St Michaels, 1-10 Enniskillen	Omagh CBS 0-10	
1974	Omagh CBS 1-11	St Michaels, 0-12 (R: 0-6 0-6) Enniskillen	
1975	St Colmans, 2-7 Newry	St Pats Cavan 1-8	

1976	St Colmans, 1-4 Newry	St Pats, Maghera 0-4	
1977	St Pats, Maghera 1-7	Abbey CBS 0-8	
1978	St Colmans, 1-10 Newry	St Pats, Maghera 1-3? or 79	
1979	St Colmans, 0-7 Newry	St Pats, Maghera 0-5	
1980	St Pats, Maghera 3-9	Abbey CBS 3-6	
1981	St Colmans, 1-3 Newry	St Pats, Maghera 0-4	
1982	St Pats, Maghera 1-7	Abbey CBS 1-6	
1983	St Pats, Maghera 2-10	Abbey CBS 0-8	
1984	St Pats, Maghera 1-9	St Marys CBS, Belfast 0-6	
1985	St Pats, Maghera 2-9	St Michaels, Lurgan 1-1	
1986	St Marys CBS, 1-8 Belfast	St Pats, Maghera 0-6	
1987	Abbey CBS 2-6	St Colmans, Newry 0-8	
1988	St Colmans, 3-5 Newry	St Pats, Maghera 1-9 (Rs: 0-5 0-5; 2-7 2-7)	
1989	St Pats Maghera 4-10	St Colmans Newry 4-9	
1990	St Pats Maghera 3-6	St Colmans, Newry 1-5 (R: 0-6 0-6)	
1991	St Pats, 2-7 Dungannon	St Colmans, Newry 1-9	
1992	St Michaels, 1-8 Enniskillen	St Pats, Dungannon 0-9	
1993	St Colmans, 0-10 Newry	St Pats, Maghera 1-5	

ROLL OF HONOUR

St Colmans, Newry 16; St Pats, Armagh 13; St Pats, Cavan 11; St Pats, Maghera 8; St Macartans 7; Abbey CBS 4.

Note: St Pats, Maghera first participated in the MacRory Cup in 1970. Martin O'Neill, the former Northern Ireland soccer captain, scored five points for St Malachys, Belfast in the 1970 final. 14-year-old Dermot McNicholl scored 1-3 for Maghera in the 1980 final. He went on to play in another 4 finals, captaining winning teams in 1983-84. While still at the school Mc Nicholl won an All Star and played for Ulster and Ireland. Greg Blaney captained the winning St Colmans team in 1981. James McCartan scored 3-2 for St Colmans in the 1989 final but still ended up on the losing side.

31. THE HOGAN CUP: ULSTER IN ALL-IRELAND FINALS

1946	St Pats, Armagh 3-11	St Jarlaths, Tuam 4-7	
1947	St Pats, Armagh 3-8	St Jarlaths, Tuam 4-10	
1948	St Pats, Cavan 3-3	St Mels, Longford 4-7	
1949-56		Competition Suspended	
1957	St Colmans, 0-4 Newry	St Nathys (Ballaghadereen) 1-7	
1965	St Columbs, 0-11 Derry	Belcamp OMI (Dublin) 1-7 (R: 0-9 0-9)	
1967	St Colmans, 1-8 Newry	St Jarlaths, Tuam 1-7	
1970	St Malachys, 1-13 Belfast	Col.Chriost Ri (Cork) 4-5	
1971	St Marys CBS, 1-13 Belfast	Col.Chriost Ri 1-7	
1972	St Pats, Cavan 2-11	St Brendans (Killarney) 1-5	
1975	St Colmans, 1-7 Newry	Carmelite College 2-3 Moate	
1978	St Colmans, 2-4 Newry	St Jarlaths, Tuam 2-11	
1980	St Pats, Maghera 1-8	Carmelite (Moate) 0-12	

1984	St Pats, Maghera 2-3	St Jarlaths, Tuam 0-10	
1986	St Colmans, 3-10 Newry	St Davids (Artane) 0-7	
1988	St Colmans, 1-11 Newry	St Mels, Longford 1-7	
1989	St Pats, Maghera 2-15	Colaiste Chriost Ri 1-6 (R: 1-5 0-8)	
1990	St Pats, Maghera 1-11	St Jarlaths, Tuam 0-13 (R: 1-4 0-7)	
1993	St Colmans, 2-10 Newry	St Jarlaths, Tuam 1-9	

HOGAN WINNING MANAGERS:
1946 Fr. Rouahan at St Pats, Armagh.
1965 Fr. Ignatius McQuillan at St Columbs, Derry.
1967 Fr. John Treanor and Gerry O'Neill at St Colmans, Newry.
1971 Bro. L.P.Nolan at St Marys CBS, Belfast.
1972 Fr. Benny Maguire at St Pats, Cavan.
1975 Ray Morgan at St Colmans, Newry.

1986/88/93 Ray Morgan with Pete McGrath at St Colmans, Newry.

1989-90 Adrian McGuckin at St Pats, Maghera.

Note: Adrian McGuckin managed all of Maghera's MacRory Cup wins. In 1986 St Marys, Belfast won the MacRory Cup but St Colmans, Newry, winners of the Rannafast Cup, represented Ulster in the Hogan Cup. Because of a different age ruling Ulster teams usually lose some players from MacRory to Hogan Cup games.

32. THE HOGAN CUP: ULSTER ALL-IRELAND WINNING TEAMS

1946 ST PATS, ARMAGH: Eamon Caherty, Benny Dargan, Jim Devlin, Brendan O'Neill, Pat O'Neill (c), Eddie Devlin, Felix O'Kane, Malachy Dargan, Larry Higgins, Peter McGrath, Iggy Jones, Gerry O'Neill, Pat Smith, Larry Donegan, Tom Gribben. Subs: Kevin Moran, Vincent Cullen, Brian O'Kane, Sean McGrath.
Special Note: Iggy Jones scored 3-4 in the final.

1965 ST COLUMBS, DERRY: Joe Cassidy, Michael Trolan, Brendan Dolan, Michael P.Kelly, Colum Mullan, Malachy McAfee, Tom Quinn, Harry McGill, Peter Stevenson, Chris Browne, Paddy McCotter (c), Tony O'Doherty, Eamonn Small, Seamus Lagan, Brendan Mullan.

1967 ST COLMANS NEWRY: Ciaran Lewis, John Gribben, Sean J.Moore, Sean McCann, Jimmy Smyth, Noel Moore (c), Jimmy Donnelly, Tony Quinn, Paddy Turley, John Purdy, Peter Rooney, Con Davey, Martin Murphy, Sean McMullan, Des Rice.

1971 ST MARYS CBS, BELFAST: Kevin O'Loan, Paul McKiernan, Gerry Cullen, Conor Smyth, Gerry McHugh (c), Sean Sands, John McKiernan, Phil Shephard, Pat Armstrong, Frank Toman, Paul Growcott, Ciaran Donnelly, Canice Ward.

1972 ST PATS, CAVAN: Aidan Elliott, Pat McGill, Eamonn Gillic, John Sweeney, Ollie Brady, Gerry Smith, Ciaran O'Keeffe, Sean Leddy, Charlie O'Donoghue, Niall Brennan (c), Brian Brady, Hugh Reynolds, Michael English.

1975 ST COLMANS, NEWRY: Pat Donnan, Michael Connolly, Pat McGivern, Michael Sands, Jim McCartan, Declan McConville, Cathal Strain, John McCartan, Tom Treanor, Noel Rodgers, Declan Rodgers (c), Jim McIlroy, Michael McDonald.

1986 ST COLMANS, NEWRY: Brendan Tierney, Mark Mooney, Larry Duggan, Mark Matthews, Peter Morgan, Martin Magee, Stephen McGrane, Ian Hall, Brian McCartan, Martin Burns, Ollie Reel, Cathal Murray, Ronan Fitzpatrick, Paul Fegan (c), James McCartan.

1988 ST COLMANS, NEWRY: Eamonn Connolly, Barry Hynes, L.Duggan, Barry Fearon, Pat Tinnelly, Mark McNeill, M.Matthews, Gerard Reid, Eamonn McKay, Paul McCartan, J.McCartan, Paul O'Hare, O.Reel (c), Tom Fegan, Gareth McCaugherty.

1989 ST PATS, MAGHERA: John Murtagh, Gregory Simpson, Paddy McAllister, Dermot O'Neill, Barry McGonigle, Terry Bradley (c), Karl Diamond, Anthony Tohill, Joe McCullough, Roderick Skelly, Brian McCormick, Dermot Dougan, Ryan Murphy, Eamonn Burns, Eunan O'Kane.

1990 ST PATS, MAGHERA: J.Murtagh, Kevin Bateson, Ronan McCloskey, G.Simpson, Martin McGonigle, B.McGonigle, K.Diamond, B. McCormick, Hugh Mullan, E.O'Kane, D.Dougan, E.Burns (c), Geoffrey McGonigle, R.Murphy, Philip McGuigan. Sub: Kevin Ryan for McGuigan.

1993 ST COLMANS, NEWRY: Martin Doyle, Kevin O'Reilly, Ronan Hamill (c), Sean Cunningham, Finbar Caulfield, Mark Rowland, Gary Farrell, John Morgan, Paul McShane, Aidan McGivern, Diarmuid Marsden, James Byrne, David McCall, Martin Sherry, Des French.

Note: Hogan teams were 13-a-side in the 1970s.

VOCATIONAL SCHOOLS

33. ULSTER IN ALL-IRELAND VOCATIONAL SCHOOLS FINALS

1966 FERMANAGH 2-7	Kerry 2-2	1981 DERRY 1-11	Cork 2-6
1967 TYRONE 2-6	Kerry 1-7	1984 DONEGAL 3-9	Longford 2-3
1968 ANTRIM 6-7	Galway 1-4	1985 DONEGAL 3-8	Cork 1-4
1969 TYRONE 0-8	Dublin 1'4	1987 Donegal 2-9	Kerry 2-13
1970 TYRONE 3-11	Clare 2-7	1988 TYRONE 1-9	Mayo 1-4
1971 Antrim 0-9	Mayo 2-4	1989 TYRONE 0-13	Mayo 1-6
1974 Tyrone 1-7	Wicklow 2-7	1990 Cavan 0-7	Kerry 0-11
1975 Tyrone 0-11	Mayo 1-15		
1979 DERRY 1-5	Mayo 0-6 (R: 2-3 0-9)		
1980 DERRY 2-8	Wicklow 0-6		

HURLING

34. ULSTER SENIOR HURLING CHAMPIONSHIP FINALS 1901-49

1900-1	Antrim (Walk over)			1928	Antrim 4-5	Down 1-5
1902	Derry 2-7	Antrim 2-5		1929	Antrim	
1903	Antrim bt	Donegal		1930	Antrim 10-4	Down 2-0
1904	Antrim 0-12	Armagh 0-4		1931	Antrim 4-10	Derry 0-1
1905	Antrim			1932-	Donegal 5-4	Antrim 4-5
1906	Donegal 5-21	Antrim 0-1		1933	Antrim 1-7	Donegal 2-1
1907	Antrim bt	Derry		1934	Antrim 3-4	Donegal 2-2
1908	Derry 2-8	Cavan 0-2		1935	Antrim 7-9	Donegal 1-2
1909	Antrim bt	Donegal		1937	Antrim 6-7	Donegal 3-2
1910	Antrim bt	Donegal		1938	Antrim 3-5	Donegal 2-2
1912	Antrim	Monaghan		1939	Antrim 9-8	Down 4-2
1913	Antrim 3-33	Monaghan 0-0		1940	Antrim 4-4	Down 1-3
1914	Monaghan 4-3	Antrim 1-0 (R: 2-0 2-0)		1941	Down 5-3	Antrim 2-5
1915	Monaghan 1-5	Antrim 1-2		1943	Antrim 6-8	Down 2-0
1916	Antrim 3-1	Monaghan 1-1		1944	Antrim 7-3	Monaghan 0-1 (R: 5-7 6-4)
1923	Donegal 7-1	Antrim 3-0		1945	Antrim 8-2	Donegal 2-4
1924	Antrim 5-3	Donegal 4-0		1946	Antrim 6-3	Armagh 2-1
1925	Antrim 5-4	Donegal 4-5		1947	Antrim (Walk over)	
1926	Antrim 4-3	Cavan 3-1		1948	Antrim (Walk over)	
1927	Antrim 5-4	Cavan 3-3		1949	Antrim (Walk over)	

35. ULSTER SENIOR HURLING CHAMPIONSHIP 1989-93

1989	Down 6-7	Derry 1-13			Antrim 3-14	Down 3-10
	Antrim 2-16	Down 0-9		1992	Down 9-18	Derry 0-10
1990	Down 1-22	Derry 0-4			Down 2-16	Antrim 0-11
	Antrim 4-11	Down 2-11		1993	Antrim 0-24	Down 0-11
1991	Down 6-13	Derry 2-10				

36. TEAMS IN ULSTER HURLING FINALS 1989-93

1989 ANTRIM: Niall Patterson, Ger Rogan, Terence Donnelly, Dessie Donnelly, James McNaughton, Dominic McKinley, Gary O'Kane, Paul McKillen, Terence McNaughton, Brian Donnelly, Aidan McCarry, Sean Paul McKillop, Donal Armstrong, Ciaran Barr (c), Danny McNaughton. Subs: Ger Holden for O'Kane, Dominic McMullan for McKillen, Aidan Murray for Rogan.

DOWN: Noel Keith, Kevin Coulter, Paddy Dorrian, Seamus Fay, Paul Coulter, Martin Mallon, Paddy Branniff (c), Danny Hughes, Philbin Savage, Noel Sands, Gerard Coulter, Chris Mageean, Barry Coulter, Hugh Gilmore, Brendan Coulter. Subs: Martin Bailie for Barry Coulter, Paul McMullan for P.Coulter.

1990 ANTRIM: N.Patterson, G.Holden, D.Donnelly, D.McKinley (c), John Carson, Declan McKillop, A.Murray, Jim Close, P.McKillen, B.Donnelly, A.McCarry, S.P.McKillop, Alistair McGuile, C.Barr, Olcan McFetridge. Subs: Noel Murray for McGuile, G.O'Kane for D.McKillop, Mickey Sullivan for McKillen.

DOWN: N.Keith, K.Coulter, P.Dorrian, P.Branniff, M.Mallon (c), G.Coulter, C.Mageean, John McCarthy, M.Bailie, D.Hughes, N.Sands, Barry Coulter, M.Blaney, Philbin Savage, P.Coulter.
Sub: Hugh Gilmore for B.Coulter.

1991 ANTRIM: N.Patterson, Paul Jennings, D.McKinley (c), D.Donnelly, G.Rogan, J.McNaughton, D.McKillop, S.P.McKillop, P.McKillen, J.Carson, C.Barr, D.Armstrong, A.McCarry, T.McNaughton, J.Close. Sub: G.O'Kane for Close.

DOWN: N.Keith, K.Coulter, P.Dorrian, P.Branniff (c), M.Mallon, G.Coulter, P.McMullan, M.Bailie, J.McCarthy, D.Hughes, C.Mageean, P.Coulter, M.Blaney, Pearse McCrickard, N.Sands.

1992 DOWN: N.Keith, K.Coulter, G.Coulter, P.Branniff, M.Mallon, P.McMullan, Dermot Woods, D.Hughes, Gary Savage, Gerard McGrattan, Greg Blaney, P.Coulter, M.Blaney, M.Bailie, N.Sands (c). Subs: C.Mageean for M.Blaney, P.Savage for P.Coulter.

ANTRIM: N.Patterson, Ronan Donnelly, D.McKinley, J.McNaughton, D.McKillop, G.O'Kane, P.Jennings, P.McKillen, T.McNaughton (c), S.P.McKillop, A.McCarry, D.Armstrong, Alistair Elliott, C.Barr, J.Close. Subs: Seamus McMullan for Jennings, J.Carson for T.McNaughton, D.Donnelly for Armstrong.

1993 ANTRIM: Pat Gallagher, S.McMullan, D.McMullan (c), Eoin McCloskey, R.Donnelly, D.McKinley, J.McNaughton, P.McKillen, P.Jennings, A.Elliott, Gary O'Kane, S.P.McKillop, J.Close, T.McNaughton, Gregory O'Kane.

DOWN: N.Keith, Stephen McAree, G.Coulter,

P.Branniff, M.Mallon, P.McMullan, D.Woods, D.Hughes, G.Savage, G.McGrattan, M.Bailie (c), Dermot O'Prey, M.Blaney, Jerome McCrickard, N.Sands. Sub: B.Coulter for McCrickard.

37. ULSTER IN THE ALL-IRELAND HURLING CHAMPIONSHIP

(Semi-final except where marked)
1900-1949

1900	Antrim 0-1	Galway 3-17
1901	Antrim lost to	Wexford
1902	Derry 0-6	Dublin 6-19
1903	Antrim lost to	Kilkenny
1904	Antrim 2-3	Cork 4-18
1905	Antrim 1-9	Dublin 2-8
1906	Antrim 1-3	Kilkenny 7-21
1908	Cavan 0-3	Dublin 3-12
1909	Derry 0-3	Kilkenny 3-17
1910	Donegal withdrew.	
1911	Antrim 1-1	Kilkenny 3-5
1912	Antrim lost to	Limerick
1923	Donegal 0-1	Limerick 7-4
1924	Antrim 3-1	Dublin 8-4
1943	Antrim 3-3	Kilkenny 1-6
	Final Antrim 0-4	Cork 5-16
1944	Antrim 3-1	Dublin 6-12
1945	Antrim 1-6	Tipperary 5-9
1946	Antrim 0-7	Kilkenny 7-11
1947	Antrim 0-5	Cork 7-10

1948	Antrim 2-6	Dublin 8-13
1949	Antrim 1-4	Tipperary 6-18

1984-93
(Q/F = Quarter-final, S/F = Semi-final)

1984	S/F: Antrim 2-5	Cork 3-26
1985	Q/F: Antrim 3-12	London 1-15
	S/F: Antrim 0-12	Offaly 3-17
1986	S/F: Antrim 1-24	Cork 7-11
1987	Q/F: Antrim 3-14	London 1-15
	S/F: Antrim 2-11	Kilkenny 2-18
1988	S/F: Antrim 2-10	Tipperary 3-15
1989	Q/F: Antrim 4-14	Kildare 0-7
	S/F: Antrim 4-15	Offaly 1-15
	Final Antrim 3-9	Tipperary 4-24
1990	S/F: Antrim 1-13	Cork 2-20
1991	Q/F Antrim 5-11	Westmeath 1-5
	S/F: Antrim 1-19	Kilkenny 2-18
1992	S/F Down 1-11	Cork 2-17
1993	Q/F: Antrim 3-27	Meath 4-10
	S/F: Antrim 1-9	Kilkenny 4-18

38. ULSTER TEAMS IN ALL-IRELAND FINALS

1943 ANTRIM: John Hurl, John Currie, Kevin Murphy, Willie Graham, Paddy McGarry, Jimmy Walsh (c), Pat McKeown, Jackie Bateson, Noel Campbell, Danny McKillop, John Butler, Joe Mullan, Kevin Armstrong, Danny McAllister. Sammy Mulholland. Sub: John McNeill for Walsh.

1989 ANTRIM: Niall Patterson, Gary O'Kane, Terence Donnelly, Dessie Donnelly, James McNaughton, Dominic McKinley, Leonard McKeegan, Paul McKillen, Dominic McMullan, Ciaran Barr (c), Aidan McCarry, Olcan McFetridge, Donal Armstrong, Brian Donnelly, Terence McNaughton. Subs: Danny McNaughton for McMullan, Declan McKillop for O'Kane, Mickey Sullivan for McKinley.

Attendances 1943 - 48,843; 1989 - 65,496.

39. SENIOR TEAM MANAGERS

ANTRIM: Danny McAllister 1960s, Frank Smith, Joe Duffy, Neilly Patterson, Gilbert McIlhatton, Jim Nelson 1970s, Neilly Patterson, Sean McGuinness 1984-86, Jim Nelson 1986-

DOWN: A Selection Group, with a representative from each of the three clubs, was the norm until Joe McCrickard from Leitrim was appointed manager. The post stayed out of the Ards with Sean Holywood 1984-89 and Sean McGuinness 1989-

40. ALL-IRELAND B CHAMPIONSHIP FINALS

1974	Antrim 3-13	Kildare 1-26
1978	Antrim 1-10	Down 2-6
	ANTRIM 1-16	London 3-7
1981	ANTRIM 3-17	London 3-14
1982	ANTRIM 2-16	London 2-14
1983	Down 2-13	Kerry 3-16
1984	Down 1-9	Kerry 1-16
1985	Down 1-13	Meath 3-18
1988	Down 1-7	London 2-6

Note: By virtue of winning two All Ireland B finals in a row in the early eighties, Antrim were admitted automatically to the senior competition. The Ulster Senior Championship was re-started in 1989.

41. RAILWAY CUP

(Semi-finals except where marked)

1944	Ulster 3-1	Munster 9-3	1968	Ulster 3-8	Leinster 5-10
1945	Ulster 3-1	Leinster 2-3	1970	*Prelim.* Ulster 3-6	Connacht 2-6
	Final Ulster 2-0	Munster 6-8		Ulster 3-6	Munster 6-14
1946	Ulster 1-7	Connacht 4-14	1971	*Prelim.* Ulster 1-4	Connacht 4-11
1947	Ulster 0-0	Munster 9-7	1976	Ulster 0-12	Leinster 6-15
1948	Ulster 4-2	Leinster 5-5	1977	Ulster 3-6	Munster 3-17
1949	Ulster 2-7	Connacht 5-7	1978	Ulster 1-13	Leinster 3-17
1950	Ulster 3-2	Munster 9-4	1979	Ulster 0-11	Leinster 1-19
1951	Ulster 0-2	Leinster 7-9	1980	Ulster 1-10	Munster 4-16
1952	Ulster 3-0	Connacht 7-6	1981	Ulster 1-8	Munster 5-13
1953	Ulster 1-5	Munster 8-6	1982	Ulster 2-5	Leinster 3-15
1954	Ulster 1-1	Leinster 8-7	1983	Ulster 1-8	Leinster 3-16
1955	Ulster 2-4	Connacht 5-10	1984	Ulster 1-7	Munster 3-21
1956	Ulster 2-6	Munster 5-13	1985	Ulster 2-6	Munster 3-16
1957	Ulster 2-5	Leinster 7-7	1986	Ulster 0-11	Munster 1-19
1958	Ulster 3-3	Leinster 8-10	1987	Ulster 0-15	Connacht 5-13
1960	Ulster 5-3	Leinster 8-6	1988	Ulster 1-8	Leinster 1-13
1961	Ulster 1-2	Munster 3-13	1989	Ulster 1-22	Munster 3-31
1963	Ulster 3-5	Munster 9-7	1990	No competition.	
1965	Ulster 3-2	Munster 3-11	1991	Ulster 1-6	Connacht 1-11
1966	Ulster 3-7	Leinster 6-14	1992	Ulster 2-6	Connacht 0-7
1967	Ulster 2-6	Munster 6-11		*Final* Ulster 1-8	Munster 3-12
			1993	Ulster 0-21	Munster 0-18

42. ULSTER TEAMS IN RAILWAY CUP FINALS

1945 Michael McKeown, Billy Feeney, John Butler (Antrim), E O'Toole (Monaghan), Pat McKeown (Antrim), Brian Denvir (Down), M Butler (Antrim), Oliver Keenan (Down), Noel Campbell, Dessie Cormican, Kevin Armstrong, Larry McGrady (Antrim), John White (Down), Chris Mullan, Sammy Mulholland (Antrim). Subs: Danny McAllister for O'Toole, John Butler (Mitchells) for White.

1992 Pat Gallagher (Antrim), Kevin Coulter (Down), Dominic McKinley (Antrim), Paddy Branniff, Martin Mallon (Down), Paul Jennings, James McNaughton (Antrim), Paul McMullan, Chris Mageean, Danny Hughes (Down), John Carson, Aidan McCarry, Olcan McFetridge (Antrim), Seamus Downey (Derry), Ciaran Barr (Antrim), Noel Sands (Down). Subs: Noel Keith for Gallagher, Martin Bailie for Carson, Gary O'Kane for Coulter, Declan McKillop for McCarry.

43. RAILWAY SHIELD FINAL 1987

Ulster 3-20   Munster 3-18 (aet)
Team: N.Keith, D, McKinley, T. McNaughton, P. McMullan, Paul Doyle (Armagh). M.Bailie, M. Mallon, P. McKillen, C. Mageean, B. Donnelly, D. Donnelly (c), C. Barr, S. Fay, D. McNaughton, P.

Savage. Subs: Mick O'dowd (Monaghan) for B.Donnelly, Jimmy Darragh (Antrim) for McMullan.

Note: Eddie Donnelly was Ulster manager from 1986-91. Sean McGuiness is now in charge.

44. ULSTER ALL STARS

1988 Ciaran Barr CHF (Antrim).
1989 Dessie Donnelly LCB, Olcan McFetridge LHF (Both Antrim)

1991 Terence McNaughton MF (Antrim).
1992 Gerard McGrattan RHF (Down).

45. ULSTER ALL STAR REPLACEMENTS

1972 Niall Wheeler (Antrim)
1975 Eddie Donnelly (Antrim)
1976 JIm Corr (Antrim)
1977 Eddie Donnelly (Antrim)
1985 Brian Donnelly (Antrim)
1987 Dessie Donnelly (Antrim)

1988 Martin Bailie (Down), Paul McKillen (Antrim).
1989 Danny McNaughton, Olcan McFetridge (Both Antrim).
1990 Terence McNaughton (Antrim).
1991 Ciaran Barr, Olcan McFetridge (Both Antrim).

CLUB HURLING

46. ULSTER CLUB CHAMPIONSHIP FINALS

1972	Loughgiel 3-8	Portaferry 1-12	1983	Ballycastle 4-11	Ballygalget 2-3
1973	Rossa 2-9	Ballycran 3-2	1984	Ballycastle 1-14	Ballycran 1-3
1974	Balllycran 3-5	Sarsfields 3-2	1985	Cushendall 0-19	Ballycran 0-10
1975	Ballygalget 4-6	Ballycastle 1-9	1986	Ballycastle 1-14	Lavey 1-8
1976	Ballycran 0-8	Rossa 0-7	1987	Cushendall 3-10	Ballycran 1-6
1977	Rossa 1-13	Ballycran 2-6	1988	O'Donovan Rossa 0-13	Lavey 0-11
1978	Ballycastle 2-14	Portaferry 2-7	1989	Loughgiel 1-14	Portaferry 2-9
1979	Ballycastle 0-11	Ballycran 0-8	1990	Dunloy 0-17	Ballygalget 2-4
1980	Ballycastle 1-20	Ballycran 0-13	1991	Cushendall 1-16	Portaferry 2-4
1981	Cushendall 7-19	Portaferry 3-5	1992	Cushendall 2-12	Ballygalget 1-10
1982	Loughgiel 1-9	Ballygalget 0-9			

47. ULSTER IN ALL-IRELAND CLUB FINALS

1980	Ballycastle (Antrim) 1-8	Castlegar 1-11 (Galway)
1983	Loughgiel (Antrim) 2-12 (R: 1-8 2-5)	St Rynaghs 1-12 (Offaly)
1989	O'Donovan Rossa 0-12 (Antrim)	Buffers Alley 2-12 (Wexford)

TEAMS IN FINALS

1980 BALLYCASTLE: Paul Smith, Kevin Boyle, Kevin Donnelly, Gerard McAuley, Seamus Donnelly (c), Terence Donnelly, Dessie Donnelly, Terence Barton, Stephen Boyle, Brian Donnelly, Phelim Watson, Peter Boyle, Peter Dallat, Eddie Donnelly, Olcan Laverty. Sub: Michael Dallat.

1983 LOUGHGIEL: Niall Patterson (c), Martin Carey, P.J. O'Mullan, Sean Carey, Eamonn Connolly, Paddy McIlhatton, Aidan McNaughton, Mick O'Connell, Gerard McKinley, Paddy Carey Jnr, Dominic McKinley, Brendan Laverty, Paddy Carey Snr, Aidan McCarry, Seamus McNaughton. (Note - Martin Coyle and Brendan McGarry played in the drawn match).

1989 ROSSA: Paddy Quinn, Ger Rogan, Damien Murray (c), Mark Barr, Adrian Murray, Mark Reynolds, Sean Collins, Jim Fagan, Jim Close, Donal Armstrong, Ciaran Barr, Paul Ward, Noel Murray, Jim Reilly, Collie Murphy. Subs: Paddy Rogan, Sean Shannon, Chris Condon.

MINOR HURLING

48. ULSTER MINOR FINALS

1930 Down 9-7	Monaghan 0-6		1965 Antrim 7-3	Armagh 0-1
1931 Antrim 5-0	Down 3-1		1966 Antrim 6-6	Tyrone 1-3
1932 Down 3-5	Antrim 2-1		1967 Down 5-2	Tyrone 4-2
1935 Antrim 7-7	Down 3-1		1968 Antrim (Walk over)	
1936 Antrim 6-3	Down 3-0		1969 Antrim 2-11	Down 4-3
1937 Antrim 5-7	Donegal 2-2		1970 Antrim 4-12	Down 0-5
1938 Antrim beat	Donegal		1971 Down 5-11	Derry 4-4
1939 Antrim 11-2	Down 0-0		1972 Down 2-8	Armagh 2-4
1940 Antrim beat	Derry		1973 No Records	
1941 Antrim			1974 Derry 3-6	Armagh 2-8
1946 Antrim 8-7	Donegal 0-2		1975 Armagh 3-8	Down 3-6
1947 Antrim 10-4	Down 0-0		1976 Down 5-12	Tyrone 1-3
1948 Antrim 15-6	Donegal 0-0		1977 No records	
1949 Antrim			1978 Down 4-9	Derry 1-11
1950 Antrim 4-3	Armagh 1-3		1979 Derry 3-8	Monaghan 2-4
1951 Antrim 12-2	Down 0-1		1980 Derry 1-5	Armagh 1-4
1952 Antrim 7-8	Down 1-1		1981 Derry 3-6	Armagh 1-4
1953 Antrim 11-14	Donegal 1-0		1982 Derry 1-14	Armagh 2-2
1954 Antrim 9-9	Down 1-3		1983 Derry 5-10	Monaghan 0-6
1955 Antrim 5-4	Armagh 2-2		1984 Down 3-6	Antrim 1-11
1956 Antrim 7-4	Down 1-3		1985 Down 3-6	Antrim 2-9
1957 Down 4-1	Antrim 3-3		1986 Antrim 2-9	Derry 1-10
1958 Antrim 10-5	Down 0-2		1987 Antrim 6-9	Down 0-6
1959 Antrim 11-6	Donegal 0-2		1988 Antrim 2-10	Down 2-8
1960 Antrim 16-4	Donegal 1-0		1989 Down 3-8	Antrim 2-8 (R: 2-11 3-8)
1961 Antrim 11-5	Donegal 4-4		1990 Derry 4-11	Antrim 1-8
1962 Antrim 12-7	Donegal 2-3		1991 Derry 3-10	Antrim 2-11
1963 Antrim 6-12	Donegal 1-1		1992 Antrim 0-12	Down 0-7
1964 Antrim 11-11	Armagh 0-0		1993 Antrim 2-13	Down 1-9

LEINSTER MINOR CHAMPIONSHIP FINALS

1979 Antrim 1-9 Kilkenny 5-13   1980 Antrim 1-10 Wexford 1-12

UNDER-21 HURLING

49. ULSTER UNDER-21 FINALS

1965 Antrim 4-5	Down 2-7	1980 Antrim 4-16	Down 0-9
1966 Antrim 4-5	Down 0-8	1981 Antrim 2-9	Down 1-5
1967 Antrim 3-8	Down 2-7	1982 Antrim 9-14	Down 4-5
1968 Down 7-6	Armagh 2-9	1983 Down 2-7	Antrim 0-7
1969 Down 5-17	Antrim 2-11	1984 Down 1-14	Antrim 0-15
1970 Antrim 6-12	Down 2-10	1985 Down 1-12	Antrim 1-10
1971 Down 5-11	Antrim 2-9	1986 Derry 3-9	Down 1-2 (R: 2-9 2-9)
1972 Antrim 4-9	Down 1-11	1987 Derry 2-7	Antrim 0-9
1973 Antrim 3-13	Down 3-3	1988 Antrim 6-11	Down 1-4
1974 No records.		1989 Antrim 4-18	Down 0-4
1975 Down 3-10	Antrim 1-3	1990 Down 2-9	Antrim 2-6
1976 Antrim 1-8	Down 0-5	1991 Antrim 2-19	Down 2-6
1977 Down 3-7	Antrim 0-9	1992 Antrim 3-11	Down 3-4
1978 Antrim 5-18	Down 3-9	1993 Derry 2-13	Antrim 1-8
1979 Antrim 9-13	Down 2-2		

JUNIOR HURLING

50. ULSTER JUNIOR FINALS

1949 Armagh 4-7	Down 3-3	1970	
1952 Antrim 4-6	Down 0-2	1971 Donegal 2-7	Derry 0-5
1953 Antrim 2-11	Donegal 1-2	1972 Donegal 5-3	Monaghan 5-1
1954 Antrim 7-3	Down 1-3	1973 Armagh 3-10	Down 1-6
1955 Antrim 4-15	Down 0-4 (R)	1974 Derry 3-5	Armagh 1-7
1956 Down 4-6	Donegal 3-5	1975 Derry 0-4	Armagh 0-3
1957 Antrim 7-11	Down 3-5	1976-82 Played as Division 4 of NHL	
1958 Antrim 3-4	Down 1-3	1983 Cavan 2-11	Donegal 2-6
1959 Antrim 8-7	Donegal 3-2	1984 Derry 2-12	Monaghan 1-7
1960 Down 2-5	Antrim 1-7	1985 Cavan 4-7	Derry 0-5
1961 Antrim 4-7	Down 1-3	1986 Monaghan 1-14	Fernamagh 1-10
1962 Down 3-7	Donegal 2-2	1987 Monaghan 3-10	Fermanagh 1-6
1963 Antrim 6-12	Armagh 2-4	1988 Monaghan 2-12	Cavan 2-8
1964 Down 9-7	Antrim 4-7	1989 Donegal 3-12	Monaghan 0-9
1965 Armagh 3-7	Down 4-2	1990 Armagh 3-10	Fermanagh 1-10
1966 Antrim 3-13	Down 6-3	1991 Armagh 2-7	Fermanagh 1-4
1967 Down 6-6	Monaghan 1-5	1992 Down 1-9	Fermanagh 0-8
1968 Antrim 5-8	Donegal 0-3	1993 Down 2-9	Tyrone 1-11
1969 Antrim 5-16	Donegal 3-8		

ULSTER IN ALL-IRELAND JUNIOR FINALS

1963 Antrim 3-6   London 4-7   1964 DOWN 3-2   London 1-3